Yorkshire from AD 1000

Charles,

With best wishes,

David

A Regional History of England

General Editors: Barry Cunliffe and David Hey

For full details of the series, see pp. xiv–xv.

Yorkshire
from AD 1000

David Hey

Longman
London and New York

Longman Group Limited
Longman House, Burnt Mill, Harlow
Essex CM20 2JE, England
Associated companies throughout the world

Published in the United States of America
by Longman Inc., New York

First published 1986

British Library Cataloguing in Publication Data

Hey, David
   Yorkshire from AD 1000. – (Regional history of England)
   1. Yorkshire – History
   I. Title   II. Series
   942.8′1   DA670.Y6
ISBN 0-582-49211-4 csd
ISBN 0-582-49212-2 ppr

Library of Congress Cataloging in Publication Data

Hey, David
   Yorkshire from AD 1000.

   (Regional history of England)
   Bibliography: p.
   Includes index.
   1. Yorkshire – History   I. Title.   II. Series.
   DA670.Y6H47   1986   942.8′1   85–11032
   ISBN 0–582–49211–4
   ISBN 0–582–49212–2 (pbk.)

Set in Linotron 202 10/12pt Sabon Roman
Produced by Longman Singapore Publishers (Pte) Ltd.
Printed in Singapore.

Contents

List of plates

List of figures

List of tables

Acknowledgements

Any book of this nature, covering as it does the whole of Yorkshire over a thousand years of history, must draw heavily upon the labours of scholars past and present. The extent of my debt is obvious from the list of publications cited in the bibliography. One of the greatest pleasures of historical research is to discuss approaches and findings with fellow workers in the field, to share enthusiasms and to absorb (often unconsciously) the ideas of other researchers and writers. It is also my great fortune to teach groups of adult students who are a constant source of stimulus and challenge and who help to clarify ideas and identify problems. Most of the material assembled in the book has been used in courses that I have taught during the past twelve years for the University of Sheffield's Division of Continuing Education. I would like to thank the many friends who have helped in their various ways.

Thanks are also due to the many archivists and librarians who have been of assistance over the years, particularly those at the Borthwick Institute of Historical Research, the Yorkshire Archaeological Society, the various archive bodies set up by the new county and district councils in 1974 and such national repositories as the Public Record Office, the British Library and the Bodleian Library. Documentary research and fieldwork have taken me to every part of my native county. I hope that this familiarity with places 'on the ground' is evident in the writing.

I am indebted to the following for permission to reproduce copyright material: The Athlone Press Ltd for Table 4 from table 3.1 p. 338 *The Yorkshire Gentry from the Reformation to the Civil War* by J. T. Cliffe (1969) © The Athlone Press; Cambridge University Press for Table 3 from table 13 pp. 48, 49 & 148 *Winchester Yields: a study in medieval agriculture productivity* by J. Z. Titow (1972) and data for Tables 1 & 2 from pp. 61, 139, 212 & 375 *The Domesday Geography of Northern England* ed. Darby & Maxwell (1962). I am also grateful to the following for their permission to reproduce plates which appear in the text: The Department of Tourism, York (1.3 & 3.1); East Yorkshire Borough Council (3.3); Dr Shiela Edwards (2.1); Hull Central Library, Humberside County Council (4.1); The Royal Commission on National Records (England) (1.1 & 3.4); North Yorkshire County Library (Unné photograph collection) (1.4, 2.3 & 2.4); Scarborough Borough Council (1.2); Sheffield Central Library (2.2, 2.5, 5.1, 5.2, 5.3, 5.4, 5.5 & 5.6); The Sutcliffe Gallery, Whitby (4.2); and The Yorkshire and Humberside Tourist Board (1.5).

Glossary

assart   a close of pasture, meadow or arable land newly cleared from the
   wastes or woods
beck   brook
berewick   outlying farm within a manor
bordars   smallholders, especially those who had cleared marginal land
bovate   one-eighth part of a carucate (*see below*); an oxgang
caput   the major settlement within a manor
car, carr   low-lying marshy land marked by trees, especially alder or willow
carucate   a measure of plough land that varied (according to the nature of the
   soil) from about 100 to 120 acres
castellanies   large, compact lordships that were controlled from a major
   castle
Danelaw, the   that part of England occupied by the Danes; the boundary was
   agreed in AD 878
feoffee   trustee of a charitable estate
garth   close, paddock, yard
gate   way, road
gill   ravine
holme   flat meadow ground by a river
ing   low-lying meadow prone to flooding
keld   spring
nabb   shoulder of a hill
prebend   endowment of land, etc. to support a canon or a member of a
   cathedral chapter
ridding   clearing
royd   clearing
scales, scholes   temporary shelter, shieling
sett   mountain pasture, shieling
soke   large multiple estate
sokeland   outlying property within a soke (*see above*)
stall   cattle shed
thwaite   clearing, farmstead or hamlet
toft   homestead
tourn   court
vill   the basic unit of settlement for taxation and other administrative
   purposes
wapentake   subdivision of a county, for administrative, judicial and military
   purposes (known elsewhere as a *hundred*)

General preface

England cannot be divided satisfactorily into recognizable regions based on former kingdoms or principalities in the manner of France, Germany or Italy. Few of the Anglo-Saxon tribal divisions had much meaning in later times and from the eleventh century onwards England was a united country. English regional identities are imprecise and no firm boundaries can be drawn. In planning this series we have recognized that any attempt to define a region must be somewhat arbitrary, particularly in the Midlands, and that boundaries must be flexible. Even the South-West, which is surrounded on three sides by the sea, has no agreed border on the remaining side and in many ways, historically and culturally, the river Tamar divides the area into two. Likewise, the Pennines present a formidable barrier between the eastern and western counties on the Northern Borders; contrasts as much as similarities need to be emphasized here.

   The concept of a region does not imply that the inhabitants had a similar experience of life, nor that they were all inward-looking. A Hull merchant might have more in common with his Dutch trading partner than with his fellow Yorkshireman who farmed a Pennine smallholding: a Roman soldier stationed for years on Hadrian's Wall probably had very different ethnic origins from a native farmer living on the Durham boulder clay. To differing degrees, everyone moved in an international climate of belief and opinion with common working practices and standards of living.

   Yet regional differences were nonetheless real; even today a Yorkshireman may be readily distinguished from someone from the South-East. Life in Lancashire and Cheshire has always been different from life in the Thames valley. Even the east Midlands has a character that is subtly different from that of the west Midlands. People still feel that they belong to a particular region within England as a whole.

   In writing these histories we have become aware how much regional identities may vary over time; moreover how a farming region, say, may not coincide with a region defined by its building styles or its dialect. We have dwelt upon the diversity that can be found within a region as well as upon common characteristics in order to illustrate the local peculiarities of provincial life. Yet, despite all these problems of definition, we feel that the time is ripe to attempt an ambitious scheme outlining the history of England's regions in 21 volumes. London has not been included – except for demonstrating the many ways in which it has influenced the provinces – for its history has been very different from that of the towns and rural parishes that are our principal concern.

In recent years an enormous amount of local research, both historical and archaeological, has deepened our understanding of the former concerns of ordinary men and women and has altered our perception of everyday life in the past in many significant ways, yet the results of this work are not widely known even within the regions themselves.

This series offers a synthesis of this new work from authors who have themselves been actively involved in local research and who are present or former residents of the regions they describe.

Each region will be covered in two linked but independent volumes, the first covering the period up to AD 1000 and necessarily relying heavily on archaeological data, and the second bringing the story up to the present day. Only by taking a wide time-span and by studying continuity and change over many centuries do distinctive regional characteristics become clear.

This series portrays life as it was experienced by the great majority of the people of Southern Britain or England as it was to become. The 21 volumes will – it is hoped – substantially enrich our understanding of English history.

Barry Cunliffe
David Hey

A Regional History of England

General Editors: Barry Cunliffe (to AD 1000) and David Hey (from AD 1000)

The regionalisation used in this series is illustrated on the map opposite.

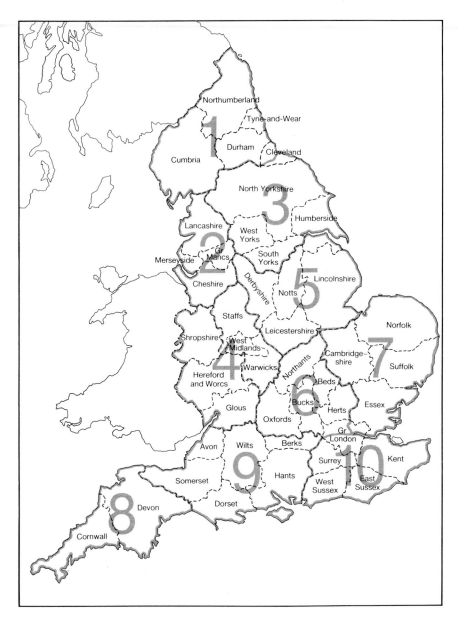

1. The Northern Counties
2. The Lancashire/Cheshire Region
3. Yorkshire
4. The Severn Valley and West Midlands
5. The East Midlands
6. The South Midlands and the Upper Thames
7. The Eastern Counties
8. The South West
9. Wessex
10. The South East

In memory of my parents and brother,
who lived in Yorkshire

Introduction

Yorkshire was by far the largest county in England until it was broken into five parts in 1974. It had over 3.75 million acres within its bounds and covered about an eighth of the whole country. The West Riding alone was bigger than any other English county, and the North Riding came fourth in size. Yorkshire stretched from the river Tees in the north to the Humber in the south, and from the east coast to the highest points of the Pennines, reaching in one place to within ten miles of the Irish Sea. The date that it became a county cannot be fixed precisely, but it appears to have been created during the late tenth or the early eleventh century, about the same time as the Danelaw counties of Derbyshire, Leicestershire, Lincolnshire and Nottinghamshire came into being. The Wessex shires were probably formed as far back as the eighth century, and the west Midland counties during the early tenth-century campaigns of Edward the Elder, but the northern Danelaw shires were later. They took their names from the military centres that became their county towns; thus Yorkshire was named after Jorvic, which is how the Vikings pronounced Eoforwic, the Anglian name of the traditional capital of the North.

The territory that became Yorkshire had achieved an identity long before it became a fully fledged shire, for it seems to have been the district settled by the Danish army under the leadership of Healfdene, who captured York in 867. The *Anglo-Saxon Chronicle* states that in 876 'Healfdene shared out the land of the Northumbrians and they proceeded to plough and to support themselves'. Healfdene may well have taken over a recognizable unit or perhaps a group of territories, just as other Danes did in East Anglia three years later. It is difficult to see how the small armies of the ninth century could have done otherwise. Certainly, the southern border of the new Yorkshire followed more or less the same course as the previous frontier of the Anglo-Saxon kingdom of Northumbria. In 830 when the Northumbrians submitted to Ecgbert of Wessex the ceremony took place near their frontier at Dore, which remained the county boundary until recent times. When Edmund of Wessex succeeded Athelstan in 940 he soon had to accept that his power did not extend

1

beyond the Mercian–Northumbrian border, which ran from Dore to Whit-well and so on to the Humber, probably along the line of the later county boundary.

The south-western frontier was formed by the river Sheaf, which has given Sheffield its name, and by the Meers Brook, a stream whose name has been applied to a Victorian suburb of the city. The names of both these watercourses are derived from words signifying a boundary. Immediately to the east the border followed the Shire Brook and part of the river Rother and then continued along the present northern fringes of Derbyshire and Nottinghamshire. Shortly after the Norman conquest, however, the county boundary was altered so as to incorporate extra settlements within the new lordship of Doncaster, which defended an important crossing of the Don. Land

---

Figure i Yorkshire's south-eastern boundary

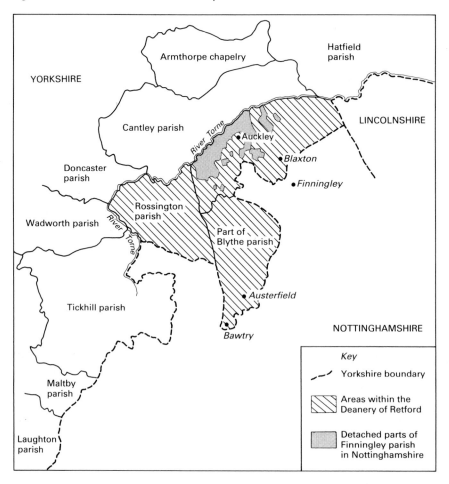

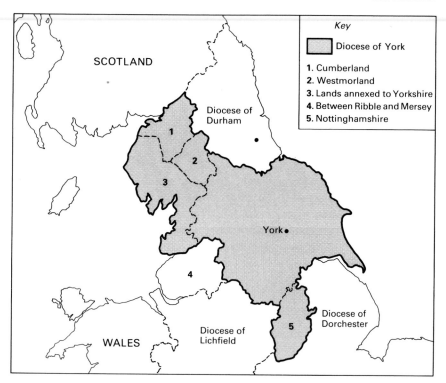

Figure ii   Yorkshire and the Diocese of York in 1086

communication between Yorkshire and southern England was restricted to a fairly narrow passage between the Pennine hills in the west and the marshlands in the east, and the Normans were naturally concerned about the old Roman route which formed the basis of the Great North Road. The pre-Norman arrangement of territories south of Doncaster can be recognized because it was partly preserved for ecclesiastical purposes until modern times. Auckley, Austerfield, Bawtry and Blaxton remained attached to the Nottinghamshire parishes of Blyth and Finningley, and together with the parish of Rossington they formed part of the deanery of Retford within the archdeaconry of Nottingham, instead of being grouped with other south Yorkshire parishes within the deanery of Doncaster. As each of these settlements lay just south of the Torne, this small river probably served as the original southern boundary of the county.

Some readjustment of the north-western border may also have taken place during the Norman period. Yorkshire was the only one of the six northern counties to have been created before the Norman Conquest; Lancashire, Cheshire and Westmorland did not come into being until well into the twelfth century. In 1086 the Yorkshire folios of Domesday Book included

3

the Lancashire lands that lay north of the Ribble, as well as part of south Westmorland and an estate in south-west Cumberland that formerly belonged to Earl Tostig. Each of these districts (together with the whole of Copeland, which was not included in the Domesday survey) remained within the diocese of York and the archdeaconry of Richmond long after the creation of the north-western counties. In the absence of firm evidence, however, it is impossible to say whether or not they were once regarded as forming part of the county of Yorkshire.

Yorkshire's three ridings take their distinctive name from the Viking word 'thrithing', meaning a third part. Only the former north Lincolnshire kingdom of Lindsey, with its north, south and west ridings, was divided in a similar manner. Perhaps the Yorkshire Ridings were created from territories that already had some unity before the Danes arrived. We may speculate, for example, that the West Riding was the result of the union of Elmet and Craven, but proof is lacking. York, of course, remained independent of all three parts. In turn the ridings were divided into wapentakes, which saw to the raising of armies, the levying of taxes, the maintenance of law and order, and to property transactions. Wapentake was a Scandinavian word which was derived from the symbolic manner in which weapons were flourished to signify agreement to the decisions of the open-air public assemblies. In other parts of the Danelaw similar administrative units in Derbyshire, Leicestershire, Lincolnshire and Nottinghamshire were also known as wapentakes. They seem to have been created from the amalgamations of smaller units known as hundreds (though, confusingly, in later times the words wapentake and hundred were interchangeable in the north Midlands). By the time of the Domesday survey of 1086 the change to wapentakes was already complete in the North and West Ridings and was in various stages of completion in the rest of the northern Danelaw. At that time, the East Riding was still divided into eighteen hundreds, but these were gradually converted into six wapentakes during the course of the next 80 years. Dickering wapentake, for instance, was first recorded in 1166 when it covered roughly the same area as the three Domesday hundreds of Burton, Hunthou and Turbar (*VCH East Riding*, II 1974: 2–3).

York had been the ecclesiastical capital of the North during the Roman Empire, and as far back as 314 its Bishop had attended the Council of Arles. After the pagan phase of Anglian settlement Christianity once more became the official religion of the region on Easter Day 627, when Paulinus baptized King Edwin of Northumbria at York and became the province's first Archbishop. The medieval diocese of York covered not only the territory included within the Yorkshire section of Domesday Book, but also the county of Nottinghamshire, which formed one of the five archdeaconries. The origins of this arrangement are to be found in mid-tenth-century grants which were designed to compensate the Archbishop for his loss of revenue during the Danish wars. In 956 Archbishop Osketel obtained a large estate centred upon

Southwell, and two years later he received the equally generous gift of Scrooby and Sutton near the Yorkshire border. When the county of Nottinghamshire was formed, it seemed a sensible arrangement to place the whole of this new unit under the ecclesiastical jurisdiction of the Archbishop of York. A more unusual step to increase revenue and help provide stability was taken in 972 when St Oswald, Bishop of Worcester, was allowed to retain his Midland diocese upon his appointment as Archbishop of York. The sees of Worcester and York were held jointly until 1016 and the arrangement was revived for a short time in 1040. Though the decision was indefensible canonically, it had a political justification during a turbulent period of York's history (Stenton 1947: 430).

The other archdeaconries comprised Richmond in the north-west and three that corresponded closely to the county's ridings under the names of Cleveland, York and East Riding. The rural deaneries into which the archdeaconries were divided did not assume their final form until the Norman period. Deanery boundaries within the Danelaw normally followed those of the wapentakes, and in Leicestershire the relationship was almost exact. Yorkshire practice varied from area to area. In Cleveland the ecclesiastical units usually differed from the civil ones. In the archdeaconry of York only Ainsty took its name from a civil area; Craven was an ancient name, and Doncaster and Pontefract deaneries each combined two wapentakes and shared another one between them and took their names from towns at the centres of new Norman lordships. And although the four East Riding deaneries borrowed the names of the wapentakes of Buckrose, Dickering, Harthill and Holderness, these civil units were not created until the twelfth century (YASRS CVII 1943: viii–x).

The history of Yorkshire has been deeply influenced by the great variety of soils and geological formations that are found within the county. Life on the Pennines or the North York Moors has always been a very different experience from life in low-lying agricultural districts such as Holderness and the Humberhead Levels. In many ways farmers in the Vale of York have had more in common with their counterparts in the Midland Plain than with the miners, steel workers and textile workers of their own county. No major part of England can be regarded as a self-contained region with common characteristics. Nevertheless, Yorkshire people have acquired a belief in themselves as a breed set apart from the rest, and this sentiment has proved more powerful than these great differences in ways of life. Those living beyond the county boundary have long acknowledged this separate Yorkshire identity, though they have usually done so in phrases far removed from the eulogies that Yorkshiremen have bestowed upon themselves. A tyke was a common sort of dog, but whereas Yorkshire people accepted the name as a term of praise for the tenacious attributes of the terrier, outsiders have used it as a term of abuse for a snarling, obstinate fellow. 'The indigence of Yorkshire are strong, tall, and long legg'd', wrote John Aubrey in the seventeenth century, 'they call 'em

5

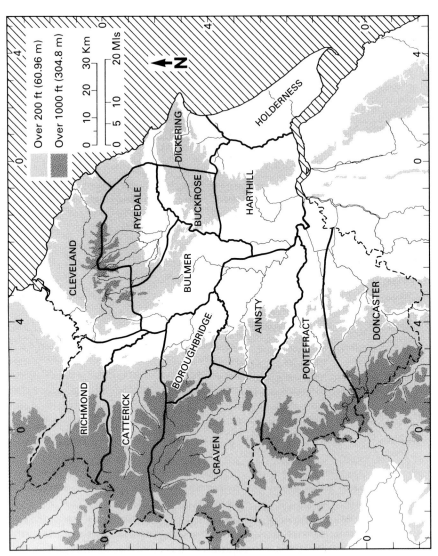

Over 200 ft (60.96 m)

Over 1000 ft (304.8 m)

N

30 Km
20
10
0

20 Mls
10
5
0

CLEVELAND

RYEDALE

PICKERING

BUCKROSE

HOLDERNESS

HARTHILL

BULMER

RICHMOND

CATTERICK

BOROUGHBRIDGE

AINSTY

PONTEFRACT

DONCASTER

CRAVEN

Figure iii Deaneries

opprobriously long-legd tyke.' The contemporary phrase 'To put Yorkshire of a man' meant to cheat or deceive him (Halliwell 1904: 874, 948).

In the west of the county the Pennine peaks rise to 2,415 ft at Whernside, and some parts have over 70 inches of rain per annum. Defoe described this range of hills as 'the English Andes', but no name was generally given to them before Charles Bertram (1723–65) cleverly forged a medieval manuscript with Roman-sounding names, including *Alpes Penina*, after which the Pennines was quickly accepted as an authentic ancient name. The Yorkshire Pennines are divided into two geological series. The northerly parts, from the Stainmore Pass in Teesdale as far south as Craven are mainly composed of Carboniferous Limestone, which produces spectacular natural scenery, rich lead veins, upland heaths and rough hill pastures. South of Skipton the limestone gives way to the sandstones and shales of the Millstone Grit measures, with extensive peat bogs and drier parts marked by heather. The Pennines were amongst the last parts of England to be settled; some hamlets are recorded in Domesday Book, but many more are the result of medieval assarting. Except in the more fertile dales that penetrated the hills, farmers concentrated upon livestock and earned extra income from a craft. Some areas prospered through having this dual economy, and upper Calderdale became one of the wonders of the Tudor age, for contemporaries were astonished that so much wealth could be generated in such bleak countryside. During the Industrial Revolution many Pennine dales were transformed into mill towns, while the hills above were enclosed with stone walls to extend the limits of cultivation or to preserve enormous stretches of moorland for grouse shooting. Further east, the gentler slopes of the Coal-Measure Sandstones supported medieval market towns, villages, hamlets and scattered farmsteads in a pleasant countryside before they too were altered almost beyond recognition by industrialization. In 1769 Arthur Young wrote, 'The country between Sheffield and Barnsley is fine, it abounds with the beauties of landscape', but when William Cobbett came the same way two generations later he remarked, 'All the way along from Leeds to Sheffield it is coal and iron and iron and coal.' The West Riding had lagged behind the two other ridings in its early development, but by the nineteenth century its population had far outstripped the rest.

In Queen Anne's reign the North York Moors were described as 'very barren grownde and covered with ling and bent throughout'. This bleak plateau, much of it over 1,000 ft, provided only the roughest grazing, and even the dales have never afforded an easy living. The farmers here had limited opportunities to combine husbandry with a craft and were always amongst the poorest and most backward in the country. Nor did William Camden, the Elizabethan antiquary, think much of Yorkshire's other hilly district, the Wolds. After noting that the lowland parts of the West Riding were 'pretty fruitful', he wrote, 'The middle is nothing but a heap of mountains, called Yorkeswold.' The verdict was too harsh, for though the High Wolds were given over to sheep-runs and rabbit warrens, the lower slopes supported

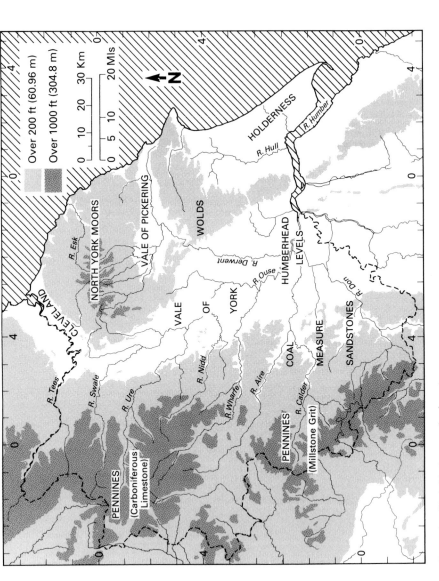

Over 200 ft (60.96 m)

Over 1000 ft (304.8 m)

20 Mls

30 Km

←N

HOLDERNESS

R. Humber

R. Hull

VALE OF PICKERING

WOLDS

NORTH YORK MOORS

R. Esk

CLEVELAND

R. Derwent

HUMBERHEAD

LEVELS

R. Ouse

VALE

OF

YORK

R. Teas

R. Swale

R. Ure

R. Nidd

R. Wharfe

R. Aire

COAL

MEASURE

SANDSTONES

R. Don

PENNINES

(Carboniferous

Limestone)

PENNINES

(Millstone Grit)

R. Calder

Figure iv Yorkshire's natural sub-regions

nucleated villages with large, arable fields. This crescent-shape range of chalk hills, stretching from the Humber to Flamborough Head and rarely rising above 800 ft, has long been a sheep-and-corn district with a character of its own. The numerous prehistoric features in the landscape attest to its popularity with settlers over the centuries.

Framed within these hills lie the vast Vale of York and subsidiary vales such as those of Pickering, Mowbray and Cleveland, flat farming land with only 24 inches of rain per annum. Upon entering Yorkshire, Henry VIII was taken to Scawsby Lees to see 'one of the greatest and richest valleys' that Bishop Tunstall had found 'in all his travels thro' Europe'. Farming systems varied according to the quality of the soils, which ranged from the fruitful earths covering the Magnesian Limestone belt to the ill-drained carrs of the Humberhead Levels and parts of the Vale of Pickering. All the Pennine rivers except the Tees find their way into the Ouse and the Humber, which was a great benefit in terms of inland transport but a serious problem in terms of drainage. Light, well-drained soils produced good crops, but elsewhere it made more sense for the farmers to concentrate on livestock. Wherever possible, each community tried to balance its resources; the townships and parishes of the Vale of Pickering extended in long, narrow strips onto the North York Moors, and in the south of the county various parishes had detached pastures in Hatfield Chase and other low-lying moorland areas.

Beyond the Wolds lies another rich agricultural district that was formerly troubled by drainage problems.

Lordynges, ther is in Yorkshire, as I gesse
A mersshy contree called Holdernesse

Chaucer's opening lines from *The Summoner's Tale* give an outsider's immediate reaction to an area where slow-moving streams and hundreds of meres once produced a watery surface. Now only Hornsea Mere is left, but in the Middle Ages the special character of Holderness was emphasized by the fact that it was almost an island, remote from the rest of England except by sea, cut off by the extensive carrs of the Hull Valley in the west and the Earl's Dyke to the north, and constantly eroded along its North Sea and Humber shores. Every slight rise supports a straggling village that has been rebuilt in brick during the eighteenth and nineteenth centuries. Daniel Defoe could find nothing remarkable along the coast – 'not a port, not a gentleman's seat, not a town of note' – but along the banks of the Humber splendid churches reflected the medieval wealth of the ports and market towns. In the Middle Ages this was one of the most prosperous parts of the country.

The changing fortunes of these natural sub-regions or *pays* forms the framework of this history of Yorkshire from the creation of the county to its destruction nearly a thousand years later. But even within these districts the life story of one community is often very different from that of its neighbour.

Thriving settlements are found next to villages which have disappeared completely, sprawling industrial communities and trim estate villages nestle side by side, and old market towns continue to fulfil their ancient role in a county that has some of the most populous cities in Britain. This variety of experience will be our central concern.

Chapter 1

The Early Middle Ages: Foundations and Growth

Anglo-Scandinavian Settlement

At the time of the Domesday Survey of 1086 England had a population of 1.5 to 2.25 millions. In Lennard's memorable phrase, it was already an old country, for it had as many settlements as were to be found scattered throughout the land 700 years later (Lennard 1959: 1). In Yorkshire the Anglian and Viking settlers had occupied not only the most fertile soils but also the second-best sites in poorly drained areas, so that by the eleventh century opportunities for further expansion were limited to the moors, the marshes and some of the remaining woodlands. Domesday Book records 1,830 settlements in Yorkshire, but as some outlying villages and hamlets, particularly in the West Riding, were unnamed berewicks of large estates, even this figure is too low. The West Riding had about 740 recorded settlements, the North Riding 649, and the East Riding 441 (Darby and Maxwell 1962: 7, 92, 170). In the North and East Ridings the pattern of settlement in the eleventh century was remarkably similar to the present scatter, and in the county as a whole more than four out of five of the towns, villages and hamlets that have ever existed had been founded by the time of the Norman Conquest. The property values recorded for 1066 show, moreover, that Yorkshire was fairly wealthy by national standards and that the East Riding was comparable with Lincolnshire, one of the richest counties at that time (Brooks 1966: 55).

The impact of the Vikings on the previous Anglian settlement pattern is evident from the county's place-names. Jensen maintains that 'the semantic content and linguistic form of the names indicate most Scandinavian place-names in Yorkshire must have been coined by Viking settlers at a time when they were still speaking their native language' (Jensen 1978). In the North Riding 223 out of the 649 Domesday Book settlement names are of Scandinavian origin and a further 66 are either hybrids or English names influenced by Scandinavian speech. The East Riding has a similar proportion, but the Viking presence was less pronounced further inland in the West Riding, except in the countryside around York and Doncaster. In north-western parts of the county place-names suggest that by the eleventh century the local inhabitants were the same mixture of Norwegians, Irish-Norse and Strathclyde Britons as were to be found in neighbouring Cumbria. In the north-east, however, the river Tees appears to have been a major cultural barrier, for both the place-names and the distribution of surviving Viking-age sculptures show that the Vikings did not penetrate far into the Anglian kingdom of Northumberland, which was centred on Bamburgh (Bailey 1980: 33).

A Viking place-name does not, of course, prove that a settlement was founded by the Vikings, for invaders may have renamed an old place. Streanaeschalch became Whitby, and numerous hybrid names like Barkston or Thurlstone denote Anglian settlements that took the names of their new owners. Archaeological evidence, particularly that of Viking-age sculpture, suggests that the Vikings sometimes settled in existing villages and left the names as they were. It is therefore difficult to draw any firm conclusions about the extent of fresh colonization by the Vikings. Much of the land that was only second best had already been settled by the Anglians, and place-name scholars no longer regard *by* and *thorpe* as reliable indicators of new settlements. The place-name elements *thwaite, royd, scholes* and *sett* provide firmer evidence of the clearing of marginal land, and so do the numerous Scandinavian names given to fields and minor topographical features, such as *toft, garth, holme, car, nabb, gate, keld, beck* and *gill*. Many of these minor names were created after the Norman Conquest and cannot be assigned to a particular century. Though the Vikings eventually adopted Old English, they kept much of their own vocabulary and pronunciation. Numerous common words in modern English have a Viking origin, but William of Malmesbury, the twelfth-century chronicler, noted that in his day northern dialect was unintelligible to people from the South of England.

Profound Scandinavian influence on the development of the English language, law and agrarian custom indicates that considerable numbers of Viking immigrants eventually settled in eastern and northern parts of the country. In Cumbria and north Yorkshire the most intriguing physical survivals from the Viking age are the stone crosses and hog-back tombstones that have been found in churchyards, or where they have been re-used as rubble or common building stones within the fabric of churches themselves. Whereas Anglian sculpture was the product of monasteries, Viking-age sculpture was a lay art, with knotwork as the dominant motif and with various shapes and designs that were peculiar to certain localities. Scandinavian mythology depicted on sculptured stones includes pagan stories of Wayland the Smith, Sigurd the Volsung (especially dragon-killing and heart-roasting) and Thor's fishing expedition. A Leeds' shaft combines Christian and pagan features by showing Wayland escaping with his wings and tools, accompanied by evangelists and ecclesiastics. During the 1867 restoration of Brompton church no less than eleven hog-back tombstones were discovered. Such three-dimensional monuments are often over four feet long and are shaped like a building with walls and a roof; at each end beasts cling onto the gables and bite into the ridge. End-beasts dominate the sculptures only within a ten-mile area between Brompton and the Tees, but hog-backs are distributed widely over north Yorkshire and Cumbria. They appear to be the distinctive art of Norwegian and Irish-Norse settlers from *c*. 920 to 1066 (Bailey 1980, *passim*).

Evidence of the Church's continued presence throughout the troubled years of the Viking invasions, despite the violent plundering and destruction of the monasteries, is provided by stones carved in the Anglian tradition which have been found at an old monastic site at Stonegrave Minster on the edge of the North York Moors (Firby and Lang 1981). Their stylistic connections are not with local secular workshops but with other Anglian ecclesiastical centres, especially those further west, and although they are not earlier than the Viking invasions they pre-date the eleventh-century fabric of the church. Elsewhere, the discovery of Viking weapons in Christian churchyards and the relative lack of pagan grave goods suggest that the new settlers soon accepted native religious customs. Viking York was ruled by a Christian king from *c*. 882 to 895. Nevertheless, the Viking invasions undoubtedly proved a considerable setback to organized Christianity, and Archbishop Wulfstan II (1002–23) constantly preached the dangers of pagan practices. Between 900 and 1066 the monastery at Burton on Trent was the only one in existence north of that river, and the nearest monastery to York was at Peterborough over 100 miles away. But while monastic life in the North was obliterated by the Vikings, some Anglian parish churches survived; there is little evidence of looting, nor of the destruction of churches inspired by pagan hatred of Christianity (Bailey 1980: 14). Early minster churches at Conisbrough, Ledsham and Masham retain architectural features that appear to pre-date the first Danish invasions. Such churches were normally associated with royal estates; Conisbrough's name means 'the King's stronghold' and the distribution of its dependent estates at the time of Domesday Book indicates that it was once the centre of an ancient lordship which stretched south from the river Don to the boundary of Northumbria. The scatter of parishes that still owed allegiance to Conisbrough after the Norman Conquest suggests that St Peter's Church was the original minster for the whole lordship (Hey 1979: 29–32). Despite the fission of its estate and parish Conisbrough affords a good example of continuity from the Anglian era through the Viking age to the time of the Normans and beyond.

The recovery and expansion of organized Christianity throughout the country after the first Viking invasion is indicated by the amount of Anglo-Scandinavian architecture that survives from the period 950–1100. At St Bartholomew's Church at Aldbrough, in Holderness, for example, a simple circular disc built into the nave wall as a sundial has the inscription 'Ulf had this church built for himself and for Gunwara's soul'. Firmer dating evidence is available at St Gregory's Church at Kirkdale, in a secluded and picturesque spot near Kirkby Moorside, where a similar sundial proclaims that 'Orm the son of Gamal, bought St Gregory's Church when it was broken and fallen, and had it made anew from the ground in honour of Christ and St Gregory, in the days of Edward the King and Tostig the earl', i.e. between 1055 and 1065. Some large quoins and a number of carved stones re-used as common building material came from the earlier church and its graveyard, and the nave walls and the arches leading into the tower and chancel survive from Orm's eleventh-century rebuilding. Several neighbouring lords in Ryedale, notably at Appleton le Street and Hovingham, rebuilt their churches about the same time so in this area at least the parish system was complete before the Norman Conquest. Domesday Book refers to 167 churches in Yorkshire, but historians have long recognized that this figure is a serious under-recording. The church at Aldbrough is not mentioned, nor is that at Wharram le Street, where the tower, parts of the nave, and the foundations of the chancel all apparently pre-date the Norman Conquest.

Mercian influence is evident in the 'long and short' quoins of two late Anglo-Saxon churches in south Yorkshire, at Bolton on Dearne and Laughton en le Morthen. Laughton is a particularly instructive example of how much had been achieved by Anglo-Scandinavian settlers before the Norman Conquest. The settlement lies on the fertile soils of the Magnesian Limestone belt that had proved so attractive to early colonists. By 1066, when Earl Edwin of Mercia was lord of the manor, 54 carucates or about 6,000 acres of arable land had been brought into cultivation in and around Laughton and its dependent hamlets, and a large parish had been carved from territory that had been dependent upon the ancient minster at Conisbrough. The parish lay between the prehistoric and Roman Ricknield Street in the west and the county boundary in the east and south, with detached portions scattered in the neighbouring township of Wales. However, the northern and southern halves of the parish were almost separated by the independent township and parish of Dinnington, and the mother church at Conisbrough retained detached portions at Anston. Though Laughton had broken away from Conisbrough by the eleventh century, these topographical clues hint at its former subserviency.

Plate 1.1   All Saints Church, Hovingham. Hovingham Church stands near the gates of Sir Thomas Worsley's mid-eighteenth-century hall, its nave and chancel rebuilt in 1860 but its Anglo-Saxon tower intact. Early Anglo-Saxon churches had a gabled porch at their west end, and some of these, including those at Bardsey and Ledsham, were subsequently heightened and converted into towers. Bell towers were not introduced into England until the tenth century.

The large stones in the lower stage of the tower at Hovingham probably come from an earlier building; the huge side-alternate quoins are arranged in typical early-Northumbrian fashion. Part of a ninth-century Anglian cross is incorporated in the upper stage of the west wall, and until 1924 the carved slab that now serves as a reredos to the altar in the south aisle was used as common building stone high in the south wall.

The tower was probably completed not long before the Norman Conquest. It is topped by a Norman corbel-table and a modern pyramid roof. The tower is unbuttressed, is divided by string courses of square section, has two-light bell openings separated by mid-wall shafts, a course of stones laid in herringbone fashion, and a western doorway that are all typical of late Anglo-Saxon work. As this is a Northumbrian church it does not have the pilaster strips and long-and-short quoins that distinguish the Mercian style.

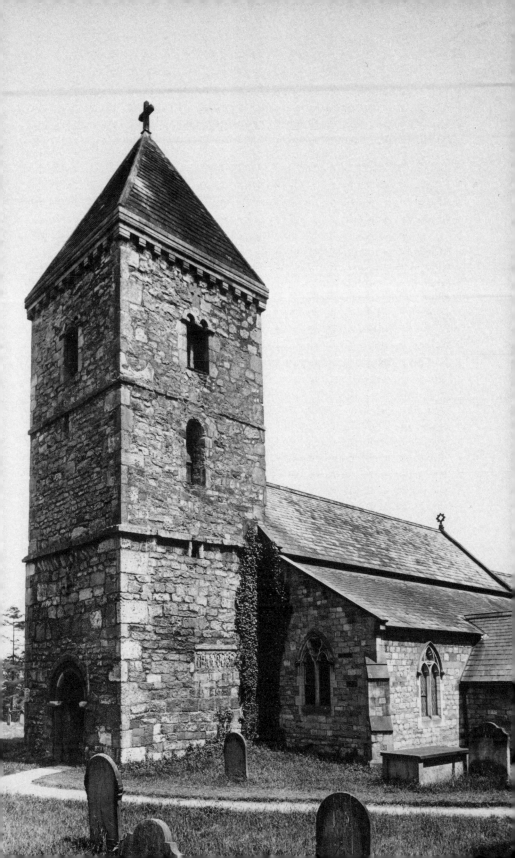

The Morthen part of Laughton's name is another intriguing survival, for it refers to the 'moorland district with a common assembly', which was probably an early Viking organization before the wapentake system was fully developed. Nearby Aston, Brampton and Dinnington were also described at various times as being 'in the Morthing', and the ancient meeting place of this former open-air assembly can be located in a hill meadow on the prominent ridge that separates the villages of Morthen and Upper Whiston (Hey 1979: 25–6, 37–41). The district name continued in use long after it ceased to have any practical meaning.

Yorkshire's complex medieval pattern of manors and parishes was largely in existence by the late Anglo-Scandinavian period. In south Yorkshire the disintegration of the old royal estate at Conisbrough produced a number of small pre-Conquest estates held by thegns. The fragmentary nature of some of these estates is clear from their entries in Domesday Book. Doncaster, for instance, was divided into three small manors, at least one of which is referred to in the 1002–4 will of a Mercian nobleman, Wulfric Spott. Wulfric also owned part of the township of Wales, 'the territory of the Welshman', which had been divided into at least two and possibly three manors by 1066. Mid-nineteenth-century maps show that these properties were associated with the three different parishes of Laughton, Treeton and Harthill, and that they were scattered either as single strips or as small blocks of land throughout the township. The fragmentary nature of the Domesday Book ownership pattern was still evident in the reign of Queen Victoria. The same phenomenon can be observed a few miles away at Kirk Sandall, where the western wall of St Oswald's church is thought to be eleventh-century work. The 1,637 acres of the parish were divided into three separate blocks, with 650 acres at Sandall, 490 acres at Streetthorpe (whose name is derived from the Old Norse personal name, Styrr), and 497 acres of detached marshland at Trumfleet. In 1066 Earl Harold's lordship of Conisbrough included two carucates at Kirk Sandall, two carucates at Streetthorpe, and 1 carucate 3 bovates at Lond Sandall. All these territories formed part of the parish of Kirk Sandall, which still owed some allegiance to Conisbrough's church after the Norman Conquest, even though Conisbrough was some 8 miles away in the west. Intermingled with Harold's possessions at Long Sandall, however, were 6 carucates 5 bovates belonging to Scotecol and half a carucate shared by Ulsi and Rainald, and these formed part of Doncaster parish, which separated Sandall from Conisbrough (Hey and Magilton 1983).

A striking parallel to Sandall is provided by the parish of Warmsworth on the opposite side of Doncaster. The parish was small with just over 1,000 acres. Until the Second World War the church stood alone, half a mile from the village, just inside the parish boundary. The earliest surviving deeds show that the village and its open fields had acquired their shape by the late thirteenth or early fourteenth century, and a 1726 estate map, together with Ordnance Survey maps of the second half of the nineteenth century, offer evidence that

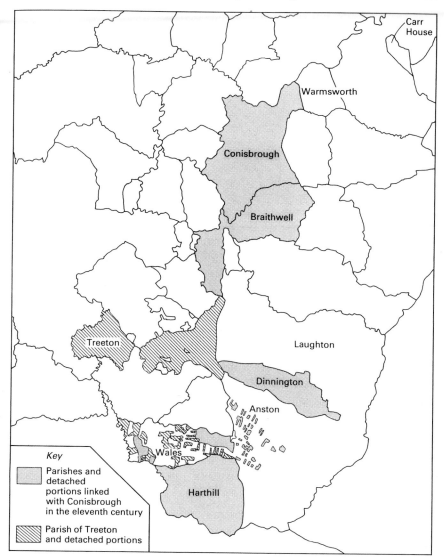

Figure 1.1   South Yorkshire parishes

the village was deliberately laid out on a regular plan. Domesday Book records two manors, and later manorial history reveals that one manor was dependent upon the lordship and parish of Doncaster, that the other had severed its links with Conisbrough by the early twelfth century at the latest, but that Castle Farm remained within both the lay and ecclesiastical jurisdiction of Conisbrough. Despite the replanning of the village the properties of the two manors and of Castle Farm were intermingled within the open fields. No firm

17

dates are available, but as Warmsworth is derived from a Mercian personal name it is possible that the village was replanned and renamed during the century before the Norman Conquest when Mercian lords were penetrating southern Northumbria (Hey and Magilton 1983).

This disintegration of old estates during the Anglo-Scandinavian period was happening all over Yorkshire and many similar examples could be cited. Nevertheless, the Yorkshire folios of Domesday Book reveal the continued existence of ancient, extensive lordships alongside the newer, smaller holdings. Large multiple estates known as shires in Anglian Northumbria and as sokes in the Scandinavian era contained out-lying properties called berewicks and sokelands that were controlled from a head village or caput. In Domesday Book 64 per cent of the Yorkshire entries were linked in such estates; for example, Gilling had 9 berewicks and 19 sokelands, and Wakefield had 8 berewicks and 14 sokelands (Darby and Maxwell 1962: 4, 88). Riponshire, Sowerbyshire, and several other multiple estates retained the English description of shire long after the Norman Conquest. Hallamshire had 16 Domesday Book berewicks, Howdenshire had 18 berewicks and 7 sokelands, and Allertonshire had 11 berewicks and 24 sokelands. Professor Glanville Jones has suggested a hierarchy of multiple estates, with the earliest having their caput near an Iron Age fort or a Roman settlement (Sawyer, ed. 1976: 15–40). One of his outstanding examples of an early estate is Burghshire, which extended from the Pennine hills down to the lower valleys of the Ure, the Nidd and the Wharfe; by this means a satisfactory balance was achieved between rough moorland and woodland pasture on the one hand and large expanses of good-quality arable on the other. Aldbrough, the caput of Burghshire, was built on the site of Isurium Brigantum, the fortified Roman cantonal capital of the Brigantes; this was the burh which gave the shire its name. Domesday Book records 135 vills within this shire, of which 60 were wholly or partly royal vills. By that time two royal multiple estates were centred on Aldbrough and Knaresborough (later, the headquarters of a royal hunting forest), but the intermixture of berewicks and sokelands suggests that they once formed part of a single estate. Most shires had been truncated long before 1066, and although Yorkshire has disappointingly few pre-Conquest charters and wills to provide enlightenment upon these matters, it is clear that in the late Anglo-Scandinavian period the pattern of landownership was complex. On the eve of the Norman Conquest Earls Morcar, Edwin and Harold, the Archbishop of York and the Bishop of Durham formed a group of big landowners, but a large number of thegns held numerous middling to small estates.

Even after the Norman Conquest customary services and renders on northern manors were relatively light. According to an 1185 inquest at Temple Newsam tenants who held one or two bovates paid yearly 30*d.* per bovate, two hens and twenty eggs, and every year they ploughed and harrowed four days for the lord, mowed hay one day, and worked four boon days in the autumn;

they also washed and sheared sheep for two days, repaired the millpond and transported new millstones. Similar light services were demanded on the Templars' estates at Skelton and Colton in the West Riding and at Allerthorpe in the East Riding, and on other manors as far apart as Burton Agnes (East Riding), Kirkby Moorside (North Riding) and Harewood (West Riding) (Kapelle 1979: 66–7). These were the traditional customs of the soke and the shire. Specific tasks were performed at certain times of the year but northern countrymen were not obliged to do weekly work on the lord's land. Manors with large demesnes were not characteristic of medieval Yorkshire, and as in eastern England large numbers of farmers were relatively free. The Yorkshire place-names Dringhoe and Dringhouses are derived from a Scandinavian word for a comparatively well-off farmer, and though drengs generally disappeared after the Norman Conquest, as late as 1265 six properties at Burton Agnes were still said to be held 'in drengage' (*VCH, East Riding*, II 1974: III). Two-thirds of the population recorded in the Yorkshire folios of Domesday Book were free villeins, and in only a few settlements did the proportion fall below half. In the North Riding villeins amounted to 79 per cent of the recorded population, in the East Riding 73 per cent, and in the West Riding 54 per cent. Most of the rest of the recorded population were described as bordars, who were probably smallholders who had made new clearings at the edge of settlements. In the West Riding, where pioneers still had ample opportunity to advance the cultivation of moors and woodlands, bordars numbered one in three of the recorded population, but in the other two ridings, where most of the available land was already farmed, they numbered less than one in five (Darby and Maxwell 1962: 36–7, 118–20, 194–5). No serfs are recorded in the Yorkshire folios of Domesday Book, but later references suggest that this omission is misleading. Commenting on Swein's invasion, the Archbishop of York, Wulfstan II wrote, 'often a slave binds very fast the thegn who previously was his master, and makes him a slave' (Finberg, ed. 1972: 476).

On the best arable lands Anglo-Scandinavian farmers cultivated their village fields right up to their parish boundaries. By the eleventh century Holderness villages were as thick upon the ground as they are at the present day. Domesday Book portrays Holderness as one of the most densely populated parts of England, with little land left for development. Very few settlements, except those on the eastern slopes of the Wolds between Cave, Cottingham and Beverley, retained any woodland, and the corn-growing land was already fully tilled. In the large township of Kilham the acreage under the plough at the time of the Domesday Survey corresponds exactly with the 384 oxgangs or bovates that were being farmed there in 1729 (Harvey 1983: 101). Many other Holderness communities had cleared their land as far as their parish boundaries before the Norman Conquest. A grant from King Cnut to the Archbishop of York of an estate in Patrington in 1033 mentions many boundary points that can be identified with those of the medieval parish boundary (Farrer, ed. 1914: 23–7). Only in waterlogged areas, such as the marshy district between Wawne, Sutton, Rise and Routh, were the boundaries not agreed until as late as the thirteenth century.

In Edward the Confessor's reign numerous freeholders (the Domesday survey records 45 different names) held land in Holderness, often jointly or in small parcels. Upon the Norman Conquest all these men lost their land to Drogo, otherwise known as Dreu de la Beuvrière, a Flemish supporter of William the Conqueror; only estates belonging to the Church remained outside his control. The place-name Holderness hints at the possibility that a similar unity may have prevailed immediately after the Danish invasions of the ninth century, for a 'hold' was a Danish nobleman who could wield considerable territorial power. Dr Mary Harvey has suggested that this era was the time when the distinctive field systems of Holderness came into being (Harvey 1983). Their marked regularity of form certainly implies that they were imposed from above over the whole district as part of a planned policy. Documents shed no light on the form and organization of these fields until the thirteenth century, but as large tracts of arable land had been brought into cultivation here by 1066 it is feasible that the Holderness field systems were already ancient by that time. Cornfields were laid out in long, parallel lands, which were often over 1,000 yards long, and in some townships over a mile long. Despite this length the arable was usually divided into only two fields, and these fields acted as the cropping units. The Holderness arrangement was therefore very different from the classic three-field system of midland England, where strips frequently changed direction to suit the local topography and where the cropping units were sub-divisions of the fields, known as furlongs. In Holderness furlongs were few and large, and within any one field system their structure was similar; each contained the same number of lands and each had the same proportion of broad and narrow lands lying in the same relative position to each other. Recent work on Northamptonshire suggests that such systems may not be unique, and that long lands were an early feature of even those midland townships which by the twelfth century had developed a classic open-field system (Rowley, ed. 1981). In Holderness, however, the original system was never modified into a complex pattern of short lands and small furlongs.

In addition to a regular physical lay-out, the sequence of ownership in Holderness was the same in each furlong and field, a method known as 'sun-division'. For example, lands at Skeffling, Halsham and Brandesburton in 1227 were said to be 'lying everywhere to the sun' (English 1979: 195), and at Preston each of the two open fields was divided into seven 'bydales' which were laid out in regular order from east to west, with the same pattern of ownership in each bydale (Harvey 1978). This method of laying out lands 'towards the sun' is also recorded in thirteenth-century charters for the Magnesian Limestone parishes of Barnburgh and Harthill in south Yorkshire, and in adjoining parts of Derbyshire and Nottinghamshire (Postles 1979: 1–23). However, the West Yorkshire Archaeology Survey has discovered similar evidence, mainly from the thirteenth century, from villages and hamlets in every part of their modern county, from Burney in the north, Wadsworth in the far west, Old Lindley in the south-west, Tyersall and Ulvesthorpe in the centre, Chevet, Wintersett and Woolley in the south-east, and Castleford, Colton, Ledston and Shippen in the east. This was not an area of intensive Viking settlement, nor is there any correlation here between 'sun division' systems and place-names (Faull and Moorhouse, eds 1981: 197–8).

Holderness villages have none of the regularity of their fields. Many are strung out over a mile in length and appear to have a composite or polyfocal structure, a physical arrangement that matches the Domesday evidence which shows that in 1066 most villages were divided into two or more estates. The English names of many Holderness villages imply that the Danes were content to take over and add to existing settlements without replanning the tofts and crofts associated with the village houses. The Wolds villages, too, are irregular in shape, but here again the arable was usually laid out in two large fields with long lands (Harvey 1983). Except on the High Wolds soils throughout this area had been tilled long before the Norman Conquest, and though the name of the Wolds had been derived from its primeval woodland, no wood remained at the time of the Domesday survey. A grant of an estate at Newbald on the western edge of the Wolds reveals that in 963 the 30 carucates recorded in Domesday Book were already being cultivated. On the chalk Wolds the Newbald estate boundary ran through dry valleys and along a 'dyke' or prehistoric embankment, and was aligned upon prehistoric mounds; off the hills it followed watercourses and the limits of the arable fields. Its line can be identified as that of the medieval parish boundary (Allison 1976: 60–1).

In the Vale of York some large stretches of woodland survived the onslaught of generations of Anglian and Scandinavian settlers. The wooded district to the north of York later formed the Norman Forest of Galtres, and the woods in the low-lying, watery countryside between the Ouse and the Derwent were preserved until the district ceased to be a royal forest in 1235. The waterlogged carrs towards the Ouse and the Humber were also sparsely settled, yet even here diking and draining had begun before the Norman Conquest. In central parts of Yorkshire the open arable fields occupied far less territory than in the Wolds and Holderness.

Dr June Sheppard has shown that at Wheldrake some 350 acres of arable land surrounding the village had been enclosed by a turf dyke by 1140 at least; 350 acres were sufficient to support about fifteen to twenty households before new assarts could be reclaimed from the forest after 1235. She has also reconstructed a regular pattern of sixteen original plots arranged around the village street, and has suggested that this plan originated either in the Anglo-Scandinavian period or possibly shortly after William's harrying of the north in 1069–70 (Sheppard 1966). Central Yorkshire provides numerous examples of regular, planned villages arranged around a street or green, sometimes with associated field systems laid out by the 'sun-division' method. Unfortunately, the origins of these plans cannot usually be placed in a firm historical context; in fact it is clear that they range fairly widely in time. In lower Wensleydale East Witton village was not replanned until the late thirteenth or early fourteenth century and in the East Riding Wawne was not laid out on regular lines until the fifteenth century (Allison 1976: 80–1). Dr Sheppard believes that the majority of such plans were implemented before 1200. She has applied Swedish techniques of metrological analysis to identify the dimensions of village tofts and field units shown on seventeenth- and eighteenth-century maps and to interpret these dimensions in terms of multiples of ancient units of measurement, particularly the 18 ft perch. Even where bovates had gone out of cultivation by the time of the maps the integrity of basic tenurial units has been remarkably preserved over the centuries. In eighty-nine of a sample of 182 villages that have some elements of a regular plan, that is 48 per cent, the medieval fiscal assessment of the village was related directly to the length of frontage of each toft. The origins of these assessments and measurements may take us back well before the Norman Conquest (Sheppard 1974: 118–35).

Many small settlements with single-field systems had been established high on the Pennine hills by the Anglo-Scandinavian era, if not before. In addition to the unnamed berewicks of Hallamshire, Domesday Book records three small estates on the edge of the moors in south-west Yorkshire. At 700 ft a small plot of cultivated land at Onesacre had been named after a Viking, at 850 ft Holdworth was the enclosure of an Anglo-Saxon Halda, and at 900 ft Ughill had taken its name from either an Anglo-Saxon Ugga or a Viking Uggi (Smith 1961: 224–8). Further north, the townships that formed the Graveship of Holme within the huge manor of Wakefield were already recognizable to the compilers of Domesday Book. East of the river Holme they recorded Cartworth, Hepworth, Wooldale, Fulstone and Thurstonland, and to the west Holme, Austonley, Thong, and possibly Yateholme. Each of these settlements was perched high above the deeply incised valleys of the river and its tributary streams, which formed the township boundaries until reorganization in Victorian times. At 1,000 ft Holme had almost reached the limits of cultivation, with steep, infertile ground fit only for rough grazing rising beyond to 1,900 ft at the county boundary. Although each township had some common arable land, this was a pastoral area, some of which was farmed only on a temporary basis. Within Wooldale township the common Viking place-name Scholes is derived from a shepherd's summer hut or hovel. Not far away, Upper Denby had the only vaccary or cattle-farm recorded in the Yorkshire Domesday folios, but in this Pennine area there were surely already many more.

The great majority of Yorkshire people lived in the countryside, but Domesday Book shows that the county capital was already a bustling place, second only to London in size and importance. York had developed rapidly as an urban community under the Anglians and its economy boomed under the direction of Scandinavian merchants and craftsmen, its population doubling in size. York was one of the greatest centres of North Sea trade and a large and prosperous town by contemporary standards. Between the Danish invasions and the Norman Conquest York and Chester appear to have been the only mint towns north of the Trent. Viking-age coins found at York are inscribed with forty Scandinavian, thirteen English and five Celtic names, suggesting that 'the integration of the settlers with the native population was far less complete in York than in any other part of England in which the Vikings settled' (Smart 1968). *The Anonymous Life of St Oswald* describes York *c.* 980 as a densely populated city with rich Scandinavian merchants, but with many poor buildings. By the reign of Edward the Confessor, York had between 1,600 and 1,800 houses and at least fourteen churches, of which the tower of St Mary Bishophill Junior is the outstanding survivor. The York Vikings had soon adopted Christianity, and Guthfrith, their second king, was buried in the Minster. Carved grave-covers and other stone sculptures have been found under and near the Minster in a large Viking-age cemetery. *The Law of the Northumbrian Priests*, compiled by Archbishop Wulfstan I (1002–23) in his later years, shows that the behaviour of the clergy in this populous city was not all that it should have been, however. Wulfstan instructed them not to frequent taverns, to have only one wife, not to put 'unsuitable things' in church, not to bring weapons into church, not to celebrate in wooden chalices nor to say mass before the church was consecrated, but to 'love and honour one God . . . and entirely cast out every heathen practice' (Aylmer and Cant 1977: 18).

The name York is derived from the Scandinavian Jorvic, and many of the city's street names retain the Scandinavian element 'gate'. Property boundaries first defined a thousand years ago survived into modern times. The Vikings constructed the curving Micklegate, the 'Great Street' which descended through the former Roman colonia on the west bank of the river to the Ouse bridge (the only bridge across the Ouse until 1863) and into the commercial heart of Jorvic around Coppergate, Castlegate, Ousegate and Pavement. In 1972 a group of Viking leather-workers' premises were unearthed in Pavement, and four years later excavation began on the now-famous Coppergate site. The dramatic discoveries included three Viking-age timber buildings set side by side at right angles to the street and running back towards the river Foss. Coins found in their earth floors date their construction to *c.* 960–85, and it is thought that they fell into decay some time during the eleventh century. Foundation beams were laid out a few feet below ground level, and walls consisting of several courses of horizontal plank cladding were supported on the inside by squared uprights. They are undoubtedly among the best preserved Viking-age buildings ever discovered by excavation. The woodworkers' waste which littered the site shows that Coppergate was indeed 'the street of the coopers'. Associated finds include antler combs, glass beads, amber jewellery, bone objects, brooches and dress pins, fragments of clothing and hundreds of pairs of leather shoes. In quantity the finds have more than doubled the total number of Viking artefacts previously found in Britain, and their quality has emphasized the creative aspects of Viking life that have to be set alongside the

thuggery and brutality. Jorvik offers tremendous scope for further excavations, with prime sites in and around King's Square and King's Court (a
possible royal palace) and at 'Earlsburgh' near St Mary's Abbey ruins in the
Museum Gardens (possibly the residence of the earls after 954); it is known
that the nearby church of St Olave was built for Earl Siward, who died in 1055
(York Archaeological Trust 1978: 10–14). The manner in which the Vikings
heightened and strengthened the old Roman and Anglian defences of the city
can be seen at the other side of the Museum Gardens.

The Norman Conquest

The power of the Irish Sea Vikings declined after 954 when Eric Bloodaxe was
killed in battle on the heights of Stainmore, the gateway to York via the Vale of
Eden. From that time onwards the Wessex kings struggled to re-establish
English control of the North, and they appointed earls and archbishops from
the South to discourage separation. But the North was still a borderland open
to invasion, and three times in the early decades of the eleventh century
Malcolm II of Scotland invaded Northumbria. The Scots remained a serious
threat until Earl Siward defeated Macbeth in 1054. Meanwhile, in 1013 the
Danes had reappeared in the Humber, intent under Swein's leadership on the
conquest of all England. They were joined by Uhtred, Earl of York and
Northumberland, for Danish armies could still depend upon support for
Danish separation in the North. Swein died at Gainsborough in 1014 and was
buried at York, though his body was later removed to Denmark. Cnut, his son
and successor, slew Uhtred treacherously at Wighill in 1016 and killed
Edmund, King of the English, in battle. A Danish leader was now ruler of all
England, but the North was still not well integrated into the rest of the country
and royal power there remained weak. The memory and to some extent the
outlook of the old kingdom was preserved (Kapelle 1979: 14–15).

Siward, the last great Scandinavian Earl of York, ruled Yorkshire
without great difficulty for 22 years. He ended the Northumberland revolt in
1042, secured his frontier with Cumbria, and in 1054 invaded Scotland to
defeat Macbeth. Upon his death in 1055 his young son, Waltheof, and another
northern contender for the succession, Cospatric, were both considered
unsuitable by King Edward. The Confessor preferred Tostig, third son of Earl
Godwin of Wessex, as his new northern earl. The appointment was unpopular
in the North, and Tostig's reckless levying of heavy taxes in a region that
traditionally had been taxed lightly soon led to disaster. In 1065 the North
revolted and Tostig was ejected from his earldom. The rebels made the
conciliatory move of inviting an outsider, Morcar, brother of Earl Edwin of

Mercia, to become their new earl, but Tostig found a powerful supporter in King Harold Hardrada of Norway, who had his eyes on the English throne. Their forces sailed up the Humber and the Ouse to Riccal, and on 20 September 1066 they defeated Morcar and Edwin's army at Fulford on the outskirts of York. Five days later King Harold Godwinsson arrived hot-foot from the South to deal with this threat to his new kingdom, and at Stamford Bridge, in what proved to be the last major battle that the Vikings fought on English soil, both Tostig and Harold Hardrada were killed. King Harold Godwinsson had then to return immediately to the south coast to face a separate threat of invasion. On 14 October 1066 he lay dead on the battlefield at Hastings, and on Christmas Day William the Conqueror was crowned the new king of England.

It soon became clear that William's greatest difficulty in securing his new kingdom would be in the North. There, in the spring of 1068, Edwin and Morcar rose to protest against his taxation levies of 1067 and 1068, just as previous northern leaders had revolted against Tostig. William feared the possibility that northern England might become an independent territory centred on York, supported by either the Danes or the Scots. At that time the North was remote from London and difficult to reach, so its continued inclusion within William's kingdom was by no means guaranteed. William marched to York, and having found that the rebels had withdrawn when their allies failed to support them, he left a garrison of 500 men under his sheriff, William Malet, in a hastily constructed motte-and-bailey castle. William's withdrawal from York in 1069 signalled a fresh rebellion, however. The Norman army at Durham was massacred and a large-scale northern revolt seemed likely. William returned to sack York and kill hundreds of rebels. William fitz Osbern, a trusted and outstanding soldier, was put in command, and the defences were strengthened by the construction of a second castle on the other side of the Ouse. It is impossible to say which castle came first, but they can be identified with the structure that became known as York Castle (which was strengthened in the thirteenth century by the addition of Clifford's Tower) and with the mound known as Baile Hill or the Old Baile, which stands further south just inside the city walls.

The northern rebels retreated into the hills to await support from the Danes. In September 1069 they attacked the Norman strongholds and killed William's soldiers. The Danes prepared a winter base in the Isle of Axholme at the head of the Humber, but William arrived before their fortifications were complete and drove them back across the river. He then had to deal with a minor rebellion in Staffordshire before he could advance on York. For three weeks the Yorkshire rebels held the northern bank of the Aire, but William's army eventually forded the river far upstream and marched onto York through the hills. They spent Christmas in the devastated city and then came to an agreement with the Danes, who abandoned their base and sailed home. The immediate threat to William was over, though it was not obvious at the time that the great Viking era was almost at an end, and the northerners still threatened to resume their guerilla tactics from the hills as soon as the Conqueror returned to London or Normandy. William decided that it was therefore time to destroy the rebels by a ruthless campaign of unparalleled severity, the infamous 'harrying of the North'.

William's army went into the hills to kill any rebels they could find, and in cold blood they devastated the Vale of York and the adjoining valleys so the guerillas would have neither food nor support. A terse entry in the *Anglo-Saxon Chronicle* for 1069 says that William 'laid waste all the shire'. Orderic Vitalis, a well-informed and unbiased chronicler who was born in 1075, wrote

Nowhere else had William shown so much cruelty. Shamefully he succumbed to this vice, for he made no effort to restrain his fury and punished the innocent with the guilty. In his anger he commanded that all crops and herds, chattels and food of every kind should be brought together and burned to ashes with consuming fire, so that the whole region north of the Humber might be stripped of all means of sustenance. In consequence so serious a scarcity was felt in England, and so terrible a famine fell upon the humble and defenceless populace, that more than 100,000 Christian folk of both sexes, young and old alike, perished of hunger. (Chibnall 1969: 231–3)

In a similar vein Symeon of Durham wrote that William devastated the North

throughout the winter and slaughtered the people . . . It was horrible to observe in houses, streets and roads human corpses rotting . . . For no-one survived to cover them with earth, all having perished by the sword and starvation, or left the land of their fathers because of hunger . . . Between York and Durham no village was inhabited.

According to Symeon, the countryside lay desolate for nine years, uninhabited except for bandits and wild animals, and those who did not die of famine were reduced to eating dogs and cats (*Rolls Series*, Vol. 75 1885: 188). The Normans massacred farmers, destroyed their dwellings, burned the previous year's harvest, smashed ploughs and tools, and slaughtered livestock. The harrying of the North was the most brutal campaign ever recorded in the annals of Yorkshire.

The long-term effects of the harrying are not easy to determine. The problem revolves around the interpretation of 'waste' entries in the Domesday survey, which was made seventeen years later. Inaccuracies, discrepancies and omissions make the Yorkshire folios an unsatisfactory text. Yorkshire was the most northerly county to be covered by the survey, and its size and manorial complexity caused the scribes many difficulties. No less than 40 per cent of the entries are concerned with berewicks and sokelands of manors, and (as in some other counties) information about two or more places is often combined in a single statement.

The difficulties of interpretation are increased by the unique Summary or Recapitulation, which must have had a separate origin from the Text, for the recorded names are markedly different in form and disagreements are common (Finn 1972: 16–22). Some places were not named in the Text because they were silently included in the entry for the head vill of a manor; nineteen places in the West Riding are mentioned only in the Summary (Darby and Maxwell 1962: 11). On the great archiepiscopal estate at Sherburn in Elmet, however, neither Text nor Summary names or numbers the berewicks, though contemporary sources record at least twenty (Stevenson 1912). The Domesday record of churches and woodland is also deficient, and as the clerks were concerned only with the arable side of farming, statistics relating to livestock were omitted. Domesday Book clearly is not a complete record.

The waste entries in the Yorkshire folios can be summarized as follows:

Table 1.1   Waste vills in Yorkshire in the Domesday survey of 1086

	Wholly waste	Partly waste	Total waste	Total entries in text	Percentage waste
North Riding	217	150	367	639	57.58
East Riding	67	93	160	424	37.38
West Riding	196	71	267	719	36.37
Yorkshire	480	314	794	1,782	44.5

(The figures are taken from Darby and Maxwell 1962: 61, 139, 212)

Waste vills were recorded in most counties, but the number in Yorkshire is remarkable. Wholly and partly waste manors formed 22 per cent of the total in Cheshire (half the Yorkshire total), 20.3 per cent in Derbyshire, and 18.2 per cent in Nottinghamshire. In Cheshire, where some settlements may have suffered from Welsh raids as well as from Norman harrying after the Mercian revolt, additional information for the year 1070 reveals that by 1086 the county had recovered to the level of waste recorded on the eve of the Norman Conquest.

Table 1.2   Waste vills in Cheshire, 1066–86

	Wholly waste	Partly waste	Total waste
1066	41	11	52
1070	135	27	162
1086	41	17	58

(The figures are taken from Darby and Maxwell 1962: 375)

Shropshire had made a similar recovery by the time Domesday Book was compiled. Why had Yorkshire not recovered in the same way? Either the harrying was of exceptional severity, or the waste entries have a different explanation. Dr Wightman has argued that in Domesday Book waste does not always mean devastated, deserted or valueless, but was often an administrative term used for manors that ceased to exist after the Norman Conquest because of amalgamation, or in cases of doubtful or undecided ownership (Wightman 1975). For instance, in the Text Penistone was entered not only under the King's possessions but also under Ilbert de Laci's, though it is clear from the Summary that here was only one estate. The explanation seems to be that Penistone was granted by the King to Ilbert during the making of the survey and that therefore the clerk wrote off one estate as waste. Moreover, some manors described as waste nevertheless had a value. Helperby, for example, was said to be waste without any ploughs, yet a farmer there paid six shillings rent, Ilkley was described as waste yet had a church and a priest, and Whixley was written off as waste even though it had two churches. The distribution of waste vills in Yorkshire does not support the claim that the waste was all due to William's harrying, nor does it lend weight to Bishop's ingenious theory that after 1069–70 tenants were forcibly removed from unproductive areas to resettle more fertile lands (Hunt, Pantin and Southern, eds 1948). Little or no waste is recorded along such major invasion routes as the lower reaches of the Ouse or the approach to Stamford Bridge from Bridlington, while on the other hand plenty of waste vills are recorded in Holderness and parts of south Yorkshire, which lay well away from the areas that suffered from the harrying. Waste entries in north-west Yorkshire coincide very closely with the wapentakes of Ewecross and Staincliffe, whereas just across their boundaries many inhabited vills are recorded (Raistrick 1968: 83–4). Domesday Book does not therefore seem a reliable guide on this matter. Could a comparatively small army really have done sufficient damage for so much land to remain devastated seventeen years later? Can we really believe that no less than 480 settlements, that is 27 per cent of those recorded in the Yorkshire folios of Domesday Book, were deserted for at least seventeen years, yet nearly all of them were subsequently resettled with their former place-names and boundaries intact?

Many personal names of a pre-Conquest character appear in charters that date from the later eleventh century to the thirteenth century. The vigorous northern literary tradition in the Middle English period and its distinctive dialect also suggest the survival of an Anglo-Scandinavian population (Barrow 1969). The relative scarcity of Norman place-names implies that the new settlers came in only at the top rank. Domesday Book shows that at this level, however, the Norman take-over in Yorkshire was virtually complete. As Professor Le Patourel has written, 'It is only as one works through this remorseless catalogue of Normans that the magnitude of the revolution is brought home to one' (Le Patourel 1971). Even some of the sub-tenants had come over from France, and those English thegns who survived usually retained only a fraction of their former estates, and then as tenants of some Norman lord. William also suppressed the Earldom of York and reduced the Province of York to a dependency of Canterbury. When Archbishop Ealdred died in 1070 he was succeeded by Thomas, a canon from Bayeux; the new Bishop of Durham was also a Norman.

Norman Castles

Immediately after the Conquest the Normans used forced labour to erect hundreds of private castles up and down the country. In the absence of documentary evidence in this poorly recorded period it is difficult to distinguish these earthworks from similar structures erected during the civil wars of the reign of King Stephen, and castle place-names have to be treated with care for they may refer to earlier structures dating back as far as the Iron Age. The *Anglo-Saxon Chronicle* says of William, 'Castles he caused to be made, and poor men to be greatly oppressed', and of Stephen's reign, 'They filled the whole land with these castles. They sorely burdened the unhappy people of the country with forced labour on the castles. And when the castles were made they filled them with devils and wicked men.' The majority of these earthworks were abandoned in more stable times; at Castle Hill, Bardsey, pottery found during excavation was restricted in date to the twelfth and thirteenth centuries, and at Beighton (then just inside Derbyshire but now part of south Yorkshire) reference was made in the early fourteenth century to 'the tower of the former castle'. Fieldwork and local historical research are still adding to the list of Norman military earthworks, and the West Yorkshire Archaeological Survey has recently concluded that a combination of minor place-names, field-names and medieval surnames suggests that at least fourteen minor castles still await discovery in that part of Yorkshire (Faull and Moorhouse, eds 1981: 736, 739).

The simplest Norman defensive structure was a ringwork enclosed by a ditch. Such earthworks may have been an early form, a hasty, short-time deterrent; at Burton in Lonsdale a ringwork was later converted into a motte-and-bailey castle, and at Castle Hall Hill, Mirfield, another earthwork may have been adapted in a similar manner and given a bailey which now forms the cemetery of the adjoining church. Each structure was constructed to fit the local topography, though this may be less obvious now than it was in the eleventh or twelfth century. Two miles north of Doncaster the deserted motte-and-bailey at Langthwaite looks difficult to defend, but it was presumably once surrounded by marshy land. The Fossards, lords of the soke of Doncaster

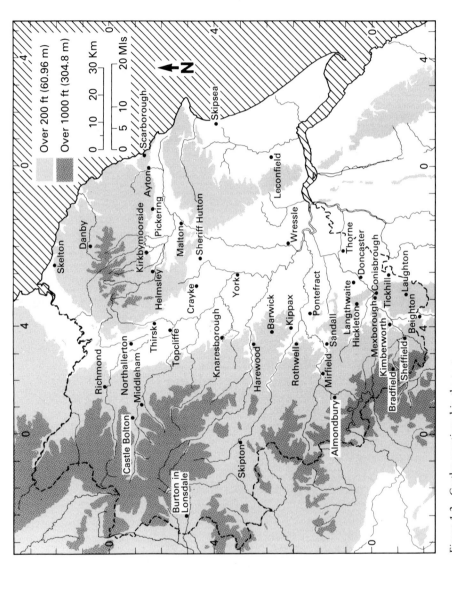

Over 200 ft (60.96 m)

Over 1000 ft (304.8 m)

0   5   10   20   30 Km

0   10   20   MIs

N

Skelton

Danby

Kirkbymoorside

Ayton

Pickering

Helmsley

Malton

Sheriff Hutton

Scarborough

Skipsea

Leconfield

Wressle

Thorne

Doncaster

Conisbrough

Laughton

Tickhill

Beighton

Sheffield

Bradfield

Kimberworth

Mexborough

Hickleton

Langthwaite

Sandall

Mirfield

Pontefract

Kippax

Rothwell

Barwick

Almondbury

Harewood

York

Crayke

Knaresborough

Topcliffe

Thirsk

Middleham

Northallerton

Richmond

Castle Bolton

Skipton

Burton in Lonsdale

Figure 1.2   Castles mentioned in the text

and great Yorkshire landowners, thought it a suitable place to protect the approach to Doncaster, where they had erected another castle on the foundations of a Roman fort and an Anglo-Scandinavian burh. Such castles acted not only as a place of refuge but as an administrative centre and as a base from which a wide area could be controlled.

Not all Norman castles were constructed near major roads and important river crossings; some were built in remote places high on the hills in order to subdue the native population. The lords of Hallamshire had their headquarters at Sheffield Castle, but they thought it prudent to have a moorland base seven miles away at Bradfield. Perhaps their first choice of site was Castle Hill, a natural protuberance at nearly 1,000 ft above sea level, which may have been adapted as a small oval ringwork, but soon they started to build one of Yorkshire's most impressive motte-and-baileys on nearby Bailey Hill. Though the 60 ft high motte and the curving rampart of the three-quarter acre bailey are now covered with trees, the earthwork is still an awesome sight, especially in winter. It commands extensive views across the valley and is protected by a wide ditch, and on the western side by a rocky precipice. In time, the earthwork on Bailey Hill had a significant effect on the local settlement pattern, for a church was built alongside it and the hamlet of High Bradfield (or Kirkton) grew up nearby. A local legend, which is typical of a type that harks back to an early dispute, maintained that the church was originally intended for Low Bradfield, but that each night supernatural forces re-erected it on the present site. An Anglo-Saxon cross, which now stands inside the church, was found in Low Bradfield, so there may be some truth in the old story.

Fears of invasion from Scotland or Cumbria, or perhaps of fresh attacks by the Vikings, and worries of further revolts in the north led the Normans to occupy Yorkshire as a border zone. William created compact lordships to support major castles, even where this meant a complete regrouping of estates. In the Welsh Marches he brought into existence the two large lordships of Chester and Shrewsbury and in the North-West he grouped all the lands north of the Ribble into Roger de Poitou's new honour of Lancaster. Northern England had an unusually large number of compact lordships known as castellanies, which defended the Pennine crossings and the entrances to the Vale of York. In 1086 the whole of Yorkshire was divided between only 28 tenants-in-chief and king's thegns, whereas the smaller, neighbouring county of Lincolnshire had at least 69. Ambitious, competitive, ruthless men who were determined to hang on to what they had got were deliberately chosen to establish Norman control over this vulnerable area.

In 1071, shortly after the harrying of the North, work began on a castle at a new site of great strategic importance high above the river Swale, a site that took the appropriate Norman name of Richmond, the 'strong hill'. The honour of Richmond was one of the three largest feudal holdings that William created, with 440 dependent manors in many parts of England; the Yorkshire section of the lordship formed an unusually large and coherent estate of 199 manors and 43 outlying properties, which together established a powerful military presence in the north-western part of the county near the junction of the main routes coming out of Scotland into the northern Vale of York. Richmond was granted to Alan the Red, or Alan Rufus, a cousin of the Count of Brittany, and it continued with this Breton family until 1399. Herringbone masonry and other stylistic details suggest that the curtain wall, the original gatehouse and Scolland's Hall were completed by the end of the eleventh century. Scolland's Hall is the earliest example of this type of domestic accommodation within a castle courtyard in the whole of Europe; it stands two storeys high and the principal rooms on the first floor were reached by an outer staircase. It remained the chief residence within the castle even after a majestic and well-preserved keep was raised more than 100 ft high over the gatehouse during the third quarter of the twelfth century. The keep's strange position at the castle entrance is unique, and it seems to have been built purely for military purposes. Richmond was also the first English castle to have projecting mural towers to improve its defences; two of the three towers remain, and one contains the tiny castle chapel. An extensive open space or outer bailey stretched beyond the castle walls to deny cover to an attacking army, though much of this space has since been built upon. It kept the name of The Bailey after its transformation into a market place, and its curving line is well preserved by shop frontages. Royal grants of 1313 and 1341 authorized the building of town walls above the bailey defences, but now only two sections of walling and the remains of two of the four bars survive.

Richmond was not mentioned in Domesday Book, but the name is recorded in a charter of 1109–14 and the borough that nestled under the protection of the castle is referred to in a document of 1136–45. The properties or burgage plots of the townsmen radiated from the market-place and along the two extramural developments of Bargate and the significantly named Frenchgate. Richmond was also made an important ecclesiastical centre as the focal point of a vast archdeaconry. Holy Trinity Church, the centrepiece of the market-place, contains some Norman work within its fourteenth-century tower, but it was described by John Leland at the end of the Middle Ages as merely a large chapel. The parish church of St Mary's stands to the rear of Frenchgate, well away from the castle, but the reasons for this inconvenient choice of site are not clear. It may have served a pre-Norman settlement (as at Pontefract or Leeds), or it may have been built at the edge of the new town when the restrictions of the market-place site of Holy Trinity became obvious (as at Doncaster); it has Norman nave arcades and a dedication that was popular in Norman times. Much of the architecture and the plan of eleventh- and twelfth-century Richmond is remarkably well-preserved today.

At the other end of the county the threat of invasion from the sea was countered by the restructuring of Holderness into a single compact lordship (with the exception of the estates held by the Archbishop of York and the

Bishop of Durham). The new lord was Drogo or Dreu de la Beuvrière, a Fleming who had accompanied William at Hastings but who soon returned to the continent, perhaps in disgrace. By 1087 William had regranted the new honour to Odo, a fellow countryman from Aumale in north-east Normandy. Odo's headquarters was at Skipsea, where a massive motte rises nearly 50 ft from the fields, with an 8 acre bailey protected by high banks. The site was once surrounded by a glacial mere, and its present desolate condition dates from the suppression of a rebellion in 1221, when Henry III ordered its destruction. A cluster of houses near the southern entrance marks the position of a small Norman borough that failed to survive the dismantling of the castle. The lords of Holderness did not give their knights compact blocks of land, but their scattered possessions were nevertheless much larger in total than similar estates elsewhere in Yorkshire; by 1200 most Yorkshire knights' fees ranged in size from 5 to 27 carucates, but in Holderness they averaged 48 carucates, despite the fact that this was one of the richest parts of the county (English 1979: 139, 142). No doubt the Normans were concerned to prevent any further Danish invasions via the east coast and the Humber. For them, Yorkshire was a border region which needed exceptional measures and a firm hand.

The central Vale of York was dominated by great estates based on the four mighty castles of Pontefract, Wakefield, Conisbrough and Tickhill. Two of these castles were at the centres of ancient lordships; two were the centres of new Norman honours. The new honour of Pontefract occupied almost the whole of the wapentakes of Staincross, Osgoldcross, Agbrigg and Morley and parts of Barkston Ash and Skyrack. This enabled it to guard the principal crossings of the Pennines; particularly the Aire Gap, and to control the north–south roads that were funnelled between the western hills and the marshlands of the Humberhead Levels. Pontefract Castle was built on the old Roman road from Doncaster to Catterick and the eastern boundary of the honour more or less followed the alternative route north from Doncaster to York. The King granted this new lordship to Ilbert de Laci from Lassy, south of Bayeux. Pontefract takes its name from the old French words *pont freit* for broken bridge (hence the local pronunciation Pomfret), for the castle and its borough were built on a new site some distance away from the pre-Conquest manorial centre at Tanshelf. The new name was not recorded in Domesday Book, and the burgesses who were already established under the protection of the castle were numbered with the inhabitants of Tanshelf. Pontefract was also made the head of a deanery.

Similar developments can be observed at Tickhill, where a new Norman honour guarded the southern boundary of Yorkshire and the northern entrance to the Midland plain. The honour comprised 163 manors in Nottinghamshire, 54 in south Yorkshire, and many others scattered elsewhere, principally in north-east Derbyshire. William entrusted this estate to Roger de Busli from Bully-en-Brai near Neufchâtel. A massive motte was raised upon Tica's hill and a new town was laid out beyond the castle green or outer bailey. The burgesses recorded in Domesday Book appeared under the old name of Dadsley, which is commemorated today by Dadsley Lane and by Dadsley Well Farm to the north of the town. In 1102 the castle was forfeited to the crown, together with the castles of Arundel, Bridgnorth and Shrewsbury, after Robert de Belleme, the Earl of Shrewsbury, had fought on the losing side against Henry I. During the course of the twelfth century the motte-and-bailey castle was given stone defences. In 1129–30 a curtain wall was raised and a gatehouse of a simple type, with a wooden ceiling and no portcullis, was built into the rampart. Between 1178 and 1182 Henry II erected a multi-sided keep (dismantled in 1648) on top of the motte, and about that time the original curtain wall was rebuilt or encased with ashlar stone. King John spent well over £300 on strengthening the castle, but it was not developed further after his reign. Immediately behind the castle fishponds were dug out and a hunting park created. At Richmond, Pontefract and Tickhill Norman enterprise had a profound effect on the subsequent medieval history of Yorkshire. Tickhill replaced Strafforth as the centre of the wapentake, but Doncaster was made the head of the deanery.

The Yorkshire manors which formed a substantial part of the new honour of Tickhill were taken from the old lordship of Conisbrough, the 'King's stronghold' which guarded an ancient crossing of the River Don near the southern border of Northumbria. Despite these losses, the lordship of Conisbrough still had subsidiary estates in 28 townships within Strafforth wapentake at the time of the Domesday Survey, and it continued to play an important role alongside its new neighbour at Tickhill. During the 1170s and 1180s Hameline Plantagenet erected an impressive 90 ft high keep on the same plan as that of his smaller castle at Mortemer on his estates in Normandy. The Conisbrough keep survives almost to its full height and is one of the earliest examples of the cylindrical plan, which had first been attempted in this country at Orford in Suffolk. Hameline Plantagenet had married the heiress of the Warennes who had acquired vast estates at the time of the Norman Conquest. William de Warenne, who hailed from Varennes near Dieppe, was a distinguished commander at Hastings. He had other castles at Lewes, Reigate, Castle Acre and at Wakefield, where another Northumbrian lordship was preserved and strengthened to help control the troubled North. The manor of Wakefield's chief military and administrative centre was on a commanding hill at Sandall, where recent excavations have shown that the motte was originally surmounted by a circular timber keep, that the bailey was protected by a wooden palisade, and that within the enclosed area stood a timber aisled hall with a small square kitchen. From the thirteenth century onwards the lords rebuilt the castle in stone (Mayes and Butler 1983).

These huge castellanies were too large to administer from single centres, so certain powers were delegated to officials in other strongholds. Thus, the honour of Tickhill had subsidiary bases at Mexborough and Laughton en le

Morthen, where impressive motte-and-baileys remain. The earthworks of some of these lesser castles are amongst the most interesting in the county. The western parts of the honour of Pontefract were managed from a dramatic hill-top site at Almondbury, which rises abruptly to 900 ft and is a natural landmark for miles around. After centuries of disuse the prehistoric fort that had given the settlement its name was adapted by the de Lacys into a Norman castle. The inner rampart of the prehistoric fort was built up with shale to provide the outer defence, the bank and ditch of the earliest camp on the site were redefined to separate the outer from the inner bailey, and a deep new ditch was dug to isolate the motte. Almondbury's status within the honour declined after about 1200, but the castle was maintained throughout the fourteenth century and an accompanying borough was laid out within the outer bailey.

The regular pattern of burgage plots revealed by recent aerial photographs confirms the evidence of a 1634 map, where the words 'The scite of the towne' are written across the part showing the bailey. In 1322 Henry Irnehard paid 1*d.* rent for 'one burgage which he holds freely there', and from at least 1294 Almondbury held a market each Monday and a three-day annual fair. The old borough site is now deserted and the present settlement is clustered around All Hallows church half a mile or more away. Despite having no architecture that can be dated before the thirteenth century, the church probably marks the site of the Anglo-Saxon settlement that had been founded near the disused prehistoric earthwork, for it served an enormous moorland parish that stretched between the Colne and the Holme as far west as the county boundary on top of the Pennines. The village around the church continued to flourish despite the rival attraction of the new borough which was perched alongside the Norman castle on the old earthwork, and the villagers eventually saw both town and castle abandoned. The northern parts of the honour of Pontefract were originally administered from the substantial ringwork-and-bailey that lies adjacent to the eleventh-century parish church at Kippax. Later building platforms have been recognized with this ringwork, but no stone defences have been found. Some time during the early thirteenth century Kippax appears to have lost most of its functions to yet another fortified centre nearby at Barwick, where an Iron Age hill fort was converted into a Norman stronghold. In time, it too was replaced by a new centre at Rothwell (Faull and Moorhouse, eds 1981: 735–7).

The estates of these new castellanies were reasonably compact, but other Norman lordships interpenetrated one another in complicated patterns. The 215 manors held by Robert, Count of Mortain, the half-brother of William I, were scattered throughout Yorkshire. William II continued the castellany policy and extended his authority much further north. In Yorkshire he created the new honour of Skipton and gave it to Robert de Rumily. The full extent of Norman reorganization in Yorkshire is not revealed by Domesday Book because at that time some of the largest lordships, including the Mowbray fee, had not achieved their final form (Le Patourel 1971). Norman power in the

North of England remained uncertain until the reign of Henry I, for until then it did not extend to the limits of the old Anglo-Scandinavian kingdom nor into the far north-western parts of the county. Moreover, few Yorkshire castles were built in stone before the twelfth century and many were without substantial keeps until the late Norman period.

Yorkshire has a notable collection of fine castles begun by Norman barons. At Scarborough William, Count of Aumale, built on a dramatic headland that rises between two bays, on a site settled by prehistoric man and used by the Romans as a signal station. The count had been created Earl of Yorkshire after his prominent part in the 1138 Battle of the Standard near Northallerton, which had stemmed a Scottish invasion, and for a time he was

Plate 1.2 Scarborough Castle. The dramatic headland upon which the castle is set was occupied in prehistoric times and used by the Romans as a signal station. An impressive Norman curtain wall and a sturdy keep defended the only part of the headland that was vulnerable. The wall dates from about 1130 and the keep from 1158–69, when Henry II made it a royal castle. During the thirteenth century the defences were strengthened further by a barbican.

The castle was never taken in battle, but after Parliament's victory in the Civil War the western wall of the keep was demolished. In 1746, after Bonnie Prince Charlie's invasion of England, the Mosdale Hall in the outer bailey was converted into a barracks.

The town which grew up around St Mary's Church and the harbour below the castle achieved borough status about 1163. The Old Town was soon enlarged by the creation of Newborough, which in the eighteenth century became a fashionable spa resort.

the most powerful man in Yorkshire. His castle at Scarborough had a keep built between 1158 and 1169 and an extensive curtain wall. At Middleham an early Norman earthwork, which had been erected to guard both Coverdale and the road from Richmond to Skipton, was replaced in the twelfth century by a much larger castle some 500 yards away. Here, during the 1170s, one of the largest keeps in the country was built on a 40 ft high motte surrounded by a formidable ditch. The keeps at Conisbrough and Tickhill were erected about the same time. Meanwhile, throughout England, a lesson learned during the Crusades was put into practice, when curtain walls were strengthened and given sturdy towers. At Bowes, on the other hand, a royal castle built in the 1170s and 1180s by Richard the engineer was not supported by a curtain wall, but consisted simply of a keep.

At Pickering Castle, where a large shell keep of the 1220s surmounts a spectacular motte, the surviving buildings date from *c.* 1180 onwards. This was the headquarters of a great honour whose berewicks stretched 24 miles from north to south and 6 miles from east to west. It was also the administrative centre of the royal forest of Pickering. William I's brutal penalties for the illegal killing of game in royal forests remained in force until the 1217 Forest Charter checked the worst abuses. As Domesday Book does not record any Yorkshire forests it is possible that here, as in Cumbria, they were the creations of William Rufus. Though the term 'forest' merely implies an area set aside for hunting and not necessarily one that was thickly wooded, ancient woodland nevertheless usually formed the forest core. The Domesday Book information on Yorkshire woodland cannot be trusted, for curious gaps and inconsistencies appear, but the general impression that much of eleventh-century Yorkshire was only thinly wooded and that many settlements had no woodlands at all is probably accurate. Even within the Norman forests tracts were grazed and cultivated by tenant farmers.

Knaresborough Castle was the administrative centre of a forest which had probably been in existence for some time before it was first recorded in 1167. This forest covered most of lower Nidderdale, and together with the area known as the liberty on the other side of the Nidd it formed the honour of Knaresborough. In time two parks were enclosed within the forest and a third outside it. The 2,250 acre Haverah Park was probably created by William de Stuteville, who became lord in 1173, and the 1,100 acre Bilton Park (together with the 1,200 acre Haya Park beyond) was enclosed in the mid-thirteenth century by Richard, Earl of Cornwall and brother of King Henry III. Keepers or foresters also had charge of woodland preserves within the forest at such places as Oakdene, Harlow and Fulwith (Jennings, ed. 1967: 47–8). Yorkshire's other famous forest once covered most of the wapentake of Bulmer and was known as the Forest of Galtres. As its name is a Danish one meaning 'boars' brushwood', it may have been a hunting ground long before the Norman Conquest. It was within an easy ride from York, and though its size was reduced considerably during the reign of Henry II it remained a royal forest

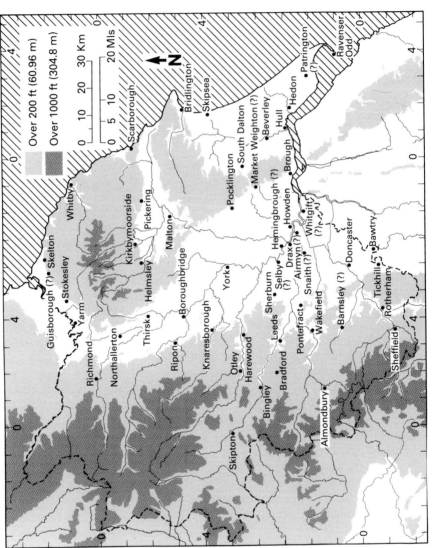

Figure 1.3   Norman boroughs

until the 1630s. An early record notes that in 1251 a justice of the forest was ordered to kill a hundred bucks in Galtres and to have them well-salted for the King's use. Bowland Forest was the fourth of the Yorkshire forests in existence at the beginning of Edward III's reign, and in addition the county had numerous chases, the hunting grounds of barons and more lowly lords. The Norman aristocracy were preoccupied with hunting and war and every castle had either a chase or park nearby. Thus, the Warennes had a deer park on the hill side near their castle at Conisbrough and a chase at Hatfield several miles away on the edge of the turf moors; they also hunted in those Pennine dales which formed part of their great manor of Wakefield, in and around Holmfirth and in Calderdale, where the hunt is commemorated in such place-names as Buckstones, Deerstones, Doestones and Roebucks.

New Towns

Norman lords were also active in founding new towns, and many of the most populous places in Yorkshire can trace their urban origins to the eleventh or twelfth centuries. York was already an outstanding centre and by far the largest town in the North at the time of the Conquest, but in 1086 (if Domesday Book is to be believed) only four other settlements within the county had claims to urban status and even they were hardly distinguishable from the surrounding villages. The Domesday clerks noted burgesses only at the Norman castle-boroughs of Pontefract (Tanshelf) and Tickhill (Dadsley) in the West Riding and at Bridlington and Pocklington in the East Riding. Over the next two centuries, however, the great expansion of the national economy encouraged the creation of many more towns, so that by 1300 (and probably long before) Yorkshire had well over forty urban centres. Of course, medieval towns were very small by later standards and rarely contained more than 1–2,000 people, and often much less. They were distinguished from rural settlements by their weekly markets and annual fairs and by the measure of independence enjoyed by the burgesses, which included the right to own their plots of land. Founding a new town was a speculative business and some, like Skipsea, were doomed to failure, but many others prospered either as entirely new plantations on virgin sites or as conscious developments of existing villages. Naturally, the earliest were established under the protection of a castle.

Although Tickhill's 31 Domesday Book burgesses were recorded under the old name of Dadsley, there is little doubt that the new town had already been sited half a mile to the south of the previous settlement on the edge of the castle green. The main streets radiate from the market-place, with Castlegate forming a dog-leg towards the castle and Northgate petering out in a double bend so as to pick up the alignment with Dadsley. The road heading eastwards from the market-place was referred to in a parliamentary survey of 1649 under the item 'The Burgar or gate rent payable within a certain streete . . . called Sunderland'; the name signifies land sundered or set apart from the castle, perhaps by the deep and curving ditch that was an early feature which was later filled to allow the extension of a narrow burgage plot (Magilton 1979). Patterns of medieval burgage plots at Tickhill are seen best between Castlegate and St Mary's Road, but are also evident east of Northgate as far as a broad footpath leading to Tithes Lane, and from Westgate to Pinfold Lane in the north and to Mill Dyke in the south. The final form of the medieval town plan is well preserved, but its origins and development await further archaeological investigation. The previous Anglo-Scandinavian communities in Dadsley and the surrounding hamlets were served by All Hallows Church on a knoll a few hundred yards north-west of Tickhill, but by the thirteenth century the prosperous townsmen decided to build a new church dedicated to St Mary on a more convenient site at the edge of the growing town and the castle green. Because of its relatively late foundation St Mary's can be glimpsed only occasionally from the main streets of the town. Tickhill was a successful plantation and by 1377 ranked eighth amongst the nation's newly created urban centres, with 680 taxpayers (Beresford 1967: 267).

Tickhill and Pontefract have much in common. At Pontefract the new town which was laid out to the west of the castle soon replaced the older manorial centre of Tanshelf, which guarded the crossing over the Aire. The broad central street of Micklegate acted as the market-place, and the town was enclosed by the curving lines of Walkergate and Back Northgate, probably just within the outer defences of the castle. Northgate and Southgate lay parallel to Micklegate and they too curved at their western ends (as Finkle Street and Baxtergate) to meet just inside the old west gate. Professor Maurice Beresford has suggested that the pre-urban settlement of Kirkby lay around the church of All Saints (a typical Anglo-Saxon dedication) just beyond the north-eastern edge of the town and that Tanshelf stretched towards the meeting place of the wapentake at Osgot's Cross, next to where St Giles's Church now stands. Then during the 1250s the Norman castle-town was enlarged by the creation of the additional borough of West Cheap around St Giles. In this part of Pontefract the streets still have the names that they have acquired over centuries of market activity – Market Place, Wool Market, Shoe Market Street, Corn Market, Beast Fair, Horse Fair, Roper Gate, Salter Row and Middle Row – and the whole area is 'as good an example as one could find anywhere in England of a former market place now encroached upon by streets' (Beresford 1967: 525). St Giles was founded as a chapel-of-ease of the original parish church of All Saints, but the inconvenient position of the latter and the damage it suffered during the Civil War led eventually to a reversal of roles. Pontefract was a very successful Norman creation. In 1377 it had 1,085 taxpayers and was second only to Hull amongst the new towns of medieval Yorkshire.

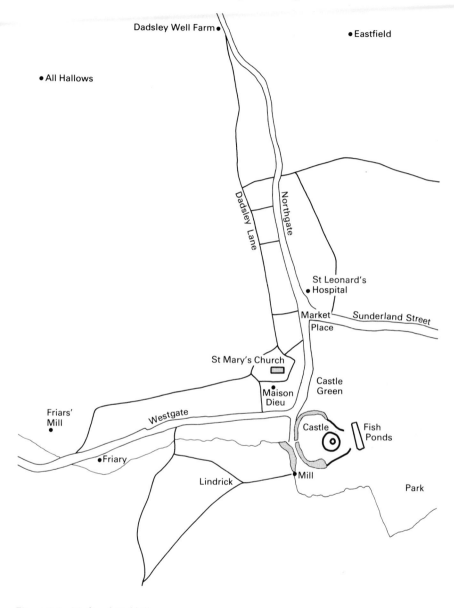

Figure 1.4   Medieval Tickhill

Successful and not so successful towns were also founded near to Norman castles at Almondbury, Harewood, Helmsley, Kirkby Moorside, Knaresborough, Malton, Northallerton, Pickering, Richmond, Scarborough, Sheffield, Skelton, Skipsea and Skipton, and of course in all other English counties as well. Sometimes, however, the topography of a medieval town is rather more complicated. At Wakefield the town grew around the ancient centre marked by the parish church, well away from Sandall castle, and at Thirsk the towering Perpendicular church of St Mary and the nearby site of the former Mowbray Castle are remote from the busy market town on the opposite bank of the Cod Beck. Presumably, church and castle were the focal points of the original settlement, the Thirsk whose name is derived from an Old Norse word for fen. However, by 1145 at the latest a Norman town had been established around the enormous rectangular market-place at the other end of Kirkgate (Beresford 1967: 518–19).

At Doncaster the Normans reoccupied an old Roman site at a strategic crossing of the river Don. A motte-and-bailey castle was raised above the Roman fort of Danum and its successor, the Anglo-Scandinavian burh, and a town was laid out over the Roman civilian settlement. Richard I's borough charter of 1194 confirmed the townsmen's existing privileges, and a royal charter, which extended the fair from two to three days, added to previous market rights. Medieval burgage plots have been traced in Frenchgate, High Street, St Sepulchre Gate, Baxter Gate and Scot Lane, and the street pattern in the centre of the town has been moulded by the town ditch (which had been dug out by 1215) and the earthen rampart which was thrown up alongside it. In the Middle Ages water from the Cheswold, the original course of the river Don, flowed along this ditch, which was not filled in until 1734. Four substantial stone gates at St Mary's bridge, St Sepulchre Gate, Hall Gate and Sun Bar marked the entrances to the town. An enormous market-place in the south-east corner of the town lay conveniently near the wharf, which for nine months of the year could be reached by light craft venturing up the Don. Like many other early market-places it formed an extension of a churchyard. Doncaster's original parish church, St Mary Magdalene's, stood on the site now occupied by the Victorian Corn Exchange, an area known formerly as the Maudlens. It declined in status when St George's Church was built upon the ruins of the motte-and-bailey castle when that earthwork became redundant. St Mary Magdalene's became a chantry chapel, was dissolved at the Reformation, and was subsequently converted into an Elizabethan town hall and grammar school. The demolition of these buildings in 1846 caused quite a stir, for to everyone's surprise they were found to incorporate substantial remains of the Norman church, including much of the nave arcades and clerestories. Doncaster's markets and fairs eventually became nationally famous, for the town was a natural regional centre served not only by traffic along the river but by the Great North Road and other important highways into the heart of the West Riding. In 1467 Doncaster became fully incorporated with a ruling body consisting of a mayor, 12 aldermen and 24 common councilmen, and soon the corporation acquired manorial rights over the surrounding rural settlements that lay within the soke of Doncaster (Hey 1979: 51–4).

By no means all the new Norman towns were founded near castles. Thirteenth-century Beverley was similar to Doncaster in being enclosed by a ditch and an earthen bank with bars at the principal entrances. On the western side of the town the road known as The Leases still follows the line of this ditch. Beyond lay the open fields, the extensive common pastures, and to the south the archbishop's park. Beverley minster had been refounded in the 930s by King Athelstan as a college of secular canons on the site of John of Beverley's early eighth-century monastery. Though Domesday Book does not mention any burgesses, the high value of the manor immediately before the Norman Conquest implies that the settlement was a sizeable one. Certainly, Beverley was a town by the reign of Henry I, when the annual fair was extended from two to five days. A large triangular market-place tapered from the minster towards the area still known as the Wednesday Market, and though much of this space has since been built upon, Highgate and Eastgate evidently mark its old boundaries. Extra land was needed to accommodate the growing commercial activities, and a new Saturday Market (now the main market square) was laid out beyond the original settlement and given a chapel-of-ease dedicated to St Mary. In 1269 St Mary's was elevated to parochial status, and before the close of the Middle Ages it had become one of the finest parish churches in the land. Another chapel-of-ease stood near the navigable river Hull and was dedicated appropriately to St Nicholas, the patron saint of seafarers. This river formed the main artery for Beverley's trade, which by the twelfth century included exports of local cloths to Europe (Allison 1967: 228–36).

Over in the West Riding, in November 1207 Maurice de Gant founded a new town in his manor of Leeds, the successor of Loidis, an estate of some importance as far back as the days of the Celtic kingdom of Elmet. The Anglo-Scandinavian village lay in and around Kirkgate and was served by St Peter's Church. Gant's town was grafted onto the western edge of this settlement, by the river crossing, with the broad market street of Briggate leading up to Headrow; the pattern of many of the 60 medieval burgage plots is preserved on the ground as long, narrow innyards and Victorian arcades (Beresford 1967: 524). Sixteen miles to the south of Leeds the new town of Barnsley was sited even further away from its parent village, an Anglian settlement which had acquired the name of Old Barnsley by 1280. The monks of the Clunaic priory of St John of Pontefract, who had been granted the manor in 1156, decided to establish a market town half a mile away at the junction of the Leeds–Wakefield–Sheffield road and the highway which came down from Richmond and Halifax to Rotherham and London. An ancient thoroughfare from the Cheshire salt wiches to Doncaster passed close by to the south. Eastgate, Southgate, Westgate, High Street and Church Street were set out in an orderly fashion, and weekly markets and annual fairs were held in Fair Field to the west of the church and also down the broad slopes of Market Hill. In 1249 the monks obtained a charter for an additional weekly market and an annual fair at the bottom of the hill on May Day Green, which at that time formed the southern limit of the town. The new settlement prospered, for it was well-placed and had no rivals nearby, but it was not until the reign of Queen Victoria that the ecclesiastical arrangements were altered to take account of the town's success and Barnsley was elevated to the rank of a parish instead of forming a chapel-of-ease within the huge medieval parish of Silkstone (Hey 1979: 57–8).

Medieval burgesses have also been located in Guisborough, Otley, and Stokesley, which are easily recognizable as successful market centres, in Sherburn, which has lost its market rights, in Bingley, Bradford and Rotherham, which have since grown into industrial towns, and in the ports of Whitby and Yarm (Beresford and Finberg 1973: 184–92). Yarm's name is derived from a word meaning a fish pool, no doubt a dam for catching fish that had been constructed within a loop of the Tees eighteen miles up river. Yarm is recorded in Domesday Book and the position of the Norman and eighteenth-century church of St Mary Magdalene on the river bank away from the market-place and the grid pattern of the town centre suggests that a small port thrived here before the creation of the borough. The 1,198 acres of Yarm township remained a chapelry of Kirk Levington until the nineteenth century, despite the success of the new town. A borough was in existence here by 1273, and in 1295 the burgesses were called upon to return a member of Parliament. Certain clues point to an even earlier urban origin, for the Blackfriars had a house here by 1266, and the Hospital of St Nicholas had been founded before 1141 by the second Robert de Brus, lord of the manor of Yarm. The town was designed with a regular pattern of narrow streets or wynds and a broad, curving High Street, which accommodated the Thursday markets and annual fairs. Bishop Skirlaw's bridge of *c.* 1400 took traffic from York and Thirsk across the Tees, while along the road from Richmond came pigs of lead and, in later times, corn and firkins of butter bound for London. Large granaries and warehouses were built in East Row at the height of Yarm's prosperity. The Tees was tidal up to four miles beyond Yarm, and the town prospered until the eighteenth century when it lost its river trade to Stockton, which had the advantage of deeper waters further down the river (Wardell 1957).

At the opposite end of the county Bawtry's history provides many points of comparison with that of Yarm. A new town was laid out during the late twelfth or early thirteenth century, and by the second quarter of the thirteenth century Bawtry was a borough with regular markets and fairs. The church of St Nicholas stands beyond the grid pattern of the town alongside the former wharf on the banks of the river Idle and was probably the focal point of an earlier settlement; a Roman fort stands guard on the other side of the river. Down the Idle to the river Trent at Stockwith went Derbyshire lead and millstones and south Yorkshire metalware, until the river Don was made navigable in the eighteenth century and the Chesterfield canal opened a direct link to Stockwith. The wharf is now overgrown and forgotten, but Wharf Street survives and the original winding course of the Idle still forms the county

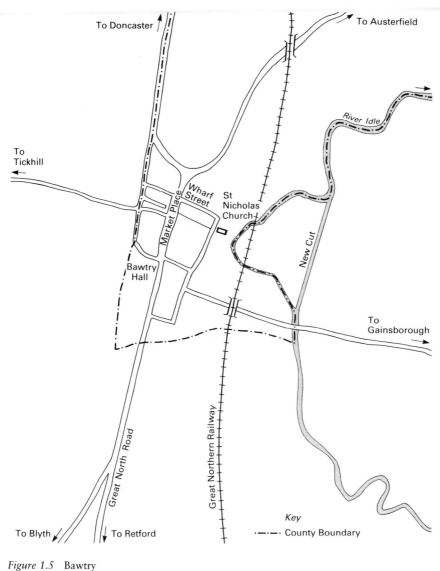

Figure 1.5 Bawtry

boundary. The medieval town was planted between the river in the east and the Roman road in the west and was surrounded on three sides by the county of Nottinghamshire; indeed, St Nicholas's Church was a chapel-of-ease of the Nottinghamshire parish of Blyth. The Roman road was diverted into a huge, rectangular market-place, and Bawtry thrived as a thoroughfare town half-way between Retford and Doncaster on the Great North Road. Even though most of Bawtry's buildings date from a renewed period of prosperity in the

1780–1840 stagecoach era, the topography of the medieval town can still be traced on the ground (Hey 1980: 105–13).

The river Ouse was a great commercial highway whose importance to York was recognized by the compilers of Domesday Book. For most of its course it was tidal, and many of its tributaries were navigable for light craft. River traffic could get as far inland as Doncaster on the Don, Knottingley Mills on the Aire, Stamford Bridge on the Derwent, and Tadcaster on the Wharfe. The northern limit of navigation was Boroughbridge on the river Ure, where the local lords had the right to weigh and load pigs of lead and to levy tolls on goods borne by river as far as York. Aldborough was an Anglian burh that was developed within the walls of Roman Isurium, but Boroughbridge was a new town laid out on 95 acres of narrow land to the south of a bridge that was built over the Ure about 1145. As a surveyor of 1631 expressed it, 'The borough lieth within the said Manor of Aldborough and is part thereof, being compassed about with the Demesnes and fields of Aldborough and having no demesne, fields, or other lands' (Beresford 1967: 523–4). The streets were arranged in a grid pattern around the market-place, and by 1165 the town had achieved the status of a borough. It flourished not only as an inland port but as a thoroughfare town where the Great North Road was joined by the road from York. The present bridge is the eighteenth-century work of John Carr, widened later, and nothing remains above ground level of the twelfth-century settlement other than fragments of the ornate Norman doorway of the chapel of St James, which was rebuilt in 1852. As at Bawtry, the permanent effects of decisions taken eight centuries ago are to be found in the network of streets around the market-place.

Down river from York staithes or landing-places were constructed near the Archbishop's seat at Cawood and close to the abbey at Selby. A village was recorded at Selby in 1030, but upon the foundation of the abbey in 1069 the settlement was altered out of all recognition. A broad market-place was laid out beyond the west gates of the abbey and commercial activities no doubt spilled over into the wide Micklegate, which led to the abbot's staith on the Ouse. A few miles further on, the old course of the river wound its way past the tall spire of Hemingborough church. The place-name, the Anglo-Saxon work in the nave, and the presence of a small medieval market indicate some past importance, but Hemingborough was over-shadowed by Selby and Drax, where another new borough was established by the middle of the thirteenth century. Two miles further on, at the confluence of the Ouse and the Aire, a long line of houses on the east bank of the Aire marks the position of the small town of Airmyn that the abbot of St Mary's, York, had founded by 1253 on the edge of the parish of Snaith. On the opposite side of the river in the parish of Drax, Little Airmyn occupies the site of an earlier settlement that was recorded in Domesday Book, and whose name means 'the mouth of the Aire'. Booth-ferry bridge is the lowest bridging point over the Ouse; the place-name suggests that ferrying was important before the construction of a bridge, for this was the principal southern exit from the East Riding. Another ferry at Airmyn enabled travellers to cross the Aire, and it was as a small port and ferry town that Airmyn survived even though it did not flourish (Beresford 1967: 521–2). Goole, of course, did not become a port until the nineteenth century, and in the Middle Ages was only a creek and tiny hamlet, but a few miles further on there was another ferrying point at Whitgift, and here the abbot of St Mary's York, obtained a charter for a weekly market and an annual fair, but took no steps to create a borough.

Travellers along the Roman Ermine Street were ferried across the Humber at Brough. The place-name may refer to a Roman settlement or to a later burh, but in the Middle Ages Brough was only a small village without a church of its own, on the edge of the parishes of Brantingham and Elloughton. In 1239 the Archbishop of York obtained a charter for a Thursday market and a St Matthewtide fair, and burgesses were invited to settle. Time soon showed that they were unable to compete with the merchants of Yorkshire's most successful medieval new town a few miles down the river at Kingston upon Hull, and Brough must be reckoned as one of the urban schemes that failed (Beresford 1967: 510). Hull's success also worked to the detriment of Hedon, Patrington and Ravenser Odd. Patrington was not sited favourably for river traffic, though it had a haven for light craft and the Archbishop of York as lord of the manor. Its wonderful fourteenth-century church is known throughout the land, and as late as 1650 a survey of the manor spoke of the 'Tolls and profits of a weekly market kept every Tuesday within the said town of Patrington together with the anchorage of vessells coming within the Haven', but then these profits were valued at only £1.

The history of Ravenser Odd is an exceedingly strange tale. The suffix Odd refers to a headland at the mouth of the Humber, now washed away by the sea. Ravenser, Old Ravenser and Ravenser Odd were three separate places in 1297, but as all three have been eroded it is impossible to determine their relative situations. A vivid account by a government inquisition states that about 1235 the action of the North Sea caused sand and stones to accumulate at the tip of the Spurn peninsula and that here fishermen began to dry their nets. When a ship was wrecked on the headland one enterprising man built a hut from the timbers and sold meat and drink to sailors and merchants. Soon after these humble beginnings the Count of Aumale founded a borough here; it is first recorded in a charter that can be dated between 1241 and 1249 which granted Meaux Abbey half an acre of land 'in the borough of Odd near Ravenser'. By the 1260s over a hundred burgesses, trading largely in herrings and other fish, had settled here. The chronicler of Meaux Abbey described it as 'distant from the mainland a mile or more. For access it had a sandy road no broader than an arrow's flight yet wonderfully maintained by the tides and the ebb and flow of the Humber.' But the sea eventually took away that which it had provided. The single causeway was breached (perhaps in the great storm of 1256) and Ravenser Odd became an island. As such it thrived for another three generations, and the borough returned members of Parliament in 1300 and 1337, but in 1346 two-thirds of the town was said to have been washed away by the sea; about two hundred houses had been destroyed in this way during the previous dozen years. In the words of the Meaux Abbey chronicler,

> All men daily removing their possessions, the town was swiftly swallowed up and irreparably destroyed by the merciless floods and tempests. This was an exceedingly famous borough devoted to merchandise and very much occupied with fishing; having more ships and burgesses than any on this coast.
>
> (Beresford 1967: 513–14; English 1979: 211–12)

During the first half of the twelfth century the Counts of Aumale had also founded a borough-port at Hedon, the 'heather-covered hill' at the southern end of the parish of Preston. The town was laid out on a grid pattern, and at the height of its prosperity boasted three churches and was three times its present size. St Augustine's, the only church to remain, bears witness to the wealth generated by trade in wool and hides, for it is known as the king of Holderness, to Patrington's queen. However, the narrow creek leading down to the Humber did not allow sufficient passage to withstand competition from Hull, and in time it became silted up. Hedon's rival had been established at the confluence of the Hull and the Humber during the third quarter of the twelfth century by the monks of the Cistercian abbey at Meaux. At first the place was known simply as Wyke, meaning a creek, and it did not acquire the name of Kingston upon Hull (or Hull as it has always been known for short) until Edward I's purchase of the manor in 1293. The monks marked out a new town on a grid pattern, blocked the last few hundred yards of the old course of the river Hull, and dug a new straight channel to provide better access to the estuary. Down this tributary came goods from Holderness and the Wolds, and reloading facilities were made available for traffic that had sailed down the Ouse; for example, in 1193 wool contributed by Yorkshire monasteries towards Richard I's ransom was gathered at the 'portum de Hulmo'. In John's reign Wyke (as it was still known) ranked sixth amongst the seaports, and by the end of the thirteenth century only London and Boston had more trade by sea. The Abbot of Meaux had acquired markets and fairs, and in 1293 the town had 55 occupied tenements.

Wyke's history was already a success story before Edward I purchased the manor 'to increase the fitness of the port for ships and traffic' (Beresford 1967: 511–16). The advantages of sustained royal interest soon became obvious, for the king provided new approach roads from Beverley and York, enlarged the quay, built a new water mill, extended the duration of markets and fairs, and established a mint and an exchange. In 1299 Edward granted the townsmen a borough charter with freedom from tolls throughout the kingdom, and in 1331 they achieved complete independence. From 1304 onwards Hull returned members of Parliament, and by that time the De la Poles had begun to build their family's great fortune in the wool trade. Royal privilege ensured the town's growth, and in 1296 bailiff's accounts speak of 50 new plots beyond the old settlement of Wyke, probably fronting those streets that lie to the west of Holy Trinity. It is true that a rental of 1320 shows that only 21 of these plots were then occupied, but later that century the burgesses were sufficiently prosperous to enclose their town with a massive wall and towers in what seems to have been England's first public work undertaken in brick (Platt 1976: 43). Holy Trinity Church was also rebuilt in this material from the early fourteenth century onwards, and by the time its tower was completed about 1500 it was the largest church by area in England. Nevertheless, it remained a chapel-of-ease in the parish of Hessle until 1661.

York

The only other walled town in medieval Yorkshire was of course the county capital. The area enclosed by walls was still more or less that of the Roman legionary fortress together with the colonia to the south of the Ouse. The Normans heightened the Anglo-Scandinavian banks which surmounted the old Roman walls and guarded the principal exits with bars or gateways. Norman archways are incorporated in the present Micklegate and Walmgate bars and in Bootham Bar, which was built on the site of its Roman predecessor. During the thirteenth and early fourteenth centuries the citizens built the present walls along 2¾ miles of the ancient banks. No other town in England has maintained its walls so well, and despite the necessary renovations of the last two centuries much original work survives. During the thirteenth and fourteenth centuries the bars were redesigned and the new Monk Bar replaced the north-eastern exit which had been used since Roman times. Walls were not needed to defend the whole of the eastern approach to the city, for this part was controlled by the two Norman castles on either side of the Ouse. Baile Hill had fallen into disuse by 1268, but York Castle was greatly strengthened between 1245 and 1270 by the addition of Clifford's Tower and by the damming of the Foss to create a lake and a huge fishpond. At their greatest extent the walls had four great bars, six posterns and 44 towers. Within the walls the medieval street plan was not very different from today's, though only two bridges crossed the Ouse and the Foss. York was a busy commercial and administrative centre, second only to London in terms of wealth and population, with crowded market-places and much coming and going along the highways and the river. Suburbs sprawled beyond the walls, especially alongside the principal

Plate 1.3 Bootham Bar, York. Bootham Bar is the only York gate to stand on the site of a Roman predecessor. Fragments of the north-west gate of the legionary fortress of Eboracum survive nearby. Bootham Bar is Norman in origin but it was redesigned in the thirteenth or fourteenth century when the city walls took their present form and it has subsequently been much restored. The plain, round-headed arch is thought to be late eleventh century. It was once defended by a barbican (as at Walmgate Bar) but this was demolished in 1832.

The walls of St Mary's Abbey (foreground, left) once joined the city walls at Bootham Bar. The Archbishop of York held markets and fairs beyond the bar and in the eighteenth century Bootham became a fashionable suburb.

thoroughfares, and beyond lay the common pastures, notably the Knavesmire, Hob Moor and Heworth Moor, which survive still.

When Thomas, the treasurer of Bayeux, became Archbishop of York in 1070, 'he found everything deserted and waste' after the harrying. According to Hugh the Chanter, only three of the seven canons who served the minster were left 'in the burnt city and ruined church'. The recent excavation of St Helen's churchyard has shown that skulls of this period are of a markedly different type than before, suggesting immigration into the devastated city, perhaps from the Yorkshire countryside (Magilton 1980). Thomas restored and reroofed the minster church and rebuilt the refectory and dormitory, only to see them destroyed in 1079 by Danish invaders. He resolved to build an entirely new church, and this was probably completed before his death in 1100. The walls were 7 ft thick and included much re-used Roman masonry that had been plastered and painted with red lines to simulate new ashlar blocks. Perhaps up to this time Roman buildings had still been standing in the vicinity, but now the ancient lay-out of the legionary fortress, especially that of the principia or headquarters building, was abandoned so as to allow the new church to have the correct liturgical alignment. Thomas's 362 ft long building was set at 45° across the Roman site and comprised an aisleless nave, crossing and transepts, and choir, with three apses at the eastern end. After the church had been seriously damaged by fire on 4 July 1137, Archbishop Roger of Pont L'Évêque constructed a new choir and crypt and added two western towers which were not replaced until the early fifteenth century (Aylmer and Cant 1977: 25–6, 114). Very little of the Norman church survives above ground level, though the eight-bay crypt remains. The earliest work on a grand scale is to be found in the transepts, which date from the time of Archbishop Walter de Gray (1216–55). Their most famous feature is the Five Sisters window, composed of five tall lancets with austere grisaille glass and Purbeck marble shafts.

The archbishops owned the manors of Otley, Ripon and Sherburn (West Riding), Malton and several places around the Forest of Galtres (North Riding), and Beverley, Fridaythorpe, Patrington, Riccall and Swine (East Riding). They once held other estates but Thomas was generous in his grants of property to the canons who served the minster; in Hugh the Chanter's words, 'He gave vills, lands and churches himself and restored those which others had taken away.' Eventually nine English medieval cathedrals were served by secular canons rather than by monks, an arrangement that began about 1090 in the cases of York, Salisbury, Lincoln and London. The four leading members of the chapter – the dean, precentor, chancellor and treasurer – were each housed near the archbishop's palace behind the minster, and the other canons were provided for with funds from separate endowments known as prebends. The range of wealth among the thirty-six prebends was enormous; at the top of the scale the York treasurership and the prebend of Masham (which had been founded in the late twelfth century by Roger de Mowbray for a kinsman) were considered two of the richest plums in Christendom. Henry I made the substantial endowments of the prebends of Driffield and Laughton en le Morthen, for he considered the minster an important centre of loyalty. The Norman kings rarely visited the north and relied upon the Archbishop of York and the Bishop of Durham, together with their chapters, to help control this border region. Though it would have suited Henry I politically to have had only one see, he did not contest the Pope's decision in favour of Archbishop Thurstan's campaign to regain the independence from Canterbury that York had lost at the time of the Norman Conquest.

About 1260 the masons who had worked on the north transept began to build the octagonal chapter house, the largest of its type in England. Lavish use of Purbeck marble shafts, outstanding stiff-leaf and naturalistic foliage, and a distinctive pyramidal roof supported by its original wooden vault help to make this a thirteenth-century masterpiece. The chapter house was the administrative centre where each prebend could have his say in general policy and everyday affairs. During their absences from York the canons relied on the thirty-six vicars choral to be their deputies. From 1252 onwards the vicars choral were organized as a largely self-governing body and in 1421 they were formally incorporated as a college. Their accommodation at the Bedern, some 150 yards east of the minster, was in separate chambers with a common dining hall and a chapel. Recently excavated and partly restored, the Bedern was the first such institution to be established at any English secular cathedral (Aylmer and Cant 1977: 90).

Medieval York had at least thirty-nine parish churches and numerous small chapels, in addition to various religious houses and charitable institutions. All these were built of stone, but domestic houses were mostly timber-framed. A hoard of coins from Edward the Confessor's reign found within the construction of a timber-framed house in High Ousegate suggests an early date for this building but this is a rarity, for hardly anything survives from before 1300. A Norman stone building forms the core of a wing of Gray's Court, and down a passage leading off Stonegate an upstairs window and the faint outline of a first-floor hall and undercroft are all that remain of a twelfth-century stone house (York Archaeological Trust 1978: 16). Otherwise, the earliest domestic buildings in York which can be dated with confidence are the rather humble two-roomed dwellings in Our Lady's Row in Goodramgate, which were erected in 1316 for artisans.

Very little is known about the daily lives of York citizens during the twelfth and thirteenth centuries, but one particular group was so distinctive and provoked so much hostility that their activities are recorded in more detail. Professor Barrie Dobson has provided a vivid account of 'the single most famous incident in the history of the medieval English Jewry', the massacre and mass suicide of York Jews on the night of 16 March 1190 (Dobson 1974). Jews had been brought into England by William the Conqueror, but it was not until the middle of the twelfth century that they began to settle in provincial towns.

Until his death in 1186 Aaron of Lincoln dominated all substantial money-lending by Jews in both Lincoln and York, but afterwards York financiers such as Benedict and Josce came into their own. The Jewish community in York seems to have been concentrated in Coney Street, and the place-name Jewbury presumably marks the site of their extramural cemetery. Though the community was never larger than forty households it became the most famous provincial Jewry in medieval England and was without a serious rival in the north. Josce was secure enough to offer mortgages on 20 year terms and to lend money to the king, to the dean and chapter, and to many rural landowners. He was leader of the York Jewish community when Henry II, the royal protector of English Jews, died on 6 July 1189. Henry's successor, Richard I, was the hero of the crusading propaganda that helped to whip up anti-semitism.

In February 1190 the heightening of religious passion during Lent following Richard's departure on the third crusade led to mob violence against the Jews of King's Lynn and Norwich, but these outbreaks were mild compared to the savagery of events in York a few weeks later. Rioting and plundering forced the Jews to retreat into the castle keep, but even there they were not safe from the hatred of the mob. The castle was set on fire, and, as it seemed that the Jews would all be murdered, fathers cut the throats of their wives and children and then were in turn killed by their rabbi. At daybreak the 'wretched remnant of the Jews' emerged from the burnt-out castle and appealed for mercy in return for Christian baptism, but although they came out under promise of safety they were all massacred. The ringleaders of this outrage were nearby rural landowners who had become greatly indebted to the Jews. The most notorious were Richard Malebisse of Acaster Malbis and Copmanthorpe, William Percy of Bolton Percy (the head of a junior line of this illustrious family), Alan Malekale, Marmaduke Darell and Philip de Fauconberg; they belonged to the middle baronage and had close ties of blood and acquaintanceship, but they did not escape justice. Jews soon returned to York and were able to enforce payment of debts and mortgages. By 1218 they formed one of the ten specially protected English urban communities. They prospered remarkably during the second and third quarters of the thirteenth century, and in 1255 were assessed at a higher rate than the Jews of any other provincial English city. During the reign of Edward I, however, the fortunes of all Jewish communities declined, and in 1290 the King expelled them all from England.

Parish Churches

Religious fervour was put to a more constructive use in the provision of parish churches. The Normans provided a major new impetus to building, enlarging existing churches such as Conisbrough and Laughton, and erecting many new ones. Even in a poor parish like St Helen's, York, the strength of the Christian faith inspired constant rebuilding, as recent excavation has shown. The creation of new manors after the conquest and the subsequent recovery and increase of the population meant that churches were needed where none had existed before, but by 1200 the medieval parish system was complete. Yorkshire had over five hundred medieval parish churches, and Norman work survives in about half of them. A great number of churches containing Norman features survive in small parishes where the population did not expand in the later Middle Ages, particularly in places where fertile soils had attracted early settlers and villages were thick on the ground. Where settlements continued to grow, churches were enlarged and rebuilt, so now only parts of their Norman architecture survive, or else, as at Rotherham, the size of the previous Norman church can be judged only from its foundations. Yorkshire's early Norman churches were built in the style of their Anglo-Scandinavian predecessors. At Burghwallis, for instance, the nave and chancel are constructed of unsquared pieces of Magnesian Limestone arranged in attractive herringbone patterns with huge, side-alternate quoins which have perhaps been re-used from an earlier church. The building belongs to the period of the 'Saxo-Norman overlap' which continued throughout the eleventh century and into the twelfth. A few miles further north at Kippax the tower, nave and chancel each have the tall and relatively narrow proportions of the pre-Conquest style, and several sections of walling are arranged in herringbone fashion. Another eleventh-century example on the Magnesian Limestone belt is the tower of St Bartholomew's Church at Maltby, which has side-alternate quoins instead of buttresses, triangular-headed openings and some patches of herringbone masonry. Other 'overlap' churches have unusually broad western towers which may have supported a timber superstructure (Ryder 1982).

The Castle Howard estate village of Bulmer has a parish church that has been greatly altered over the centuries, but the side-walls of the nave, together with the lower part of the north chancel wall, are of the 'Saxo-Norman overlap' period, and the head of an Anglian wheel cross suggests an even longer history. Bulmer was the head of a wapentake and a deanery, and fittingly the church of St Martin has a dedication that is usually reckoned to be very early. On the Wolds at Weaverthorpe pre-Conquest traditions lingered on until the early twelfth century, with a tall, slim tower in the old style and Norman nave and chancel; a sundial set in the tympanum over the south door tells that the church was built by Herbert the Chamberlain of Winchester. By the middle of the twelfth century the Normans had introduced a more confident style with richly carved features. Yorkshire possesses some outstanding rural churches from this period, and they are especially to be found in the central Vale of York. One of the best known is St John the Baptist's church at Adel, a small building consisting only of nave and chancel and a bellcote 'renewed' in 1839. The eaves

Plate 1.4   Norman door, Stillingfleet Church. All the major styles of English medieval architecture can be found at St Helen's church but it is the south door which is justly famous. By the middle decades of the twelfth century the Normans were building and decorating even their small rural churches with more confidence. The door at Stillingfleet is thought to date from the 1160s. Dragons, fabulous beasts biting a roll-moulding, human heads, zigzag and other designs provide a display to strike a parishioner with awe as he or she entered the church.

The ironwork on the wooden door may be contemporary with the masonry, but it may well be even earlier. It appears to depict a ship of the Viking era.

are supported by a corbel table carved with fanciful heads, and the small slit windows, deeply splayed on the inside, rise above a decorative string-course in the usual manner. The main entrance (in the south-western position that became traditional from the Norman period onwards) is an elaborate piece of display with intertwined bands and leaves, animals, zigzag and beakhead decoration and the figure of Christ between the symbols of the evangelists in the gable. No other county has as much beakhead decoration as Yorkshire.

Another twelfth-century church of national importance is St Mary's,

Birkin, which is larger than Adel, having an unbuttressed tower at the west end and a rib-vaulted and pilaster-buttressed apse to the east, as well as a fourteenth-century south aisle. Its Norman decoration includes a corbel table, large shafted windows above a string course, and a fine south doorway with zigzag, beakhead and medallions with ornamental motifs. At a more humble level the little church at Adwick upon Dearne has never been enlarged or restored and still possesses a rare Norman bellcote. Norman towers have usually been heightened or replaced, but a striking example can be found at Campsall, and pleasing combinations of Norman and later work can be seen a few miles away at Arksey and Brayton. Other outstanding West Riding examples of Norman craftsmanship include the decorative doorway at Fishlake, a tomb-chest of *c*. 1140–60 at Conisbrough, and carvings depicting a baptism scene and the four seasons on the font at Thorpe Salvin. In the East Riding notable Norman churches are to be found at Newbald and Kirkburn, and Stillingfleet has a memorable doorway complete with original twelfth-century ironwork. In the North Riding, although numerous churches have Norman features, no complete building is outstanding.

Many villages found that their Norman churches were adequate for their needs in later times. More often than not the introduction of the Early English Gothic style at parish church level meant simply the insertion of lancet windows or other minor architectural features rather than large-scale rebuilding. Nevertheless, at Skelton Yorkshire has the most perfect small Early English church in the country. The building was erected about the middle of the thirteenth century in a style close to that recently employed at York minster, and it is probable that Roger Haget, the York treasurer, was largely responsible for the project. The nave has only two bays, with narrow aisles set under the continuation of the steep slope of the roof; at the top a bellcote marks the division between nave and chancel. Throughout, the arches are deeply moulded and the carvings were made to the latest stiff leaf and dog tooth designs. In the East Riding Early English work on a greater scale can be seen in the parish churches at Filey and Hedon, and in the North Riding at Bossall.

Yorkshire's three great collegiate churches were also rebuilt in the thirteenth century. Medieval Yorkshire had twenty-one secular colleges of priests who were not bound to any particular monastic rule. Such colleges were founded within the diocese of York long before the Norman Conquest at Beverley, Ripon and Southwell (Nottinghamshire), and afterwards at Howden. Each was associated with a market town and grew rich with the early-medieval expansion of the economy. After Wilfrid's seventh-century monastery at Ripon had been destroyed by fire in 950, it was refounded as a collegiate establishment. Some of its architectural features may date from the late twelfth century, but the famous west front is of the 1220s; Ripon was elevated to cathedral status in 1836. Beverley minster has a similar story. St John of Beverley's early eighth-century church was refounded by Athelstan as a collegiate establishment about 935, after it had been destroyed in Viking raids. By the thirteenth century it had assumed cathedral-like proportions, with some of the best Early English work in Yorkshire. The third great collegiate church at Howden had belonged to the Bishops of Durham and was made collegiate in 1267. Rebuilding began almost immediately, firstly in the transepts, then the choir and nave; the west front was completed by 1306–11 and the crossing tower almost 100 years later. Since the dissolution of the college and the decay of the market town, however, this fine church has become partly ruinous. The roof and upper walls of the choir collapsed in 1696, two generations later the roof of the chapter house fell in, and gradually the nearby episcopal manor house became a ruin. St Peter's Church is now a poignant sight, reflecting in one unforgettable scene the ambition and splendour of the medieval church and the crushing of this ideal at the end of the Middle Ages.

Monasteries

Yorkshire's greatest medieval glory is its collection of monasteries. The early Vikings had plundered and destroyed Anglo-Saxon sites in such an effective fashion that they left no monastic life north of the Trent. One of the most positive achievements of the Normans was to re-establish northern monasticism. By 1500 Yorkshire had eighty-three religious houses, including some of the finest abbeys in the land. The rule of St Benedict of Auxerre (480–534), which had been revived on the continent during the first half of the eleventh century and had been taken up with particular zeal in Normandy, was the first to secure a foothold in England. The Benedictine impact was such that by the Dissolution 245 of their houses had been established. In 1069 King William I founded Selby Abbey, the first new monastic house in Yorkshire and soon one of the richest Benedictine establishments in the North. Abbot Hugh de Laci began work on the present structure about 1100, and judging by the distinctive, incised patterns on the sturdy nave piers he probably employed the master mason who had been responsible for similar work at Durham Cathedral. Selby Abbey remains the finest Norman ecclesiastical building in Yorkshire.

One of the Conqueror's knights, Reinfrid, was deeply moved by the desolate sight of the ruins of Hilda's seventh-century abbey at Whitby, which the Danes had destroyed in 867. He took monastic vows at Evesham, and together with Aldwin (subsequently prior at Durham) set out to restore the historic, ruined monasteries at Monkwearmouth, Jarrow, Whitby and York. Whitby was refounded on its majestic cliff-top site as a priory about 1078 and as an abbey a generation later; the present ruined shell dates from the

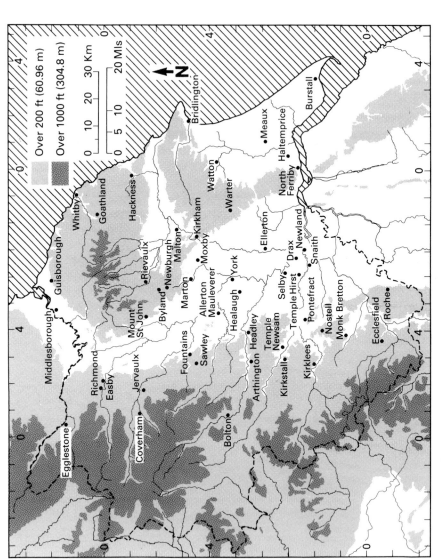

Figure 1.6 Yorkshire's religious houses mentioned in the text

thirteenth and fourteenth centuries. On the other side of the North York Moors, another ancient monastic site at Lastingham was resettled from Whitby in the late 1070s. Work must have begun almost immediately on the remarkable crypt and superstructure, for after only a decade the monks moved to York, where William Rufus had founded St Mary's Abbey on what was probably the site of the former monastery of Galmanho. The beautiful limestone ruins of the abbey church date from 1271, though earlier work is known from the foundations. By the thirteenth century the abbot's lodge was already a large building and the abbey was enclosed by its own precinct walls, which after 1318 were adorned with towers and gatehouses. The northern and eastern sections of these walls survive intact and are of special interest to military historians as a few of the battlements retain grooves for the shutters that afforded some measure of protection for the bowmen. Architectural evidence of York's other monastic houses survives only at Holy Trinity, Micklegate, where the Benedictine priory that Ralph Pagnell founded in 1089 as a cell of the Norman abbey of Marmoutier was later converted into one of York's many parish churches.

The first generation or two of Norman barons frequently granted English estates to monastic houses in their native land. Marmoutier established cells to administer their property at York, Allerton Mauleverer and Headley, and Aumale had a cell at Burstall. Ecclesfield priory is a rare thirteenth-century survival of an alien cell. Early in the twelfth century an estate at Ecclesfield had been given by William de Lovetot, lord of Hallamshire, to the Norman monastery of St Wandrille. When alien institutions were dissolved by Richard II the property passed to the new Carthusian priory of St Anne, near Coventry, and upon the Dissolution the building was converted into a superior farmhouse and given the name of Ecclesfield Hall. English Benedictine houses also established cells at outlying properties. Whitby had four at Goathland, Hackness, Middlesbrough and York; Selby had a cell at Snaith; and in 1137 St Mary's, York, established nine or ten monks at St Martin's priory, Richmond, now marked by three of the walls of the Norman chapel and other fragmentary ruins.

Norman kings and barons also gave enormous support to the Cluniacs, a reformed Benedictine order that had been founded at Cluny in Burgundy in 910. Cluniacs placed much emphasis on liturgy and the splendour of their setting. Their first English house, Lewes Priory, was also by far their richest. Founded by William de Warenne after a visit to Cluny, it was endowed with extensive properties, including possessions from Warenne's Yorkshire estates. However, the order was not as successful as on the Continent and most English houses were small. One of the most important was Pontefract Priory, which Robert de Laci founded near his castle about 1090; it housed twenty-seven monks in 1279, but now nothing survives above ground level. About 1154 Monk Bretton Priory was founded as a daughter of Pontefract, when Adam fitz Swein gave seven acres of land at Lundwood near Bretton village, but in 1281 the monks changed their allegiance and accepted the Benedictine discipline. The East and North Ridings remained unaffected by the Cluniac movement, and Arthington Nunnery was the only other Cluniac house in Yorkshire.

By about 1090 the first wave of enthusiasm had petered out in the North. Much of the renewed inspiration of the early twelfth century came from the canons of St Augustine, or the Austin Canons as they were generally known in England. Their aim was to provide not a strict monastic order but a common life for priests, and their houses were mostly of modest size. They began in Italy and France in the late-eleventh century, established themselves at St Botolph's Priory, Colchester, in 1103, and soon attracted royal patronage. Archbishop Thurstan encouraged their activities in the North, and seven houses were established in Yorkshire before 1140. Nostell Priory, founded in 1114–19 by Archbishop Thurstan and endowed by King Henry I, was one of the two earliest and most important Austin houses in the country, but now the only standing remains are of two late-medieval ranges of outbuildings. The contemporary Bridlington Priory, founded by Walter de Gant, eventually became a large establishment with a 333 ft long church. The nave is still in use, and the vaulted undercroft of the prior's lodging and the fourteenth-century gatehouse survive. About 1119 another early Austin priory was established at Guisborough by the generous endowment of Robert de Brus, ancestor of King Robert Bruce and brother of the first Prior. In time Guisborough Priory acquired a wide reputation for its strict observance of religious life; the remains of the east gable give some idea of the proportions of the 352 ft long church. Two other Austin houses, Bolton and Kirkham, are now picturesque ruins in rural situations on river banks. Bolton Priory was founded in 1120–21 by William Meschin and his wife, Cecilia, at Embsay, four miles away, but the land proved unproductive and in 1154–55 the monks moved to Bolton, to the spot that was later eulogized by Wordsworth, Turner and Ruskin. Kirkham Priory was founded about 1122 by Walter L'Espec and had eighteen canons at the Dissolution, compared to Bolton's average of fifteen. Yorkshire's other twelfth-century Austin houses were established at Warter, Drax, North Ferriby, Marton, Healaugh and Newburgh, and a late foundation at Cottingham in 1322 moved to Haltemprice three or four years later.

In England the deepest monastic influence came from the Cistercians, the order of white monks founded at Cîteaux in Burgundy in 1098 on the austere principles of the early Benedictines. By 1200 more than a hundred Cistercian houses had been established in England and Wales. Wealth and luxury were renounced and gifts of prosperous manors refused; all the monks desired was a gift of uncultivated land on the edge of moor, marsh or wood. Their architecture was as austere and simple as their ceremonies; their ideal was the frugal, devotional and meditative life. The system depended upon a great number of lay brothers who did manual work but no study and who worshipped in the abbey church only at the beginning and end of each working day. These farmers, herdsmen and builders played a vital role in Cistercian organization and expansion. The first English house was at Waverley in Surrey (1128), but it was in Yorkshire that the Cistercians achieved their greatest success. In March 1132 Walter L'Espec, Lord of Helmsley and founder of Kirkham Priory, brought thirteen monks from Clairvaux to the Rye Valley, and at Rievaulx established the most famous Cistercian house in twelfth-century England. By the 1140s Rievaulx housed three hundred monks and lay-brothers, and daughter houses had been established at Dundrennan, Melrose and Warden in Scotland and Revesby in Lincolnshire. In its heyday in the later years of the rule of St Ailred (1147–67) Rievaulx had 140 monks and over five hundred lay brothers. Ailred was the greatest monastic figure of his time, friend of kings, author of religious and historical works, saintly leader and efficient administrator. The monastery's high spiritual reputation was matched by that of its architecture, and heavy debts were incurred by a building programme that lasted for over a century. Building stones were floated on rafts along the old course of the Rye from Penny Piece quarry to a specially constructed wharf, and a magnificent 370 ft long church was constructed on an unusual north–south axis on the steep slopes of the valley. Only at Fountains are there more extensive remains of an English Cistercian abbey.

Inspired by the foundation of Rievaulx, in March 1132 thirteen Benedictine monks from St Mary's Abbey left York to start a new Cistercian house in desolate Skeldale. Archbishop Thurstan had given them a large tract of uncultivated land, watered by pure springs or fountains. The first winter was harsh and morale was low, but in 1135 they were joined by Hugh, former Dean of York, who brought financial resources and a library. Fountains soon grew in size and fame into one of the most celebrated Cistercian houses in England, and by far the richest. By 1150 seven daughter abbeys had been established, one as far distant as Norway. Fifty years later Fountains had more than fifty monks and over two hundred lay brothers. Despite the ravages of the Dissolution, it is architecturally the most complete Cistercian abbey in England, as famous in our own day as it was in the Middle Ages. Almost equally famous was Byland Abbey, just four miles across Scawton Moor from Rievaulx. The community had come together in 1134 in Calder in Cumberland, but four years later had retreated in face of Scottish invaders to Hood, near Thirsk. Finding this site too small, they moved in 1143 to Ryedale to take possession of a grant from Roger Mowbray, and in order to obtain their desired solitude they removed the village of Byland to a new position over a mile away. Still their travels were not yet over, for as they were less than two miles from Rievaulx the two communities could hear each other's bells. In 1147 they finally moved to the present site, which they had laboriously cleared by rooting out the woods and by digging enormous drainage ditches. Thirty years later Byland's thirty-six monks and hundred lay brothers had gained a wide spiritual reputation. Their spectacular church was finished by 1225, and the ruins of the monastic complex now

afford an almost perfect example of the Cistercian method of arrangement (Butler and Given-Wilson 1979: 237–42).

Two other Yorkshire Cistercian abbeys are of particular architectural interest. The austerity of Kirkstall remains a permanent memorial to early Cistercian endeavour. Forced by unproductive land and robbers to evacuate their original settlement at Barnoldswick, the community established themselves at Kirkstall in 1152 as a daughter house of Fountains and eventually grew to thirty-six monks and many more lay brothers. Wealth generated by the wool trade paid for the buildings that were erected over the next generation or so, and as little rebuilding took place in later times and Kirkstall escaped massive destruction at the Dissolution, the abbey provides the clearest illustration of the Cistercian's use of the Romanesque style. The eastern parts of the church at Roche Abbey rank with the cathedrals at Canterbury and Wells as the earliest known examples of Early English Gothic. Roche was founded in 1138 from Newminster in Northumberland (itself a daughter of Fountains) on a remote uncultivated plot on the common boundary of the parishes of Laughton and Maltby. Here in the 1170s the monks built their abbey with beautiful local limestone. Three storeys high and rib-vaulted, the abbey church was not entirely Gothic in concept, for its walls are thick and the blind recesses of the triforium do not achieve the lightness and space associated with later buildings. It suffered badly at the Dissolution, but Lancelot Brown's landscaped setting has enhanced the beauty of this lonely site. Yorkshire's three other Cistercian abbeys were also substantial institutions, at Sawley (founded from Newminster in 1147), Jervaulx (re-established in 1156 on a site now marked by extensive ruins), and Meaux (founded in 1150 from Fountains). The great Holderness abbey of Meaux had sixty monks and ninety lay brothers in 1249, but now there are no buildings above ground, nor at the daughter cell of Otteringham.

In addition to the great abbeys, the Benedictines and Cistercians each established a dozen or so nunneries in Yorkshire. By 1133 St Clement's had been founded as a Benedictine house in York, and Handall as a Cistercian nunnery 12 miles north of Whitby. Another Cistercian house at Kirklees may

---

Plate 1.5 Rievaulx Abbey. One of the medieval glories of Yorkshire, Rievaulx Abbey was founded in 1132 by Walter L'Espec, lord of Helmsley, who invited thirteen monks from Clairvaux to establish the first Cistercian house in the county. In time it became one of the largest and most famous abbeys in England.

The Norman buildings were plain and severe in the usual Cistercian manner. Most of the Norman nave has collapsed but some twelfth-century work remains in the transepts. During the thirteenth century the abbey was rebuilt in the new Early English Gothic style. The seven-bay chancel (to the right of the picture) is particularly memorable and the domestic buildings also date mostly from this period. The abbey follows the standard Cistercian plan but the usual east–west orientation had to be abandoned to accommodate the buildings in the narrow Rye valley.

By the eighteenth century the picturesque ruins were widely admired and Thomas Duncombe constructed a terrace on the adjoining hill with Ionic and Doric temples and with frequent glimpses of the medieval abbey in the valley below.

date from 1138. During the 1140s new foundations were few, but the 1150s saw a rapid advance to twenty-four Yorkshire nunneries (Burton 1979). Nunneries may have seemed unimportant religious houses to contemporaries, for they were poor and small, with usually only twelve nuns under a prioress; their remains are insubstantial. Small nunneries were also founded at Moxby by the Austins and at Arthington by the Cluniacs.

The Premonstratensian order of canons was founded in 1120 at Prémontré in France and first established in this country at Newholme (Lincolnshire) 23 years later. By the time of the Dissolution the canons had created thirty-one English abbeys and three nunneries. This priestly order combined manual labour with devotion and scholarship in remote places on the Cistercian model. They had three abbeys in Yorkshire and another at Beauchief, which was incorporated within the county in the twentieth century. Easby Abbey was founded in 1151 by Roald, Constable of Richmond, for the usual thirteen canons, but by 1392 the numbers had more than doubled; the picturesque ruins on the banks of the Swale have an unorthodox arrangement with the church in the middle. Next in time was Coverham Abbey, which was refounded at the close of the twelfth century after a false start about 1187 at Swainby. Soon afterwards, in 1198 Egglestone Abbey was established from Easby. The other regular order of canons was the Gilbertines, the only one to originate in England. Their standards were high and they provided numerous orphanages and leper hospitals. They began in 1131, when Gilbert, priest of the Lincolnshire parish of Sempringham, built a small convent next to his church for seven local women. Most of the twenty-seven Gilbertine houses were in Lincolnshire, but four were established in Yorkshire. Ellerton Priory and St Andrew's, York, have gone completely, but there are substantial remains of St Mary's Church at Old Malton and a well-known site in the East Riding at Watton. Eustace Fitzjohn founded Watton Priory as a double house about the middle of the twelfth century. Excavations have revealed the plan of the entire 600 ft long complex, the western parts for nuns and the eastern parts for canons, close by the prior's attractive fifteenth-century brick house, which survives intact with angle turrets and a remarkable oriel window.

By about 1220 the great period of monastic growth in England had come to an end. Religious houses were numerous and widespread, and so much property was in monastic hands that almost every landowner would have had a man of religion as his neighbour (Platt 1978: 61). The religious included not only the monastic but the military orders that had been created after the capture of Jerusalem in 1099; the Knights of the Hospital of St John of Jerusalem and the Knights of the Temple, who guarded holy places and protected pilgrims. The Hospitallers had Yorkshire estates at Beverley, Mount St John, and Newland near Drax, and the Templars at Temple Newsam, Templehirst and eight other places. Their establishments were small and have left hardly any remains, for normally their properties were let out to rent. Medieval religious life has left much more substantial remains in the form of its hospitals. Of the 90 known sites 72 were urban; Beverley had 10 hospitals at different times, and York had 19. The ruins of St Leonard's hospital at York confirm that it was the largest in Yorkshire. It was the successor to the tenth-century St Peter's Hospital, refounded and rebuilt during the twelfth century, and large enough to accommodate 229 sick people in 1280. The surviving ruins are of the vaulted undercroft of the large infirmary hall and the first-floor chapel.

The friary was another widespread urban institution, a new form of religious life in the thirteenth century that abandoned rural isolation and deliberately sought contact with society. In 1221 the Dominicans became the first preaching order to reach England, and six years later they had become established in York, where they eventually had sixty members. Dominican friaries were also built at Beverley (by 1240), Scarborough (by 1252), Pontefract (1256) and Yarm (by 1266). The Franciscans had also arrived in York by *c.* 1230, and later at Scarborough, Richmond, Beverley, Doncaster and Hull. Austin Friars had put down roots in York (by 1240), Tickhill (*c.* 1260) and Hull (1317), and the Carmelites at York (1253), Hull (1289), Scarborough (1319), Doncaster (1350) and Northallerton (1356). The Crutched Friars and the Friars of the Sack also gained a temporary foothold, but did not flourish.

English monks were celebrated not only for their spiritual life but for their farming activities, particularly for the vast flocks of sheep which they pastured on the hills and in the marshes. Fountains Abbey had up to 18,000 sheep on Malham Moor and thousands more elsewhere in the Dales. The Benedictines had built up large flocks in parts of England during the eleventh and twelfth centuries, but it was the Cistercians who acquired vast tracts of moorland and extensive pasture rights for huge numbers of sheep. For example, in 1158 Rievaulx Abbey obtained pasture for 1,000 sheep in the parish of Folkton on the northern edge of the Wolds, and about the same time Meaux Abbey was granted pasture for 800 sheep in Myton, 860 sheep at Warter, 300 at Beeford and 200 at Hatfield; by the 1270s they had 11,000 sheep and 1,000 beasts in Holderness (*VCH East Riding*, II 1974: 171; English 1979: 198, 200). Other Cistercian monasteries received numerous twelfth- and thirteenth-century grants of pasture in the West Riding, usually for 200–300 sheep, and vast sheep-runs were created in the North-West; Fountains Abbey held over 90 square miles of Wharfedale around Kilnsey, enclosed within a continuous boundary, and by the thirteenth century the Fountains moorland sheep pastures were clearly demarcated from those of Bolton and Salley Abbeys. In Yorkshire, more than in any other region of England, monks were great sheep-masters. Even so, it is important to remember that laymen also farmed sheep on a considerable scale. In 1273–75 the grain sales on the Holderness manors of Isabella de Fortibus amounted to less than £100, but the sales of her wool totalled about £460; shortly afterwards the family owned at least 7,000 sheep in the Holderness marshes. Another example, much lower down the social scale, is that of a middleman, Thomas of Westhorpe, who had over

2,700 sheep and sixteen sacks of wool at Ebberston in the Vale of Pickering in 1366, compared with a contemporary flock of 1,307 sheep belonging to Whitby Abbey. In the West Riding some of the largest flocks were kept in the rich arable parishes so that sheep could manure the land. A 1287 grant of pasture for 240 sheep at Chevet speaks of a permanent sheep-fold enclosed by ditches, and elsewhere folds and temporary hurdles are mentioned frequently (Waites 1967; Faull and Moorhouse, eds 1981: 762–3).

In the Middle Ages sheep were valued not only for their wool and mutton but also for ewe's milk, especially in the form of cheese. However, it was the wool that brought in the big profits. Much was sold to clothiers from Beverley and York and the other English cloth-manufacturing towns of the thirteenth century, but the lucrative markets lay abroad where cloth was produced on a much larger scale, particularly in Italy and in northern France, Flanders and Brabant. The great Italian merchant houses of Florence, Lucca and Siena made contracts with English monasteries by which they paid in advance for wool that would be delivered years ahead. Occasionally, monasteries got into difficulties under this system; in 1284, for instance, Kirkstall Abbey was £5,250 and 59 sacks of wool in debt, but by 1301 this debt had been reduced to £160 and the abbey's livestock had been built up to 4,000 sheep and 600 head of cattle. Wool was England's greatest export commodity, and Yorkshire monasteries commonly held contracts with more than one firm at the same time. The larger monastic bodies also acted as middlemen for the smaller religious houses and for laymen; thus, wool from Arden Nunnery in the Hambleton Hills was sent to Byland Abbey's main woolhouse at Thorpe Grange ten miles away, and Guisborough Priory had a woolhouse within a few miles of its sheep stations on the North York Moors and its lowland granges. Hull and York were the country's chief wool markets and ports, and the York suburb of Clifton was a major collecting point alongside the Ouse, where Italian agents inspected the wool and saw that it was properly packed and weighed 'without cocked and black guard, grey scab, clacked and all vile fleeces (Waites 1967; Miller and Hatcher 1978: 231).

Monastic estates were built up during the twelfth and thirteenth centuries by grants from the faithful, usually of land that had to be assarted from the waste. Byland Abbey was granted the right to pasture 360 sheep in Upper Whitley with 'all necessaries from the wood for making their sheep-cote in Kottrode, and for making a hedge and enclosure round the sheep-cote'; Kottrode means the clearing around the cot or hut. In *c.* 1185–93 Kirkstall Abbey acquired an estate in Seacroft and wood 'to make their hedges and to build folds and sheep houses on my land when they have need', and a *c.* 1212 grant to Pontefract priory of a grange or barn, with pasture for 200 sheep in Shippen near Barwick in Elmet, stated that 'this grange, with the plot on which it is situate, I have given to the monks to shelter their sheep'. The Cistercians developed the grange system to farm their outlying estates, particularly their arable holdings in the lowlands. The granges varied greatly in size and situation, but in the early years when capital was limited they were generally simple and were worked only by lay brothers and small groups of hired labourers. Earthworks which can be found alongside such Yorkshire granges as Cayton, Kildwick, Morker and Sutton have been identified as the foundations of labourers' houses.

The monks were not firmly committed to any principle of isolation and did not normally depopulate existing settlements, except much later in the fifteenth century when arable lands were enclosed for sheep pastures. However, the nature of their grants meant that they were often cut off from village communities on the edges of the wastes. In 1160–72 Meaux Abbey was granted half a carucate of land and pasture for 300 sheep 'outside the ditches of the town' of Dunnington on the moor towards Beeford. The site of Moor Grange is well-marked by a water-filled moat, and by 1396 an arable estate of 408 acres had been established by drainage, reclamation and further grants. On the Wolds at Octon, Meaux Abbey consolidated another grange of 434 acres with virtually unlimited pasture, and at Skerne built up their largest grange of all, with lands covering 1,417 acres. From the late thirteenth century onwards many granges were rebuilt on the scale of small contemporary manor houses, with hall, chamber, kitchen, chapel, barn and other outbuildings. In the lowlands they were often laid out on a simple double-courtyard plan, with the domestic range separate from the great court, as at the Cistercian foundations at Balk, Cayton, Melsonby, Morker, Octon, Skiplam and Suttons, the Gilbertine grange at Rillington, or the Augustian settlement at Willerby (Platt 1969: 40–1, 50–7, 72, 88). The monks played a prime role in the development of the medieval Yorkshire economy, not only as sheep and cattle farmers but as converters of the waste into arable land; moreover, in the West Riding they were prominent in the mining and smelting of iron.

Chapter 2

The Later Middle Ages

Yorkshire c. 1300

Agriculture

Between the time of the Domesday Survey and the opening decades of the fourteenth century, England's population more than doubled and may well have trebled. The twelfth and thirteenth centuries provide clear evidence of a massive increase in population throughout the country. If we take at face value the suspect figures from the Yorkshire folios of Domesday Book then the county's population growth appears to have been the fastest in England; even after the Scottish invasions of the early fourteenth century and after the ravages of the Black Death the total number of people living in Yorkshire at the time of the 1377 poll tax returns was about seven times higher than that recorded in 1086. Such a contrast is no doubt exaggerated, but the dynamics of growth are clear. At a minimum over 3¼ million people were living in England about 1300, and the true figure was probably much higher.

'In general', wrote Professor Postan, 'England's population in the thirteenth century was predominantly agricultural, her agriculture was in the main arable, her arable villages were in the main composed of customary tenants' (Postan 1972: 131). Such tenants held family farms and earned a subsistence income, many of them having a customary bovate or carucate of 10–15 acres of arable land, with grazing and other rights on the commons. Postan has estimated that this size of holding would provide a family of five with about 2,000 calories per head each day in an average year. Some wealthier families had accumulated a few bovates and were able to employ labourers, to sub-let parts of their estates, and to sell their surpluses at neighbouring markets and fairs. Other families at the opposite end of the scale were smallholders or cottagers, even in the years before the Norman Conquest. Their numbers grew steadily in the subsequent 250 years when much new land was asserted from the wastes to accommodate the rising population. By the late thirteenth century, when documentary sources provide firm information, cottagers with less than 5 acres of land could be found in large numbers in many parts of Yorkshire. At Kirkby Moorside, where 60 out of 240 tenants were cottagers and at Thoralby, where cottagers numbered 51 out of about 80 tenants, moorland assarts were presumably the source of new land, but similar-sized groups of smallholders were found at Cottingham in the Hull valley (137 cottagers out of 365 tenants), and in the Vale of York at Buttercrambe (62/134), Riccall (45/82) and Stillington (45/87). Taken as a whole, these cottagers formed about 40 per cent of the tenantry, a proportion similar to that found in most other parts of England (Miller and Hatcher 1978: 54).

In the country at large, smallholders accounted for at least 1½ million people and may well have totalled 2½ million. Everywhere the impression is of a growing number of families living on the margin of subsistence, a rural proletariat whose wages failed to keep pace with rising rents and prices. Some of these families turned to industrial occupations or to crafts and trade, but most undoubtedly suffered from under-employment. As in many Third World countries today where the population is increasing at an unprecedented rate, national economies may expand rapidly in terms of aggregate products and incomes, yet the lot of the individual may hardly improve or even worsen. When population levels soar and the same primitive farming techniques are employed, living standards are lowered.

During this period of expansion, however, 'England took a long step away from serfdom and towards greater independence and freedom' (Postan 1972: 143–54). Most Anglo-Scandinavian countrymen were of dependent status, but even before the Black Death labour services had virtually disappeared north and west of a line extending from the Wash to the Severn. In Yorkshire labour services had traditionally been light, and during the twelfth and thirteenth centuries money rents became increasingly the principal service, whether in the Pennine foothills and sandstones of south-west Yorkshire or on the Wolds at Little Weighton, where it was said in 1328 that labour services had been converted into money payments 'from ancient times' (Miller and Hatcher 1978: 124). The story was not one of continuous progress, but in common with other northerners medieval Yorkshiremen were not as sorely burdened as some of their contemporaries on manors further south.

Throughout western Christendom the majority of medieval countrymen were small-scale farmers dependent upon their own labour and upon the produce of their own fields and livestock. Prolonged spells of bad weather and sudden epidemics emphasized the precariousness of life and the annual importance of the harvest. Though starvation was relatively rare, malnutrition and disease were commonplace. Contemporary opinion held that England was a rich land, but from a later point of view her farmers were equipped with only a backward technology. In this era of technological inertia new ideas were adopted very slowly, and then they usually involved the management rather than the use of land. In Yorkshire, as in most parts of England, cereals were the farmers' major concern. Despite the relatively small population, large acreages had to be devoted to crops as yields were so low. Modern farmers expect to get at least three times as much wheat and barley from their seed as did their medieval predecessors, and at least five times as much oats. From the limited amount of information that we have for medieval Yorkshire, only the barley yields in Holderness approached Walter of Henley's ideal of an eight-fold harvest; here the yields were amongst the highest in the country.

Table 1.3   Yield ratios of grain per seed

Manors or estates	Period	Wheat	Barley	Oats
Harewood	1266–89	3.5	3.5	2.1
Keyingham	1263–91	4.6	5.2	2.8
Little Humber	1263–91	5.4	7.8	2.9
Easington	1263–91	3.2	6.0	2.4
Bolton	1301–14	4.8	4.9	2.7
Malham	1301–14	4.1	4.7	2.5

(After Miller and Hatcher 1978: 216.)

The low quality of the available seed, the limitations of shallow ploughing and the difficulties in eradicating weeds, together with the lack of underdrainage on heavier soils and a shortage of manure meant that much heavy labour was needed to produce even such modest results. Livestock farming was no more productive than arable husbandry. The dairy herd at Bolton priory produced only 72 lbs of butter and cheese per cow, and annual milk yields of 120–50 gallons per cow were only about one-sixth of a modern farmer's expectations. During the 1260s and 1270s a herd of twenty-five cows at Harewood produced an average of seventeen calves each year, but even this modest figure was higher than the one calf per two cows at Bolton priory and the two calves per five cows on the other side of the Pennines in the Lacy vaccaries in Blackburnshire. By 1300, if not before, many estates throughout the country were falling behind their previous levels of productivity. Some of the newly won assarts did not maintain their fertility for long, and even some of the old-cultivated lands witnessed a decline in their yields. Miller and Hatcher have pointed to an appreciable fall in the average expectations of life during the century before the Black Death and have commented that in some of the more populous and old-settled parts of the country famine conditions had become almost endemic by the early fourteenth century (Miller and Hatcher 1978: 78, 217).

By 1300 Yorkshire farmers had reached the present-day limits of cultivation on the Pennines. In the limestone dales, particularly in Wharfedale and Wensleydale, steps of lyncheted fields climbing the steep hillsides still bear silent witness to the efforts of farmers who brought marginal land under the plough. On the Pennine edges of the huge manor of Wakefield a vivid picture of a pioneer farmer is provided by a 1309 entry in the court rolls, when William the son of Thomas of Hallamshire paid a shilling entry fine and 6*d.* per annum rent 'to take an acre of new land from the waste of Hepworth in front of his door'. The process of assarting is well recorded in the twelfth and thirteenth centuries, but it was probably just as active in earlier times, and in parts of the Pennines such activity was resumed after the withdrawal from the margins which followed the disasters of the fourteenth century. Thus, in 1440–41 Edward of Ryles, Agnes his wife, and Richard their son were given permission by the lord of Sheffield 'to pluck up by the roots and clear away, in all lands that could be ploughed, thorns, brambles and thicket'. Ryles may perhaps be identified with Rails in the Rivelin Valley and with the local surname Ryalls. William and Isabella Ryol and Agnes Ryall, widow, were recorded in the 1379 poll tax returns for Sheffield.

Royd was the usual name for a Pennine assart. Thus, a clearing made in 1307 in Wakefield manor was said to be 'called rodeland because it was cleared from growing wood'. In remote areas where manorial control was weak colonists often did not bother to get formal permission to settle, and although many isolated farmsteads are recorded for the first time in documents of the twelfth to the fourteenth century it is impossible to give a precise account of the progress that was made. Judging from terms used in contemporary documents, these assarts were normally enclosed by a ditch and a hedge. At Lawrence Field on the Derbyshire border the enclosure is formed by a ditch and a bank of vertical stones. Stone walls were a much rarer feature of the landscape than they are today, though in a thirteenth-century charter the Rye Croft on the bleak Pennine slopes at Ughill was said to be enclosed by a stone wall. In more hospitable territory further east, hedgerows were preferred; for instance, a 1338 lease of a furlong of arable land on the coal-measure sandstones at Birstall refers to 'thorns for making hedges', probably hawthorn. Stone walls became much more common during the seventeenth and eighteenth centuries and were extensively used during the era of parliamentary enclosure, but in the Middle Ages they may have formed only the principal boundaries and property divisions.

The amount of corn that was grown on the Pennines by medieval farmers was much greater than in later times. Unfavourable climatic and soil conditions meant that the usual crop was oats, which was sown in spring and harvested late, sometimes following a winter-sown crop of rye. In areas of low population densities and extensive pastures such simple rotations satisfied subsistence needs. Most, if not all, Pennine hamlets had one or more 'townfields' devoted to crops. In south-western parts of the county townfields can be identified (though in many cases the evidence is post-medieval) at Bradfield, Brightholmlee, Carlecotes, Cat Hill, Dungworth, Ecklands, High Lee, Hoylandswaine, Hunshelf, Ingbirchworth, Midhope, Rough Birchworth, Scholes, Snowden Hill, Stainborough, Stannington, Wigtwizzle and Worrall. At Rough Birchworth, where a settlement at 800 ft above sea level was recorded in Domesday Book, the pattern of the long narrow 'lands' or strips of the townfields has been fossilized by the stone walls that were built when the fields were enclosed by agreement. A little further north, in 1297, Agnes of Denby paid 6*d.* at the manor court of Wakefield for a licence to take three acres of land in the west field of Upperthong, and ten years later when the same court tried a case where a woman said she had been attacked, her hedge broken and her grass consumed by cattle, the defendants claimed that she had wrongfully enclosed land 'in which they ought to common in open time'. The West Yorkshire Archaeological Survey has also noted references to arable land in the field of Shibden hamlet (1317), to the common field of Leventhorpe, a hamlet of Thornton (1339), and the arable fields of Scoles in Cleckeaton township (1483).

The origin of hamlet townfields is obscure, but they were probably developed from earlier assarts. Royds Moor in the parish of Whiston is named after a royd which had been cleared by the third quarter of the twelfth century; by the following century charters were referring to lands that lay in the arable fields of the small settlements of Rodes. Here, as elsewhere, it appears that individual assarts were eventually incorporated into communal town-fields. Marginal land at the edges of the arable core was occasionally brought into cultivation and then given several years to recuperate while other marginal land was tilled. These outer fields were sometimes referred to as foreland, and in west Yorkshire the term has been found at Stanbury near Haworth (1422) in the extreme west, as well as in central and eastern parts at Barwick (1258), Addingham (1313), Otley (early fourteenth century), Leeds (1357), Methley (1376) and Lofthouse (1425), (Faull and Moorhouse, 1981, 659–68).

A few miles north-west of Sheffield the townfields of the Pennine hamlet of Ughill rose to over 1,000 ft above sea level. Ughill was recorded in Domesday Book, but no further documentation is available until the late thirteenth century from when sufficient charters survive to suggest that the area under cultivation was similar to that shown on Thomas Jeffreys's map of Yorkshire 500 years later. In a pre-1290 charter Henry, the son of Adam of Ughill, granted to his sisters, Matilda and Beatrice, one acre of land in the fields of Ughill, of which half lay upon the Lee and butted upon Albrayrood. Arable lands lay intermingled in the open fields, and another charter that mentions a piece of meadow in the grasscroft 'between the meadow of John of Ughill on both sides' suggests that the common meadows were divided into doles. Immediately beyond the townfields a common wood stretched from 'the west side of the house of Thomas the son of Hugh of the Wood', perhaps in the vicinity of the present Woodhouse farm in the direction of small wood on the slopes towards Ughill. Rye Croft lay to the west of the settlement and other assarts had been cleared beyond the townfields as far north as Withanley House. One thirteenth-century charter refers to 'part of that moor which lay between the old dike [which presumably marked the original limit of the arable] and the new dike and butted upon the new land of Thomas of Wyhenlee'; another charter refers to 'two acres of land in the field of Ughill at le

Wythenleye, as then enclosed'. Even in this bleak and inhospitable territory the limits of cultivation had been reached before the end of the thirteenth century.

A different type of farming, with more emphasis on pastoral activities, was practised in north-western parts of the Pennines, where the Carboniferous Limestone soils provided extensive pastures. At Malham it was agreed in 1264 that the owner of an oxgang of land could pasture up to six oxen, six cows with their young of less than three years, four mares with their young, 200 sheep, five she-goats, one sow with her young of one year, and five geese. Here too, however, sufficient corn was grown to satisfy subsistence needs (Baker and Butlins, eds 1973: 173). Insights into the workings of a pastoral economy on the Lancashire border are provided by an agreement made during the reign of King John between William Mowbray and Adam of Staveley, which acknowledged that the forest of Mewith belonged to William, but allowed Adam and his men of Ingleton and of High and Low Bentham certain common rights including pannage for pigs and the collection of wood for building and burning. Beasts belonging to Adam and his men could graze in the forest by day but had to be collected each night, and the Bentham men were allowed to graze twenty mares and their foals around the clock. Cattle belonging to William and his men of Burton in Lonsdale were also permitted to graze within the forest bounds and William was given leave to make lodges and vaccaries for breeding cattle. Another three vaccaries belonging to Adam were stationed on Whernside, Souther Scales and Birbladewith (YASRS, XLIV 1911: 8).

In western parts of Yorkshire *scales* or *scholes* is a common minor place-name of Viking origin denoting a shieling or temporary shelter. Souther Scales takes its name from an Old Norse byname, Sutari. Some shelters may have been for charcoal burners or other itinerant craftsmen, but most accommodated pastoral farmers in search of summer pastures. In time these shelters became permanent and some formed the nucleus of a settlement. An equally common name is the Old Danish *booth*, which had much the same meaning and which came to be applied to a cowhouse, a herdsman's hut or an outlying hamlet. Fulwood Booth and Old Booth, Bradfield, may perhaps be identified with two vaccaries belonging to Sheffield castle, which in 1184 were restocked with forty cows, four bulls and eight oxen; certainly Fulwood Booth was a manorial vaccary in later times. Such activities were organized on a much larger scale further north, where place-names such as Birstall, Heptonstall, Kirkstall, Saltonstall and Wainstalls are derived from Old English *stall*, meaning a cattle-shed.

The main vaccary sites of the manor of Wakefield lay within the graveship of Sowerby high on the Pennines. Each farm had 24–30 acres of grazing land for upwards of forty animals all the year round, and in 1309 the farm at Over Saltonstall was enclosed with 'a good fence' which had cost 8 shillings to repair. Cattle farms were principally concerned with producing oxen as draught beasts for sale in distant parts. The 'Wakefield Gate' which linked the vaccaries on the moorland edges of the upper Calder valley with the manorial centre must at times have been a busy drove road, for all the cattle were taken to Wakefield to be marked and sold (Faull and Moorhouse, eds 1981: 758–61). Similar large-scale organizations geared to a market economy is evident at Bolton Priory, where in 1297 the four hundred strong herd included 189 cows, valued for their calves and dairy produce, all under the control of a central stockman (Kershaw 1973: 97–103). Other Pennine pastures were vast sheep-runs, with monastic flocks running into thousands, but elsewhere the total number of sheep owned by small farmers may well have exceeded the better-recorded flocks on the demesnes. R. E. Glasscock has estimated that in the country as a whole there may have been eight million sheep during the early fourteenth century (Darby, ed. 1973: 150).

As the clearing of moorland and woodland was being pursued actively at a time when surnames were being formed, many of the isolated farmsteads that were established on the Pennine hills during the early medieval period were the source of distinctive family names. Though some go back to at least the twelfth century and others were not formed until Tudor times, most Yorkshire surnames became hereditary between 1275 and 1425. The scattered nature of settlement and the relatively small population at this time meant that the West Riding acquired a large number of distinctive names, many of which had a single family origin. Dr G. Redmonds has shown that upper Calderdale was a particularly prolific source of distinctive surnames derived from place-names. Upper Calderdale comprised the enormous medieval parish of Halifax, which stretched 15 miles from north to south and was the largest in England. More than three-quarters of the West Riding's distinctive locality surnames that were recorded in the 1379 poll tax returns were from this single parish. Although only 831 people from the Halifax area were assessed for this poll tax, well over a hundred surnames derived from minor place-names survive, and an equal number were in use for many years before they failed.

The surviving names gradually spread outwards, but they are still most numerous in or close to their place of origin. To this day the Halifax region is the main source of such distinctive surnames as Ackroyd, Bairstow, Barraclough, Boothroyd, Bottomley, Brearley, Copley, Crabtree, Gledhill, Greenwood, Haley, Hemingway, Hey, Holroyd, Horsfall, Illingworth, Lumb, Midgley, Murgatroyd, Priestley, Sutcliffe, Woodhead and many more. Names that originated at localities a little further south within the parish of Almondbury include Armitage, Beaumont, Brook, Crossland, Kaye, Lockwood, Parkin and Thewliss. Dr Redmonds has shown that even the surname Brook apparently has a single source. Other distinctive West Riding names such as Fieldhouse, Green, Moorhouse and Woodhouse seem to have had varied origins, however. On the other hand, even some surnames which have been derived from personal names have come from single families, for instance, Allott, Gillott and Wragg in the Sheffield region, Jowett around Bradford and Leeds, and Oddy in the Bowland area on the Lancashire border. Nicknames, too, sometimes had a single origin as surnames; the West Riding clothing area had numerous Teals, Tempests and Veritys, and Speight (a woodpecker) first appears in records in 1307 at Gomersal.

Though the study of surnames has revealed that medieval families sometimes migrated considerable distances and that restrictions on mobility were less than once supposed, nevertheless most West Riding families remained rooted in or near the homes of their ancestors (Redmonds 1973: *passim*). Thus, although the surname Sunderland became common in the West Riding, the Sunderland family long continued in Northowram township where Alcock of Sondreland was recorded in 1274 and Thomas of Sundirland in 1379. Likewise, within a few miles of Penistone variants can be found of the surname Bilcliff, which is derived from a site a couple of miles or so west of Penistone occupied by Upper and Lower Belle Clive farms. Local people still call the farms Bilcliff, for this was Billa's cliff, a clearing on the edge of the moors that was first recorded early in the thirteenth century. Similarly, the surname Reaney is derived from Ranah farm a mile or so away, and Bullas from Bullhouse.

The marginal nature of some of these clearings is evident from a 1334 survey of the forest of Pickering on the North York Moors. The forest justices recorded about 1,400 acres of assarts that had been cleared over several generations. Only a few acres supported both winter-sown and spring-sown grains; many more were sown simply with oats or with oats and hay; but the most common practice was for new land to be cropped intermittently or for just a few years before reverting to pasture (Miller and Hatcher 1978: 56). Farmers turned in desperation to this sort of land when the supply of fertile soils had run out, and it was the first to be abandoned when population pressures were eased by the disasters of the fourteenth century.

Woodland clearance had progressed so far by the early Middle Ages that in many places surviving resources had to be preserved and managed. Coppicing was already a common practice by the time of Domesday Book, and as the young shoots that grew vigorously from coppiced stools were known as springs many a wood acquired the name of Springwood. When the trees in Westwood in Crigglestone township were sold to four tenants of Wakefield manor in 1307 the purchasers agreed to 'cut the wood as close to the ground as possible, and to clear the place of twigs, so as not to impede the fresh growth of the wood'. Coppice woods were protected from animals by a ditch and a bank with a fence, and some of these old boundaries are still preserved. Most woods were of the coppice-with-standard type, where timber trees were spaced out amongst the coppiced underwood, but some (or parts) were subject to common grazing rights for cattle and pigs and had grassy clearings within them. Outwood, which covered most of the north section of Stanley township and part of the adjoining township of Alverthorpe, was the common wood of the townspeople of Wakefield. In the lordship of Sheffield Beeley wood was recorded in 1332; by the mid-seventeenth century, when it covered 80½ acres, it was a springwood, but amongst the plants and fungi that indicate the wood's

75

Plate 2.1 Ranah Stones Cote. Ranah comes from an Old Norse word meaning 'raven-mound' or 'raven-hill' and is one of several minor place-names on the bleak foothills of the Southern Pennines that are derived from birds and wild animals. The present building dates from the eighteenth century but a Henry of Ravenhowe lived nearby in the fourteenth century and in 1379 Thomas of Ranaw was amongst the Thurlstone farmers who paid the poll tax. The site has given rise to the local surname Reaney, which until recent times was pronounced Rainey or Rayner. Many other Pennine farms are the homes of distinctive West Riding surnames.

antiquity cow wheat can still be found growing in its grassy parts, lending support to the documentary evidence that in 1442 the lord received 20 shillings 'from the grass of the pasture in Bylleywode'. Though many woods were managed and preserved in the Middle Ages, others were felled and stubbed in a continuous process of assarting. In the parish of Penistone the minor place-names Bradshaw, Catshaw, Fulshaw and Smallshaw speak of small woods that have long since gone, and Copthurst farm on the hills south of Holmfirth reminds us of a vanished 'wood of pollarded trees' that was recorded as Coppedhirst in 1307.

During the middle of the twelfth century 140 pigs grazed in Escrick wood in the Vale of York; the tenants of the manor each had common for 10 pigs, 10 cattle and 20 sheep. The common wood covered 260 acres in 1291 and occupied roughly the same acreage five centuries later. Elsewhere in the parish assarting proceeded apace with *riddings* and *thwaites*, especially after the removal of forest law in Ouse-Derwent wapentake in 1234 and the passing two years later of the Statute of Merton, which allowed manorial lords to clear land for their own use provided 'sufficient' commons were left (*VCH, East Riding*, III 1976: 22). In Escrick's neighbouring parish of Wheldrake the arable was expanded beyond the old turf dyke to accommodate the rising population. The number of households rose from the 16 or so of the planned village to about 69 in 1316 and to 84 in 1348. Over twenty assarts had been cleared by the time that the forest laws were lifted, so that the arable was already double its original size. These early clearings were subject to common grazing rights after the crops had been harvested. Fountains Abbey established a grange in the parish and took the lead in bringing fresh land into cultivation after the removal of forest laws. Dr Sheppard has argued that it may not have been until the early fourteenth century that two or three distinct open fields were established in Wheldrake, with many of the new assarts serving as foreland. During the fourteenth century the older arable lands were reorganized as four open fields, named simply West, North-west, North and East fields. Three of the fields had fixed crop rotations, but East field formed part of the foreland or 'extra land', and during the fifteenth and sixteenth centuries much of this foreland was converted to pasture. Beyond these open fields were numerous assarts in individual closes and also the large meadows that lay in the Ings beside the river Derwent. The common pastures comprised the sandy North Moor and Rox-hall Moor and the ill-drained areas known as the Horse Marsh and the Moss (which was intercommoned with Escrick) (Sheppard 1966).

Open-field systems developed slowly as fresh land was brought into cultivation. Individual assarts were often absorbed into open-fields at a later stage, perhaps because they had been cleared as a communal activity and had been grazed in common after harvest, and perhaps sometimes because they had been subdivided by sales or by the practice of partible inheritance. The fully fledged 'Midland' field system, in which winter and spring crops were suc-ceeded by a fallow, evolved in those parts of the Vale of York where population

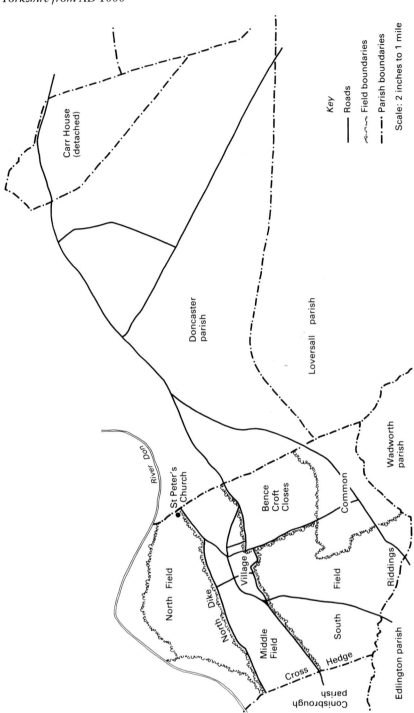

Figure 2.1 Warmsworth's open fields

growth put such pressure on the available supplies of pasture that the arable had to be farmed to a system that provided grazing on the fallow and on the stubble after harvest. The Magnesian Limestone belt, whose fertile soils provided some of the best farming in the county, adopted this system at an early date. At Warmsworth, for instance, the open fields had reached maturity by the late thirteenth or the fourteenth century (the period of the earliest surviving deeds), for by then the strips in each field had already reached the parish boundaries. The original names appear to have been the simple ones of South field, Middle field and North field. South field must have been farmed to its full extent at an early date before the parish boundaries were settled, for the south-western border of this field took a series of right-angled turns along the ends of strips abutting upon Edlington common. In 1296 South field also extended to the Cross hedge (the parish boundary in the west) and to the Conisbrough road in the north. Earlier assarts had been brought into communal ownership, for a grant of 1320 refers to one acre lying in South field in a place called 'le Ryding' and adjoining the 'Wekedike'. Ridding Closes and Weik Closes are marked together on a 1726 map, and fourteenth-century references to 'le Wykus' indicate a *wic* or dairy farm, which was separated from the open field by a ditch. Another ditch and bank, known in 1273 as the North Dike, separated the Middle and North fields and may possibly have marked the original limit of cultivation in the planned village, thus fulfilling a role comparable to the turf dyke at Wheldrake. Ridge-and-furrow patterns in steep, rough ground support the evidence of a 1335 deed that North field was ploughed beyond the dyke as far as the floodplain of the river Don, the northern boundary of the parish. About 113 acres of clayey soils, well-suited to pasture, served as a common at the south-eastern extremity of the parish. By the early fourteenth century, therefore, full use was made of the available resources within the restrictions imposed by contemporary technology (Hey and Magilton 1983).

A similar tale can be told about the Wolds, even though the remoter parts were left to sheep and rabbits. Aerial photographs have revealed extensive remains of ridge-and-furrow on the High Wolds with the characteristic headlands, balks and reverse-S-shape strips of open-field agriculture which was abandoned here during and after the fourteenth century. A sheep-and-corn system of husbandry, where barley was the major crop and the sheep manured the arable, was practised all along the Wolds. Such was the pressure on land in some places that the sheepwalks had to be safeguarded by legal agreements. When Bridlington Priory was given rights of pasture for five hundred sheep beyond the arable fields of Willerby, the donor's son agreed not to plough any land which had not been tilled previously and to restrain others from so doing. The Bridlington Priory granges at Burton Fleming and Speeton, together with those of Meaux at Dalton, Octon and Wharram and that of Malton at Mowthorpe were concerned with corn-growing as well as sheep. In 1299 Bridlington Priory farmed 'ovenhams' or foreland in the East and West fields of

Burton Fleming, where the arable extended as far as the boundaries of six neighbouring villages. Here again the limits of cultivation had already been reached (Allison 1976: 67–8).

In Holderness the framework of village fields seems to have been constructed before the Norman Conquest. In the late eleventh century Count Odo, the Lord of Holderness, claimed that nothing grew in his lordship but wild oats, but by the thirteenth century some of the best barley yields in England were being obtained and wheat was also grown. Peas and beans were also cultivated on an increasingly large scale, so that by the mid-fourteenth century legumes may have accounted for 20 per cent of arable production on some Holderness manors, one of the highest proportions in the whole of the country. Much of the peas and oats was fed to draught animals, and considerable amounts of hay were needed for the winter feed of oxen, cows, horses, and particularly sheep. In 1273–75 wool sales on the principal Holderness manors of Isabella de Fortibus amounted to about £460, compared with less than £100 raised by sales of grain. In certain parts of Holderness new land was still available for sheep pastures if capital was available for the expensive task of drainage and reclamation. One of the prime concerns was to protect the whole of the Humber coast by a series of walls so that marsh and silt could be converted to pasture and arable. That at Paull Holme was recorded in 1201, and in 1287 St Leonard's Hospital, York, had 358 acres of 'lucrative' arable at Broomfleet, 68 acres of 'fresh' pasture and another 32 acres of salt pasture beyond the banks (*VCH East Riding*, III 1976: 71). Further inland, the Counts of Aumale and the Abbots of Meaux took the lead in constructing channels deep and wide enough to take boats. Ashdyke was built in the 1160s and 1170s to convey goods from Meaux Abbey to the river Hull, and Monkdike, Skernedike and Forthdike were each recorded in the early thirteenth century.

In the Hull valley dykes were constructed to act not only as drains but as property boundaries, sometimes dividing open fields from marsh or wood, and sometimes separating neighbouring settlements. The dyke between Wawne and Sutton was built to fix a boundary between 1221 and 1235, and so was a new dyke connecting Brandesburton and Heighholme. At first, efforts to drain the freshwater swamps and to reclaim land on the coast were assisted by a slight lowering of the sea-level, but after about the year 1200 the sea rose again. By the middle of the thirteenth century serious flooding occurred around Sutton and Drypool and tidal waters penetrated as far inland as Cottingham. Nevertheless, new settlements had been established in the lower Hull valley at Newland, Sculcoates and Stoneferry and the town of Wyke had been founded at the estuary (English 1979: 198, 203–4; Allison 1976: 76–7). Though the area was not effectively drained until the eighteenth century substantial progress had been made in converting marshland into meadows and pastures. Soon, however, much that had been gained was to be lost when the sea once more obtained an upper hand. It was fortunate that by the time that happened population pressure on available resources had eased considerably.

During the Middle Ages the Holderness meres and rivers were fished for bream, pickerel, pike and vast quantities of eels. The Sutton family provided 4,000 eels per annum to the Count of Aumale as a rent for their lands at Sutton on Hull, and such payments were by no means uncommon. Domesday Book records an annual render of 7,000 eels from the Beverley fishery and a total of 6,400 eels from the eleven fisheries nearby at Leconfield. In Hatfield Chase the twenty Domesday fisheries at Tudworth each provided 1,000 eels per annum for Conisbrough castle. Fish formed a major part of the medieval diet, especially during Lent and other religious festivals and in order to supply their own needs monastic communities often constructed complex breeding tanks. Fishponds were also dug out alongside castles and manor houses or within deer parks. A diet of freshwater fish was supplemented by herring, haddock, cod and skate from the North Sea. Tithe records dating from 1414 to 1442, for example, suggest that between 34 and 35 Scarborough men owned a fleet of 70–100 vessels, mostly boats and small craft known as cobles. The most substantial men fished herring and often sailed as far as Iceland (Heath 1968).

Manorial lords also ensured their meat supply by building dovecotes, by setting land aside for coney garths, and by enclosing deer parks. The East Riding had at least thirty medieval deer parks and the two other ridings probably had similar numbers. Parks associated with castles were the earliest, and lords sometimes claimed hunting rights that went back by prescription to the Norman Conquest, if not before. Sheffield park was held by prescriptive right, and 2,461 acres were enclosed within its bounds. However, most medieval parks were created by royal licence during the thirteenth and fourteenth centuries. Tankersley park was enclosed in 1303–4 and its boundaries can still be followed along $4\frac{1}{2}$ miles of footpaths, hedges and walls; the deer were not removed until late in the eighteenth century. At Bishop Burton a high earthen bank and deep ditch that marked the boundary of the Archbishop of York's thirteenth-century park can still be followed as 'The Reins' for a mile or so around the present park. As medieval parks were economic assets and not just places for sport they were normally wooded and provided with fish ponds. They were commonly laid out near the lord's residence, but not invariably so. In south-west Yorkshire the Wortleys used their 1252 grant of free warren to create a chase upon Wharncliffe Crags, the rocky extremity of their lordship, and they did not enclose a park by their hall until the reign of Henry VIII. Chases were larger and more remote than parks and were less well-defined with banks and ditches; they were the more lowly equivalent of royal forests. John Leland described Hatfield Chase as 'forest ground, and though wood be scars there yet there is great plentie of red deere, that haunt the fennes and the great mores thereabout'; an estimated 700 deer roamed the chase in 1539. The twelfth-century first floor hall that served as a hunting lodge survives encased in a later building.

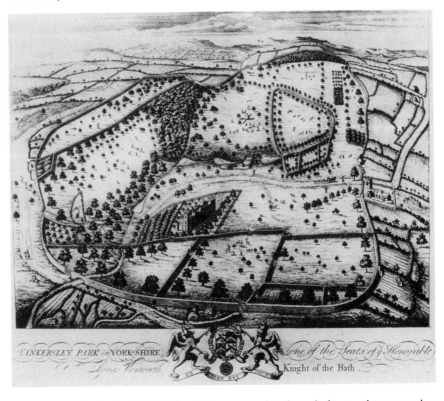

Plate 2.2   Tankersley Park. Tankersley Park was created in the early fourteenth century when Hugh de Elland obtained a royal grant of free warren. Its boundaries can still be followed along 4½ miles of footpaths, hedges and walls. This engraving was made in 1725–28 when Tankersley formed part of the Wentworth estate, just before the Elizabethan hall (which had replaced an earlier hunting lodge) was demolished and its stone re-used to build farms and barns. When Daniel Defoe came this way he saw 'the largest red deer that, I believe, are in this part of Europe: one of the hinds, I think, was larger than my horse'. The deer were removed to Wentworth in the nineteenth century when the park was given over to ironstone mining.

  The park stifled the development of the village and may have led to its desertion. On the engraving the church has been orientated wrongly for artistic effect; it was recorded in Domesday Book long before the park was made. Beyond the church the rectory was surrounded by a deep moat which probably marked the site of the original manor house. By the early eighteenth century the park was clearly enclosed by a wall and divided into paddocks, while the stream that flows through its centre had been dammed to form fish ponds. The main road from Sheffield to Barnsley skirted the park wall and was turnpiked a generation after this view was taken, but the road through the park is now merely a rutted cart track.

Industry

In some parks and chases iron-working was permitted. In 1268 the Furnivals had 'smithies' in their park at Sheffield, and in 1332 three forges were at work in Rothwell park. Six smiths were recorded at Hessle, near Hemsworth, in the Yorkshire folios of Domesday Book, and it is most unlikely that other smiths were not at work elsewhere in the West Riding. Domesday Book refers to Kirk Smeaton ('the farmstead of the smiths') and Orgreave ('the pit from which ore was dug') and to Kirkby Overblow, whose name is derived from the Old English word 'orblawere', meaning a smelter. Further evidence of medieval iron-working is provided by the numerous Cinder Hills (bloomery sites) and Bole Hills, where either iron or lead was smelted. On the northern side of Sheffield, Pitsmoor takes its name from the 'orepitts' that had been dug by 1315, and nearby Brightside is derived more obscurely from a smith's hearth that was recorded in 1171.

Lay and monastic lords exploited the minerals on their estates on the Coal-Measure Sandstones of the West Riding and in the Cleveland hills. Kirkby Overblow was an active iron-smelting centre for several centuries, and the lords of Knaresborough erected other small forges within their honour until the ironstone deposits and the fuel supply were exhausted. As early as 1304–5 a forge at an unidentified Thoresdene was abandoned 'because of the destruction of the woods' (Jennings, ed. 1970: 90–2). Further south, in the manor of Wakefield forges were at work within the common woodlands of Outwood and Hipperholme, and the Tankersley ironstone seams were exploited in south Yorkshire, where smiths, nailers and cutlers were active by the thirteenth and fourteenth centuries. A brief glimpse of one of these woodland craftsmen is obtained in 1218–19 when Roger the charcoal burner was 'outlawed for the death of Robert of Tankersley . . . He had no chattels' (Selden Soc., LVI 1937: 211). The best recorded enterprises of all are those of the Cistercians who were active on the Coal Measure Sandstones between Leeds and Sheffield. By an undated deed of the mid-twelfth century the lord of Stainborough granted all his ironstone, mines, minerals and woods to make charcoal to the monks of Rievaulx abbey, who subsequently received similar grants at Chellow, Flockton, Halton, Heaton, Shipley and Shitlington. In 1161 the Cistercians of the Lincolnshire abbey of Kirkstead were allowed to dig ironstone and to erect four forges on the borders of Kimberworth and Ecclesfield, and before 1177 Fountains Abbey had established Bradley grange near the confluence of the Calder and Colne, where they concentrated almost entirely upon iron-working. During the early thirteenth century the monks of Byland Abbey founded Bentley Grange in Emley township, some 46 miles away from the parent house, together with Denby Grange in the adjacent township of Upper Whitley in order to mine and forge iron, but the famous bell-pits that have been attributed to them are more likely to have been associated with nearby Bank furnace, which was built in 1655.

Lead had also been mined and smelted from a period long before the first written records of the industry begin; pigs of lead with Roman inscriptions have been found in the Yorkshire Dales as well as in the north Pennines and the Derbyshire Peak. The Yorkshire lead field was divided into a northern area around Swaledale, Arkengarthdale and the north side of Wensleydale, and a southern area comprising Wharfedale and Greenhow Hill. In the early Middle Ages Cistercian monasteries were prominent amongst those who exploited these mineral deposits to meet the demand for roofs and gutters for castles, abbeys, cathedrals and churches. Large parts of the Mowbray fee were granted to Fountains and Byland Abbeys. Pigs of smelted lead were dragged laboriously over land to the nearest river port, notably Yarm on the Tees or Boroughbridge at the head of the Ouse, on their way to the major distribution centres of Boston fair and London. Lead for Waltham Abbey near London and for Clairvaux Abbey in France went along these routes during the 1170s and 1180s. In 1365 lead for Windsor Castle was transported by

> two waggons, each with ten oxen, carrying 24 fothers of the said lead from Caldstones in Nidderdale in the county of York by high and rocky mountains and by muddy roads to Boroughbridge, about twenty leagues, namely for 24 days each waggon with the men taking it, 3s. per day, £7.4s.0d. And in portage and carriage of the said 24 fothers of lead from Boroughbridge both by land and water to the city of York, about sixteen leagues, namely for each fother 2s.4d., 54s. And payment to Adam Candeler of York for portage, boat-hire and carriage for the said 40 fothers of lead from the said city of York to London . . . £26.13s.4d.
>
> (Raistrick and Jennings 1965: 23–31)

The relatively low cost of water transport compared with land transport is evident.

In 1274 mineral coal mined at Hipperholme was referred to in the Northumberland manner as 'sea-coal' to distinguish it from charcoal. The name does not imply that local coal was exported, for the West Riding was too landlocked to compete with the North-East. Peat was an important alternative source of fuel for other parts of Yorkshire, and 'turves' from Inclesmoor were taken up the Ouse to York and down the Humber to heat the brick-kilns of Kingston-upon-Hull. Peat was also dug on the Pennines and on commons further east. Nevertheless, there is sufficient documentary evidence to suggest that coal was mined by numerous small concerns in the early Middle Ages within the manor of Wakefield and the honour of Pontefract and further south around Silkstone and Barnsley. As well as satisfying local domestic needs, miners dug coal to fuel the smithy fires of the Sheffield cutlers and rural nailers and the kilns of local potters. Though pottery was mainly an urban industry, well evidenced in York, Doncaster and Scarborough, the wares of a fourteenth-century rural pottery at Upper Heaton, near Huddersfield, have been found 35 miles away in the Yorkshire Dales (Manby 1965). By 1300 industrial activities formed an important part of the rural economy, especially in the West Riding, where in addition to the occupations mentioned above, the manufacture of cloth often provided farmers and labourers with a second source of income.

Until the late twelfth century the English cloth industry appears to have been almost entirely urban. York and Beverley organized their trade through a guild system and ranked in importance with the leading export centres of eastern England. By about 1300, if not before, the towns of Hedon, Masham, Northallerton, Ripon, Selby, Whitby and Yarm were also involved in cloth manufacture, together with such West Riding urban centres as Leeds, where Simon the Dyer was active in 1201. Even in this early period, however, the balance was shifting in favour of West Riding rural communities, where a cottage industry was free of restrictions imposed by urban guilds and where by-employments were an essential means of support for the growing population. The rural population concentrated upon producing cheap kerseys like their counterparts in the East Anglian village which had given this fabric its name (Heaton 1965: 1–8; Crump and Ghorbal 1935: 25–6).

The West Riding had the inestimable advantage of rivers that fell steeply from the Pennines to provide water power for the fulling mills. Water-wheels had of course been used to drive corn mills in much earlier times, and Domesday Book records a minimum of 92 Yorkshire mills (40 in the West Riding, 30 in the East Riding, and 22 in the North Riding). Windmills and fulling mills were not introduced into England until the second half of the twelfth century, and the first English references are both found in Yorkshire documents dated 1185. In that year a post mill was recorded at Weedley, near South Cave, and a fulling mill is mentioned in a survey of the Knights Templars' lands at Temple Newsam. Previously, cloth was scoured, thickened and felted by 'walking', i.e. trampling it under foot. The old name continued in use, and the site of the fulling mill recorded at Oxspring in 1306 is still known as Walk Mill Bank. The surname Walker was derived from this trade (John the Walker of Emley and John Fuller or Walker of Golcar were recorded in 1316) and the surnames Lister and Webster arose from the trades of dyeing and weaving (Robert the Lister was living in Ossett in 1274 and Thomas Webster in Skipton in 1303). Fulling mills were erected in many parts of Yorkshire and are referred to at Pocklington in 1260, Knaresborough 1284, Hoyland 1290, Thorpe Arch 1301, Aysgarth 1302, Stokesley 1302, Pickering 1302, Aberford 1327 and Alwoodley 1327, but they were most numerous on the banks of West Riding rivers and streams. Calverley had five fullers at work in the 1250s, and by the end of the century the best sites on the Aire, Calder and Colne had long been occupied (Heaton 1965: 5–7). By 1300 much of the Yorkshire countryside had an industrial tinge and England as a whole supported far more small-scale industries than it did at the time of the Norman Conquest.

Plague, War and Famine

By 1300 most of England's available land, including much that was only of marginal value, had been brought into cultivation. The continued increase of the population could not be supported by the primitive technology of the time, and the country was on the verge of a Malthusian crisis in which plagues, famines and wars drastically reduced the number of inhabitants seeking land and food. It is clear that this crisis came to a head well before the Black Death and that the years 1315–22 witnessed a series of harvest failures and livestock disasters almost without parallel in the history of English agriculture. A poor summer in 1314 was followed by an exceptionally wet summer in 1315, when heavy, persistent rains fell from May till autumn. The hay and corn harvests were ruined and the weakened population succumbed to disease. According to the Lanercost chronicler, 1316 saw 'such a mortality of men in England and Scotland through famine and pestilence as had not been heard of in our time. In some of the northern parts of England, the quarter of wheat sold for 40 shillings', whereas three years earlier the average national price had been about five shillings a quarter. The chronicler went on to note that in the winter of 1319–20

> the plague and murrain of cattle which had lasted through the two preceding years in the southern districts, broke out in the northern district among oxen and cows, which after a short sickness generally died; and few animals of that kind were left, so that men had to plough that year with horses.

As the climate deteriorated and sea levels rose, much of the land that had been laboriously reclaimed was lost. Meaux Abbey suffered considerable losses in Holderness. At Orwythfleet near Easington 33 acres of grassland were submerged by the Humber between 1310 and 1339; at nearby Tharlesthorpe about a third of the 90 acre grange was saved by a costly sea-wall built in the 1350s, but by 1400 the whole estate had disappeared. At Hornsea Burton, where Meaux Abbey held 26 acres of arable in 1334, only an acre or so was left by the end of the century. Hoton township disappeared under the sea during the course of the fourteenth century, and in 1396 Hyth, to the east of Skipsea, was said to have been totally destroyed (Sheppard 1912: 87–193). Three churches crumbled away before the ravages of the sea and had to be rebuilt with cobbles and rubble on safer sites further inland. Hollym church was rebuilt in 1488, in 1469–70 a Perpendicular Gothic church at Skeffling replaced a predecessor which had succumbed to the sea, and though a new church was begun at Withernsea in 1444, by Henry VIII's reign it too was 'much decayed'. Nearby, material eroded from the North Sea and Humber coastlines formed the sandy headland of Spurn Point, whose shape was frequently changed by the impact of gales and tidal waves.

Trouble of a different kind came in the same years, for after their famous victory at Bannockburn in 1314 Scottish armies plundered deep into the heart of Yorkshire. An enquiry into the devastation they had caused at Knaresborough in the summer of 1318 reported that 140 of the town's 160 houses had been burnt. In 1318 and 1319 marauding armies reached as far south as Pontefract. Dr I. Kershaw's study of the Bolton priory estates in Craven has shown how these invasions coincided with natural disasters and brought the local economy to its knees. The torrential rains of the summers of 1315 and 1316 so ruined the harvests that in some cases less corn was reaped than seed had been sown. Total demesne output and tithe collection amounted to a little above half the normal returns, and the monks had to buy wheat at five times the normal price. A flock of over 3,000 sheep was reduced to 1,005 and in the following year to 913, for sodden pastures and lack of hay meant that numbers could not be maintained and that survivors were at risk from epidemics. As wool was the priory's chief cash crop, the loss was serious. When the first of the Scottish armies arrived in 1318, the prior retreated across the hills to Blackburnshire, and his tenants fled with their livestock and personal belongings. At Halton Grange the demesne and tithe corn was stolen or burnt. Throughout the district the Scots destroyed buildings and took cattle and hostages. The following year they returned, sweeping aside Archbishop Melton's hastily gathered army at Myton on Swale, and repeating the depredations of 1318; Halton Grange may have lost all its 43 oxen. More trouble was in store, for in 1319–20 the great cattle murrain, which had been raging in the South for the previous two years, at last reached Yorkshire. It was the final straw for the monks of Bolton Priory. By 1321 the remaining stock of oxen had fallen from 139 to 53, and the rest of the cattle had been reduced from 225 head to 31. Though some of this fall may have been the result of sales, murrain was chiefly responsible. In 1320 Bolton Priory was abandoned and the monks sought refuge in other monasteries. Nevertheless, they were resilient enough to return five years later and to begin work on rebuilding their church in the new Decorated style (Kershaw 1973: *passim*).

It is now possible to pinpoint 1315, 1316, and 1321 as years of harvest failures in Yorkshire, to identify 1313–17 as the period of sheep murrain and 1319–21 as the time of cattle plague. Not since the harrying of the North by William I's armies had the country experienced so much misery. The immediate impact of these disasters is reflected in the massive tax reliefs granted to settlements in many parts of the six northern counties. In Cleveland deanery the assessment was lowered from £608 to £347.13s.10d., in Bulmer from £663.9s.4d. to £334.12s.8d., in Ryedale from £600 to £315.6s.8d. and in the East Riding deanery of Buckrose from £373.2s.0d. to £222.2s.0d. (Robinson 1969). In the northern Vale of York many communities had their tax assessments lowered by 50 per cent or more, and it is significant that few places in the

North Riding have churches that were rebuilt in the Decorated style of the first half of the fourteenth century; only Thornton Dale is of much interest. Records of the 1341–42 tax known as the Inquisition of the Ninth confirm this picture, for over 80 North Riding settlements had waste and uncultivated land and many of the marginal settlements were deserted. All but four parishes in Cleveland deanery recorded waste, and in Bulmer deanery eleven parishes noted that land which had been tilled at the time of a previous tax assessment in 1291 was now uncultivated. At Alne 200 acres lay unploughed, worth nothing, and another 1,000 acres were worth no more than 2d. each; at Easingwold 200 acres were untilled for lack of a plough team; at Ronaldkirk 40 carucates were no longer cultivated; at Danby a third of the arable lay waste; and at Bowes, Brignall and Marske 17 carucates had been destroyed by the Scots (Baker 1966). The East Riding returns unfortunately do not survive, but early-fourteenth-century manorial surveys reveal vacant holdings and uncultivated ground in the High Wolds (Beresford and Hurst 1971:7). Far fewer places lay waste in the West Riding than in the North Riding, but even in areas well to the south of the Scottish invasion routes the rural economy had begun to contract long before the Black Death. At Almondbury it was claimed in 1322 that herds had been reduced by murrain and by the troubles brought about by the Earl of Lancaster's revolt, and at Sheffield ten years later all 240 acres of demesne arable lay uncultivated. On the grits and sandstones of south-west Yorkshire the 1341 tax was commonly assessed at only two-thirds of that of 1291, and in some settlements at half or less; at Penistone and Hoyland a major share of the arable lay waste, and at Silkstone 340 acres of arable had not been tilled (Postles 1979).

It is clear from the national tax returns of 1334 that the wealthiest counties were in southern and eastern England. The East Riding was more prosperous than the rest of Yorkshire, but in national terms was only at the middle of the scale. The overwhelming importance of agriculture is obvious from the fact that the richest areas contained the most fertile soils, while from an urban point of view the most successful places were ports or cloth-manufacturing centres. London paid £11,000 in tax, Bristol paid £2,200, and York was ranked third with an assessment of £1,620. York's chief northern rival was the country's fourth city, Newcastle upon Tyne, which paid £1,333. Two parts of Yorkshire were comparable in wealth with the South and the East, namely the districts centred on York and on Beverley and Hull. Beverley's assessment of £500 placed the town 20th in the national scale, Hull was 33rd with £333 and Cottingham 35th with £330. Scarborough also paid £333, and other towns which paid over £225 included Pontefract (£270) and Doncaster (£255) (Darby, ed. 1973: 139, 181-82). The resources of the West and North Ridings cannot be measured satisfactorily in terms of tax per square mile because of their vast amount of moorland, but it is clear that these parts of Yorkshire were still relatively poor; nevertheless, the Magnesian Limestone belt, with its fertile arable lands, ranked with much of the East Riding.

The great building enterprises in the century before the Black Death were in precisely those areas which paid most tax in 1334. At York work began on a new nave for the Minster in 1291 and culminated in Ivo de Raghton's great west window of 1338. At Selby Abbey the beautiful seven-bay choir of 1280–1340 has the entire range of Decorated tracery types, and the design of the east window had far more influence on local styles than did the contemporary work at York Minster. The county's other great Decorated churches are all in the East Riding, at Beverley, Hedon, Howden, Hull and Patrington, names that immediately conjure up images of some of the noblest medieval buildings in the country. In the same riding Cottingham and Skipwith have notable Decorated work, and at Bainton, where the rector, William of Brocklesby, was active during the second quarter of the fourteenth century, the church is a complete example of work of this period. In the West Riding the great age of church rebuilding still lay in the future with the Perpendicular Gothic style, but on the Magnesian Limestone belt extensions were made or structures redesigned in Decorated fashion at Owston, South Anston, Thorpe Salvin and Wadworth, and a little further east at Barnby Dun and at Fishlake, where Richard Mauleverer rebuilt the chancel in the 1350s. Yorkshiremen abandoned the Decorated style after the completion of the Flamboyant east window at Fishlake and the construction in 1358 of the east window at Welwick, in Holderness, where the tracery has a hint of the new Perpendicular style which was to carry all before it during the next two centuries.

The Black Death reached Yorkshire in the spring of 1349 and was virulent during the months of June, July and August. During that year eleven churchyards, including eight in the North Riding, were specially dedicated for the burial of the county's plague victims. The national pattern of mortality was enormously varied, and diseases other than bubonic plague were also rampant, with children and adolescents particularly likely to succumb. Some places were unaffected, but at Meaux Abbey only ten of the forty-two monks and seven lay-brothers survived. The crowded towns suffered worst, but even in the Forest of Knaresborough death rates appear to have reached 40–45 per cent, and in both lower Nidderdale and the upper Calder valley about 40–45 per cent of holdings were vacated upon the death of tenants (including those who died of more normal causes) in 1349–50 (Fieldhouse and Jennings 1978: 29–30, 58–59). In the diocese of York the death rate of beneficed clergy at this time was 39 per cent, though as the nature of their occupation exposed them unduly to the infection they may not have been truly representative of the total population. The clerical death rate was only 21 per cent in the moorland deanery of Cleveland, but it reached 45 per cent in the archdeaconry of York and climbed to 61 per cent in the Wolds deanery of Dickering. At Middleton on the Wolds about 60 acres were 'lying waste and untilled' in 1350 'owing to the great mortality', and in 1352 at Boynton (where nine farms had been devastated by the flooding of the Gypsey Race in 1327) 21 of the 29 bovates of land which belonged to one estate were said to be waste and the windmill lay in ruins. Nearby Easton and Garton had suffered in a similar manner. In 1354 Dickering villages had their tax assessments reduced by over two-thirds, and twenty-four others had their contributions reduced by between one-third and two-thirds. Flotmanby, at the foot of the Wolds, paid no tax at all in 1354 and seems to have been one of the few villages that was completely depopulated by the Black Death; this community was never recorded again, and the character- istic earthworks of a deserted medieval village can be seen near the hall. Barthorpe, near Acklam, may also have been destroyed at a stroke, but gradual decay was much more common, with shrunken villages set on a course of steady decline. Others survived as hamlets, and some eventually recovered (Allison 1976: 99–103).

Pestilence returned during the 1360s and 1370s. The major epidemic of 1361–62 is sometimes referred to as the children's plague, possibly because this section of the population had not acquired immunity during earlier attacks and was therefore more likely to succumb, or perhaps the young were vulner- able because this epidemic was a different killer disease. One-third of the beneficed clergy of the deaneries of Richmond and Catterick died in that year. Another major epidemic visited Yorkshire in 1374 and bubonic plague re- mained endemic with repeated local outbreaks throughout the fifteenth cen- tury. The timing, effects and precise nature of these recurrent diseases are in doubt, for the evidence is patchy, but it is clear that the national population was reduced drastically by these continued assaults. In the parish of Wheldrake, for example, the number of households fell from 84 in 1348 to 73 in 1361 and to 56 in 1394, and the hamlet of Waterhouses alongside the river Derwent was abandoned. Everywhere in England the population pressure eased and mar- ginal land was allowed to revert to a waste condition.

Falling population levels meant that more land was available for all. The late-fourteenth and fifteenth centuries saw the rise of relatively wealthy farm- ing families who engrossed holdings and founded dynasties of yeomen and minor gentlemen; they were constrained only by the higher wages they had to pay and by the lower rents which they could charge their sub-tenants. The average holdings of all countrymen increased in size during the fifteenth century and the economic condition of the great majority of the rural popula- tion improved considerably. Those families which survived the pestilences were better off than they had been before 1349, both in legal status and in their standard of living. Labourers also benefited for demand outran supply and the Statute of Labourers (1351), which tried to regulate wages, could not be enforced. In the early 1360s the giving and taking of excess wages was a frequent offence tried at the Yorkshire sessions of the peace. The 1381 rising, which found support in Yorkshire, particularly in the towns of Scarborough, Beverley and York, did not accelerate this process, for by then the gains were already secure.

The Black Death and other pestilences of the fourteenth century rarely obliterated the population of a village community at a single visitation, but many settlements were weakened and made more vulnerable to the designs of enclosing landlords. For example, in the East Riding wapentake of Dickering the Black Death affected Hilderthorpe so badly that its tax quota was reduced by over 60 per cent, but later tax returns show that the process of depopulation was a gradual one. At nearby Auburn the tax quota in 1354 was reduced by 55 per cent, but it survived as a 'very beggarly village' until Elizabethan times (*VCH., East Riding, II* 1974: 92, 201). The pace of depopulation did not quicken until the middle years of the fifteenth century, a hundred years or so after the Black Death. Some villagers were forced to leave by ruthless landlords who sought greater profits in rearing cattle and sheep than they could make by growing corn, but in other parishes landowners had no alternative to pastoral farming, for they were unable to find tenants to work the land. Large profits could be made from wool, but the reduced national level of population meant less demand for corn. In these conditions the more ambitious, fortunate or grasping freeholders and tenants prospered by consolidating their own holdings and by leasing the demesne land of absentee landlords. Many of England's yeomen families emerged from the ranks of manorial tenants during the fifteenth century.

At least 375 of Yorkshire's medieval villages were vacated by their inhabitants, though some of these settlements did not expire until the seventeenth century. No less than 171 of these were in the North Riding, particularly in the northern Vale of York, the Vale of Pickering and the Howardian hills; 129 were in the East Riding, especially on the Wolds and in adjacent parts of north Holderness; and 75 have been identified in the West Riding (Beresford and Hurst 1971: 69). In the country as a whole well over 2,000 deserted medieval villages have been located. Yorkshire was amongst the areas hardest hit, together with the Midland Plain counties and Lincolnshire and Norfolk. Yet vast though this number is, it does not tell the whole story, for the number of shrunken sites is far greater than the number of deserted ones. Moreover, in those parts of the West Riding where settlements were scattered throughout the countryside an unknown number of small hamlets and isolated farmsteads were abandoned.

Villages of every size were susceptible to destruction. The fenland settlement of Haldenby had 117 tax-payers in 1379, but its site is now deserted. The Wolds village of Cowlam had fifty-four people who paid the poll tax in 1377, and presumably it had once been even larger for in 1352–54 its tax quota was remitted by over 50 per cent, but by the early eighteenth century only two shepherds lived there and church services had to be held in the ruined chancel, which was the only part of the church still standing (Beresford and St Joseph 1979: 124-26). On the whole, however, villages that were depopulated were small even before the Black Death and the land which they occupied was usually inferior. Manorial lords found it easier to enclose arable lands where communities were small and poor, especially if the villagers were tenants rather than freeholders. Professor Beresford had considered the 1334 East Riding tax assessments by wapentake and has shown that villages which became deserted in Dickering were assessed at only 46 per cent of the sums paid by their neighbours, in Holderness 52 per cent, Howdenshire 53 per cent, Buckrose 64 per cent and Harthill 74 per cent. Nevertheless, small villages sited on marginal land sometimes managed to survive. Villages were secure if they were founded alongside good quality arable land or if their economy was already based upon pastoral activities. Woodland and moorland communities with small enclosed fields and extensive common pastures were tenacious enough to survive and did not attract the attention of large-scale graziers.

On the high chalk Wolds the graziers were in their element. The large amount of ridge-and-furrow patterns revealed by aerial photographs confirms that the High Wolds were tilled extensively in the Middle Ages before the change to sheep farming. Then, at least 12,000 acres were used as unenclosed sheepwalks and rabbit warrens until the era of parliamentary enclosure. Eastburn had shrunk to three houses by 1671, and by the end of the seventeenth century was one great sheepwalk 'not divided by fences and ditches'; Arras was reduced to a single farmstead but was not hedged before 1770; and a similar tale could be told at Cottam and Riplingham. The fullest story of all is being revealed at Wharram Percy, one of the Wolds' spectacular sites and now the most famous deserted medieval village in the country. Wharram is first recorded in Domesday Book, but excavations over the past three decades have shown that the history of settlement in this parish goes back a great deal further. Indeed, the excavating team report that it is 'beginning to look as though the basic plan of the medieval village was determined by the layout of the Romano-British fields'. Wharram Percy was a large parish of some 9,500 acres, comprising five separate medieval settlements, each of which had its own open fields. A deed of 1384 shows that the arable lands in the Raisthorpe fields were arranged by the sun-division method. Wharram village also had a planned element, dating from the twelfth century when houses were built on the bank high above the original nucleus around the church. Wharram received a severe blow from the Black Death and over 60 per cent of its tax quota was remitted in 1354, but its decay was gradual until its final desertion some time in the late fifteenth century. In 1517 the government enquiry into enclosures made during the previous thirty years reported that the lord had 'put down four ploughs and allowed four houses to decay'. About the same time three of the parish's other four townships suffered a similar fate and were converted to sheep pastures. The side aisles of Wharram church were demolished and the nave arcades were blocked up. Only the township of Thixendale survived, and until 1879 its inhabitants continued to trudge three miles over the Wolds to their church services.

Another classic site, well-marked by the grassy mounds and hollows of former houses and lanes, is that of East Tanfield on the banks of the Ure between Ripon and Masham. It stands in the northern Vale of York, another prime target of the graziers. East Tanfield had seventeen families taxed in 1301 and at the peak of its prosperity probably had twenty-two. Manorial accounts show that the place had begun to shrink by the 1440s, and the 1517 enquiry noted that 400 acres had been enclosed during the past generation, that eight houses had been demolished and thirty-two people evicted from their homes. The enquiry was concerned only with what had happened since 1488, by which time the main period of conversion to sheep and cattle farming was over, nevertheless it provides a great deal of evidence about what was happening all over Yorkshire. The report noted 29 cases involving 3,660 acres in the West Riding, 30 cases concerning 2,628 acres in the North Riding, and 25 cases relating to 1,560 acres in the East Riding; in all, the commissioners investigated 84 cases in Yorkshire involving the enclosure of 7,848 acres of land and the demolition of 232 houses or cottages (Beresford 1955: 217).

At Norton Conyers, a mile or two from East Tanfield, another medieval village site can be located in the park that stretches away from the hall. The village was a healthy size in 1377, when forty-nine persons were taxed, and tenants of the manor still lived there in 1569. The early-sixteenth-century house was remodelled by Sir Richard Graham during the reign of Charles I and given its distinctive Dutch gables, and perhaps it was about this time that the village disappeared; it was not marked on a map of 1690. The 1517 enquiry noted a number of cases where arable lands had been enclosed to create or extend manorial parks, and many a great house owes its privacy and uninterrupted view to the decay or removal of a village. Allerton Mauleverer, Harewood and Ribston are examples that immediately spring to mind. At Cridling, where twenty-two dwellings were recorded in 1425, the entire village site was enclosed within a park by Henry Vavasour, and at Thrybergh the commissioners noted that Richard Reresby had enclosed 60 acres of pasture and wood and 26 acres of arable land into the park that now forms a golf course. At Temple Newsam the enquiry revealed that the remaining four dwellings had been demolished and 80 acres enclosed; the nearby settlements of Skelton and possibly Colton were also absorbed into the estate that surrounded the mansion. Other deserted sites are marked not by a hall but by an isolated church, such as the early-fourteenth-century chapel which stands alone in a flat landscape at Lead, or the medieval church at Frickley where the surrounding fields now once more support fine crops of corn. Frickley was already a small village by 1334 and its population comprised only 23 taxpayers in 1379; a rental of 1426 shows that it was farmed on a three-field system (Kirkfield, Millfield and Clough field), and the village struggled on until the middle years of the seventeenth century. All Saints' Church survived because of the attention of the squires of Frickley Hall and because it also served the neighbouring community of Clayton. Likewise the splendid little Norman church at Adel continued in use because it served Eccup and because in time Adel was resettled. Others were less fortunate and have disappeared as completely as their villages.

Rural market centres suffered a similar fate. In the Middle Ages England probably had three or four times as many market-places as today. The holding of weekly markets and annual fairs was of course an essential function of a medieval town, but as the national population and economy expanded during the thirteenth century many rural lords obtained royal licences for similar privileges in their villages. In Emley, where the old market cross still stands at a road junction, William of Woodhall obtained a charter in 1253 for a Thursday market and a four-day May fair. In the same year the lord of Hooton Pagnell received a royal grant of a Thursday market and a three-day fair at the feast of St Lawrence, the patron saint of the local church, and the cross that was erected is still mounted on steps in the village street. Scores of places received similar grants and many other centres claimed a prescriptive right from time immemorial. In the East Riding wapentake of Dickering, to take a fairly typical example, Bridlington had a market grant in 1200, Burton Agnes a 1257 Tuesday market and fair, Carnaby a 1299 Thursday market and two six-day fairs, Filey a 1221 Friday market, Flamborough an undated market and fair, Humanby a market by 1231, Kilham a thirteenth-century market and fair that was 'of little note' by 1778, Lowthorpe a 1304 Friday market and fair, Nafferton a 1304 Thursday market and fair, Thwing a mid-thirteenth-century Wednesday market and fair, and finally Bempton may have had similar privileges at some unknown date, for in 1767 one of its open fields was known as Market Dale (*VCH, East Riding*, II 1974: *passim*). Not all these markets were necessarily in existence at any one time. The fourteenth-century pestilences and the national decay of the economy brought many of them to an end.

In most cases it is difficult to pinpoint the date of decline, but the example of Campsall on the Magnesian Limestone may be rather typical. In 1293–94 Henry de Laci, lord of the honour of Pontefract, obtained charters for markets and fairs at Pontefract, Almondbury, Bradford and Campsall. The Campsall rights were for a weekly Thursday market and an annual four-day fair in July around the festival of St Mary Magdalene, the patron saint of the village's imposing Norman and Gothic church. Campsall was probably still acting as a local market centre in 1379, when a chapman and twelve craftsmen paid the poll tax, but some time during the following two centuries these activities withered away. In 1627 a surveyor reported that, 'The towne of Campsall had in tymes past the priviledge of a markett, which is now decayed and lost by discontinuance.' The name Market Flatt, which is inscribed upon a map of *c.* 1740, provides the only clue as to where the old markets and fairs were held. Elsewhere, the laying out of a medieval market-place sometimes had a permanent effect on the topography of a village, even though the market stalls have long since disappeared. South Cave is an East Riding example where the original village was clustered around the church, but where a new nucleus was provided half a mile away when a medieval market-place was established on the former Roman road from Brough to York; the new settlement eventually overshadowed the old.

The decay of the national economy and the decline of population affected England's towns as well as its villages and small market centres. By the second half of the fifteenth century York, Beverley, Hull, Scarborough, Richmond, Ripon and Tickhill, and probably others, were feeling the effects of economic stagnation. This malaise came on gradually and is difficult to pinpoint, but it overcame some of the most successful towns of the early Middle Ages. Kingston-upon-Hull is a good example. By the middle of the fourteenth century the town had justified Edward I's faith in its potential; nearly all the sites within the walls had been occupied and many of them had been subdivided. Moreover, Hull was the home of the De la Pole brothers, England's most spectacularly successful merchants and money-lenders. Richard and William de la Pole first appear in local records in 1316 as burgesses and in 1321–24 as the chamberlains in charge of the town's finances when Hull was fortified in face of the Scottish threat. During the early 1320s Richard was in effect the King's agent in Hull, but in 1328 he moved to London and was soon elected an alderman of Bishopgate. William remained based in Hull but expanded his operations into the sphere of national finance and became an indispensable agent of the crown. In this way he acquired a large estate and gained considerable political influence; his son, Michael, was made Earl of Suffolk in 1385. 'No other family rose so far, so fast and then managed to retain its position for so long' (Horrox 1983: 43). The family played little part in the subsequent fortunes of Hull. Henry VI granted the town a charter of incorporation in 1440, but it soon began to feel the chill of recession. The monopoly of the Hanseatic League drove Hull merchants from the Baltic ports. Exports of wool fell sharply, until by 1460 they were less than a quarter of their value of fifty years previously. In 1462 only about fifty ships entered the port of Hull from abroad, principally foreign-owned ships from Antwerp and Calais (Davis 1964: 4). By 1465 the rents of the expensive High Street properties had fallen and worse was soon to come as trade decayed and population levels declined. By 1527–28 most rents had dropped to at least half their 1465 level (YASRS, CXLI 1983).

York also fell victim to the late-medieval recession. In the mid-sixteenth century its population was a third less than its early-fifteenth-century peak of over 12,000. In better times York had been England's leading provincial city. On five occasions between 1298 and 1338, during the time of the Scottish wars, and again in 1392 it served as the country's administrative capital with the King in residence and Parliament in session. Between 1200 and 1450 York was at the height of its prestige as a centre of ecclesiastical as well as secular administration, an inland port and market town through which lead and wool were exported and food and luxuries were imported, and a place where skilled craftsmen such as pewterers, bell-founders and glaziers were gathered. Royal charters of 1393 and 1396 gave York the status of a county borough, and the city government 'emerged as a hierarchical, tightly-knit and powerful organisation' (Prestwich 1976). By that time the various trade guilds, which had been created from the twelfth century onwards, were also of great importance in the town's social and economic affairs.

Cloth-making and international commerce were of relatively little importance in early-fourteenth-century York, for rural weavers provided fierce competition and alien merchants dominated the export trade in English wool. However, from the middle years of the fourteenth century English wool merchants penetrated new overseas markets. When Calais became the continental staple for wool exports in 1363 two York men were appointed to the ruling body. During the following decade York merchants were responsible for 1,600 of the 2,700 sacks of wool exported from Hull, whereas fifty years earlier they had exported only 200 sacks. This blossoming trade was matched by a general expansion of York's economy during the second and third quarters of the fourteenth century and a marked increase in population. In 1377 York ranked second to London, for its population had topped 10,000, a 50 per cent increase since 1348. By 1400 the city had even more people, the cloth-making industry had fully recovered, and York merchants handled more than half of Hull's wool and cloth exports and about a third of her imports. But in the fifteenth century this expansion came to an end; overseas trade with the Baltic and Gascony ceased to be as profitable and competition from West Riding clothiers became more intense. After 1420 York's population declined, the setbacks in the economy were not offset by gains in other sectors, the wealthiest merchants ceased to make huge profits from foreign trade, and even the inhabitants of York began to dress in country cloth. The depths of the recession were reached in the third quarter of the fifteenth century, and in 1487 the corporation admitted to Henry VII that 'Ther is not half the nombre of good men within your said citie as ther hath beene in tymes past' (Bartlett 1959). Throughout western Europe contracting populations meant less demand for goods and therefore economic decline. York was not alone in its suffering.

One part of late-fifteenth-century Yorkshire fared much better than most, however. While cloth-making declined in York, Beverley, Ripon and the Vale of York, it began to flourish in the huge parish of Halifax and adjacent areas. Cheap woollen kerseys, used particularly for hose and stockings, had long been manufactured in the West Riding, but the 1379 poll tax returns suggest that the Halifax–Bradford district was then of little importance. By 1473–75, however, the parish of Halifax was second only to York in the number of woollen cloths counted by the ulnage collectors (Heaton 1965: 68–76). During the sixteenth century the ancient trade of the Suffolk market town of Kersey decayed, but by that time kerseys were being exported from Halifax all over western Europe. Kerseys had become the distinctive product of the upper Calder valley.

Security and Warfare

The troubles of the early fourteenth century were aggravated by a breakdown in law and order and by the criminal activities of such outlaw bands as the Coterels of north Derbyshire. Violence was met with violence and many manorial lords erected their own gallows. Some sites are remembered by place-names such as Gallows Hill, which characteristically appear on old manorial boundaries, and the notorious Halifax gibbet survived until 1650. When the law was ineffective, men defended their rights by force and went about armed. In 1428 the ecclesiastical court at York considered an incident in a Dales parish when the porch of Holy Trinity church, Coverham, had been obstructed by weapons during service time. A more blatant act of aggression occurred at Aberford in 1346, when William Bosville of Micklefield brought an armed gang to terrorize the inhabitants, steal their property, violently interrupt a sheriff's tourn, and commit other 'enormous trespasses'. About the same time James and Arthur Bosville murdered John Bingham in Aberford Church. A Yorkshire JP, Sir John Eland, tried his best to control outlaw bands, but on 29 October 1350 he was murdered at Brighouse by a gang led by Adam Beaumont, William the son of Thomas of Lockwood, William of Quarmby and Thomas the son of Thomas Lasci. A few months later the same brutal gang murdered Sir John's son and namesake. They were never brought to trial, but their infamy lived on and was commemorated by the (largely fictitious) sixteenth-century ballad, *The Eland Feud*, which was written to warn Sir Henry Savile, Sir Richard Tempest and other Yorkshire gentry of the grave consequences of bitter quarrels (Kaye 1979).

Men were therefore conscious of security when they built their manor houses. In lowland parts, especially on the ill-drained clays of the Vale of York and Holderness, the chief defensive element was the moat. By 1282, for example, Baynard Castle at Cottingham was said to be 'well constructed with a double ditch enclosed by a wall'. Yorkshire moats usually date from the thirteenth and fourteenth centuries, especially from 1250 to 1325, that is from the period of maximum public disorder (Le Patourel 1973). Moated manor houses were sometimes the obvious successors of Norman motte-and-bailey castles; at the Percy manor of Topcliffe the earthworks are close together, and just to the north of Doncaster the Radcliffe moat was constructed on the opposite bank of a stream from Castle Hills. As licences to crenellate multiplied during the reign of Edward I other moats were constructed by minor lords and monastic institutions and in remote places moats enclosed the property of freeholders. Prestige was as important as security, for the defensive element was often minimal and people were sometimes more concerned with aping their social superiors. Yorkshire moats were from 4 ft to 15 ft deep and they surrounded buildings which ranged from castles to timber-framed houses. At

Thorpe in Balne an extensive moat enclosed not only the manor house and its farm buildings but also fishponds and a Norman chapel-of-ease, for the parish church at Barnby Dun was difficult to reach across the river. Markenfield Hall, three miles south of Ripon, is the only fortified medieval manor house in Yorkshire to have survived reasonably intact. The stone buildings and complicated moat system probably date from just after 1310, when a licence to crenellate was obtained by the Markenfield family. With defence in mind, the main hall was placed on the first floor and reached by an external stair and porch. The hall and chapel windows are of a similar Geometric design to their famous counterparts at Stokesay Castle in Shropshire, and a spire-capped stair turret and some original chimney stacks rise above the battlements.

In highland areas, especially in the northern Pennines and the Scottish borders, men fortified their properties with tower-houses, where the normal rooms of a medieval manor house were arranged vertically instead of horizontally. Mortham Tower, the medieval seat of the Rokebys in Teesdale, began as a fourteenth-century tower and grew into a picturesque courtyard manor. In Craven Farnhill Hall was built in the early fourteenth century as a ground-floor hall block with four slender angle turrets but was later given a three-storeyed solar wing which was virtually a separate tower house. In Wensleydale Thomas Metcalfe built Nappa Hall about 1460 with a west tower as the main unit, a central hall, and a lower east tower containing the service rooms. Other surviving fifteenth-century examples include Ayton Castle near Scarborough, Lawrence Hammerton's Hellifield Peel on the Pennines, and Sir Richard Conyer's Cowton Castle, which stands isolated on a hill above the contemporary and equally solitary South Cowton church; the towers of Aske Hall, Bolling Hall and Bolton on Swale Old Hall are now part of much larger houses. All these are of stone, but Riccal manor house is a fifteenth-century brick tower house with a lookout room at the top of a turret, and another brick example is found far from the highlands at Paull Holme, near the banks of the Humber; it dates from the 1480s and defence was obviously in the builder's mind, for the sturdy tower had a portcullis and was surrounded by a moat. Other medieval manor houses concerned with defence were arranged around a courtyard. Barforth Hall and Scargill Castle are two fifteenth-century examples just south of the Tees, and in south Yorkshire Denaby Old Hall was 'built partly of lath and plaister, on three sides of a square court'. At the demolished Wombwell Old Hall a solid tower formed the centrepiece of the

---

Plate 2.3   Mortham Tower. This picturesque fortified house in Teesdale was the medieval seat of the Rokeby family. It began as a mid-fourteenth-century pele tower and was extended in the fifteenth century into a courtyard manor house with the tower in the north-west corner. The gateway, walls and battlements and the upper part of the tower date from the fifteenth century. Thomas Rokeby's new quarters included a Great Chamber (remodelled in the seventeenth century) and a Great Hall to the right of the tower. The hall has been considerably altered and at one time served as a barn, but it still has two of its original roof trusses. In the eighteenth century Sir Thomas Robinson built his Palladian Rokeby Hall nearby.

western range. These courtyard manor houses were humbler versions of fourteenth-century quadrangular palace-castles such as Bolton and Sheriff Hutton (Ryder 1982: 108–22).

Although they were still built to endure a siege, late-medieval castles were very different from their Norman predecessors. By the early fourteenth century the old idea of a keep as the principal fortification had been abandoned and at Skipton Robert Clifford replaced the Norman fortress with a sturdy gatehouse and six massive round towers set close together to protect other ranges of building. The new, smaller castles of the later fourteenth and fifteenth centuries were often built on the sites of Norman motte-and-baileys. Some were larger versions of the tower-house. At Crayke the Bishop of Durham built a four-storey block known as the Great Chamber, at Whorlton a tower and a gatehouse were erected upon a broad motte, and at Harewood Sir William Aldburgh used his 1366 licence to crenellate to build a single block containing hall and kitchen on the ground floor, solar and chapel on the first floor, and bed chambers and garderobes in the small angle towers of the top storey. Other contemporary castles were palaces arranged around a courtyard, with four massive corner towers to deter aggressors. The Latimers's early-fourteenth-century castle at Danby is the earliest Yorkshire example, but the best preserved is Bolton Castle in Wensleydale, and the greatest was Sheriff Hutton on the edge of the Forest of Galtres.

A motte-and-bailey castle at the village of Hutton had been constructed about 1140 by Bertram of Bulmer, Sheriff of York, and a Norman church had been built alongside. The manor passed through the female line to the Nevilles, who enclosed a park in 1335 and established a weekly market in 1378. Four years later John Neville obtained a licence to crenellate a lofty palace fortress at the west end of the village, with angle towers four and five storeys high and intermediate ranges that reached almost the same height. John's son, Ralph, was created Earl of Westmorland by Richard II and the Nevilles rivalled the Percies as the most powerful family in the north. Ralph's numerous offspring were connected by marriage to most of the leading families in the land, and his grandson was known as the king-maker. John Leland 'saw no home in the north so like a princely loggings', but by 1624 the building was ruined, and now only the fantastic, eerie shapes of the wrecked towers and gatehouse remain to attract the traveller's eye. On the edge of the Wensleydale moors, however, the visitor can still experience much of the original impact of forbidding medieval might. In 1568 Sir Francis Knollys called Bolton Castle 'the highest walled house that I have seen', but thought of it as a house rather than a castle. Sir Henry Scrope, Chief Justice and Chief Baron of the Exchequer, consolidated the family's Wensleydale estates in the early fourteenth century and Sir Richard, the first Lord Scrope, erected the castle. Sir Richard was also responsible for the park, the small church of St Oswald's, and possibly the village, which was laid out in two rows alongside an oblong green. Work on the castle began in 1378 when John Lewyn, the chief mason, signed a contract. Leland was informed that draughts of oxen were posted at regular stages to bring the necessary timber from the Cumberland Forest of Ingleby and that it took eighteen years to finish the building. Three of the four mighty corner towers and much of the three-storeyed ranges that enclose a rectangular courtyard survive almost to their full height.

The contemporary Wressle Castle in the Vale of York was built to a similar plan by Sir Thomas Percy. Leland thought 'the house is one of the most propre beyound Trente . . . al of very fair and great squarid stone'. Wressle was the main Yorkshire seat of the mighty Percy family, the major landowners in the county after the Duchy of Lancaster. At the beginning of the fourteenth century the Percies had properties only in Yorkshire, Lincolnshire and at Petworth, but Henry Percy purchased the Northumberland estates of Alnwick and Warkworth and was rewarded for his active part in the Scottish wars by large grants of confiscated estates in the Borders. In 1308 he fortified two of his Yorkshire manor houses, at Spofforth and Leconfield. Leland wrote that Leconfield

is a large house, and stondith withyn a great moteyn one very spatius courte. 3 partes of the house, saving the meane gate that is made of brike, is al of tymbre. The 4 parte is fair made of stone and sum brike. I saw in a litle studiying chaumber ther called Paradice the genealogie of the Percys. The park thereby is very fair and large and meately well woddid. Ther is a fair tour of brike for a logge yn the park.

In the West Riding the Percy family held the manors of Healaugh, Leathley, Linton, Spofforth and Tadcaster, as well as lands in Craven, Ribblesdale and Langstrothdale; in the North Riding they held Asenby, Gristhwaite, Kirk Leavington, Seamer, Throxenby and Topcliffe; and in the East Riding their possessions comprised Arras, Catton (with a 350 acre park), Gembling, Leconfield, Nafferton, Pocklington, Scorborough, Wansford, Wasplington and Wressle. Henry Percy's grandson and namesake became the first Earl of Northumberland, Earl Marshal of England, and warden of the northern marches, and was connected by kinship with nearly all the leading families of the North. By that time the Percies were one of the leading families in the land. In 1399 Henry IV, the son of John of Gaunt, Duke of Lancaster, dethroned his cousin, Richard II, and later that year murdered him at Pontefract Castle. At first the Percies supported the new king, but they were soon involved in disastrous rebellion. In 1403 Henry Hotspur, the son of the Earl of Northumberland, was killed while leading the rebel forces at Shrewsbury; two years later Archbishop Richard Scrope was executed after the battle of Shipton Moor, north of York; and in 1408 the rebellion was brought to an end when Earl Henry was killed at the battle of Bramham Moor near the Great North Road, when the Percy forces from north Yorkshire were defeated by a smaller army of Yorkshiremen commanded by the county sheriff, Sir Thomas Rokeby.

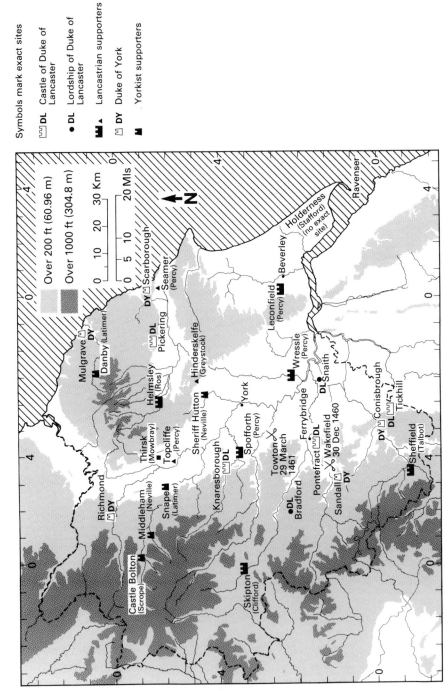

Symbols mark exact sites

⌂ **DL**   Castle of Duke of Lancaster

● **DL**   Lordship of Duke of Lancaster

▲   Lancastrian supporters

⌂ **DY**   Duke of York

■   Yorkist supporters

Over 200 ft (60.96 m)

Over 1000 ft (304.8 m)

0   5   10   20   30 Km

0   10   20 Mls

N

Scarborough

Seamer (Percy) ▲

Mulgrave ⌂ **DY**

Danby (Latimer)

Helmsley ■ (Ros)

DL Pickering

Hinderskelfe ▲ (Greystock)

Leconfield ● (Percy)

Beverley ●

Holderness (Stafford) (no exact site)

Ravenser

Wressle ■ (Percy)

DL Snaith

Thirsk (Mowbray)

Topcliffe ▲ (Percy)

Sheriff Hutton ■ (Neville)

● York

Spofforth ■ (Percy)

Ferrybridge

Pontefract ⌂ **DL**

DY ⌂ Conisbrough

⌂ **DL** Tickhill

Richmond ⌂ **DY**

Middleham ■ (Neville)

Snape ■ (Latimer)

Knaresborough ⌂ **DL**

Towton 29 March 1461

Bradford ● **DL**

Wakefield 30 Dec 1460

Sandall ⌂ **DY**

Sheffield ■ (Talbot)

Castle Bolton (Scrope) ■

Skipton ■ (Clifford)

Figure 2.2   The Wars of the Roses

Earl Henry's head was displayed on a tower in the middle of London bridge, then the rest of his body was quartered, pickled in spices, and exhibited in Lincoln, York, Newcastle and Berwick.

The final period of dynastic conflict seriously to affect Yorkshire was the Wars of the Roses, which began in 1455 with the Battle of St Albans and ended thirty years later with Henry VII's triumph at Bosworth. Edward III's younger sons had been created Dukes of Clarence, Lancaster, York and Gloucester, and most of the crown property in Yorkshire had been granted to John of Gaunt, Duke of Lancaster, and to Edmund Langley, Duke of York. When John de Warenne, eighth and last Earl of Surrey, died without legitimate issue in 1347, his Yorkshire lordships of Conisbrough and Wakefield, together with all his other estates north of the Trent, were forfeited to the crown and were then given to the Duke of York. Likewise, in 1372 the estates that the crown had acquired after the execution of Thomas, Earl of Lancaster, fifty years earlier, were granted to the Duke of Lancaster. They included the great honours of Pontefract, Tickhill, Pickering and Knaresborough, the lordships of Bradford and Snaith, and parts of Yorkshire that lay adjacent to the honour of Clitheroe. The Duchy of Lancaster passed back to the crown when John of Gaunt's son was crowned Henry IV in 1399, and the Duke of York's estates were engrossed when Edward IV became king in 1461.

The East and West Riding nobility overwhelmingly supported the Lancastrian cause, but loyalty in the North Riding was divided. The Nevilles of Sheriff Hutton and Middleham threw in their hand with the house of York and were backed by the Scropes of Bolton, the Latimers of Danby and Snape, and the Mowbrays of Thirsk and Burton in Lonsdale. On the Lancastrian side the Nevilles' chief rivals, the Percies, were supported by the Cliffords of Skipton, Ros of Helmsley, Greystock of Hinderskelfe, Stafford of Holderness, and Talbot of Sheffield. Yorkshire was the stage for two of the major encounters of the wars, at Wakefield and Towton. On 30 December 1460 Richard, Duke of York and many of his followers were killed after foolishly leaving the security of Sandal castle to fight a Lancastrian army that was perhaps five times as large. The Duke's severed head was crowned with gold paper, attached to a pole, and set above Micklegate Bar, 'so York may overlook the town of York'. But at Towton on 29 March 1461 the Yorkists got their revenge in one of the decisive battles of the wars. Edward, the new Duke of York, marched from London towards the Lancastrian camp near Tadcaster, and though his forces were held for a time by 'Butcher' Clifford's army at Ferrybridge, they eventually broke through and won a major victory at Towton. The grisly heads of the Yorkist leaders were removed from the bars of York and replaced by those of their enemies, and the Duke of York was crowned as Edward IV. His throne was far from secure, however, and when the 'kingmaker', Richard Neville, Earl of Warwick changed allegiance in 1470 and released Henry VI from prison, Edward was forced to flee to Holland. Next year he returned via Ravenser and the Humber, and although the citizens of Hull refused him entry he was encouraged by the support of Beverley and York and went on to kill both Henry VI and Warwick. The leading Yorkshire families who had backed the Lancastrian cause had their estates confiscated.

The achievements of the Tudors in reasserting law and order and in bringing the North firmly under central control is evident when seen against this feuding background. But much of the savagery and treachery involved only the more ruthless and grasping of the barons and their armed retainers. Other men refused to get involved in the scheming and bloodshed. A good example of a squire who did not get entangled in these quarrels but who devoted his energies to consolidating and enjoying his inheritance was Richard Clervaux of Croft on the banks of the Tees. Clervaux was proud of his role as a leading member of the ancient gentry of Richmondshire, he worked hard at building up his estate, and he cared about his reputation (Pollard 1978). The enormous tomb-chest in the south aisle of the Perpendicular church of St Peter's at Croft is a fitting memorial to him.

Perpendicular Gothic Churches

The communities that escaped the full rigours of the fourteenth-century mortalities and which were not seriously weakened by economic decline continued to enlarge their churches and to redesign them in contemporary styles. The lavish display of the Decorated period gave way to the last phase of English Gothic, a style dubbed Perpendicular by later analysts, a native development that made no concessions to the Italian Renaissance and which inspired church builders for two hundred years until the Reformation brought such activities to an end. In the later Middle Ages wealthy people rarely gave to monasteries but sought instead to improve their parish church or to attach their private chantry chapel to an aisle or chancel, where a priest was employed to sing masses for departed souls. At least three-quarters of the Yorkshire chantries that were recorded at their dissolution were founded after the Black Death, and the fashion was particularly popular in the late fifteenth and the early sixteenth centuries. The north chapel of Harpham Church contains the memorials of the St Quintin family, including the best brass in the East Riding; at Worsbrough the wooden monument to young Roger Rockley, who died in 1534, is gruesome to modern eyes for his skeleton is depicted underneath his living image; and in estate villages chancels as well as chapels sometimes look like the private mausoleums of the squirearchy. St Martin's Church at Burton Agnes displays the monuments of the Griffiths and the Boyntons, and All Saints, Harewood has six medieval alabaster tomb-chests with recumbent figures commemorating local lords.

The heraldic devices of donors often help to date a church in the Perpendicular style. The arms of John of Gaunt, Fitzwilliam, Eastfield, Sandford and White date the tower of St Mary's, Tickhill, to 1373–93, though John Sandford's will shows that the work (possibly the fine crown) was not complete in 1429. The nave was heightened about the same time as the tower and given a range of clerestory windows; the foliage of the capitals and the unusual manner in which the nave arcades are designed with ogee arches and crocketed finials suggest an early phase of Perpendicular Gothic. The large window over the chancel arch helps to make the interior as light and spacious as merchants' churches in East Anglia. Merchants' marks are displayed in the nave, and in 1390 a local merchant, Richard Raynerson, left 100 shillings 'to the works of the church of Tickhill'. But within a generation or so of this bequest Tickhill appears to have entered its phase of late-medieval decline, for plans to vault the tower were never completed. In other parts of Yorkshire the cost of Perpendicular rebuilding was borne by single families. In 1412 Katherine de Burgh and her son John gave the mason Richard Crakehall 170 marks and a gown to demolish St Anne's, Catterick, and to erect the present chancel, nave, aisles and tower on a fresh site nearby. The rector of All Saints, Bolton Priory, paid for the rebuilding of his church which was completed in 1424, and at Thrybergh the rector inherited the manor and rebuilt both the chancel and nave of St Leonard's during the middle years of the fifteenth century. At St Michael's, Cowthorpe, which was consecrated anew in 1458, the memorial brass to Brian Ronclyff and his wife shows the couple holding a large model of the church they had built, and an inscription formerly commemorated their pious act.

A leading role in the new style of building was naturally taken by the master masons of York Minster. After seventy years of activity the minster's Decorated nave was completed in 1361 and work began on a new east end. William Hoton the younger, who had succeeded his father as master mason in 1351, provided designs in the new Perpendicular style but made a conscious attempt to harmonize with the earlier work in the nave. The presbytery which he and his successor, Robert Patrington, built onto the east end of the late Norman choir between 1361 and 1373 contains some of the earliest Perpendicular work in the north of England. A shortage of funds seems to have delayed work on the new choir until 1390, but King Richard II is known to have contributed 100 marks in 1395 and the five bays designed by Hugh Hedon in a fully developed Perpendicular style were completed by 1405. Bishop Skirlaw of Durham, a Yorkshireman with an eye on the vacant archbishop's seat, then paid for the immense east window, which was finished within three years. This masterpiece of John Thornton, the Coventry glazier, is 76 ft high and 32 ft wide, contains 1,680 square feet of stained glass, and is undoubtedly a 'major monument of European glass painting (Aylmer and Cant 1977: 365). When Thornton finished his work the minster was a Gothic whole with Norman work visible only in the crypt. The next project was to raise a huge central tower, designed by William Colchester and paid for by Bishop Skirlaw. Masons' marks suggest that most of the central lantern was built before 1450, but fears of a collapse prevented any work above roof level. By 1430 it had been decided to concentrate on the two western towers instead. William Waddeswyk, the designer, was obviously influenced by French examples. The south-western tower was finished by about 1450 and its twin was completed during the next two decades. Plans to build a dominant central tower and spire were abandoned and after the interior of the crossing had been painted the minster was reconsecrated on 3 July 1472.

By the middle of the fifteenth century Beverley minster was also of cathedral size. Sir George Gilbert Scott considered it the finest Gothic church in the world. Beverley also has the good fortune of possessing one of England's most beautiful parish churches. The rebuilding of St Mary's in Perpendicular style covered the years from about 1400 until the splendid tower was completed in the 1520s. Both minster and parish church have an outstanding collection of carved misericords. The golden age of East Riding church building lasted from the thirteenth century until well into the Perpendicular period. At St Mary, Cottingham, where the nave had been built in Decorated style, a Perpendicular chancel was finished by 1384 and then work began on a crossing tower. At Holy Trinity, Hull, it was the chancel that had been completed in the Decorated period; here, a new nave was built between 1389 and 1418 and a crossing tower had reached its full height by the end of the century. At the port of Hedon the fine church of St Augustine was given a crossing tower during the first half of the fifteenth century, and good Perpendicular towers were also erected in the East Riding market towns of Great Driffield, Holme on Spalding Moor and Pocklington. Walter Skirlaw, Bishop of Durham from 1388 to his death in 1405, was an influential patron in the early phase of Perpendicular rebuilding. Howden was one of the bishopric's possessions, and there Skirlaw built the chancel, the lower part of the crossing tower, the choir transepts, a small chantry chapel and the chapter house. In 1401 he built St Augustine's church in his native village of Skirlaugh, a building that is a perfect example of early Perpendicular architecture in the style of a college chapel. The design of the distinctive openwork parapet that crowns the tower was copied in such distant places as Coxwold and Tickhill, and in York at All Saints Pavement, and perhaps inspired the slightly different design on the eastern arm of York Minster, which was the model for St Martin le Grand at York, the Greyfriars tower at Richmond, the nave and chancel at Coxwold and the entire roofline of the North Riding's finest church at Thirsk. Spires were less in favour in Yorkshire, but a beautiful example at Laughton en le Morthen, which was built to a unique design when William of Wykeham was prebend of Laughton in the later fourteenth century, is one of the county's medieval glories, and Hemingborough's spire is one of the most amazing of all, rising 126 ft above the tower to a full height of 189 ft.

During the course of the fifteenth and early sixteenth centuries many

Plate 2.4   St Mary's Church, Thirsk. St Mary's is the finest church in the North Riding. It stands proud and aloof from the market place for its site had been chosen for worship before the market was founded in the early Middle Ages. It is approached from the centre of town along the gentle curves of Kirkgate, and the first view of it leaves an abiding memory.

Rebuilding began in the 1430s with the tower, followed by the nave and its aisles and finally the chancel, which was completed about 1460. St Mary's is therefore a remarkably complete example of the mid-fifteenth century Perpendicular style of Gothic architecture. The openwork parapet and pinnacles give it an air of distinction. This is a feature copied from York Minster and the Greyfriars tower at Richmond and which is also found at Coxwold.

parts of the West Riding, especially those involved in the textile trades, became prosperous enough to rebuild their churches on a scale that matched those in the East Riding. The first stage of an ambitious programme at Rotherham was begun in 1409 when the Archbishop of York granted an indulgence to all those parishioners who contributed towards the cost of a new tower; by the 1480s Rotherham had one of the finest town churches in Yorkshire. The arms of several local families from the rural parts of the parish were visible at the time of a 1585 visitation, but the most notable benefactor was Archbishop Thomas Rotherham, a native of the town, who built the south chancel chapel in 1480 and shortly afterwards founded the nearby College of Jesus. Bradford, Doncaster, Halifax, Sheffield and Wakefield soon followed Rotherham's example, and by the third quarter of the fifteenth century many rural parishes were also rebuilding. In the lowlands to the east of Doncaster the Norman church builders had used cobbles and boulders collected from local glacial deposits, but now sufficient wealth was available to import ashlar blocks of beautiful Magnesian Limestone from quarries several miles to the west. The tower of St Cuthbert's, Fishlake, bears the badge of Edward IV on its south side and can therefore be dated to 1461–83, and in the neighbouring parish of Hatfield the tower of St Lawrence's Church displays the shield of Sir Edward Savage, keeper of Hatfield park and master of the game during the reign of Henry VII. On the Magnesian Limestone belt the elaborate tower at Sprotborough was said to have been of new construction when William Fitzwilliam made a bequest in 1474, and belfries of almost identical design nearby at Conisbrough and Wadworth were presumably contemporary and may even have been built by the same team of masons.

The way in which new designs were copied in neighbouring churches can be seen in the fashion for corbel tables below the tower parapets at Bardsey, Batley, Methley and other churches in central parts of the West Riding. It can also be observed in Pennine parishes which were now populous and wealthy enough to rebuild on a large scale. In a score of Craven churches, notably Dent, Kirkby Malham, Sedbergh and Skipton, the fashion was for long, low buildings with straight-headed windows and rather short, sturdy towers. Some northern towers are quite massive and seem to have been built to guard against further Scottish invasions; the most famous example is St Gregory's, Bedale, where the upper chamber has a fireplace and garderobe, and where portcullis grooves can still be seen at the foot of the tower stair. However, the finest Pennine churches are in the south of the county, where profits from the cloth and metal trades supplemented those from agriculture at all levels of society. An indulgence for the repair of Almondbury Church was granted in 1486, and the inscription on the nave ceiling says that the work was completed in 1522.

At Silkstone the crossing tower was pulled down in 1479 and a new tower at the western end was finished by 1495. Penistone and Bradfield churches were rebuilt about the same time, and many of the masons' marks on Silkstone tower can also be found a few miles away at Darton and Royston.

According to an inscription on a wall-plate the Chancel of All Saints, Darton, was completed in 1517 by 'Thomas Tykyll, prior of Monk Bretton and patron of this church'; the name and tower were rebuilt in contemporary style by the parishioners. The most splendid of this group is St Mary's, Ecclesfield, which Roger Dodsworth, the seventeenth-century Yorkshire antiquary, thought was 'the fairest church for stone, wood and glass' that he had seen in a rural parish. Here the Carthusian monks of St Anne's Priory at Coventry (who had succeeded the abbey of St Wandrille in Normandy as rectors when alien priories were dissolved by Richard II) collaborated with the parishioners from about 1480 to 1520 to erect a building that was worthy of a town church. By the reigns of the early Tudors the West Riding could no longer be considered to be poorer and more backward than other parts of the county.

Late-Medieval Houses

The great wealth of a few medieval families and the poverty of the masses is nowhere more apparent than in the surviving domestic buildings. Mighty barons and prosperous manorial lords could afford to use stone or brick, but everyone else built with timber (almost always with oak) or with the humblest of materials such as cobbles or mud. The cottages of ordinary countryfolk are known only from the excavation of deserted village sites. Normally of just one room they were open to the roof and had a central hearth but no chimney and just a few, narrow, unglazed windows; a cottage at Wharram Percy measured only 20 ft by 10 ft. A typical dwelling probably consisted of a crude cruck frame reared on rubble foundations (to prevent damp and for stability) and infilled with cheap local materials. Even in the East Riding, where few crucks or other timber-framed houses survive, documentary evidence shows that buildings were erected in this tradition; thus in 1368 John of Sewerby provided four posts, a hearth, 20 spars and straw thatch to enable his tenants to build a house (*VCH, East Riding*, II 1974: 98), and a survey of Settrington in 1599 reveals that all the houses and cottages were reared on crucks (YASRS, CXXVI 1960). In 1297 Peter the Shepherd paid a sixpence fine in Wakefield manor court for permission to buy a house from Geppe Stock and to re-erect it at Milnthorpe, near Sandall. Thirty years later Walter Gunne bought a house in Stanley township from another villein and then sold it to Thomas Tanner, who 'uprooted it' and took it out of the manor; the court fined him one shilling for buying the house without licence (Faull and Moorhouse, eds 1981: 808). Just across the Derbyshire border, the lord of Norton leased his manor to William Shemyld in 1400, but 'reserved to himself the right of breaking down old houses and of carrying them away and selling them' (Hall 1914: 120). In North

Yorkshire the Bedale manor account rolls for the second quarter of the fifteenth century indicate that all the thirty buildings mentioned were timber-framed structures on stone footings, with upper walls infilled with wattle and daub and roofs either thatched or stone-slated. At Snape, $2\frac{1}{2}$ miles further south, the houses were of poorer quality, with entire walls composed of wattling and rendered with mud. At the same period and in the same district, therefore, the quality of vernacular building could vary enormously; even a single community could have widely different standards of housing (Harrison and Hutton 1984: 4–6).

The majority of Yorkshire's surviving timber-framed buildings are not immediately recognizable from the outside, for they have been subsequently encased in stone or brick. Many have been discovered by intensive fieldwork in recent years. A great number are Elizabethan and Stuart rather than medieval, but on the fringes of the southern Pennines a notable collection of houses and barns were erected during the second half of the fifteenth century and the first quarter of the sixteenth. Together with neighbouring Perpendicular churches, these buildings highlight the emerging prosperity of the cloth-manufacturing district in the West Riding, in contrast to the stagnating economy of places, particularly in the East Riding, which had formerly been the wealthiest in the county. In the country as a whole, only Kent has a better selection of late-medieval houses within a limited area than those of the yeoman-clothiers of the Halifax district. This is not because other counties have since replaced their old stock; rather, the number and quality of surviving structures from any one period reflects the wealth of the area at that time (Mercer 1975: 3–14). The visual evidence also supports the belief that the national economy entered a period of decline about half way through the reign of Henry VIII and did not recover until mid-way through the reign of Elizabeth.

Though in Midland and southern England surviving cruck frames date back to the thirteenth century, in the North such early survivors are rare. Nearly a hundred base-cruck structures have been discovered south of the Trent, but so far the only northern examples are Baxby manor house, Husthwaite, and the much-restored Canons' Garth at Helmsley; both supported a crown-post roof and date from about 1300 (Harrison and Hutton 1984: 21–3). Documentary evidence for cruck structures becomes available in the fifteenth century. In 1432 a house at Holdworth Ing in Ovenden township was built on eight crucks and roofed with slatestones, and in 1495 the Abbot of Whitby repaired his house at Goathland 'after the manner of the country' with 'three pairs of forks', a typical alternate name for crucks. By the early sixteenth century cruck frames were used in most, if not all, parts of Yorkshire for humble dwellings and farm buildings. An Elizabethan survey of the Wharfedale manor of Cracoe reveals that nearly all the houses and barns were erected in this manner. In south Yorkshire dendrochronological dates have recently been assigned to a 1539 cruck-framed house in Stannington, a demolished building of the 1540s in Fulwood, a Stannington barn of 1588, and a demolished cruck of the 1630s at Waleswood. In 1638 Hugh Mellor of Shiregreen left his son Hugh 'two paire of Crookes Allredie broken' and other timber with which to build a smithy. The majority of surviving examples date from the fifteenth to the seventeenth centuries, but the tradition lingered on in the humblest buildings until the eighteenth century. The cottages and barns that have survived were later encased in stone, or sometimes brick, when the original walls were in need of repair. The Pennine fringes of south-west Yorkshire and the North York Moors and adjoining parts retain great numbers of crucks, but such structures were once widespread in the county (Hey 1979: 106–12; Ryder 1982: 123, 134–5).

At Green Farm, on the hills above Stocksbridge, a six-bay cruck barn has stone walls adorned with the names of William and Sara Couldwell and the

Plate 2.5 Hawksworth's Cote Cruck Barn, Midhope. This two-bay cruck barn on the edge of the southern Pennines was photographed just before it was demolished about 1903. The later stone walls and roof have been dismantled, leaving only the crude timber framework of the original building. The cruck blades are held together by a tie-beam at mid level and the whole structure has been hoisted onto stone footings to give extra height and to prevent rising damp. The weight of the roof is supported by the cruck blades with the aid of a ridge beam and sturdy purlins. Extra space has been gained at the lower side by the construction of a simple aisle. All the joints are supported by wooden pegs. Many similar barns and a few cottages can still be found locally, but their timber-frames are hidden behind later stone walls. Most Yorkshire crucks date from the fifteenth, sixteenth and seventeenth centuries.

date 1688, but inside the building it is clear that the timber frame is earlier than the stone walls which have been built around it. The farmhouse was also reclad in stone in the eighteenth century, two hundred years or more after it was built as a sturdy timber-framed building with a king-post roof. Post-and-truss buildings such as this overlap with crucks both in time and space, though generally speaking they belong higher up the social scale. The earliest surviving timber-framed building in Yorkshire is probably the long barn that the lords of Hallamshire built at Whiston. The posts, arcade plates and connecting braces of the original five southern bays display carpentry techniques that are not found anywhere else in the county and which are paralleled in Essex barns of the early thirteenth century. At Shore Hall and Dean Head in the parish of Penistone two aisled barns with collar-rafter roofs appear to date from the fourteenth or fifteenth centuries, and a similar but unaisled barn at Nether Haugh, north of Rotherham, is late-medieval. Early collar-rafter roofs were not confined to the lowland zone of England, as was once thought, but were constructed even on the edge of the Pennines. Netherfold farmhouse at Thorpe Common has been dated by dendrochronology to 1495. Sturdy Pennine barns with king-post roofs, such as those at East Riddlesden Hall and Dives house, Dalton, tend to be later, and many are post-medieval.

During the late fifteenth and early sixteenth centuries many West Riding families acquired sufficient wealth from the textile trades, and occasionally from other industries, to rebuild their homes on a scale comparable with those of south-east England. They had king-post roofs with ridges and purlins sturdy enough to support heavy, stone-slated roofs, and close-studded walls decorated with diagonal patterns, especially in the gable ends. Gentry houses such as Elland New Hall, Shibden Hall and Thornhill Lees Hall had two-storeyed cross-wings and a central hall that was open to the roof. The Wickersley family's Broom Hall at Sheffield, a typical example of this type, has been dated by dendrochronology to 1507 ± 9. The standard of carpentry in these gentry houses was very high; two roofs at Calverley Hall were given a display of hammerbeams, a technique that was rarely employed in the North of England. But as a group the collection of houses built by the yeomen-clothiers of the Halifax district are of much greater interest. Well over twenty examples have been recorded from the second half of the fifteenth or the first quarter of the sixteenth century. As some of them are in clusters of two or three in a village or hamlet such as Boothtown, the owners' wealth obviously did not come solely from the land. 'This concentration of substantial houses of late-medieval character within a very small area appears to be unparalleled elsewhere in England' and no doubt reflects the intense development of the textile trades (Mercer 1975: 16). A few houses of this type have been recognized further south at Shelley Woodhouse and Barnby Hall and around Huddersfield, but they are nowhere near as common there as in the medieval parish of Halifax. Their most distinctive feature is the use of aisles (a characteristic element of earlier buildings elsewhere), usually in the form of a single aisle to the rear of the hall. Though they have the normal arrangement of a central hall, cross passage, service wing and solar wing, all under one roof, they are not easy to recognize from outside as they have been clad in stone and heavily disguised. Their central halls were open to their king-post roofs, but instead of an open hearth they had a stone reredos at the lower end, with a timber and plaster smokehood. Vale of York houses had similar features, so by the later Middle Ages Yorkshire yeomen no longer lived in smoke-filled rooms.

The sixty or so timber-framed houses discovered in the Vale of York date from *c.* 1450–1680 and have a wide variety of plans. Their common features include collar-rafter roofs, close-studded walls and usually an aisle or an outshut at the rear or the end. The fifteenth-century examples have open halls, but the later ones are storeyed. Another type of roof, the crown-post, is common in southern England, but is also found in houses in York and such other medieval towns as Beverley, Ripon, Scarborough and Tickhill, and more rarely in the countryside; a four-bay house at Woodall on the southern boundary of the county, for instance, has a well-preserved crown-post roof which has been assigned to the late fourteenth century (Ryder 1982: 130). In York fifteenth-century houses in the Shambles and other streets have crown-post roofs and jettied upper storeys, and a building just off Goodramgate has the typical features of the 'Wealden houses' that are so common in Kent. York in particular was open to influences from southern England, but the county as a whole has a far larger and more varied collection of medieval buildings than was realized until recently. The evidence of the buildings refutes the idea that the whole of Yorkshire was part of a 'backward North'.

The Medieval Scene

During the late Middle Ages Yorkshire was administered by a mosaic of different authorities. The county had a high sheriff who presided over the county court, a coroner and numerous minor officials based at York Castle. The county capital was also the centre of ecclesiastical administration and jurisdiction for the northern province. In 1396 the city of York was given county status with its own sheriff, and the authority of the mayor and corporation was extended beyond the city to include the whole of the wapentake of Ainsty. Hull was also granted county status in 1440, and other enclaves included the palatinate liberties of Beverley and Ripon with their own JPs, and the incorporated boroughs of Doncaster (1467), Pontefract (1484) and Scarborough (1485). Commissions of peace were held not on a county basis but in each of the three ridings, where the quarter sessions met at convenient market towns. The JPs, who had wide judicial and administrative

113

powers, were local gentry who sat on the bench only at sessions held in their own wapentakes. Though they had lost their judicial powers, the wapentakes long continued as the bodies responsible for assessing and collecting taxes and raising musters. The smallest unit of local government was the township, whose origins may go back to Celtic times. Sometimes a township covered the same area as an ecclesiastical parish, but many average-sized parishes consisted of two or three townships, and moorland parishes had many more; the West Riding had about six hundred townships to 170 parishes at the end of the Middle Ages (Smith 1970: 128). Quite independently of this system, the manorial courts dealt with tenures, dues, land transactions, farming practices and petty law and order; manorial boundaries, particularly those in western parts of the county, rarely coincided with those of the township or parish.

The early Robin Hood legends have much to say about the corruption of the legal and administrative system. Robin Hood was 'a yeoman hero for a yeoman audience' who was probably based on a local outlaw in thirteenth-century Barnsdale; the stories about the sheriff of Nottingham were possibly added from a separate group of tales (Dobson and Taylor 1976). The forest of Barnsdale, in which the earliest ballads are set, was not a forest in either the legal or literal sense, but a small, obscure part of the Magnesian Limestone belt. The *Lyttel Geste* mentions Doncaster, Kirklees priory, Wentbridge and a minor place-name, 'the Saylis', which can be identified with Sayles Plantation 500 yards east of Wentbridge. The place was a notorious spot for medieval travellers, for here the Great North Road divided into two branches, one heading for Boroughbridge and the North via Pontefract and Wetherby, and the other for York via Wentbridge and Sherburn. The area is now marked by 'Robin Hood's Well', an early-eighteenth-century monument designed by Sir John Vanbrugh.

In the fourteenth century the carriage of goods from Westminster to York took ten to fourteen days. Wherever possible, heavy, bulky goods were taken by river and along the coast, for water transport was much cheaper than land transport. The Ouse was a major thoroughfare whose navigable tributaries reached into many parts of Yorkshire. Thus, in 1534 Robert Goldsborough, a fishmonger, said in evidence that every market day he 'conveyed fresh fish from the sea to Pontefract and brought it into the market place to sell', or on rainy days, 'in an open shop opening towards the market place' (YASRS, XLI 1908: 137–41). Well-trodden 'ways' and 'gates' conveyed on such market centres, and local lanes linked farmsteads, hamlets and villages in a complicated network whose pattern has endured into modern times. Medieval people were more mobile than was once believed, though much of this mobility was restricted to a 10 or 20 mile radius around the market towns. The packmen and carriers who became so numerous in the seventeenth century were already characteristic figures; Adam the Bagger (badger) of Shelley (1308) and John Jagger of Stainland (1427) were two whose occupations gave rise to North-Country surnames. Some made regular journeys over long distances. A distinctive group of minor place-names – some still in use, others found in medieval and later records – are attached to highways that led from the Cheshire salt-works at Northwich, Middlewich and Nantwich to the market-towns of northern and Midland England.

The route from Northwich and the Longdendale valley towards Rotherham, Doncaster and Wakefield is one that can be traced with their aid. It entered Yorkshire at Saltersbrook and one branch headed towards Wakefield along the Salterway which was recorded in the fifteenth century as a boundary of the Graveship of Holme. The Barnsley–Doncaster road proceeded past Salter Croft at Dodworth, Saltersbrook at Goldthorpe and Saltergate at Scawsby, while the Rotherham route climbed the ridge to Salter Hill near Green Moor and continued along the present road through Wortley, High Green and Chapeltown to Kimberworth; eighteenth-century maps mark three widely separated fields with Salter names, which were probably recognized grazing stops. Rotherham market was approached by the 'fair Stone Bridge of iiii Arches' with a 'Chapel of Stone wel wrought' that John Leland saw about 1540. The chapel was built in 1483 and, like the mid-fourteenth-century chapel on the bridge at Wakefield, it is a rare survival. Bridges such as these were wide enough to take wheeled vehicles. When the men of Doncaster built a stone bridge over the Don in 1248 they were allowed to charge a toll on carts to pay for its upkeep. Sheffield's 1486 bridge was also wide enough to cater for such traffic, and the Hallamshire court rolls of 1446–47 noted 'the expences of 120 persons with 60 wains, and their draught-oxen coming to do boon work, carrying limestone from Roche Abbey to Sheffield castle'. Even during the Middle Ages wheeled vehicles were not confined to lowland parts of Yorkshire but were used in Pennine districts (Hey 1980: 73–4, 92, 156–9).

The study of surname origins and distributions confirms that although some Yorkshire families left the county the mobility of the great majority was restricted to short distances. As yet, outsiders rarely distinguished Yorkshiremen from northerners as a whole, but the differences between northern and southern speech were pronounced. When the first shepherd in the Wakefield mystery plays said, 'But Mak, is that truth? Now take out that southern tooth' his meaning must have been clear to his audience. About 1125 William of Malmesbury wrote, 'Almost everything about the language of the North, and particularly of the people of York, is so crude and discordant that we Southerners cannot understand it. This is because they are near to barbarian people.' His explanation was taken up in 1387 by John of Trevisa:

All the language of the Northumbrians, and specially at York, is so sharp, cutting, and abrasive, and ugly, that we southern men may scarcely understand that language. I believe that that is because they are near to strange men and aliens, that speak strangely, and also because the kings of England always live far from that country; for they are

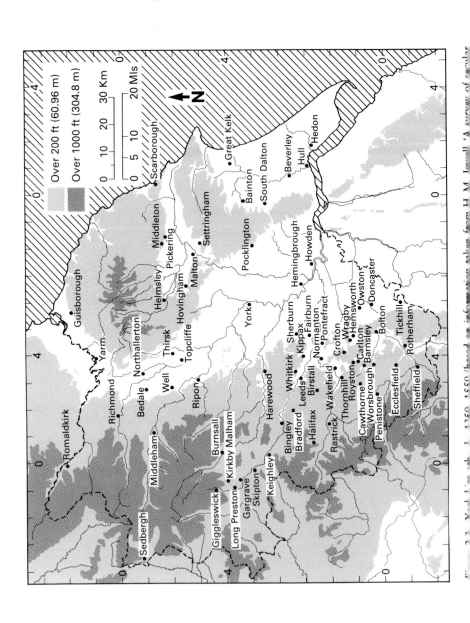

Figure 3.3 Yorkshire *ob. 1. 1250–1350* (based on information taken from H. M. Jewell, 'A survey of secular

Map legend:

Over 200 ft (60.96 m)

Over 1000 ft (304.8 m)

Scale: 0 5 10 20 30 Km

0 10 20 Mls

N

Places labelled: Scarborough, Guisborough, Yarm, Romaldkirk, Richmond, Bedale, Middleham, Sedbergh, Giggleswick, Long Preston, Gargrave, Skipton, Burnsall, Kirkby Malham, Keighley, Bingley, Bradford, Halifax, Rastrick, Leeds, Whitkirk, Harewood, York, Ripon, Well, Topcliffe, Thirsk, Northallerton, Helmsley, Middleton, Pickering, Hovingham, Malton, Settrington, Pocklington, Hemingbrough, Howden, Sherburn, Kippax, Fairburn, Normanton, Pontefract, Wakefield, Birstall, Crofton, Thornhill, Royston, Carlton, Barnsley, Wragby, Hemsworth, Owston, Doncaster, Cawthorne, Worsbrough, Penistone, Bolton, Ecclesfield, Sheffield, Tickhill, Rotherham, Bainton, South Dalton, Beverley, Hull, Great Kelk, Hedon more disposed to the south country, and if they go to the north country they go with great help and strength.

A more sympathetic note was struck by Gerald of Wales in the late twelfth century, for after observing that the Welsh sang in harmony rather than unison, he went on to say that,

> In the northern parts of Great Britain, across the Humber and in Yorkshire, the English who live there produce the same symphonic harmony when they sing. They do this in two parts only, with two modulations of the voice, one group humming the bass and the others singing the treble most sweetly. The two peoples must have developed this habit not by any special training but by age-old custom, by language which has made it second nature.

Throughout England the later Middle Ages was a time of increased educational provision and rising literacy. Northern schools were comparable with southern ones in terms of constitution, curriculum, facilities and aims (Jewell 1982). In addition to the various schools at York, 18 West Riding, 9 North Riding and 8 East Riding schools are known to have been in existence before 1500; by 1550 this number had risen to 40 in the West Riding, 16 in the North Riding and 10 in the East Riding. They varied in range from chantry schools taught by a chaplain to well-endowed colleges such as that founded in 1482–83 by Thomas Rotherham, Archbishop of York and Chancellor of England, in his native town. The Rotherham College of Jesus was served by a provost who taught theology and three fellows who taught grammar, singing, and writing and arithmetic, and it provided accommodation for six choristers and five chantry priests from the parish church; Leland described it as 'a very fair college sumptuusly builded of brike'. In the Middle Ages northern culture was largely that of the country as a whole, and northern boys such as Thomas Rotherham, John Wyclif and Roger Ascham were able to rise through the educational system to national fame.

Richard Rolle acquired a national reputation in the fourteenth century as an author of mystical works even though he remained in Yorkshire all his life, living as a hermit alongside the Cistercian nunnery of Hampole. More manuscripts of Rolle's survive than of any other English writer of his time. He was probably the author of the *Pricke of Conscience*, a moralizing summary of contemporary theology with an emphasis on death and retribution, whose fifteen signs of the end of the world are depicted in an early-fifteenth century window (possibly designed by John Thornton, the creator of the minster's great east window) at All Saints, North Street, York. The interiors of medieval churches were a blaze of colour depicting Christ, the Virgin, Saints, biblical stories and religious beliefs. York has a magnificent collection of stained glass in its minster and parish churches, and Pickering's mid-fifteenth-century wall paintings form one of the most complete surviving series in the country; they depict the coronation, annunciation and burial of the Virgin, seven scenes from the Passion and seven acts of mercy, St George, St Christopher and St Catherine, the martyrdoms of St Edmund and St Thomas Becket, Herod's feast, the Descent into Hell and the Resurrection. Decorations were not always so explicitly Christian, for some were pagan images presented in a Christian light. The 23 misericords at St Mary's, Beverley, include green men and a variety of animals as well as kings and knights, and the 68 at Beverley minster include carvings of mythical and actual beasts embodying stories and allusions that are now often lost. At York Minster mistletoe, that potent symbol of pagan mythology, was placed ceremonially on the high altar at Christmas time. Yorkshire also had a number of holy wells which were venerated in the Middle Ages and beyond for their magical cures; originally dedicated to Elen, a Celtic goddess of armies and roads, they became associated with St Helen, the mother of Emperor Constantine, who was at York when his succession was announced. St Helen was the sixth most popular saint in terms of church dedications in Yorkshire (a much higher figure than anywhere else in the country), and her wells attracted pilgrims and often had chapels alongside; the most famous wells included those at Thorp Arch (or Newton Kyme), Gargrave, Barnburgh, Eshton and Carlton, near Royston, but they were scattered widely in Yorkshire and in some neighbouring counties. The influence of the medieval Church permeated every aspect of life. In the countryside the annual farming year was arranged around the religious festivals, and in the towns the ceremonial cycle that bound society together was essentially religious. The York and Wakefield series of Corpus Christi mystery plays throw a direct and vivid light on medieval popular beliefs and on the organization of such 'ritualised recreation' (Phythian-Adams 1975).

The feudal nature of medieval society is illustrated by the account of a sumptuous feast at Cawood Castle in September 1465 in celebration of George Neville's appointment as Archbishop of York and as 'a demonstration of the power, wealth and solidarity of the great Neville clan' (Girouard 1978: 25). The guests included 7 bishops, 10 abbots, 28 peers, numerous great ladies, 59 knights and various lawyers, clergy, aldermen and esquires from all over the country. Their attendants swelled the number of people at the feast to something like 2,500 people, and the food they ate included 113 oxen, 6 bulls, 1,000 sheep, 2,000 each of geese, pigs and chickens, 12 porpoises and 4,000 cold venison pasties. Conspicuous consumption was a feature of aristocratic society long before the eighteenth century.

Chapter 3

The Tudor and Early-Stuart Era

The Medieval Background

In 1515 Yorkshire ranked twelfth amongst the English counties in terms of the amount of tax that was paid and in 1524–25 was graded eleventh (Hoskins 1976: 23). The county as a whole was much less prosperous than Kent, East Anglia and the West Country, but its most favoured parts yielded tax at the top rate of more than 40 shillings per square mile. Despite the recession that was crippling many of the greatest towns and cities in the land, York, Hull and Beverley and their rural hinterlands were still relatively populous and wealthy. Yet other parts of Yorkshire were undoubtedly poor with most of the population living at a subsistence level in humble, cruck-framed cottages with few domestic comforts, and with only a small minority of families aspiring to the rank of gentry. The lay subsidies of the 1540s demonstrate the growing importance of the West Riding and reveal a shift of emphasis away from the arable villages which had dominated the scene two centuries earlier when the 1334 subsidy had been collected. The wapentakes of Agbrigg and Morley in particular saw considerable industrial and population growth. Here the cloth industry provided poor families with extra income and enabled many richer clothiers to thrive. The proportion of people paying tax on goods valued at more than £20 was noticeably greater in this district than anywhere else, particularly in the townships of the enormous parish of Halifax, and these two wapentakes contributed a third of all the tax collected in the West Riding (Smith 1970: 29). Generous common rights, favourable manorial customs and the ease with which pastoral farming could be combined with a craft or by-employment encouraged expansion on the Pennine foothills and Coal-Measure Sandstones while other parts of the county stagnated or declined.

York was still the secular and ecclesiastical capital of northern England, the seat of the archbishop, the high sheriff and the King's Council in the Northern Parts, and the only place outside London to have a royal mint. Though it was small by European standards it was one of a handful of English provincial cities that foreigners thought worth visiting. In 1500 it looked at its

119

best, but the Reformation and the late-medieval economic recession tarnished its image. Apart from the churches of St Michael le Belfrey (1525–36) and St Helen, Stonegate (1550s) no new public buildings were erected during the sixteenth century; indeed, most reconstruction projects had been abandoned well before the Reformation. In 1400 York had ranked as the first provincial city in the land, with a population of more than 12,000, but by the 1520s it had slipped to sixth position and had less than 8,000 people. The decay of overseas trade and the urban cloth industry is reflected in the corporation's records by falling incomes from house rents and a sharp drop in the admissions of freemen. A mayor of York thought that the Halifax, Leeds and Wakefield clothiers had proved too competitive for his fellow citizens because

> not onely the commodite of the water mylnes is there nigh hand, but alsoo the poor folk as spynners, carders and other necessary work folks for the sayd webbyng may there besyds their hard labour have kyen [kine], fyre and other releif good and cheap whiche is in this citie very deare and wantyng.

Nevertheless, the collapse of York's trade was not a sudden event and as late as 1475 it remained pre-eminent in the clothing industry. The city's fortunes did not reach their nadir until the reign of Henry VIII (Palliser 1979: 203–11).

Some of England's most famous provincial towns were amongst the many urban centres which withered during the late fifteenth and early sixteenth centuries and which came to the lowest point in their fortunes between 1520 and 1570. The 1520s in particular were years of acute crisis, a decade of unparalleled hardship for towns scattered throughout England (Abrams and Wrigley, eds, 1978: 159–85). Hull was affected at this time by the decay of its cloth export trade, and Beverley and Ripon lost their former status as great manufacturing centres. Ripon was still the largest town in the West Riding, with about 2,000 people in 1532 and a wide reputation for its annual horse fairs, but only a few years later John Leland painted a gloomy picture:

> There hath bene hard on the farther ripe of Skelle a great number of tainters for wollen clothes wont to be made on the town of Ripon, but now idelnes is sore encresid in the town, and clothe making almost decayed.

Leland noted that Beverley was

> large and welle buildid of wood . . . The toune is not waullid but yet be there many fair gates of brike . . . Ther is a great gut cut from the town to the ripe of Hulle Ryver, whereby preaty vesseles cum thyther . . .

Ther was good clothing making at Beverle but that is nowe much decayid.

By way of contrast,

Wakefeld apon Calder ys a very quik market toune, and meately large; wel servid of flesch and fische both from the se and by ryvers, whereof dyvers be theraboute at hande. So that al vitaile is very good chepe there. A right honest man shal fare wel for 2 pens a meale . . . Al the hole profite of the toun stondith by course drapery . . . It standith now al by clothyng.

Bradford was 'a praty quik market toune' that 'standith much by clothing', and Leeds was 'as large as Bradford, but not so quik as it. The toun stondith most by clothing'.

'The Fate of Towns and Cities', wrote William Camden, 'is every jot as unstable as the State and Happiness of Men.' Yorkshire's ports had mixed fortunes. Bawtry was 'very bare and poore, a poore market towne' and the wharf that served south Yorkshire and north Derbyshire did not attract Leland's notice. The pier at Scarborough was 'sore decayid', but at the 'great fischer toune' of Whitby a new quay and port was under construction and the 'fischer tounlet' of twenty boats called Robin Hood's Bay had 'a dok or bosom of a mile yn lengthh'. Hedon 'hath been a fair haven town', observed Leland, 'sum places wher the shippes lay be over growen with flagges and reads . . . and the haven is very sorely decayed'. However, he concluded that the truth of the matter was that 'when Hulle began to flourish, Heddon decaied'. Some inland towns also declined in face of successful rivals; Tickhill was 'very bare' but Rotherham was 'a meately large market towne', Aberford was 'a poore thorough fare on Wateling Street' but Tadcaster was 'a good thorough fare', Boroughbridge was 'but a bare thing', Wensley 'a litle poore market' and Catterick 'a very poor towne', but Middleham was 'a praty market town', Masham 'a praty quik market town', and although Knaresborough was 'no great thing and meanely buildid' yet its market was quick. Malton too had a good market and Pontefract was 'a fair, large market towne'. (Smith, ed. 1964: vols I and IV.) But the combined population gains of the successful towns did not match the huge losses of the great cities and other declining urban centres.

Throughout the sixteenth century the English nobility retained much of the living style of their medieval ancestors. In 1521 Lord Darcy had a household of eighty people, including the sons of gentry and yeomen as well as menial servants. His contemporary, Henry Percy, fifth Earl of Northumberland celebrated Christmas and the New Year at Leconfield and Wressle in the old manner with a Lord of Misrule and visits from the boy-bishops of York and Beverley and their entourages, and entertainments that included nativity plays, minstrels and trumpeters and performing bears (Smith

1970: 85; Girouard 1978: 25). The funeral of Francis, fifth Earl of Shrewsbury, in 1560 was likewise medieval in its splendour. For five weeks his body lay in the chapel at Sheffield manor lodge before it was brought secretly to Sheffield castle for the stately procession to the parish church. The interiors of both castle and church were draped with black cloth 'garnished with scutcheons of arms', and the elaborate, four-posted hearse was adorned with banners, standards and other heraldic devices. He was buried with his ancestors in the Shrewsbury chapel on the south side of the chancel. Afterwards, 1,200 people were served with a dinner of 50 does and 29 red deer. The remains were served, with 'bread and drink in great plenty' and a dole of twopence apiece to vast numbers of the poor. Thirty years later, the funeral of George, sixth Earl of Shrewsbury, was marked by even greater pomp and ceremony (Hunter 1819: 76–8).

Northern lords continued to wield enormous power on their own estates and as representatives of the crown, but Yorkshire was too large to be dominated by the Percies or the Talbots or any other family. The crown was lord of more than half Yorkshire and the church held land throughout the county. Henry Percy, 'the magnificent' fifth Earl of Northumberland, held at least thirty-three Yorkshire manors upon his death in 1527, but during the next ten years his son, mentally incapable of responsibility, frittered away the great Percy estates in sales to meet his debts and in lavish grants to favourites. In the south of the county, however, the Talbots strengthened their hold by purchasing monastic lands and manors upon the Dissolution, and in the north-west Henry Clifford of Skipton Castle bought large estates in Craven and the major part of the Bolton Priory estate and became the first Earl of Cumberland. Medieval concepts of lordship, which stressed jurisdiction, tenure, service and obligations remained important throughout the sixteenth century, but great lords increasingly put emphasis instead on ownership, rents and profits. If they were able, they converted customary and copyhold tenures to leasehold, and especially after 1540 relied upon large entry fines to match inflation. Nevertheless, the change of attitude which stressed revenues rather than obligations developed slowly and the majority of lordships kept their basic structure intact. Numerous dependent settlements still looked to a focal township, which often had a castle and a market and which included such important centres as Pontefract, Wakefield, Richmond and Pickering.

At the beginning of Queen Elizabeth's reign six noblemen had their seats in Yorkshire and most of the county's 557 gentlemen resided upon their estates. On the eve of the civil war the number of gentry had risen to 679, of whom 195 lived in the North Riding, 142 in the East Riding, 320 in the West Riding and 22 in York. Many gentlemen were lords of manors that were dependent upon a great lordship, many earned extra income and social standing as stewards or bailiffs, and some leased demesne lands and parks. The Constables, Saviles, Fairfaxes, Gascoignes, Tempests and other gentry families were influential people in their own districts. Most were hard-headed in their response to inflation, raising their incomes by every means at their disposal. On most Yorkshire estates between 1540 and 1640 rents rose higher than the general price level. The Saviles of Thornhill raised the rents on their twelve Yorkshire manors by 400 per cent between 1619 and 1651. The struggle between landlords and tenants was often long and bitter, but examples of a more conciliatory approach can be quoted, as when Henry Tempest of Tong advised his son in 1648 to

> Oppress not thy tenants, but let them live comfortably of thy hands as thou desirest to live of their labour, that their soules may bless thee and that it may go well with thy seed after thee.
>
> (Cliffe 1969: 2–16, 39–48)

The Court of Star Chamber heard many a tale of violence involving ruthless lords and men who resorted to arms to assert or defend their rights. In 1498, for instance, two hundred people 'araid in maner of warre' had gathered on Marston Moor to pull down the pale that enclosed Miles Willesthorpe's park, and double that number 'assembled by nyght in harnes in maner of warre' to destroy more paling, to pull down a house and a water mill, to kill deer and rabbits and to dig up the rabbit warren (YASRS, XLI 1908: 166–72). Wortley park and Wharncliffe chase in south-west Yorkshire witnessed similar frenzied activity. In 1510 Sir Thomas Wortley depopulated the hamlets of Stanfield and Whitley in order to extend his chase and build a hunting lodge at the top of Wharncliffe crags, and in 1589 Sir Richard Wortley provoked further resentment by enlarging his old park and by enclosing a new park at the edge of the chase. A seventeenth-century ballad, *The Dragon of Wantley*, cast the Wortleys in the role of unprincipled aggressor.

> All sorts of cattle this Dragon did eat
> Some say he eat up trees
> And that the forest sure he would
> Devour by degrees
> For houses and churches
> Were to him geese and turkies
> He eat all, and left none behind
> But some stones, dear Jack,
> Which he couldn't crack,
> Which on the hills you will find.

The hero of the ballad was Moore of Moore Hall, who with nothing at all slew the dragon of Wantley. The occupant of Moore Hall in the 1590s was George Blount who had been amongst those who destroyed the pale of the new park and hung a deer's head with a slanderous libel in the porch of Wortley Church, and who defeated the Wortleys in a legal dispute over tithes. Gilbert

123

Dickenson, steward of the lord of Hallamshire, was the leading opponent of the Wortleys and the perpetrator of some amazing acts of vandalism. In 1593 the vicar of Ecclesfield claimed that

> there have dyvers disorders and misdemenors byn committed and donne within the said parishe of Ecclesfield in the nighte tyme as the wearyinge or killinge of this deponent's tythe Lambes there for twoe yeares together, the cuttinge awaye of the tayles of A horse and mare of his save some small parte wherein hanged dead horse heades and other bones, and saith that the said horse and mare came soe disfigured frome the said Gilbert Dicconson's howse, and further this deponent saith that there was a horse of this deponent's and a mare of one Nathaniell Smithe's in the church-yeard of Ecclesfield which said horse and mare weare in the nyghte tyme taken owte of the said churchyeard and throwen into a deepe Colepitt where they dyed. And further saith that others had their horse tayles cutt and theire fettlochs pared and shorne in the nighte tyme, and others theire flax mowen downe in the nighte beeinge but half ripe, and theire geese necks writhen and killed and laid together beefore theire dores, and others had theire sheepe barrs cutt in peeces in the nighte, and annother had his ram or tupp taken owte of his sheepe fowld and killed in the nighte tyme and the head and genitalls cutt of and sett uppon a maypole with a lewd and fylthy libell fixed to the same and that others have had theire plowes and yokes cutt in peeces, and the peeces hanged on tree toppes, others had theire stone walles overthrowen and others theire dogges and swyne killed.

Yet in 1605 Dickenson received a free pardon for his criminal activities. It is significant that his atrocities were directed against a tithe-owner and the Wortleys, and no doubt he claimed that he was meting out rough justice. It is against this sort of background that the Tudor achievement of strong central government should be seen (Hey 1975: 109–18).

Dissolution and Reformation

During a brief five-year period between 1536 and 1540 all the 650 monasteries in England and Wales were closed by order of the crown and their possessions were confiscated by the Royal Exchequer. About a third of these establishments have gone so completely that they have left no trace above ground, and the physical remains of another third are insubstantial. In Yorkshire 28 abbeys, 26 priories, 23 nunneries, 30 friaries and 13 cells were dissolved, a total of 120 institutions of all kinds. Some had been in existence since the early years of the Norman occupation, and most had begun life by the twelfth century. Yet Henry VIII was able to destroy them almost without a struggle. More than any other event, the demise of the monasteries marks the end of the period we know as the Middle Ages.

By the beginning of the sixteenth century England's monastic population had declined to about 10,000 monks and 2,000 nuns. Much of the old fervour had gone, and insufficient people were prepared to take the vows. Of course, standards varied from monastery to monastery, but few laymen regarded them with the same admiration as did their forebears; those seeking to make a religious endowment turned instead to their local parish church. A royal valuation of ecclesiastical property in 1536 revealed a great gap between a few rich establishments and the rest, for only 4 per cent had incomes of over £1,000 per annum whereas nearly 80 per cent had to be content with less than £300 a year. At St Mary's (York), Fountains, Selby and Guisborough, Yorkshire had some of the richest abbeys in England, and the heads of Selby, St Mary's and Whitby had the status of mitred abbots, ranking with a bishop; on at least two occasions they were joined in the House of Lords by the prior of Bridlington. Throughout the kingdom monks were prominent not only in spiritual affairs but as landlords, farmers, industrialists, tithe-owners and builders. Nowhere in Yorkshire was their presence so apparent as in the city of York and its suburbs, where the Minster and its dependent buildings and forty parish churches were complemented by four monasteries, a nunnery, four friaries and numerous hospitals, maisons dieu and chapels. In the county capital the impact of the Reformation was particularly sharp.

Henry's government did not start with the clear intention of destroying all the monasteries. They began cautiously by dissolving those institutions (except the Gilbertines) which had fewer than a dozen monks or nuns and an annual endowment of less than £200. Many of Yorkshire's smaller institutions escaped the first round of pillage because the county's greater monasteries had insufficient accommodation for those who would have been displaced. Nevertheless, the suppressions acted as a catalyst in turning widespread resentment at a remote central government into a spectacular rebellion known as the Pilgrimage of Grace. At first the revolt was a rising of common people whose varied grievances included high prices, the selfish policies of certain landlords, and a feeling that Henry's government was not concerned with their plight. Wild rumours insisted that Cromwell and Cranmer intended to dissolve parish churches and that prayer, fasting and charitable works would be forbidden. The plight of the smaller monasteries inflamed the situation. By October 1536 the rebellion had spread from its source in Lincolnshire into the East Riding, then it rapidly gained support in other parts of the county.

The rebels forced their local gentry to swear allegiance and to lead them into battle. Their commander was Robert Aske, a lawyer from Aughton in the Derwent flood plain, where his ancestors had lived in a motte-and-bailey castle and a moated manor house and had been buried nearby in All Saints Church.

Aske had written a defence of 'the abbeys in the north parts', praising their hospitality and alms, their masses for the souls of the dead, the places they provided for the younger children of gentlemen, and their contribution to the maintenance of roads, bridges and fen dykes, concluding that they were 'one of the beauties of this realm to all men and strangers passing through'. Aske's rebels were well received in York, for the citizens were hostile to monastic suppression and supported his restoration of the dissolved houses of St Clement's, Holy Trinity and nearby Healaugh. The rebels stayed in York for two months and held a great council before marching south to Pontefract, where Lord Darcy readily surrendered the castle. After Hull had been captured by another force, both armies advanced on Doncaster. Few of Yorkshire's leading families remained loyal to the King, but George Talbot, fourth Earl of Shrewsbury and lord of Hallamshire barred the way. On or about 9 December 1536 the Duke of Norfolk, on the King's behalf, met the rebel leaders on Doncaster bridge. Aske was promised that a Parliament would be held in York to discuss his grievances and that a free pardon would be granted to all who disarmed. Thereupon the rebels tore off the badges that symbolized the Five Wounds of the Crucified Christ and returned to their homes. Within a few months over two hundred of them were executed.

A fresh revolt gave Henry an excuse to break the Duke's promises. On 16 January 1537 Sir Francis Bigod of Settrington raised a muster in Buckrose wapentake and proposed to march on Hull and Scarborough in the false expectation that the Percies would also rise. This new twist to the story reveals the complex and contradictory nature of the rebels' motives. During the previous two years Bigod had been a member of the Cromwellian circle of advanced Protestant thinkers in London, and he saw the Pilgrimage of Grace as an opportunity to advance his plans for reform. He had written a book attacking the way that churches had been appropriated by monasteries, who then received the great tithes but gave poor value in return. In his native Yorkshire 392 of the 622 parish churches (that is 63 per cent) had been appropriated, and over a hundred of these churches were served merely by curates. Bigod's efforts were to no avail; on 10 February he was captured in Cumberland and on 2 June he was executed at Tyburn (Dickens 1959: 74–5, 90–102). Many of those implicated in the earlier revolt were also killed. Aske was hanged from the top of York Castle after being dragged through the streets on a hurdle, and Sir Robert Constable received similar treatment at Hull; he was 'so trimmed with chains', wrote the Duke of Norfolk, 'that I think his bones will hang there this hundred years'. Amongst the other prominent men who were executed were Lord Darcy, Sir Thomas Percy, and the abbots and priors of Fountains, Rievaulx, Jervaulx, Guisborough, Bridlington and Doncaster. 'Adam Sedber Abbas Jorvall 1537' is scratched on a wall in the Tower of London, a mournful reminder of those troubled times. Sedber was particularly unfortunate, for when the rebels arrived at Jervaulx to demand that he should lead them he fled to Witton Fell and then sought shelter with

Lord Scrope at Barnard Castle, but one of his monks sought to save his own skin by implicating his abbot in the plot. Jervaulx Abbey was dissolved in 1537 and the monks were ejected without pensions.

The following year the attack on the greater monasteries began. Henry's pressing need for yet more money to finance his wars encouraged him to turn a greedy eye on monastic estates and treasures. The commissioners who were sent to induce surrenders with offers of fair pensions met with only feeble opposition, for the punishment meted out to the 1536–37 rebels was fresh in memory. At Kirkstall Abbey the lead roofs were stripped and the bells recast as cannon. At Roche choir stalls were burned to melt the lead, freestone was carted away and timber sold to local families; according to Michael Sherbrook, rector of Wickersley,

> All things of price [were] either spoiled, carped away, or defaced to the
> uttermost . . . it seemeth that every person bent himself to filch and spoil
> what he could . . . nothing was spared but the oxhouses and
> swinecoates and such other houses of office, that stood without the
> walls.
> (YASRS, CXXV 1959: 123–4).

On 26 November 1539 the abbot and 31 monks at Fountains were removed and their 1,976 horned cattle, 1,146 sheep, 86 horses, 79 swine and 221 quarters of grain were sold to Sir Richard Gresham. Here, as elsewhere, a gentleman's residence eventually replaced the monastery, and outlying granges were converted into farmhouses and halls. King Henry quickly sold the estates he had confiscated to noblemen, gentlemen, courtiers, lawyers and merchants, and many a family that did not scruple to invest in the spoils was able to increase its property substantially. A few monastic churches, including such well-known examples as Bolton, Malton and Selby, were retained as parish churches, but most were despoiled and the monks were rarely heard of again. The Monk Bretton group who bought 148 books when their library was auctioned and who joined forces for at least twenty years in a house at Worsbrough were unusual survivors. The friars fared even worse, for when they were driven out in 1538 they received no pensions.

Cathedral clergy were much more fortunate and most managed to weather the storm. York Minster, however, lost a great deal of its treasure and the archbishop was compelled to exchange properties with the crown on unfavourable terms. In 1541 the archdeaconry of Richmond was taken from the diocese of York to help form the new bishopric of Chester, as part of a national reorganization involving the creation of other sees at Bristol, Oxford and Peterborough. The religious life of the city of York was altered even more drastically during the reign of Edward VI, when about a hundred chantries and nearly all the religious guilds were dissolved, the colleges of St William and St Sepulchre suppressed, and thirteen of the smaller parish churches were closed by the corporation. All over the country services were reformed and the

physical appearance of churches was altered radically in conformity with orders issued by the Privy Council. In 1548 certain ceremonies were denounced as superstitious and images were removed, and in 1550 altars were replaced by communion tables. Yorkshire congregations obeyed the government's orders promptly. In York a churchwarden's account of 1547 records that twopence was paid to a labourer who removed dirt from the church and churchyard of St Michael's, Spurriergate at the time 'the seyntts was takyn down', and at Rotherham written copies of the Edwardian service books were provided until printed copies were available. Robert Parkyn, the curate of Adwick le Street, disliked the changes immensely, but the narrative of events that he wrote in the safety of Mary's reign gives no hint of any resistance. 'Even the most traditionally minded priests were in a cowed and obedient frame of mind' (Dickens 1959: 180–3).

On the eve of the Reformation the West Riding had nearly 900 clergymen, but by the end of Henry VIII's reign their number had been reduced to 500 or 550 and at the time of Mary's accession only 250 were left (Smith 1970: 88, 92). Such were the effects of the dissolution of chantries, colleges and hospitals. At Pontefract, early in Queen Mary's reign, a townsman claimed that they had once had 'one abbey, two colleges, a house of friars preachers, one ancress, one hermit, four chantry priests, one guild priest' but now they had left 'an unlearned vicar, which hireth two priests, for indeed he is not able to discharge the cure other ways, and I dare say the vicar's living is under forty marks'. The parish priests of Henrician England have been described as men of simple faith, low incomes, inelastic minds and limited educational opportunities (Dickens 1959: 138). The reformers came not from the ranks of the priests but from above. The prime mover in the North was Robert Holgate, who was appointed archbishop in 1545 and was removed by Queen Mary nine years later; for a time he was also president of the Council of the North. A former monk and theologian, he was an able administrator and the founder of schools in York, Malton, Barnsley and his native Hemsworth (where he also endowed a hospital). Professor Dickens has characterized the population at large as practising a mundane utilitarianism and reacting to the Reformation with extreme caution and subservience. The Lollard ideals that survived were diffused thinly, but were revived by contact with continental Protestantism.

Plate 3.1 St William's College, York. The college was founded in the 1460s with the generous support of George Neville (later Archbishop of York) and his brother, the Earl of Warwick, on a site close to the east end of the minster, in order to house the chantry priests of the minster. The building is arranged in a quadrangle around a narrow, rectangular courtyard. It incorporated a chapel, a library and chambers for the priests. The ground floor is constructed of Magnesian Limestone obtained from the Huddleston quarries and the jettied first floor is timber-framed. St William's was by far the largest college for chantry priests in England's cathedral cities. At the Dissolution in 1547 it housed 28 priests and a provost.

It has been altered considerably since the Dissolution. Seventeenth-century work can be seen in the courtyard and the façade has eighteenth-century bow windows and dormers and a recent Gothic doorway. The building has been well restored in modern times.

The inhabitants of York were conventionally pious during the reign of Henry VIII, judging by the phrasing of their wills, and this conservatism was also marked under Edward VI (Palliser 1979: 249–53). In the rest of Yorkshire, however, Edwardian wills often omit any mention of the Virgin and the saints; 139 were traditional in form, but 153 were in the new style and 31 were neutral, while some that retained the saints no longer honoured the Virgin (Dickens 1959: 171–2, 207).

News of Mary's accession reached York on 21 July 1553 and the following day was received at Pontefract, Doncaster, Rotherham and other market towns. 'Wheratt', wrote Robert Parkyn, 'tholle comonalltie in all places in the northe parttes grettlie reiocide, makynge grett fyers, drynkinge wyne and aylle, prayssing God.' This good will did not last long, but the progress of the Reformation was halted for five years or so. Thirty-two heretics had been prosecuted at York during the reign of Henry VIII and 45 were tried under Mary. Protestant beliefs were not yet accepted widely, and the Elizabethan religious settlement of 1559 had a quiet reception in Yorkshire. In the county capital the corporation obeyed the injunctions slowly and reluctantly and a considerable minority continued to use Catholic forms in their wills throughout the 1560s (Palliser 1979: 243–53). Further than that they were not prepared to go. Only in Richmondshire and parts of the northern Vale of York was there fervent and widespread allegiance to the Catholic faith. Neither the Wakefield plot of 1541 nor the Seamer rising of 1549 was of more than local importance. The response to a call to arms did not worry the government unduly until the revolt of 1569–70 known as the rising of the northern earls broke out in Durham and north Yorkshire.

The rebellion was led by the Earls of Northumberland (Percy), Westmorland (Neville) and Cumberland (Clifford), the heads of the old feudal families who had long held sway in the North and who resented the extension of Tudor power in their domains. But although their revolt was overtly Catholic it failed to spark the popular response of the Pilgrimage of Grace. The earls had to pay or threaten their tenants to join them, for as Sir George Bowes, who loyally defended Barnard Castle for Elizabeth, drily observed, 'Yorkshire never goeth to war but for wages.' On 14 November 1569 the rebels occupied Durham, and for several weeks mass was celebrated amongst large congregations. Service books, English bibles and communion tables were burnt as the rebels moved south to Ripon, but their reception was lukewarm and they did not have the military strength to take York. Lacking any real sense of purpose, on 24 November they turned back to Durham. Neville eventually fled to Flanders and Percy to Scotland, but in 1572 Percy was sold to Elizabeth for £2,000, beheaded in York Pavement and his head displayed on Micklegate Bar. The last of the Percy revolts was over. The failure of the northern rebellions marked the end of the Middle Ages as surely as did the Dissolution of the monasteries and the events of the Reformation. Elizabeth was now determined to rule the North with a firmer hand and to place trusted supporters in positions of power;

on 22 May 1570 she appointed Edmund Grindall Archbishop of York and in August 1572 Henry, Earl of Huntingdon was made Lord President of the Council of the North. There can be little doubt that strong Tudor government was infinitely preferable to a semi-independence marked by feuds and lawlessness. Yorkshire's prosperity, like that of the nation as a whole, showed a marked improvement from the middle years of Elizabeth's reign onwards.

Recovery and Growth

During Queen Elizabeth's reign England recovered from its long decline and its population reached a level that had not been achieved since 1300. The beginnings of this recovery cannot be dated precisely, but the earliest parish registers show a consistent surplus of baptisms over burials by the late 1530s. This renewed growth was particularly vigorous in the western parts of Yorkshire where marginal land was being brought back into cultivation. In the Forest of Knaresborough the number of cottages on the commons was causing concern by the 1520s and particularly after 1550 (Jennings, ed. 1967: 121). In Swaledale the population rose 190 per cent from about 900 in 1377 to 2,600 in 1563, and in urban Richmond numbers increased from about 620 to 1,615 (Fieldhouse and Jennings 1978: 103). Elsewhere in Yorkshire this early growth was not as dramatic but was nevertheless significant; it has been estimated that the total population of the West Riding rose from about 75,000 in 1377 to about 100,000 early in Elizabeth's reign (Smith 1970: 2). A recent study has suggested that the period 1541–1640 was a time of moderately fast growth throughout western Europe, with England's population almost doubling from about $2\frac{3}{4}$ millions to about 5 millions (Wrigley and Schofield 1981: 160–2). This time the country was able to support such an increase without precipitating a Malthusian crisis. New industries created employment and wealth, and improved farming practices and imported corn provided sufficient food in all but the most desperate years. The Elizabethans solved the problem of how to make the relationship between population growth and economic growth a positive one.

Population growth was severely checked in the 1550s. In August 1551 43 of the 49 people buried at Halifax were said to have died of the 'sweating sickness', a variant of influenza. In 1555 and 1556 heavy, persistent rains ruined harvests and caused famines throughout northern and western Europe. The next two years saw the worst epidemics of the sixteenth century, with influenza killing 8 or 9 per cent of England's population, including 20 per cent of adults. In the West Riding woollen district burials exceeded baptisms in both 1557 and 1558, and 'plague time' is written as a marginal comment in the

Kirkburton register against the months of July, August and September 1558. Influenza was the greatest killer in the countryside, but bubonic plague was endemic in towns. York suffered from both plague and 'sweat' in 1550–52 and from the 'new ague' in 1558–59, which together reduced York's 8,000 population by a third or more to unprecedented low levels. However, York subsequently enjoyed 45 years' immunity from further attack, so that in 1589 a local gentleman could say that the city rarely suffered 'any pestylence or other infectinge sycknes' (Palliser 1979: 123–5). Doncaster, Richmond and Guisborough were amongst other Yorkshire towns that succumbed to virulent plagues. Between September 1582 and December 1583 the Doncaster burial register contains 747 entries with the letter P against them to denote plague, and milder attacks are recorded up to 1645. At Richmond plague carried off two-thirds of the inhabitants between August 1597 and December 1598; no less than 1,050 deaths by 'pestilence' are recorded in the register, but others were buried in unconsecrated ground in Castle Yard and Clarke's Green. According to an inscription in Penrith Church a total of 2,200 people died in the deanery of Richmond (Fieldhouse and Jennings 1978: 104–6).

Recovery was soon marked by high marriage- and birth-rates, but plague returned from time to time and did not disappear until 1645. Plague was still endemic in the county during the first half of the seventeenth century. York's immunity ended in 1604 when a terrible outbreak killed 3,512 people, that is, 30 per cent of the inhabitants. This was the city's last major visitation, but in 1631 plague was active at Bingley, Halifax and Heptonstall, and also at Mirfield where 139 people died that year, compared with an average of only 19 during the previous five years. In 1641, when the West Riding JPs received reports on the 'heavie visitacon of the plague' at Dewsbury and in the townships of Hipperholme cum Brighouse, Shelf and Clifton, they voted to assist them with a county rate. At Dewsbury trade and commerce were 'much decayed' and the numbers of poor on weekly relief had risen to over 270. Yorkshire was soon to be free of plague, however, and did not suffer in 1665 when stringent measures prohibited trade with London until the capital was clear of disease (Palliser 1979: 125; Drake 1962).

The battle against famine was fought with equal success, but with serious reversals in the 1580s and 1590s. The harvests of 1586 and 1587 were disastrous and mortality levels rose all over England. A poor man was 'found deade ... by famishment' in the fields outside York, and William Cecil was told that many people in the West Riding had 'peryshid this year by famyn' (Palliser 1983: 49). Burial levels were very high in the woollen districts in 1587 and 1588, and in Richmond 152 people died in 1587 and 113 the following year, compared with an average of only 39 in the previous six years and 62 in the following six (Fieldhouse and Jennings 1978: 104). The 1590s brought further hardship. In 1592 the number of burials at Hatfield was abnormally high and at Sheffield reached a record 178, but then in 1597 253 Sheffielders died. The four harvests between 1594 and 1597 were the worst consecutive series in the sixteenth century. Poor harvests in the Dales lowered resistance to the onslaught of plague in Richmondshire in 1597 and 1598; elsewhere in the county some people died of hunger. Famine deaths were recorded as late as 1623, but Yorkshire did not suffer as badly as Cumbria, Northumberland and upland Lancashire. High food prices in 1622–23 coincided with acute depression in the woollen industry and high mortality rates in Leeds and Halifax. The woollen districts also suffered badly in 1643 and 1645 (Drake 1962) but by the middle of the seventeenth century widespread starvation was a thing of the past.

England's economic recovery is evident in the revival of its export trade. By the middle of the sixteenth century the port of Hull was becoming more involved in commerce with the Low Countries and the Baltic, particularly in the products of the West Riding woollen industry. The number of cheap northern kerseys going from Hull to the Baltic rose six-fold between 1565 and 1585 and doubled or trebled again to a peak in the mid 1590s. The Baltic trade was to become all-important; between 1567 and 1687 the number of ships entering Hull from the Baltic and Norway increased five-fold (and the individual ships became much larger), but the number from the Low Countries, Germany and France remained the same. The ships that exported the kerseys returned laden with flax for the linen weavers and corn to supplement the region's own supplies; flax and corn accounted for at least 75 per cent of Hull's imports until far into the seventeenth century. Thus the port thrived as an exporter and supplier of cheap, bulky goods for a large hinterland reached by the Ouse and Trent river systems. The less-spectacular coastal trade was also important in the revival of the national economy. Every year some 50 or 60 small coasters came to Hull with foodstuffs and miscellaneous goods and coals from Newcastle, and took on board lead for London. The capital acted as the distribution centre for Yorkshire and Derbyshire lead until well after 1600, but then Hull merchants began to supply east coast ports and the Continent directly (Davis 1964: 6–13).

York's fortunes began to recover early in Elizabeth's reign. Though the city had lost for ever its pre-eminence in the manufacture of woollen cloth, by the 1580s its merchants and tradesmen were prospering. They benefited from the general revival of trade throughout western Europe and played an active role in both the home and overseas markets. Such was the extent of recovery that by the end of Elizabeth's reign York's population had risen to 11,500, making it England's third largest provincial city. London was in a league of its own with about 200,000 inhabitants, Norwich had about 15,000 and Bristol 12,000; next to York came Newcastle and Exeter with 9,000 people each. Youthful immigrants, particularly from Cumbria and the Pennines, swelled the ranks of Yorkers. Not all of them found employment, but the presence of numerous poor created little serious disorder. York's government was an open oligarchy, whose form and style remained essentially unchanged from the fourteenth to the nineteenth century. The tradesmen, craftsmen and shopkeepers who comprised the city's freemen numbered about 1,250 in the 1530s and 1540s, that is at least half the adult male population. The pewterers, silversmiths and builders were famous for miles around, and before the Reformation so were the makers of bells, stained glass, stalls and rood-screens. York was a centre of ecclesiastical and secular government and a social and commercial capital for a wide area. The freemen were deferential to the nobility and gentry who resided in their town houses for part of the year and to the wealthy and influential professional people who mostly lived and worked in the liberties outside the city's jurisdiction in and around the minster, the castle and the king's manor (Palliser 1979: 146–8, 268–71, 285–91).

York was not only the county town but the largest commercial centre in Yorkshire. The Tuesday, Thursday and Saturday markets were a magnet for local villagers, and the annual fairs attracted buyers and sellers from places many miles distant. General markets were held in the 'two faire marketsteads'

Figure 3.1 Elizabethan and Stuart York

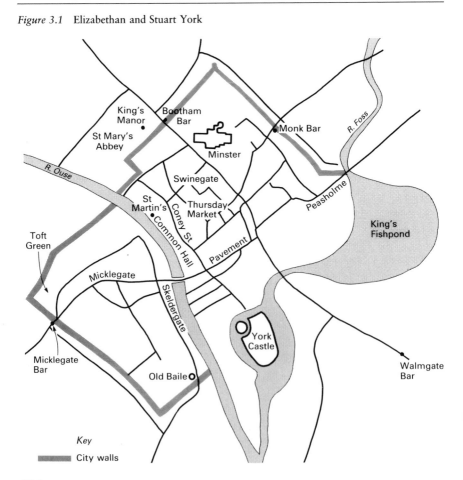

of Pavement and the Thursday Market, a malt market was held outside St Martin's Coney Street, and the stalls of the leather market were erected in the Common Hall. Fish markets were held on the two bridges, swine markets in Swinegate and Peasholme and the weekly beast market on Toft Green. In 1546 a new cloth market was opened in the Common Hall and from 1590 a horse and cattle fair was held each fortnight from Lent to Advent. Corn was bought for resale from the three surrounding wapentakes and malt from as far as Pocklington and Barnby Dun (where no doubt it had come up river from Lincolnshire). Purchasers included badgers who had travelled from Skipton and other places 30 or 40 miles to the west. Since the thirteenth century the city's two major fairs had been held in the Horsefair at Whitsuntide and the feast of St Peter and St Paul (29th June), but from 1586–87 the Whitsun fair expanded into the Thursday Market as well. The older and more important Lammas fair of the Archbishop of York lasted the two days of 31 July and 1 August. Yorkers also attended many other markets and fairs, for a charter of Richard I made them free of tolls throughout England. Thus, by the 1560s York goldsmiths and drapers were travelling to the great Stourbridge fair in Cambridgeshire and by the end of the century regular business meetings were arranged between York and London merchants at Howden fair. In Elizabethan times York was linked to the capital by a regular carrier service. River traffic remained more important than land carriage, however. Baltic iron, pitch, tar, linen, boards, wainscotting, salt, grain, oil, wine, fish and eels came via Hull as far as the Ouse bridge and some cargoes were taken further upstream towards Ripon or Bedale. York was a major distribution centre, and boats returned downstream carrying Richmondshire and Craven lead which had been weighed at the common crane in Skeldergate (Palliser 1979: 180–93).

Derbyshire lead and millstones, together with south Yorkshire metalware, were carried over land to Bawtry on the small river Idle, then taken by catches and keels to Stockwith on the Trent. Foodstuffs, Spanish steel and London hides were brought the other way. Bawtry seemed bare and poor to Leland, and the town had apparently lost its small borough status, but it began to thrive again with the recovery of trade in the Elizabethan era. The townsmen claimed free and common passage for their vessels from the burgess staith by the churchyard wall, but they had to struggle determinedly to resist the monopolistic claims of the Talbot family. George, the sixth Earl of Shrewsbury, the largest lead smelter in the country, took a lease of Bawtry manor from the crown and by 1585 was exporting over 100 tons of lead per annum from his own wharf or staith. The Shrewsburys tried to make everyone weigh lead at their weighbeam and pay for storage and passage, and law suits dragged on for over half a century. Yeomen from the parishes of Sheffield and Chesterfield testified to having traded without restraint for 35 years or more, but judgment was eventually given in favour of the lords. In 1633 Sir John Lister, a wealthy Hull merchant, purchased the manor and presided over a new period of prosperity. In 1640, for instance, Stephen and John Bright of Sheffield shipped

1,969 pigs of lead from Bawtry, and the following year 2,416 pigs. They dealt not only with Hull merchants, but directly with Amsterdam (Hey 1980: 108–11).

Market towns throughout the country began to flourish again as trade revived. Doncaster, sited a few miles along the Great North road from Bawtry, is one of Yorkshire's best examples of a regional market centre, river port and thoroughfare town. A charter of 1532 confirmed its ancient right to hold

Figure 3.2   Doncaster in the seventeenth century

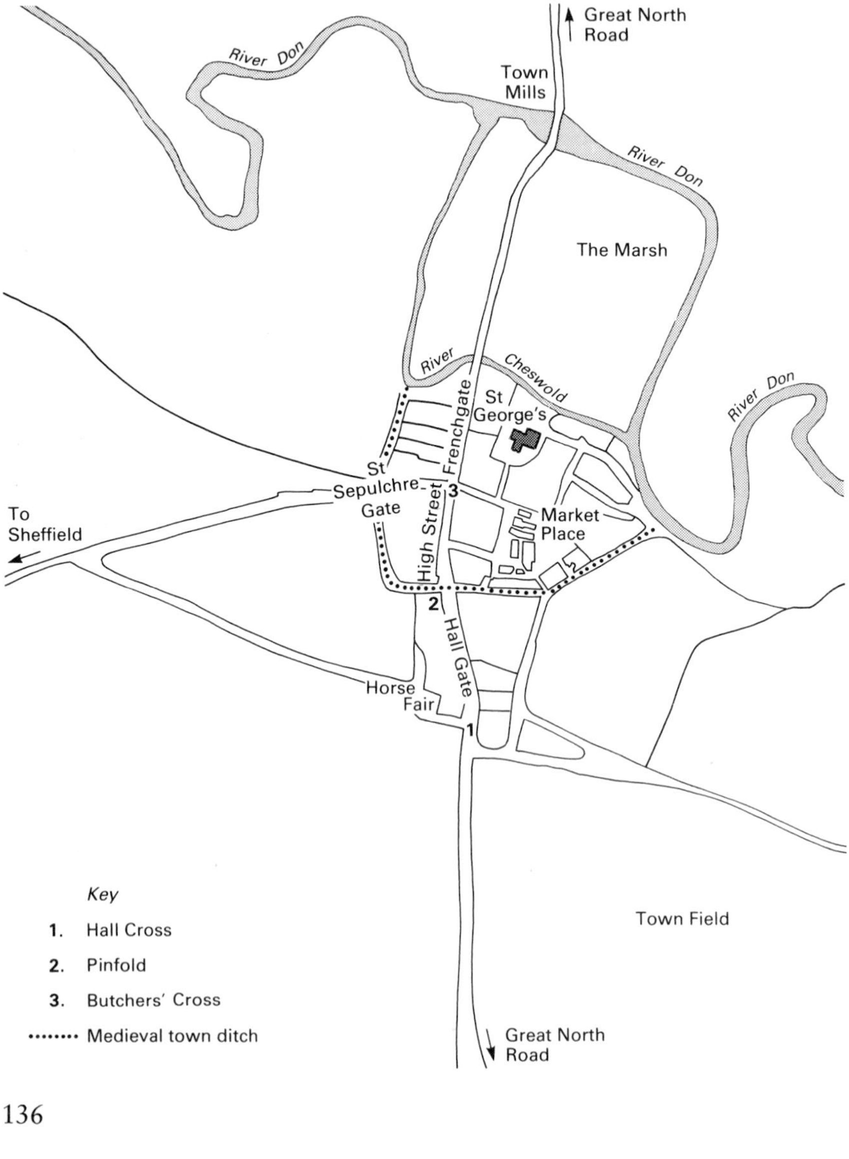

Key

1. Hall Cross
2. Pinfold
3. Butchers' Cross
••••••• Medieval town ditch

weekly markets on Tuesdays and Saturdays and two annual fairs. By James I's reign trading could no longer be confined to the medieval market place, and in 1605 the corporation agreed

> that the horse fair be held in Hallgate from the Pynfould to the Hall Crosse; that the beast fair be held in the market place; the sheep fair between the Butchers Cross and the Pynfould in Hallgate; and the swine fair in Sepulchre Gate within the bars.

In 1612 the horse fair was removed to Waterdale at the south-western limit of the town. At the heart of the old market-place was the former church of St Mary Magdalene, reduced in status to a chantry chapel and at the Dissolution converted into a town hall and grammar school. In 1615 fifteen drapers' stalls stood in Magdalen churchyard, just as their predecessors had done in 1333; here too were fish shops and stalls, a wool shop, and narrow streets such as Meal Lane and Roper Row, with shoemakers' stalls all around. The corn and beast markets and the shambles of the butchers and fishmongers attracted customers from both near and far, and the wool market grew into one of the largest in the kingdom. Sometimes as many as 6,000 fleeces were sold each Saturday during the summer. Doncaster had guilds of weavers, walkers and shearmen and of linen drapers, dyers and upholsterers, and a growing number of knitters, but most of the wool went elsewhere, principally to the West Riding clothiers. For much of the year Doncaster market could be reached by river as well as by road, and many people made a good living as middlemen or inn-keepers. Part-time employment could also bring in extra cash; when the corporation counted the number of alehouses in 1631 they found no less than 135 (Hey 1980: 170, 208).

By the 1590s both Doncaster and Richmond were noted as new centres of a stocking-knitting industry. An obscure country craft supplying local needs had been transformed into an enterprise that served London and many other parts of the kingdom. Men and women knitted coarse, thick stockings and a range of goods that was amended from time to time to meet the dictates of fashion. Their craft was just one of a host of projects inspired by the 'Commonwealth men' at the centre of government, whose aim was to make England much less dependent upon foreign exports. New crafts were introduced into places with little or no previous expertise, and established industries were changed by new techniques and ideas that were often brought in from abroad. One of the more unusual projects in Yorkshire was the opening in 1611 of alum works on the cliffs of the North Sea coast at Mulgrave, Asholme and Sandsend; within half a century alum was sold not only to English dyers and tanners but to the continent of Europe, the East Indies and the Plantations (Thirsk 1978: 37). Another successful project was pin-making; Leland found 'many pinners' at Sherburn in the 1540s, and a century later Richard Brathwait's *Barnabees Journal* reads, 'Thence to

Plate 3.2 The Wensleydale Knitters. Stocking knitting was one of the most successful projects of the Elizabethan Age. By the 1590s Richmond, Barnard Castle, Askrigg and Doncaster were recognized centres of the craft. When George Walker produced his *Costume of Yorkshire* in 1814 families in the Dales still used every spare moment to earn extra income by knitting. He wrote:

> Simplicity and industry characterize the manners and occupations of the various humble inhabitants of Wensley Dale. Their wants, it is true, are few; but to supply these, almost constant labour is required. In any business where the assistance of the hands is not necessary, they universally resort to knitting. Young and old, male and female, are all adepts in this art. Shepherds attending their flocks, men driving cattle, women going to market, are all thus industriously and doubly employed.

Sherburne, dearley loved/And for Pinners well approved.' Barnabee proceeded to Aberford 'whose beginning came from buying drink with pinning', but he observed, 'Poor they are, and very needy/Yet of liquor too too greedy.'

Urban crafts became more specialized and sophisticated over a wider range of items, and in those parts of the countryside that were geared to pastoral farming the government's policy was particularly successful. Rural crafts tended to be simple and to require little capital; they could be profitably combined with the running of a smallholding. As the rising population aspired to improved domestic and personal comfort, the demand for consumer goods became greater than ever before. Before the 1550s houses were furnished meanly with tables, benches, stools and beds, and the minimum essential cooking pots, plates and mugs. By the middle of the seventeenth century houses contained more rooms and a greater range of furniture, cooking pots made of iron, copper or brass were far more common and drinking vessels came in a

138

variety of qualities of pewter; food was more plentiful and varied, and people dressed better and more individually. A consumer revolution had taken place, a revolution that stimulated urban and rural crafts throughout the country. One of the areas to benefit most from growing demand both at home and abroad was the West Riding of Yorkshire.

Leeds set the pace for Yorkshire's towns. More than 3,000 people lived in the parish in the middle sixteenth century and twice as many in the reign of James I, mainly in the central urban township. In 1626 the whole of the parish was placed under the jurisdiction of a new corporation. Two years later a survey reported that

> Leedes is an Ancient Markett Towne . . . It standeth pleasantlie in a fruitefull and enclosed vale; upon the North side of the . . . River Eyre, over or beyond a stone bridge, from whence it hath a large and broad streete (paved with stone) leadinge directlie North and continuallie ascendinge. The houses on both sides thereof are verie thicke, and close compacted together, beinge ancient meane and lowe built; and generallie all of Tymber; though they have stone quarries frequent in the Towne, and about it; only some fewe of the richer sort of the Inhabitants have theire houses more large and capacious: yett all lowe and straightened on theire backsides. In the middle of the streete (towards the upper end wheare the Markett place standeth) is built the Court or Moote House (as they terme it) and from thence upward are the shambles, with a narrow streete on both sides, much annoyinge the whole Towne; yett for their Conveniencie, and wante of roome, not to be avoided, or placed elsewhere . . . This Mannor is all enclosed and lieth in verie small parcels as some halfe an acre, some 2 acres some more, manie lesse havinge houses scattered frequentlie and throughout the whole Lordshipp, by reason of theire great Clothinge on which trade the whole Towne, cheefely, and in a maner wholie dependeth.
>
> (Beresford 1975)

Leeds flourished as a market town and as the place where broad cloths were expertly finished by dressers, croppers and dyers.

Farming and Industry

The great variety of landscape and therefore of farming practices within Yorkshire – a wider range than in any other county in England – was commented upon by the famous Elizabethan antiquary, William Camden:

If in one place the soil be of a stony, sandy, barren nature, yet in another it is pregnant and fruitful; and so if it be naked and exposed in one part, we find it clothed and sheltered with great store of wood in another; Nature using an allay and mixture, that the entire county, by this variety of parts, might seem more pleasing and beautiful.

(Gibson, ed. 1695: col. 705)

A generation earlier, John Leland had made detailed notes upon his travels through England and Wales late in the reign of Henry VIII (Smith, ed. 1964: vols I and IV). He entered Yorkshire at Bawtry and approached Doncaster 'by a great plaine and sandy ground' and found 'very good meadow, corne and sum wood', but upon making a diversion across a great mere a mile or so wide and 'fulle of good fisch and foule' he came to Thorne, where the land was either plain, moor or fen. After returning to Doncaster he headed for Pontefract, through countryside that was 'in sum places meately woodid and enclosid ground: in al places reasonably fruteful of pasture and corne'. Within a day's journey a traveller in Yorkshire could ride through very different types of countryside. Between York and Leconfield the land was 'meately fruteful of corn and grasse, but it hath little wood'; however, a few miles further on large woods separated Beverley from Cottingham, and beyond lay 'low ground very fruteful of meadow and pasture'. Five of the six miles from Hull to Beverley consisted of 'low pasture and marsch ground' and the other mile of 'enclosid and sumwhat woddy ground'. Around Walkington Leland found 'fair champain corn ground' and between North Cave and Scalby 'low marsch and medow ground'. Walling Fen was reputedly sixteen miles in compass with many settlements in and alongside it.

During the sixteenth and seventeenth centuries most Holderness townships continued to farm their land in two enormous common fields that stretched for hundreds of acres over the boulder clays. When Brandesburton was enclosed by agreement in 1630 East Field covered 1,174 acres and West Field 1,321 acres, and it was said that 'one of the said fields used to be sowed one year and the other field another year'. At Hornsea 'all that peece of areable ground called or knowne by the name of short Goodmandale lying together in the Eastfeild . . . consistinge of 47 ridges and one baulke' was typical of the many furlongs that were ploughed in ridges and furrows. If the clay lands were drained properly good crops of wheat and barley could be grown for sale in the East Riding market towns or for export from Hull or Bridlington, and beans and peas were used for fodder. Livestock grazed in the pastures and the carrs and meadows that lay alongside meandering streams, and Holderness prospered as a corn-and-cattle district. Poor prices for corn tilted the balance towards pasture, however, and in some townships the farmers agreed to enclose their lands and to abandon the old communal methods of farming. An early example is provided by Skerne in 1596, and a later one by Patrington, where in 1650 Sir Robert Hildyard's enclosed pastures formed 131 acres in the

South field, an equally large block in the West field, 50 acres in the North field and 35 acres in Hall Marsh; these four closes 'being distinguished by their respective mounds . . . are laid together and now used as cow pasture by the inhabitants' (Thirsk, ed. 1985: 76).

Patrington also had large meadows and saltmarsh pastures and the farmers of this small market town appear to have opted decisively for livestock. At Hornsea, another coastal community with a weekly market and two annual fairs, the sea was still eroding precious land; a jury of 1609 found 'decayed by the flowing of the sea, in Hornsea Beck, since 1546, 38 houses, and as many closes adjoining', together with a stretch of common field, one mile long and 240 yards broad (Sheppard 1912: 168). Here arable farming remained important but many of the strips had been converted to grass leys to meet the increased demand for pasture. The communal system of farming was flexible enough to allow some changes, but in most villages the annual round went on much as before. Contemporary technology could not provide an effective answer to drainage problems, which were particularly severe in the Hull valley; Flaxfleet and South Cave were said in 1657 to be 'very improveable . . . much of the ground is over run with rushes . . . other meadows are overrun with sedge and coarse grass for want of scouring the drains'. Improvement still lay a long way ahead.

On the Wolds huge common fields sometimes covered all, or nearly all, of the available territory. In some places the steep slopes of dry valleys had been ploughed and escarpments brought into cultivation by flights of lynchets. The neighbouring townships of Fimber, Fridaythorpe and Wetwang were devoted almost entirely to arable farming and the deserted medieval village of Holme Archiepiscopi had been absorbed into the Wetwang common fields. At Flamborough the arable was divided into four fields and by 1570 the 'ancient custom' was for only one of them to lie fallow (Allison 1976: 115–26). Even some of the thin soils on the bleak High Wolds were farmed as outfields; in 1611 the infield below the chalk scarp at Bishop Wilton supported a two- or three-year rotation and was valued at 10d per acre, but the outfield high above was 'never sowne above once in tenn or twelve yeres' and was worth only 3d. per acre.

Most of the High Wolds was given over to sheepwalks and common pastures, however, and the worst land to rabbit warrens. The Wolds farmers concentrated on sheep and barley and to a lesser extent on cattle and wheat. Sheep were folded by night on the fallow cornfields to manure the land, their lambs sent to lowland graziers and their wool to West Riding clothiers. Deserted medieval villages provided vast sheepruns; in 1540 Jane Constable kept a flock of 400 sheep in the former common fields of deserted Caythorpe, in 1543 John Thorpe pastured 460 ewes, 300 wethers and 360 hogs at Wharram Percy, and in 1599 all of the 400 or so acres of the former Fowthorpe field were farmed as meadow and pasture. Many a village that had been weakened in the late Middle Ages finally succumbed to the grazier a century or two later. In other parishes the enclosure of common fields was a prelude to conversion to pasture; on the Low Wolds, for instance, it was stated in the mid-seventeenth century that the lord of Bessingby had recently enclosed a flatt of land and that a substantial part of the East field of Sewerby had been enclosed by the agreement of twenty or more inhabitants (*VCH East Riding*, II 1974: 19, 98). Elsewhere, convertible husbandry took the form of grass leys intermingled with the arable strips. At Thwing in 1650, for instance, 'lands or Ridges of Areable & pasture ground' were dispersed throughout the common fields of the township. Settrington's meadows and pastures were enclosed by agreement in 1668, but the common fields remained intact until 1797. A survey of 1600 records 78 houses or cottages clustered below the steep Wolds escarpment; the three arable fields covered 1,697 acres, the three common meadows 151 acres and the common pastures on the low grounds (some of which were stinted) another 916 acres. The parish was unusual in this part of Yorkshire in having 235 acres of woods divided into eight haggs. The chalk Wolds were largely demesne land physically open, but farmed by several tenants. When fully stocked the grasslands carried about 240 oxen, 550 cows and 5,500 sheep (YASRS, CXXVI: 1960).

Many Wolds parishes were dominated by a squire who was keen to maximize the profits available to a commercial farmer. In 1641 Henry Best, lord of the major of Elmswell near Driffield, wrote an unusually detailed account of his farming practices, full of shrewd, practical observations based on a lifetime's experience. Sheep were his main concern, and they occupied the first 31 pages of his text.

> Wee usually sell our wooll att home [he wrote] unlesse it bee by chance that wee carry some to Beverley on Midsummer day: those that buy it carry it into the West, towards Leeds, Hallifax and Wakefield; they bringe (with them) packe-horses, and carry it away in great packes; these wool-men come and goe continually from clipping time till Michaellmasse. Those that have pasture wooll, sell usually for 10s. and 11s. a stone; and oftentimes, when woll is very deare, for 12s. a stone; but our faugh [fallow] sheepe doe not afforde soe fine a wooll, whearefore wee seldome sell for above 8s. or 9s. a stone, unlesse it bee by chance when wooll is very deare that wee reach to 10s. a stone, or very neare.

The benefits of enclosure to such a farmer as Best are also proclaimed in the note that

> The landes in the pasture weare (att my fathers first comminge) letten to our owne tenants and others, for 2s. a lande; afterwards for 2s. 6d. a land, and lastly for 3s. a lande; but nowe, beinge inclosed, they will lette for thrice as much.
>
> (Surtees Soc., XXXIII: 1857)

Best was concerned to improve his stock and crops by trying out new ideas.

Many have alledged [he observed] that White – wheate is the best to mingle and sowe with rye, and that it will bee the soonest ripe; but wee finde experimentally that Kentish wheate is the best, or that which (hereabouts) is called Dodde-reade; and besides it is a larger corne, and a wheate that will sell as well amongst rye as the other.

He sold his oats at the Wednesday and Saturday markets at Beverley, his wheat and maslin at Malton or to the shipmasters at Bridlington quay, and his barley at Beverley and Pocklington in winter and at Malton in summer. 'Wee seldome sende fewer than eight horse-loades to the markette att a time', he wrote, with two men to guide them and to keep an eye on the 6-bushel pokes. Best knew where to get the best prices for his goods and how to use the East Riding markets and fairs to his advantage. In drier months loaded wains could get to Malton, but it was necessary to set off at three in the morning to arrive there at nine, for the corn badgers came from afar and wanted to get home before dark. Seed peas could be bought at Great Driffield or Kilham, butter at Beverley, Malton or Frodingham, and more unusual goods such as London treacle at Beverley. If the Humber was calm on Tuesdays and Fridays Lincolnshiremen would come over to Hull, where Beverley factors sold them oatmeal for resale in Brigg and other north Lincolnshire market towns.

A lot of imported corn came up the Humber, from Norfolk or abroad, and 'there was one man in Yorke that bought 3,000 quarters of barley (this yeare) all att a time, and brought it hither by shippinge; most of it hee malted himself, and the rest hee sold in the markettes'. Other imports included strong Holland cloth, brought over by merchants and sold to linen drapers, 'att whose shoppes our countrey-pedlers furnish themselves', and cheap Scottish cloth 'brought into England by the poore Scotch-merchants, and much used here for womens hand-kerchers and pockett-handkerchers'. Linen cloth was bought of pedlars 'whoe furnish themselves thereof in Cleaveland, and Blakeamoore, wheare they buy very much of this sorte; and att Newe Malton live many att whose houses one may att all times furnish themselves with this kinde of cloath'. Best himself occasionally sold yarn to the Malton weavers. His other contact with the North Riding was through the itinerant 'Moor-folk' who came to work for him at harvest time.

When John Leland crossed the North York Moors from Scarborough to Pickering he found plenty of corn and grass growing in the dales but hardly any trees. The wood belonging to the manor of Rosedale in 1649 was described as 'little and for the most parte ould Rotten Trees & underwood Fitt onely for the fyre'. Apart from the huge common wastes and turbaries, the manor was 'wholly inclosed with small and verry bad ground'. Henderskelfe park had 'much fair yong wod yn it' in Leland's time, but the park adjoining Pickering castle had only a few trees. Over a century later Blandesby park still had deer, timber and underwood, but the game within the forest of Pickering was 'almost quite decayed'. In 1651 the liberty of Pickering Lyth was said to consist 'much of grasse, moorysh grounde, meadowe and feeding grounde'. After local agreements and exchanges leading to conversion to pasture, much of the arable land in the Vale of Pickering had disappeared and the characteristic farm was now a small dairy (Thirsk, ed. 1985: 73).

In the northern Vale of York Leland found no woods worth a mention except in part of the Forest of Galtres. Much of this forest was poor scrubland or common pasture, or 'low medowes and morisch ground ful of carres'. England's lowland forests contained villages with small common arable fields, but the law restricted the amount of land that could be tilled. Spacious common pastures and lax supervision made these forests attractive to immigrant squatters. When Charles I disafforested Galtres every landless cottager was allowed four acres of good land, and in certain villages such as Huby and Easingwold the allotments were increased to six or seven acres 'in pity and commisseration'. South of Sutton-on-the-Forest Leland found 'a great plaine commune, that servith both for feeding of bestes and for turves' and near York he came across 'mervelus good corne grounde, but no plenty of wood yn neere sight'. Between Myton and Helperby he saw 'meatly good corn ground, pasture, and medow, and sum wooddes' and in Northallertonshire he discovered good corn and a great stretch of low pasture and moor. The soils of the northern vale ranged from light sands to quite heavy clays and farming practices varied accordingly. Some villages retained their common arable fields intact, yet in many others communal farming had been abandoned entirely. Many villages in this part of the county were shrunken or deserted and had long been converted to pasture. Elsewhere, common meadows were often the first to go, for their divisions were not permanent and many townships drew lots annually for the best portions. Part of the arable fields at Aldborough were enclosed in 1628 (though other fields survived till 1809), Healaugh's three fields had been enclosed by 1636, and twenty years later 1,500 acres of commons and fields at Sutton-on-the-Forest were enclosed by the agreement of their twenty-six farmers. The present pattern of long, narrow closes at Allerthorpe was created in 1640 when local farmers agreed to hedge their fields and henceforth farm them as they thought fit; some of the new enclosures there even retained the classic reverse S shape of the medieval strips and furlongs (Allison 1976: 132; Thirsk, ed. 1985: 78). By the middle of the seventeenth century perhaps 70 per cent of the rural townships in the northern Vale of York had been fully enclosed, and elsewhere extra grazing was provided by the conversion of arable strips into grass leys. In the district as a whole corn and stock were of equal importance, but the nature of the soils led to much local diversity. The area had already acquired a reputation for rearing fine horses. Leland noted that Ripon fair was 'much celebrated' for its horse sales, and by James I's reign Ripon colts were known throughout England.

The eastern and southern parts of the Vale of York were low-lying and often badly drained. Their situation did not favour arable farming and the common fields were generally insignificant compared with enclosed meadows and pastures and large common wastes. These wastes varied in character from the scrubs and woodlands of Escrick and Skipwith and the sandy heathlands of Holme upon Spalding Moor to the marshes of the Humberhead Levels. For much of the year the marshlands were under water, but in summer they provided good grazing and valuable turbaries. Few of the farms were large, for the traditional system of partible inheritance led to fragmented holdings. Generous common rights were essential to this pastoral economy, and fishing, fowling and turf-digging were crucial by-employments. However, sufficient corn for local needs was grown on the drier lands around the villages.

In 1626 Charles I employed a Dutch and Flemish company organized by Cornelius Vermuyden to improve the drainage of Hatfield Chase. Vermuyden's company received a third of the reclaimed lands and subsequently bought the crown's share, while the remaining third was partitioned amongst the local inhabitants in lieu of their common rights. The drainers decided to block the meandering southern branch of the Don and to divert the whole of the river into the straight channel that had been cut from the northern branch at some unknown date in the early Middle Ages. In 1627 Vermuyden claimed that his project had succeeded, but this was hotly denied by local farmers in Fishlake and Sykehouse whose lands were now at risk from floods. In 1630 Richard Bridges of Sykehouse wrote as 'a woefull spectator of the Lamentable destruction of my native soyle & countrie'. He told of crops destroyed, houses damaged and families distressed; 'Thus have strangers prevayled to destroy our Inheritance.' In subsequent riots foreigners were assaulted and some were killed. It was some years before the scheme was completed to everyone's satisfaction. It led to the decay of Tudworth on the disused southern branch of the Don, but it benefited the small river port and market town of Thorne and the Flemish settlers in Hatfield Levels. Beyond the Levels farming continued in much the old manner, for there the land could not be drained effectively until steam engines were employed in the nineteenth century.

Further west on the fertile lands of the Magnesian Limestone belt the demesnes of Loversall were said to be 'of great tillage' during Charles I's reign. Yet this part of Yorkshire witnessed the same trend towards pasture by the sowing of grass leys or the enclosure of common fields as did the Wolds and the clay vales. A number of settlements that had been weakened in the Middle Ages, such as Frickley and Wildthorpe, finally succumbed during the seventeenth century. Other places shrank to the size of the small estate villages which characterize the area today. Owston had about fifty freeholders in 1343, but two hundred years later it was dominated by William Adam and only a few small freeholders survived. During the reigns of the Tudors and Stuarts the social structure of many of the limestone villages changed slowly but significantly and the farming system altered accordingly. In a few villages, such as the decayed market centre of Braithwell, the freeholders were tenacious and communal farming flourished, but such parishes went against the general trend. Increased demands on pasture also led to restrictions on common grazing rights. At Hooton Pagnell stints had been agreed upon by 1570, and the best pastures at Braithwell were stinted by 1652; however, the commons at Tickhill were still unrestricted in 1649 (Hey 1979: 127–9).

Upon leaving the Vale of York for the Dales John Leland observed that the

river sides of Nidde be welle woddid above Knarresburgh for a 2 or 3 miles: and above that to the hedde al the ground is baren for the most part of wood and corne, as forest ground ful of lynge, mores and mosses with stony hilles . . . The principal wood of the forest is decayed.

In Wensleydale he noted 'the soile about is very hilly, and berith litle corne, but norisith many bestes'. In Swaledale he found 'little corne and much gresse, no wodd but linge and sum trees', and in Uredale the only corn that was grown was either oats or a northern variety of barley known as bigg, though grass was plentiful on the commons. Coverdale had even less corn and hardly any wood. Leland also noted that the dalesmen burnt ling and turves and that in the places where they cut the ling 'good grasse springith for the catel' for a year or two until it was covered again by ling. Almost a century later the justices of the peace for Richmondshire told the Privy Council that 'the greatest part' of their division 'being mountainous and consisting of grazinge' could not be self-supporting in corn.

By the end of the sixteenth century common arable fields had virtually disappeared from the Dales and much of the best meadow and pasture land had been divided into the small closes that are now so characteristic of the area. Though a little oats, bigg and rye were grown, most farmers concentrated on beef and dairy cattle and sheep and many had no arable land at all. In 1631, for instance, William Alderson of Angram in Muker had 28 cattle (12 cows, 3 heifers, 7 stirks, 5 calves and a bull), two horses and 113 sheep, but no corn. Dairying became increasingly important, and meadows were at a premium for their winter hay. The typical Dales farmer was a smallholder with 15–20 customary acres and generous common rights, who was able to keep only a few cattle and sheep, but the gentry were graziers on an ambitious scale. In 1567 Thomas Rokeby of Mortham kept nearly 1,200 sheep on the fells, in 1579 Sir William Ingleby of Ripley had a flock of 1,465, and in 1617 Sir Henry Bellasis of Newburgh priory had about 1,700 (Cliffe 1969: 52). Upon his death in 1552 Charles Dransfield, esquire, of Garrestone in Hauxwell, had nearly 1,000 sheep, 258 cattle (of which 201 were dairy cows or their young) and 51 horses (Thirsk, ed. 1967: 31). And in addition to local herds and flocks vast numbers of Scottish and northern beasts and sheep grazed on the commons as their drovers took them to lowland pastures and markets. Common grazing rights were vital to this type of husbandry, and though the moor edges had been nibbled away by intakes enormous common pastures remained. The roughest grazing was left to the sheep, but the better-quality cow pastures were carefully controlled and stinted. In winter time cattle were fed on hay in the lower closes and sheep were allowed to wander down from the moors to the better pastures; when snow lay deep on the ground the sheep were fed on holly.

Many of the great monastic estates in the Dales had been purchased at the Dissolution by landlords who increasingly thought of their property as a commercial asset. In an age of inflation they were concerned to maximize their profits from rents and entry fines. As the owner of the lordship of Richmond, the forest of Knaresborough and other properties the crown too was involved in a protracted struggle over the definition of tenure; the exact method by which a tenant held his land was crucial to the success or failure of efforts to increase revenue. The former Fountains tenants who had leases for lives or terms of years were powerless to resist demands for higher rents, but the position of tenants who held by customary tenure was much more complicated and in some cases hopelessly muddled. The crucial questions were whether the tenants enjoyed security of tenure for life and the right of their heirs to inherit, whether rents and fines were fixed or variable, and whether a tenant could sell or sub-let his holding. By the end of the sixteenth century the crown had successfully converted the manor of Grinton to 21 year leases, but had been forced to concede 40 year leases in the lordship of Richmond when customary tenure was abolished in 1571. In the Forest of Knaresborough the customary tenants won their battle, when in 1562 they were granted complete security of tenure and inheritance, subject to the payment of rents and fines. The introduction of leases on some manors also had the important consequence of abolishing the traditional system of partible inheritance in favour of primogeniture. The custom of dividing property between all the sons of a family was widespread in the Dales and had encouraged the fragmentation of holdings. Swaledale freeholders and copyholders had long inherited in this manner, but leaseholding brought this system to an end in Arkengarthdale in 1571 and possibly in the rest of the lordship of Richmond (Fieldhouse and Jennings 1978: 115–21, 135).

Population growth brought renewed pressure on the commons. By the early sixteenth century illegal encroachmentrs and unauthorized cottages were attracting attention in the Forest of Knaresborough, and by Elizabeth's reign court orders were regularly issued against them. In 1563, for instance, Brian Lawson was fined fifteen shillings for 'having common of pasture and turbary for one cottage at Menwith Hill newly erected'. But supervision was generally lax and new cottages were tolerated. After 1595 small enclosures that were announced in court and unchallenged were allowed upon payment of an entry fine and an annual rent; by the middle of the seventeenth century this rent was standardized at 4*d.* per annum. A survey of 1651 listed 159 cottages in the forest, 32 of them having illegal encroachments. Population pressure also led to the sub-division of existing houses, and even turfhouses and detached kitchens were turned into domestic dwellings. In a survey of 44 houses in Ripley and Clint 7 buildings consisted of only one room and Peter Darnbrook had decidedly old-fashioned accommodation in a 'house of four pairs of posts' with the low end serving 'for lying beasts in'. (Jennings, ed. 1967: 133–5, 349).

The poverty of cottagers and husbandmen was alleviated by earnings from textile crafts. Eighty-six of 207 Nidderdale inventories taken between 1551 and 1610 included textile equipment, yarn or fibres. Nor was it just the poor who sought extra income in this way. John Scaife, yeoman of Hampsthwaite Hollings (1580), had five cows, a horse, 21 sheep and lambs, poultry and bees, and corn and hay worth £6 as well as a loom, working gear, tenters and eight stone of wool, and most farmer-weavers had holdings of a size comparable with those of their neighbours whose sole concern was agriculture. Towards the end of Elizabeth's reign the number of weavers increased and so did the number of looms per weaving household, and linen began to replace woollen cloth as the main Nidderdale product (Jennings, ed. 1967: 162–70). In Swaledale most inventories record small quantities of wool, some of it dyed, carded and spun locally and much of it used in the knitting industry that had been established so successfully in and around Richmond. During the reign of Elizabeth Richmond's trade recovered and the town was noted for its Saturday market and fortnightly cattle fairs and for its butchers and leather workers. Wealthy hosier-aldermen collected stockings knitted in Swaledale, Teesdale, and Wensleydale and saw to their export to London. By 1625 Richmond hosiers were trading directly with Holland. Nearly 500 dozen pairs of stockings were sent abroad from Stockton in 1639, and by 1664 over 2,000 dozen pairs per annum were exported. Probate inventories show that knitting was an Elizabethan project that had been taken up with enthusiasm in the Dales. Each member of a family could help and a household normally had about three dozen pairs of stockings ready for collection. The crafts was successfully combined with pastoral farming by husbandmen and yeomen and was a vital support to the growing number of cottagers. 'Here poor people live by knitting', was Richard Brathwait's comment on Askrigg in *Barnabees Journal* in 1638. An enquiry held in Dentdale and Garsdale a few years earlier in 1634 heard that the farms were 'so small in quantity that many of them are not above three or four acres apiece, and generally not above eight or nine acres so that they could not maintain their families were it not by their industry in knitting coarse stockings'. The effects of partible inheritance were such that agriculture alone provided an insufficient livelihood (Fieldhouse and Jennings 1978: 159, 178–82; Thirsk, ed. 1967: 31).

The other major source of wealth in the Dales was, of course, lead. Leland described Grinton as 'a little market towne . . . The market is of corne and linyn cloth for men of Suadale, the wich be much usid in digging leade owre.' Small-scale partnerships of miner-farmers prospecting on the commons and working the rakes above the water-table were still the most typical enterprises, but in the early seventeenth century John Sayer of Great Worsall developed the Marrick mines in Swaledale and Sir Stephen Proctor of Fountains Hall exploited the Greenhow field by building a smelting mill and fostering a new, straggling community on Greenhow hill. Miners working this field had previously lived in villages and hamlets around the 1,000 ft contour level, but now they erected cottages and carved smallholdings out of the waste at the summit of the hill some 1,250–1,300 feet above sea level, alongside the road from Pateley Bridge to Grassington. Gentry families were able to make substantial profits from their investments in smelting. The medieval bole-hills on wind-swept gritstone edges were abandoned during the course of the sixteenth century in favour of water-powered bellows, and in 1565 William Humphray had combined such bellows with a shaft furnace to form a smelt mill. This Derbyshire innovation was soon adopted in the northern lead fields.

During the reigns of the Tudors and Stuarts the economy and character of many of the settlements in the West Riding became markedly different from those in other parts of Yorkshire. Communities that had once been among the poorest and least populous grew to be the most thriving. In the eastern parts of the West Riding some places remained purely agricultural, but elsewhere the pattern became increasingly complex. In western parts smallholders added a second string to their bow by combining agriculture with a craft. Having a dual occupation became the normal way of life. Weaver-farmers, metalworker-farmers, collier-farmers, tanners, leather-workers, charcoal-burners and other craftsmen were found in growing numbers in villages, hamlets and isolated farmsteads and cottages on the Coal-Measure Sandstones and the Pennine fringes, scattered settlements that were free from tight manorial control and regulation. Nor were the towns in these western parts restricted by guilds and corporations. Immigrants and innovators found few barriers in such open communities as these, where an insufficient livelihood could be gained by agriculture alone, but where industrial wealth increased the incomes of all classes of society.

In many West Riding communities a framework for life was still provided by the annual rhythm of the farming year organized around the church festivals. In 1574, for instance, the jurors of the manor court of Greasbrough and Barbot Hall ordered that swine should be ringed from the feast of St Bartholomew until the feast of the Purification of the Blessed Virgin Mary and yoked from Candlemas until harvest was over. Such laws were the sensible, practical decisions of experienced farmers concerned with the proper arrangement of communal agriculture. The jurors ordered the fencing of the corn fields to keep out the livestock and forbade the ploughing of common headlands and balks, the grazing of cattle in the common meadows, the felling of timber and holly (for their leaves and bark provided winter fodder), and the putting of 'corrupt cattell or scabbed horses' on the common pastures. On the Pennines many of the small common fields disappeared in this period, and on the coal-measures the common fields of such places as Shafton and Worsbrough were enclosed by agreement. Other places retained their arable strips until the era of parliamentary enclosure. In 1633, for example, Wath had three fields known as Over field, Sandygate field and Brampton sike field, which were separated from Wath wood by 'a new dike of two yeards broade and two yeardes and halfe hie', and in 1649 Barnsley had four common fields called Church field, Old Mill field, Far field and Swinill 'where the freeholders enter and have common soe soone as harvest' without stint. Barnsley also had a large, unstinted common or waste.

In other places the best common pastures were already stinted and sometimes enclosed. A Star Chamber dispute of 1524 heard that the inhabitants of the Graveship of Holme had taken in their best pastures and were driving their cattle over their moorland boundary into the township of Thurlstone; the argument ended in violence and death. A century later the Rotherham commons were said to be stinted, and in 1637 the manor court of Barwick ordered that 'None shall oppress or overcharge the Commons or wastes by putting more goods thereon in summer than they can out of the profits of their farms or tenements keep in the winter'. The West Riding also had its share of ruthless landlords such as Sir Francis Foljambe who was said in the 1630s to have enclosed three-quarters of the common between Rawmarsh and Kilnhurst and to have threatened to ruin opponents by costly litigation (Hey 1979: 125–7). The very different nature of enclosure in the West Riding woollen district is revealed by the 1633 statement of two JPs from Agbrigg and Morley wapentakes that 'generallye where Inclosures are made with us Howses are erected upon them'.

By 1560 the town of Halifax contained 520 houses and the growth of the rural population was equally remarkable.

> There is nothing so admirable in this town [declared William Camden] as the industry of the inhabitants, who, notwithstanding an unprofitable soil, not fit to live in, have so flourished by the cloath trade (which within these last seventy years they fell to), that they are both very rich, and have gained a great reputation for it above their neighbours.

James Ryder was even more fulsome in his praise in 1588:

> They excel the rest in policy and industrie, for the use of their trade and groundes, and after the rude and arrogant manner of their wilde country they surpas the rest in wisdom and wealth. They despise theire olde fashions if they can heer of a new, more comodyus, rather affectinge novelties than allied to old ceremonies . . . so that yff the rest

150

of the county wolde in this followe them but afar off, the force and welth of Yorkshier wolde be soon dubled.

The preamble to the 'Halifax Act' of 1555 (which allowed middlemen or wooldrivers to continue their trade) stated that the parish and neighbouring places

> beyng planted in the grete waste and moores, where the Fertilitie of Grounde ys not apte to bryng forthe any Corne nor good Grasse, but in rare Places, and by exceedinge and greate industrye of the inhabitantes, and the same inhabitantes altogether doo lyve by clothe making, for the greate parte of them neyther gette the Corne nor ys hable to keepe a Horse to carry Woolles, nor yet to bye much woolle att once, but hathe ever used onelie to repayre to the Towne of Halyfaxe, and some other nigh theronto, and ther to bye upon the Woolldryver, some a stone, some twoo, and some three or foure accordinge to theyre habilitee, and to carrye the same to theire houses, some iij, iiij, v, and vj myles of, upon their Headdes and Backes, and so to make and converte the same eyther into Yarne or Clothe, and to sell the same, and so to bye more Woolle of the Wooll-dryver, by meanes of whiche Industrye the barreyn Gronde in those partes be nowe muche inhabyted, and above fyve hundrethe householdes there newly increased within theis fourtye yeares past.
> (Heaton 1965: 94)

Halifax families made narrow kerseys, but further east the local product was broad cloth. In his report of 1595 'Brother Peck' was unable to find much evidence of the manufacture of 'new draperies' in Yorkshire, but noted

> At Wackefeilde, Leedes, and some other smale villages, nere there aboutes, there is made about 30 packes of brode cloths every weecke, and every packe is 4 whole clothes; the sortes made in Wackefeild are pukes, tawnyes, browns, blues, and some reddes; in Leedes of all colours.

The West Riding kerseys and broad cloths were cheap goods which were made into garments for the poorer classes. At the periphery of the woollen cloth district even cheaper cloths such as Penistones and Keighley whites were manufactured. Penistones were being offered for sale in Blackwell Hall, London, by the beginning of Elizabeth's reign, and a letter written from the capital in 1587 mentions 'a coate of penniston' that was uncomfortably hot. Nevertheless, it was the cheapness of such products that attracted the poorer customers and thus enabled many a West Riding family to make a living. Elizabethan observers found the growth of industry and population in these parts a matter of wonder and inspiration. The 'cloathing townes' began to receive national attention.

In the towns men sometimes worked full-time as clothiers for a few large-scale employers. In 1629 Leeds manufacturers were said to be 'dayly setting on worke about forty poor people in their Trade'. Amongst their number was John Harrison, the Leeds philanthropist who built St John's Church, an almshouse, a grammar school and a street of houses. In the countryside cloth-making was a family occupation with children and women preparing and spinning the yarn and men doing the weaving. Most families aimed to produce one piece of cloth per week in time for the market. Apart from fulling, all the processes of manufacture were performed at home. The trade required little capital and could easily be combined with the running of a smallholding. Fulling mills were erected in the river valleys by local gentry families such as the Kayes of Woodsome Hall and the Ramsdens of Longley Hall, who were quick to exploit any opportunity to increase their wealth through industrial and agricultural improvements. The wooldrivers and chapmen who provided the raw materials and sold the finished pieces also became a prosperous class. Wool was bought at the great fairs of Doncaster, Ripon and Pontefract, in the weekly market at Wakefield, or directly from sheepmasters such as Henry Best at Elmswell. It was said in 1588 that 'the Hallyfaxe men occupie fyne wolle most out of Lincolnshire, and there corse wolle they sell to men of Ratchedall [Rochdale]'. In 1615 it was claimed that West Riding clothiers bought wool as far afield as Lincolnshire, Leicestershire, Rutland, Warwickshire, Oxfordshire and Buckinghamshire. By that time Leeds and Wakefield were famous for their markets and for the homes of their merchants; Wakefield was the chief wool market, Leeds was the principal market for cloth. The chapmen carried the finished cloths to Hull to be exported overseas or they made regular journeys to London to the weekly cloth market at Blackwell Hall and to the great annual cloth fair near Smithfield on and about St Bartholomew's Day. The West Riding cloth trade was a great success story, but it was not one of uninterrupted progress. During the second decade of the seventeenth century, for instance, many complaints of bad trade were heard, and in the winter of 1622 a list of poor people in the parish of Huddersfield numbered 700, of whom 419 were children. But on the whole clothmaking provided steady employment for numerous smallholders and cottagers and enabled fullers and middlemen to prosper (Heaton 1965: 78, 118, 185–8; Drake 1962).

The iron industry provided further opportunities for West Riding families to increase their wealth. The Tankersley ironstone seam was mined in shallow bell-pits southwards from near the river Wharfe as far as Staveley in Derbyshire and the ore was smelted in large working units known as bloom smithies, which comprised a bloom hearth and string hearth, water-powered bellows and smaller smithing hearths. Some of these 'smithies', or 'iron mills' as they were sometimes known, appear only briefly in sixteenth-century records, but those on the river Dearne near Monk Bretton have given their name to the settlement of Smithies, and others are recorded in surviving leases. Thus, in 1607 two Silkstone yeomen took a lease of ' One Paire of Iron Smithies, Iron Mills, or Iron Forges' called Silkstone smithies, with their dams, watercourses and buildings and 'all manner of Iron Mynes and Mineralls of Iron' in Hugset wood and on the moors and commons. And in 1621 a lease of the 'Iron Smythies' in Wortley refers to 'all houses, buildings, stringe hearths, bloom hearthes', dams, water-courses, charcoal woods and ironstone mines in the neighbouring townships of Thurgoland, Dodworth and Silkstone. Excavation has revealed that Rockley Smithies, which were worked from about 1500 to 1640 comprised three water wheels, a bloom hearth, a string hearth, a reheating hearth and a possible fourth hearth of unknown purpose, with a dam and watercourses, and a site for roasting iron ore. The 1552 will of Roger Rockley refers to ironstone mining in nearby Friartail Wood, to the use of his own woods for charcoal, and to bequests to 'every of my smith's workmen' (Crossley and Ashurst 1968).

The revolutionary new technique of the charcoal blast furnace was introduced by foreign workers to the Sussex Weald in the reign of Henry VIII. A late-medieval bloomery could produce 20–30 tons per annum, but sixteenth-century charcoal blast furnaces could cast up to 200 tons per annum to be reworked at a forge into 130–50 tons of bar iron. These new furnaces soon appeared in South Wales, in the west Midlands by 1560, and on the Earl of Shrewsbury's estates at Shifnal (Shropshire) and Goodrich (Herefordshire) by 1564. The same earl probably put his first south Yorkshire furnaces into blast during the winter of 1573–74, with the aid of 20–30 workmen descended from French immigrants who had settled in the Weald. The families of Vintin, Perigoe, Dippray, Maryon, Valliance, Russell and Tyler appear in local records about this time (Awty 1981). The first Yorkshire furnaces were at Kimberworth and Wadsley, with associated forges at Attercliffe known as the upper and nether hammers. Charcoal blast furnaces made cast iron that was too brittle for the smiths, so water-powered forges wrought it into bars under powerful tilt hammers. Some forges, such as Wortley, established nearby wire-mills and slitting-mills to supply wire-drawers and nailers. During the late-Elizabethan and early-Stuart era charcoal blast furnaces and their associated forges were erected in many parts of the West Riding and Derbyshire coalfields, but the triumph of the new technology was not immediate, for the old bloomeries continued to make bar and rod iron by traditional methods.

Lionel Copley of Rotherham and Wadworth was the leading south Yorkshire ironmaster during the second and third quarter of the seventeenth century. He based his empire on leases of the Shrewsbury furnaces and forges, charcoal woods, and ironstone and coal pits in south-west Yorkshire. The charcoal blast furnace which he erected in Rockley in 1652, close to the derelict smithies, is Britain's best preserved example, standing almost to its full height. Recent excavations have located the pit for the water wheel, the bellows building and the casting pit, and have uncovered the masonry of the charging bank; the dams can be traced in part in the adjacent wood. Rockley furnace could make about 400 tons of pig iron per annum, which was average output for the improved furnaces of the mid-seventeenth century. It remained operational for a hundred years or so and was re-used during the Napoleonic wars.

Local iron was considered fit for blacksmiths, founders, nailers, and wire-drawers but of insufficient quality for cutlers and edge-tool makers. By 1614 the Sheffield manor court was insisting on the use of steel for all cutting edges, steel that had to be imported from the continent via the inland port of Bawtry. As early as 1537 the probate inventory of Henry Reynshaw of Chesterfield recorded £9 worth of unwrought Spanish 'iron', and in 1574 the bailiff of Hallamshire noted the safe delivery to the storehouses at Sheffield Castle of six barrels of steel from Bawtry. By 1645 iron was being imported from the Baltic port of Lübeck, but despite these enormous transport handicaps Sheffield triumphed over her competitors and became England's acknowledged cutlery centre. Chaucer's Miller of Trumpington had of course carried a Sheffield 'thwittel' and the tradition of craftsmanship had been long established: 'Ther be many smithes and cuttelers in Halamshire', observed John Leland. 'In Rotherham be veri good smithes for all cutting tooles.' Literary references in Elizabeth's reign praise the simple and cheap knives of the Sheffield region. Little capital was needed to set up in the trade either in the town or in the countryside, and sixteenth-century wills leave no doubt that 'stithie [anvil], hammeres and tonges, with all things belonging to the harthe' were all that were required.

Sheffield's success over its rivals is explained in similar terms to the success of the Halifax clothiers: the social and economic structure in the town and surrounding countryside and the availability of water power. Local rivers and streams are of modest size, but they fall considerably in a short distance and could therefore be dammed at frequent intervals to power cutlers' grinding wheels and iron forges. Sheffield's industrial success was based on water power long before the age of steam. By 1581 the Lord of Sheffield was renting out fifteen wheels and others had been established outside his jurisdiction. By 1637 a surveyor could report, 'These Rivers are very profitable unto the Lord in regard of the Mills and Cutler wheeles that are turned by theire streames, which wheeles are imployed for the grinding of knives by four or five hundred Master Workmen'. Grinding, of course, was not then a specialist craft (except in the scythe trade) and each cutler would rent occasional space at a wheel to grind his own blades.

During the sixteenth century the cutlery trades were organized through the manorial courts, which issued the marks by which each cutler was known. The earliest known marks were granted in 1554 to William Elles, cutler, and John White, shearsmith, but a reference eleven years later to 'the ancient customs and ordinances' suggests that the trades had long been regulated in this way. No foreign names are recorded amongst the 61 men who had been granted marks by 1569. 'Hallamshire cutts' were exported via Chester to Ireland in Elizabeth's reign, and in 1580 were sold in Worcestershire and Herefordshire by an Attercliffe packman. When the Cutlers' Company was incorporated in 1624 it was claimed that local wares were sold in 'most parts of this kingdom' and to 'foreign countries' and that the 'greatest part of the Inhabitants of the Lordship and Liberty of Hallamshire . . . doe consist of cutlers'. Scissorsmiths, shearsmiths and sicklesmiths were included amongst the 182 original members of the company, whose jurisdiction ran for six miles beyond the borders of Hallamshire. High-class wares were made in Sheffield and common pen knives in the surrounding villages, but some rural communities specialized in distinctive products. Norton parish, for instance, was the place for scythemakers; John Parker of Little Norton was described as scythesmith in 1459 and the Elizabethan parish registers record numerous scythemakers and other metalworkers, as well as iron smelters and wood colliers. By the reign of Charles I Norton men were selling scythes as far afield as Scotland and the market-towns of north-eastern England and middlemen such as the Blythes of Norton Lees had stocks of up to 2,000 (Hey 1980: 126–39).

The Norton scythesmiths were part-time farmers. Their craft was not a by-employment, nor were their farms mere appendages to a preoccupation with manufacture. Agriculture and industry were combined in a way which was so characteristic of West Riding communities in the Elizabethan and Stuart period that having a dual occupation must have been the normal way of life. In 1542, for instance, Richard Boyer of the parish of Sheffield left his children his smithy gear and hardening trough, his two wains and two ploughs 'with all things appertaining to husbandry,' a great ark in the barn, a cow, four heifers and a few sheep and lambs. In 1637 Bell Hagg farm consisted of a dwelling house, a barn and a smithy and 54½ acres of arable, meadow and pasture, with common rights on the adjacent moors, and at Cross House William Bower had 48 acres, a dwelling house of three bays, two barns of three bays, and a smithy. Of course, the poorest craftsmen had hardly any land at all; James Foster had less than an acre on the edge of Ecclesfield common and he lived and worked in a dwelling house and smithy of three bays, with a beast house and backside. But until population growth outstripped the available land most rural craftsmen were part-time farmers and some were prosperous enough to earn the description of yeoman.

> Though betwixt Cawoode and Rotheram be good plenti of wood [wrote Leland] yet the people burne much yerth [earth] cole, by-cause hit is plentifully found ther, and sold good chepe. A mile from Rotherham be veri good pittes of cole . . . Halamshire hath plenti of woodde, and yet ther is burnid much se cole.

Furthermore, 'Ther be plenty of veines of se cole in the quarters about Wakefield', and in north and east Yorkshire sea coal was purchased from

155

mines in county Durham. By Elizabethan times the people of York no longer burned wood but relied on coal and turves; they said that in 1597 turves were 'nowe the greatest parte of our fewell'. Turves were brought up the Ouse from Thorne and the other villages around the edge of Inclesmoor, together with coals from Newcastle. Meanwhile, so much coal came to York in wains from the West Riding that the causey leading to Micklegate Bar had to be repaired by a special levy (Palliser, 1979: 273). As local population levels increased so did the demand for coal, but the Yorkshire coalfield was too landlocked to compete with Northumberland and Durham in national markets. From about 1575 onwards the increased scale of mining is reflected in higher rents, but the precariousness of such enterprises in times of recession is revealed by a 1631 report on declining profits at Sheffield Park pits; the banksman blamed increased production at neighbouring pits, a mild winter, the poor quality of the coal, dear corn which meant that 'manie people was constrained to sitt with small fires rather than want bread', besides 'the great decay of the cutler trade which never was known to be so badde' and a slump in brewing (the two trades which formed the best market for Sheffield coal), and finally technical problems caused by a long earth wall in the main seam. Despite these handicaps the Park pits soon recovered their local pre-eminence.

Punchwood for pit props was supplied from local coppices; a 1642 survey of Sheffield manor noted that Burngreave was 'now felling for punch wood', Wilkinson spring had been 'lately Cutt for that and other uses' and Cooke wood had been 'cut 3 years since for punch wood'. Springwoods were managed carefully and coppiced in rotation. In the 1530s Hampole priory owned a 120-acre wood 'in which are 18 coppices called haggs, viz. 1 of the age of 18 years another of the age of 17 years and so in succession from year to year', but a century later in the Sheffield area some woods had not been cut for over thirty years and the whole of the 371-acre Greno wood had been felled at the same time. The principal purchasers of the West Riding underwoods were local ironmasters in need of charcoal. In 1637 Sheffield manor contained an estimated 2,000 acres of wood and timber (not including the trees in Sheffield Park), 'whereof there are above 16 hundred acres of spring woods besides great store of old trees fit for noe other purpose but for the making of Charkehole'. The surveyor also noted 'very stately Timber especially in Haw Parke', which was

> full of excellent Timber of a very great length and very streight and many of them of a great bigness before you come to a knott in so much that it hath been said by Travellers that they have not seene such Timber in Cristendome.

More commonly, a number of standard trees grew to full height amongst the underwood. In the 1530s Esholt priory's woods comprised the 16-acre Nunwood, 'in which are 300 great oaks growing for 200 years', the 30 acre

Bastone Cliff, which supported 200 oaks for 40 years' growth and underwood of 12 years, together with a 3 acre close with 40 oaks aged 40 years and underwood of 10 years, and a one-acre spring with 20 oaks of 40 years growth and underwood that had sprung up a year ago (YASRS, LXXX 1931: 87). Woods of the coppice-with-standards type were maintained in the old manner where a charcoal ironworks was no more than twenty miles away, but further afield woodland management was not as profitable. At Settrington on the Wolds escarpment nearly 1,600 trees were felled in the 1590s, and it was suggested in 1600 that the denuded haggs and springs should be converted to pasture. At Holme on Spalding Moor 80 acres of woods survived in 1586 but the land had been converted to arable and pasture by 1620 (Allison 1976: 131–3).

Another group with an interest in coppice woods were the tanners, who required a regular supply of oak bark. Tan pits were located on the outskirts of many of Yorkshire's medieval towns – in Fishergate at Doncaster, and by the Ponds in Sheffield, for instance – but tanning was also a rural occupation for well-to-do families. Leather was used for garments as well as footwear, for harness, horse collars, saddles and straps, for bags and bottles, and around Sheffield for bellows, grinders' belting and sheaths for knives. The supply of local hides was insufficient to meet demand, so by the late 1620s Yorkshire tanners were importing hides from London 'upp Humber and the fresh rivers there to Turnbridge and Bawtrey, and hence by land'; about 4,000 hides per annum came this way as back-carriage on boats and ships exporting West Riding goods to the capital. When Thomas Pickles, a Kirkheaton tanner, died in the 1640s, his personal estate included 'Tanned leather and dry £16, 20 country steer hides and 50 cow hides £50, Eleven score hides bought at London £220, 120 hides bought at London and not yet at Hull £150' and bark worth £20.

The growth of all these crafts and industries meant that many more horses and vehicles used the roads and that the government was forced to introduce a new system of maintenance and repair based on the parish and supervised by the JPs at the quarter sessions. From 1555 onwards each householder was obliged to work four (later, six) days a year on the roads, and unpaid parish overseers of the highways were elected on an annual basis. The most important bridges were paid for out of county rates; thus, in 1602 the West Riding JPs agreed that 48 of 'the most considerable' bridges should be kept in repair in this manner. Throughout Yorkshire, most traffic that was more than purely local headed to and from industrial sites, the market towns and the inland ports. A single horse normally carried about 240 lbs on its back but could tow up to 30 tons along a navigable river, so water transport was much cheaper than land transport for heavy, bulky goods. Nevertheless, by the reign of Elizabeth Yorkshire was connected to London by regular carrier services over land. By 1588 Doncaster corporation was employing three men to run a postal service to and from the capital, and further west carrying

157

services were so regular by 1617 that the highway from Rotherham to Mansfield via Mile Oaks and Whiston was described as 'the Auncient Rode way or London way for carryers'. Twenty years later John Taylor's *Carriers' Cosmographie* noted the usual times of arrival and departure for carriers who had converged on the capital from all over the country:

> The carriers from Sheffield, in Yorkshire, doth lodge at the Castle in Woodstreet, they are to be found on Thursdaies and Fridayes ... The Carriers of Doncaster, in Yorkshire, and many other parts in that country, doe lodge at the Bell, or Bell Savage without Ludgate, they do come on Fridaies, and goe away on Saturdaies or Mundaies.

Carriers from other parts of Yorkshire operated on a similar basis. The marked growth in internal trade in Elizabethan and Stuart times was reflected in a rapid rise in the number of inns and alehouses. A national census of inns taken in 1577 lists 239 inns and nearly 3,700 alehouses in Yorkshire; most inns were in the market towns but alehouses sprang up everywhere and were a constant concern of the JPs who tried to regulate their numbers by a licensing system. When the West Riding JPs tried to stop the spread of plague in 1638, they restrained those who sold ale and beer 'in the open street to passengers and travellers ... on the high road between Doncaster and Wentbrigg ... [who] entertain and discourse with all manner of passengers and travellers, wanderers and idle beggars'. Travellers' descriptions leave no doubt that travelling was often an arduous task; when John Taylor hired a guide to take him from Wortley to Halifax in September 1639, he found that 'the ways were so rocky, stony, boggy and mountainous, that it was a day's journey to ride so short a way'. Road technology did not improve until the eighteenth and nineteenth centuries; the parish repair system could provide only a more regular application of existing methods. Yet despite these difficulties a great deal of traffic used the roads, particularly in summer, but if necessary at all times of the year (Hey 1980: 14, 208–12).

Houses

York was no longer the flourishing city that it had been at the height of the Middle Ages, but it was still the political, judicial and ecclesiastical capital of the north, the seat of The King's Council in the Northern Parts and the home for much of the year of the Council's officials. The presidents took over the late-fifteenth-century house of the abbots of St Mary and converted it into the King's Manor, and in 1565–68 Sir Thomas Eynns, the secretary, built

Heslington Hall in the new symmetrical style with large mullioned and transomed windows and a classical doorway. But Yorkshiremen could not match the great country houses of Elizabeth's advisers, such as the Northamptonshire seats of William Cecil at Burghley and of Sir Christopher Hatton at Holdenby and Kirby; they had neither the means nor the confidence to build on a large scale until the security of Elizabeth's reign was well established. In 1587 Thomas Cecil, William's son, rebuilt Snape Castle when he gave it four sturdy corner towers like those of the 200-year-old Bolton Castle further up the dale. Towers gave a comforting sense of might and security and were retained by many an Elizabethan builder, together with battlements, great gate-houses and courtyards in the Tudor Gothic style of Hampton Court. All this was done more for display than defence and with an element of regularity provided by striking grid-patterns of glittering windows. Burton Constable Hall, built in Holderness by Sir John Constable or his son Sir Henry, has many of these features (though it was remodelled in the eighteenth century) and so did the demolished Howley Hall that Sir Robert Savile and his son John built in the West Riding in the 1580s.

Behind the symmetrical façades interiors were arranged in a traditional manner around a large central hall that was normally still open to the rafters. A passage that ran through the house separated the hall from the service rooms and the lesser chambers, and draughts and kitchen smells were kept away by a screen, which in Elizabethan times was often carved in a wonderful manner (as at Burton Agnes) with a musician's gallery on top. Beyond the dais end of the hall were parlours and the principal private room known as the great chamber, and in the larger houses a long gallery stretched all the way along the upper floor. The great chamber which Sir William Fairfax commissioned for Gilling castle some time between 1575 and 1585 is the finest surviving example in England, a showpiece of contemporary art. Barnard Dinninghof, the German glass painter, was responsible for the stained-glass windows and perhaps for the whole design. The heraldic theme of the glass is continued in the plaster frieze which depicts 443 coats of arms of almost all the Yorkshire gentry, while in a corner of the frieze the images of three male and three female musicians are a pleasing reminder of one of the uses of the room. The marquetry panelling of the walls, the ribs and hanging pendants of the plaster ceiling and the carved oak chimneypiece framing the Fairfax coat of arms complete a memorable display.

The great houses of the late sixteenth century were conscious demonstrations of the power and wealth of the leading Elizabethan families. These romantic piles with their dramatic skylines, enormous windows, formal entrances and ingenious designs reflected the arrogant spirit of the nation's rulers. North of the Trent the richest and most powerful figure was George Talbot, sixth Earl of Shrewsbury, Earl Marshal of England and husband of Bess of Hardwick. The residences of the Talbot and Cavendish families, scattered throughout the north Midlands and Yorkshire, were the inspiration

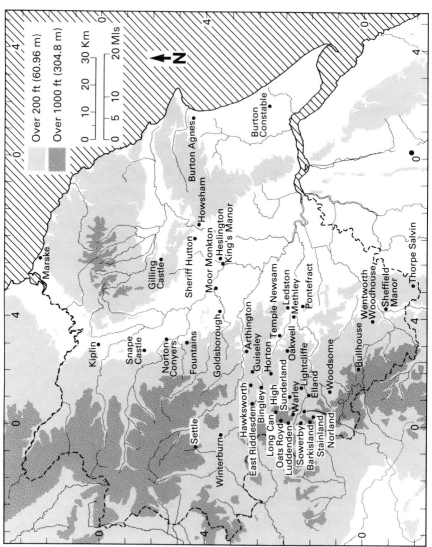

Over 200 ft (60.96 m)

Over 1000 ft (304.8 m)

0 5 10   20   30 Km

0   10   20   20 Mls

N

Marske

Kiplin

Snape
Castle

Norton
Conyers

Fountains

Settle

Winterburn

Hawksworth

East Riddlesden

Bingley

Long Can

Oats Royd

Luddenden

Sowerby

Barkisland

Stainland

Norland

Goldsborough

Gilling
Castle

Sheriff Hutton

Moor Monkton

Arthington

Guiseley

Horton

Woodsome

Bullhouse

Howsham

Heslington
King's Manor

Temple Newsam

Ledston

Methley

Sunderland

Oakwell

Warley

Lightcliffe

Elland

High

Pontefract

Wentworth
Woodhouse

Sheffield
Manor

Thorpe Salvin

Burton Agnes

Burton
Constable

Figure 3.3 Elizabethan and Stuart houses mentioned in the text

for others who had acquired the wealth and confidence to build. The old house at Chatsworth, which William Cavendish (a previous husband of Bess) had erected in the 1550s, was the chief model. Such houses were tall and compact, with chimneys and turrets silhouetted against the skyline and a long gallery at the top extending above a traditional two-storeyed hall. Only fragments survive of such once-mighty buildings as the Earl of Shrewsbury's principal seat at Sheffield Manor and Hercy Sandford's hall at Thorpe Salvin, but old illustrations and archaeological investigation have revealed some of their former importance.

Robert Smythson, who had begun his career at Longleat and Wardour Castle in Wiltshire, designed several houses for the Talbots and Cavendishes and for other leading families in the Midlands and the North, notably at Wollaton, Worksop and Hardwick. Pontefract New Hall and Heath Old Hall, two of his earliest Yorkshire buildings, have been demolished, but the county still has a major example of his work at Burton Agnes and possibly also at Fountains. The history of the two sites is very different, for Fountains Hall was built close to the ruins of a great Cistercian abbey, but Burton Agnes had been the residence of a powerful lord for many generations; the church of St Martin, tucked behind the Victorian stable block, is full of the monuments of the Griffiths and the Boyntons, and nearby is the splendid vaulted undercroft of Roger de Stuteville's Norman manor house. Sir Henry Griffith, who had spent his earlier life in Staffordshire, probably settled here in 1599 when he became a member of the Council of the North. Datestones on the house range from 1601 to 1610. Glittering bay windows, gables, finials, battlements, chimney stacks and strapwork designs adorn the front, but the symmetrical façade disguises a traditional interior arranged around a small internal courtyard, with a cross-passage and an elaborately carved oak and plaster screen separating a lofty hall from the service rooms. Another old-fashioned feature is the gatehouse, built in 1610 in the style of the Elizabethan turret house at Sheffield or Sir Mauger Vavasour's banquet house at Weston Hall in lower Wharfedale; it is one of the best Jacobean gatehouses in the country, and like the hall itself is largely of brick. But Burton Agnes was up-to-date with its long gallery on the top floor and in the Renaissance spirit of its wood-carvings, wainscotting, plaster ceilings and alabaster work (Girouard 1983: 184–8).

Fountains Hall was built about the same time, with stones from the ruined abbey, by Sir Stephen Proctor. His father, Thomas, had been granted a patent for smelting iron and lead with a mixture of charcoal, coal and peat, and had been a successful entrepreneur. Stephen Proctor was an unscrupulous and ambitious man and a zealous Calvinist. He purchased the Fountains estate in 1597, received a knighthood in 1604, and two years later obtained the lucrative post of Collector of Fines on Penal Statutes. Armed with these powers, he persecuted his Catholic neighbours in the sensitive years following the Gunpowder Plot and worried them further by endless lawsuits over land, minerals and common rights. He was much resented as an upstart of humble

Plate 3.3 Burton Agnes Hall. The great Elizabethan architect Robert Smythson designed this house for Sir Henry Griffith, who came here from Staffordshire on becoming a member of the Council of the North in 1599. Datestones show that it was built during the first decade of the seventeenth century. The glittering bay windows must have had a sensational impact. Smythson was fond of building tall houses with an irregular and dramatic skyline and a symmetrical façade. The external design masks a traditional interior with a great hall, screen and cross-passage. A long gallery ran all the way along the top storey in the front, providing a view right out to the North Sea. The only significant change to the façade has been the replacement of some mullioned and transomed windows with sashes in the eighteenth century. The grounds are enclosed by a high brick wall and a Jacobean gatehouse.

---

origins and a fervent Puritan. His house was unusually high and not very deep, for it was built against a steep bank for dramatic effect. Its architect is not known for certain, but it has the hallmarks of a Smythson design (Girouard 1983: 195–7). Fountains incorporated an Elizabethan innovation by which the servants were moved downstairs into the basement, a practice that remained normal in country house design until the present century.

Gentlemen of lesser means were neither able to employ architects nor to build entirely anew, but they sometimes had sufficient resources to refashion their timber-framed houses and to encase them with stone, even if the work had to be spread out over more than one generation. The Kayes of Woodsome Hall provide an apt illustration. Arthur Kaye inherited the manors of Farnley and

162

Slaithwaite, purchased the manor of Lingards, and bought Denby grange upon the dissolution of Byland Abbey. His son John continued to purchase property and in 1573 acquired the manor of Honley, where he erected an iron forge at Smithy Place. The Kayes owned at least seven local mills, some of them for grinding corn and others for fulling cloth, and they used their Denby grange lands for coal-mining and the quarrying of stone. They also possessed timber and coppice woods and moorland turbaries and were keen agricultural improvers. Their house was originally timber-framed and arranged in a traditional manner, but Arthur and John carried out considerable improvements. The names of Arthur and Beatrix Kaye are written in big, ornate letters over the fireplace that they inserted into their open hall sometime before 1562; a similar chimney was placed in the low parlour and the house was made more pleasant by glazing the windows and by plastering decorative patterns on ceilings. John built more chimneys, added further rooms, panelled the interior and paved the hall and courtyard. By about 1580 these improvements had been completed and the house had been encased in stone. At that time, however, it was still surrounded by a moat and John had 'made new the drawbridge'. Twenty years or so later John's son, Robert, built a north wing and a colonnade of Tuscan columns and then paved and walled the outer court (Redmonds 1982: 6–10). Robert and his son, John II, were both JPs and the new social standing of the Kayes was recognized when John III (1616–62) was made a baronet.

Two West Riding houses illustrate the different ways in which existing timber frames could determine the layout of rooms even after a building had been remodelled and encased in stone. The exterior of Oakwell Hall bears the initials of John Batt and the date 1583 but gives no clue to the antiquity of the interior, except that the thirty lights of the great seventeenth-century window illuminate two storeys; through the porch, however, is a cross-passage with service rooms to the right and a screen on the left leading into a medieval open-hall and a parlour wing beyond. The other house is Guiseley rectory, which Robert Moore rebuilt in stone in 1601. All the external details of the symmetrical façade are of this date, but an internal inspection reveals a medieval aisled hall with timber posts dividing the main block from a smaller range of rooms to the rear. Even where no earlier timber frame existed builders continued with familiar styles. The Nunnery at Arthington was built by a member of the Briggs family in 1585 to a similar plan to Guiseley rectory though there is no evidence of an earlier timber-framed building on this site. The new stone houses of the Elizabethan and Stuart gentry were rooted in the vernacular tradition, even though their visual impact must have been dramatic (Hey 1981: 22–49).

During the reign of James I Yorkshire gentlemen continued to build in styles that had been forged during the Elizabethan era. Howsham Hall, which was erected about 1619 for Sir William Bamburgh, baronet, has mullioned and transomed windows ending in glittering canted bays that seem to fill the whole of the south front, but its attractive skyline was a novel feature with regular-spaced merlons and ball finials. Several Yorkshiremen did well out of lucrative posts under the early Stuarts and were able to build on a scale that matched their official positions. Sir Richard Hutton, a judge of the Court of Common Pleas, built Goldsborough Hall about 1620, William Pennyman, one of the six Clerks of Chancery, erected Marske Hall five years later, and Sir George Calvert, a principal secretary of state, began Kiplin Hall in 1622; Calvert subsequently declared himself a Catholic, resigned his position, and as Lord Baltimore, founded the New World colony of Maryland. Sir Richard Graham, a man of humble origins who served the Duke of Buckingham and Charles I, acquired Norton Conyers through marriage in 1624 and transformed the medieval hall with delightful rows of Dutch gables; his descendants still live there.

The most powerful Yorkshiremen of this era were Sir Arthur Ingram and Sir Thomas Wentworth, first Earl of Strafford. Ingram was a native of Rothwell who devised financial schemes to keep James I and Charles I independent of Parliament and who grew enormously rich from the spoils of office. He owned estates in Derbyshire, Lincolnshire and Suffolk as well as an imposing town house behind York minster on the site of the archbishop's palace and 'a very fayre new lodge of brick' at Sheriff Hutton. His principal residence was at Temple Newsam, a former property of the Knights Templar which the Darcys had converted into one of the earliest brick houses in the West Riding. Ingram demolished the east range (for courtyards were now out of fashion) and rebuilt the house in the same severe style as the north front of Robert Cecil's Hatfield House in Hertfordshire.

Meanwhile the Wentworths were building on a similar scale. The family had resided in their ancestral village since the early Middle Ages, but it was only during the early seventeenth century that they rose to prominence in the county. Sir William became Sheriff of Yorkshire and one of James I's first baronets; his son, Sir Thomas, became Charles I's chief adviser and one of the most famous figures of his age. The Wentworths erected a brick Jacobean house at Wentworth Woodhouse in the new compact style, three storeys high with projecting wings, and with two detached lodgings and a kitchen connected to the main building by a covered passage; an Elizabethan-type banquet house stood in the garden. Sir Thomas presided here over a household of sixty-four people. He also extended the King's Manor in York and may have been responsible for enlarging Ledston Hall, a thirteenth-century grange of Pontefract Priory which had been converted to domestic accommodation after the Dissolution by the Witham family. The entrance front was given angle turrets capped with ogee-shaped domes, like those at Hatfield House and Blickling Hall, and attractive rows of Dutch gables with flat tops carrying pediments, like John Smythson's designs for Bolsover Castle and Welbeck Castle, designs which he had copied from houses in Holborn on a visit to London in 1619. New styles spread gradually from the capital to the provinces as rich families imitated the buildings that they had visited during their London season; thus in 1640 Sir Henry Slingsby of Scriven was 'much taken' by Lord Holland's Kensington home and thereupon 'took a conceite' to rebuild Red House at Moor Monkton in the Ainsty of York (Hey 1981: 50–8).

During the second and third quarters of the seventeenth century gentlemen and wealthy clothiers in the Halifax district created a unique style of domestic building. Though their gabled halls were arranged in a traditional manner, the decorative details applied to the exteriors were amazing in their virtuosity. An influential prototype was the (demolished) Methley Hall, a fifteenth-century structure enlarged between 1588 and 1611 by Sir John Savile and his son, Sir Henry. Sir John was a founder member of the Society of Antiquaries and a friend of William Camden, the author of *Brittania* (1586) and *Remains Concerning Britain* (1605); his youngest brother, Thomas, also had a considerable reputation as an authority on British antiquities. It was therefore natural for the Saviles to favour elements taken from Gothic architecture as well as classical forms. Methley was the first house in the West Riding to have an enormous hall window divided by numerous mullions and transoms. The master masons responsible for the building were probably those members of the Akroyd family whose names appear in the contemporary Methley parish register. John, Abraham and Martin Akroyd also erected the first West Riding buildings to have distinctive windows shaped like a rose or a Catherine-wheel. The original source of inspiration for these may have been Robert Smythson, the great Elizabethan architect, who in 1599 designed a circular window divided into twelve lights. The (demolished) Bradley Hall at Stainland, which the Akroyds built for Sir John Savile, had a rose-window that was undoubtedly the model for that at Barkisland Hall a generation later. The Saviles were apparently also responsible for introducing Halifax masons to the classical columns and entablatures that normally adorned the porch entrance below a rose-window, for it was Sir John's younger brother, Sir Henry, the celebrated mathematician, Greek scholar and Warden of Merton College, who invited the Akroyds and Bentleys to Oxford to extend the Merton Fellows Quad and the Bodleian Library (Pacey 1966).

The (demolished) hall at High Sunderland was the first 'Halifax house' to have classical columns. These, together with the unusual curvilinear designs of the pilasters on the garden gateways, must have caused quite a stir, for such features were surely imported from outside the region. However, Abraham Sunderland also used such aspects of the vernacular tradition as low proportions, battlements and pinnacles, string courses, and mullioned and transomed windows, and he incorporated a previous timber-framed house within his new building. When he had finished about 1629 he had combined classical and medieval features in a new, elaborate fashion which inspired the next generation of local gentlemen and clothiers to do likewise. Wood Lane Hall at Sowerby is an outstanding example of the fully developed style. The

Plate 3.4 Wood Lane Hall, Sowerby. An outstanding example of a seventeenth-century 'Halifax house', Wood Lane Hall was built in 1649 for John Dearden. It has all the architectural details that were so admired by the wealthy clothiers of this parish. The skyline is pierced by Gothic battlements and pinnacles and from the sides project a series of extraordinary gargoyles. The porch has the usual classical columns and a strange lintel that is modelled on a 1633 example at Warley. Above is a rose-window that is identical in design to one at Elland New Hall. The great hall window is also similar to the one at Elland in being divided by mullions and transoms into 27 lights. As with some other 'Halifax houses' the parlour end projects slightly to balance the porch. Despite these similarities with its neighbours, Wood Lane Hall has a character all of its own. It is built in a distinctive vernacular style that is confined to this part of the West Riding.

masons who built it for John Dearden in 1649 drew up some of the best features of neighbouring 'Halifax houses'. The finials that rest on top of the battlements resemble those at Kershaw House, Luddenden; the great hall window, the battlements and the rose-window are modelled on those of Elland New Hall; the design of the doorway lintel is similar to an earlier one at Warley; the plaster ceiling is comparable with that at Howroyde, Barkisland; the stepped windows in the gables have local parallels; and the projecting porch is balanced by the projecting parlour wing, as at Barkisland Hall and some other outstanding local houses. Nevertheless, Wood Lane Hall is triumphantly individual and decidedly Gothic in flavour. Despite their similarities no two 'Halifax houses' are alike and some seem to go out of their way to be different. The demolished Horton Hall at Bradford was a marvellously eccentric structure whose porch was extended above the rose-

166

window into a tower or observatory, where the owner, Abraham Sharpe, indulged his passion for astronomy.

The continuity of building tradition between the closing years of the reign of Elizabeth and the second half of the seventeenth century makes it difficult to date houses for which there is no firm evidence. Datestones have to be depended upon to a large degree, yet often they tell only part of the story and sometimes they are untrustworthy. A few, like the 1596 datestone on Gawthorpe Hall at Bingley, are quite early and show that many characteristic features of the style had been introduced by late-Elizabethan times. Others, such as the 1655 inscriptions on Thomas Netherwood's Giles House at Lightcliffe and Sylvanus Rich's Bullhouse Hall near Penistone demonstrate that even at the same social level owners could choose to build in a similar manner two generations later. Gabled halls cannot be dated by a progression from the simplest to the most complicated structures. Whereas the cloth trade was obviously a principal source of wealth for many owners, others profited from the exploitation of mineral resources. East Riddlesden Hall, one of the most striking houses in the West Riding, was largely the responsibility of James Murgatroyd of Warley, a wealthy clothier who acquired the property in 1638 and who also built two smaller houses nearby at Long Can and Oats Royd. Many owners aspired to the status of minor gentry, but most were content to inscribe their lintels merely with datestones and initials. John Gledhill placed his coat of arms and the date 1638 over his porch at Barkisland Hall, but the owners of Hawksworth Hall, Elland Hall, and Lower Hall at Norland adorned their rooms with the royal arms in the absence of suitable heraldry of their own.

Windows and drip-moulds were the most distinctive features of the old halls and manor houses of Yorkshire (Ambler 1913: 17–31). Halls, kitchens and parlours, and sometimes chambers as well were illuminated by large windows divided into numerous lights by mullions and transoms. Though other parts of England shared the fashion for carrying up the centre lights of gable windows, the West Riding was alone in its enthusiasm for the idea, even adopting the stepped arrangement for other windows in the top storey. Friars Head at Winterburn is a perfect example, with four small gables surmounted by finials. A common variation in Craven united the heads of triple lights into one ogee-shaped arch. Perhaps only a few masons were at work in that district, using traditional ground plans and elevations but allowing full reign to the imagination when applying fanciful details. Door heads in and around Settle were shaped in a variety of crazy curves, but even the locals thought Thomas Preston's 1679 house had gone too far, for they gave it the nickname of The Folly.

By the middle years of the seventeenth century only the humblest structures were still being built with wood. Over a century earlier John Leland had noted that in towns such as Beverley, Doncaster and Wakefield the majority of houses had timber frames and in 1577 William Harrison observed that throughout England 'the greatest part of our building in the cities and good towns ... consisteth of timber'. Town houses were often given a coat of plaster and a colour wash. Thus, when James I stopped at York on his way down from Scotland in 1603, the inhabitants were ordered by the corporation to 'painte the owteside of ther howses with some collors to the strete forwardes'. York's first completely brick house was not erected until 1610, but even in the mid-sixteenth century Yorkers were protesting against 'the great destruction of wood' within sixteen miles of the city; Thorganby, eight miles away, had insufficient wood to repair its own buildings by 1542. The owners of West Riding woods may have found it more profitable to concentrate on coppiced underwood rather than on standards grown for timber, but it is also likely that changing fashion was as important as shortage of timber in the general conversion to stone or brick, and that fear of fire hastened the change in towns. The old tradition survived longer in the countryside. When Edward Tailor added a new wing to his home in Oulton in 1611 he designed it with king-posts, struts, braces and finials to match the older parts of the building.

Timber was still valued for its decorative effect, even where lower walls were built of stone. Godfrey Bosville's mid-sixteenth century Gunthwaite barn and his (demolished) lodge at Oxspring displayed their timbers only at upper level. Other houses achieved this effect when their lower walls were rebuilt in stone; for example, the upper storey of Wormald's Hall at Almondbury appears to date from the sixteenth century, but in 1631 the ground floor was rebuilt with stone walls. At Hound Hill, the Elmhirst family's ancestral home in the parish of Worsbrough, a new stone wing in similar proportions to the earlier timber-framed building doubled the size of the house. Many other old buildings were completely encased in stone during the course of the seventeenth century and many a thatched house or cottage was given a new roof of stone slates. Leland had found Richmond and Grinton houses 'partly slatid, partly thackid', and a 1616 survey of property belonging to the Sheffield capital burgesses records a similar mixture of roofing materials; Edward Hawke, for instance, had 'a dwelling house and Barne of 5 baies whereof 4 bayes slated a workehouse 1 Bay and an old house 1 bay a hovell thatcht' and Philip Ashburrie of Owlerton had '1 dwelling house and kitchin 3 baies and an outshutt thatcht saveing the kitchin which is nue and slated an old barn of 3 baies thatcht'; marginal notes show that later in the century stone slates had commonly replaced thatch. A 1637 survey of the manor of Sheffield manor noted plenty of 'good stones for building, and slate stones for tyling or slateing of houses'. In York thatch had long been banned because of the risk of fire, and the city's timber-framed houses were roofed with tiles (Hey 1981: 9–21).

In Yorkshire the Great Rebuilding began later than in parts of southern England. Nevertheless, improved standards of comfort and construction and a remarkable increase in the quantity and quality of furniture and household equipment was evident by Elizabeth's reign. Much of this was achieved by minor structural alterations; ceilings were inserted in open-halls, parlours, chambers and service rooms were added, rooms were provided with wainscotting and boarded floors and fitted with fireplaces and glass windows. The 'iron chimneys' that superseded the old open hearths are referred to in the wills of Thomas Hinchcliffe of Carlton, near Royston (1558), of John Smythe of Worsbrough (1561) and many of their contemporaries; in 1584 Robert Howle bequeathed 'all the glass in the windows in all places in and about my new dwelling house at Attercliffe', and in 1595 William Micklethwaite of Swaithe Hall near Barnsley left 'all the slate stone which is provided towards my new kitchen . . . all my timber which is felled towards building . . . [and] all the glass standing in the windows about the house'. Throughout the land, Elizabethan and Stuart farmhouses were larger, warmer, and lighter. Such improvement was often achieved without the complete rebuilding of a house. The new crucked-framed buildings of the late-sixteenth or early-seventeenth century were probably not very different in construction from their medieval predecessors. In most parts of Yorkshire the seventeenth century was well advanced before yeomen, husbandmen and craftsmen began to rebuild their homes in stone or brick. Apart from manor houses and gentry halls few Yorkshire houses were constructed of these materials before the Civil War. The period of the Great Rebuilding of ordinary Yorkshire farmhouses was from the mid-seventeenth to the mid-eighteenth centuries.

The surviving timber-framed houses in the Vale of York that were erected during the reigns of Elizabeth or the early-Stuarts are nearly all well-built, two-storeyed houses which compare favourably with timber-framed houses of a similar size and date in the East Midlands and south-east England. Most are now encased with brick or stone and are hard to recognize, but documentary evidence suggests that they were spread fairly widely across the social scale. A detailed survey of the Ingilby estates in Ripley and its associated hamlets in 1635 described the houses of 40 of the 43 tenants; five of these (and many of the farm buildings) were cruck-framed, and the rest were timber constructions using principal posts. Six of the 35 'post' houses were of four to seven bays, 20 of three, and only nine had one or two bays; 29 houses had a chamber, and 21 of these had more than one, so they must have been substantially built. Yet all these tenants were smallholders; 31 had less than 10 acres, and only four of them had more than 20 acres; Ripley was a poorer village than most (Harrison and Hutton 1984: 8–9). In the sixteenth and seventeenth centuries Yorkshire's timber-framed farmhouses were probably more substantial than was once believed.

Harrison and Hutton's survey of over seven hundred north Yorkshire and Cleveland buildings and related documentary evidence leads them to the conclusion that a degree of continuity can be established between Tudor and Stuart farmhouses and their predecessors; in north-east Yorkshire that continuity is very clear. The traditions of plan were well-established during the late Middle Ages and were not lightly abandoned during the Great Rebuilding. The medieval longhouse, where humans and their livestock lived under the same roof but were separated by a through-passage remained popular in Yorkshire until the later seventeenth century. Twenty-seven of 100 probate inventories taken at Stillington (a large, arable township with extensive open-fields) between 1550 and 1699 had a 'low end' for cattle, crops and agricultural implements. Longhouses were not as common further west, and no example has been found in the Dales, but the farmhouse tenanted by Nicholas Sampson near Sheffield in 1611 sounds like a longhouse that had been extended, for it was described as 'One house one bay, one parler above the house, 2 baies beneath the house for beast houses,. 2 parlers newly builded 2 Chambers over the parler', with various outbuildings. The common type of seventeenth- and early-eighteenth-century farmhouse, which was entered via a through-passage with kitchen and service rooms on one side and a hearth and the main living room on the other side, seems to have descended from the longhouse plan (Harrison and Hutton 1984: 8–15, 42–64).

The Poor

The cottages of the humblest inhabitants of Elizabethan and early-Stuart Yorkshire do not survive, but scattered documentary sources reveal their nature. In 1578 the court leet of the manor of Sheffield noted a few encroachments at Owlerton; Robert Shawe had built 'a lytle house of the Lordes waste there conteyninge one Bay', for which he paid 4*d.* rent, and Widow Alfrey had built a two-bay cottage with a garden. In Sheffield town in 1616 Nicholas Shooter rented '1 small Cottage 1 bay thatcht', Hugh Milnes lived in a similar one-bay, thatched cottage in Church Lane, and Alex Hydes had a two-bay house with a slate roof in Castle Green and 'an old barn of a bay an outshutt thatcht'. In many different parts of the county poor people set up home on the wastes and commons, especially in the western parts, but even on the Magnesian Limestone belt where a survey of 1652 found 'foure poore houses built on the lords waste' at Braithwell. On the Coal-Measure Sandstones a 1638 enquiry at Cawthorne noted that nine men and two women 'being very poore people and standing need of releefe have within the compasse of fifty years last past erected poore cottages uppon the wasts within the said Mannor', and that certain freeholders had built cottages for their coal-miners. Areas with opportunities for industrial employment were particularly attractive to immigrant squatters.

The dissolution of religious houses, especially the hospitals, took away at a stroke much of the regular provision for the old and the needy. In the sixteenth century the poor were a perennial problem, a problem that became worse as the national population grew in Elizabeth's reign. York Corporation in particular were continually vexed by the task of dealing with immigrant vagabonds who entered the city in search of charity after leaving in despair the shrunken and deserted villages of the countryside. The government's answer to the administrative problem was to make each parish responsible for its own poor; by Acts of 1598 and 1601 unpaid overseers elected at Easter vestry meetings were empowered to raise local rates in order to set the poor on work, apprentice poor children and relieve the 'lame, impotent, old, blind, and such other among them being poor and not able to work'. Begging was forbidden and punished by whipping. When seven people were found guilty of being rogues and vagabonds at the Richmond quarter sessions in 1610 the women were whipped and the men were branded with a letter R. Similar punishment was meted out to eight men and four women at the Pontefract sessions in 1638 after their arrest in Wakefield. The West Riding JPs had been alarmed earlier, in 1612, about the 'greate aboundance of wandring rogues and concourse of beggers and strangers, forth of all parts of this and other countys adjoyning, more now of late than att any time heretofore'. A House of Correction established at Wakefield was said in 1614 to have 'much suppressed the number of sturdie and incorrigeable beggers and rogues and other dissolute and disordered persons', but at the Wetherby sessions in 1631 the JPs were disgruntled to find that their orders concerning beggars had been 'greatly neglected'. On the whole, parish officials were charitable towards their own deserving poor but were concerned to keep out immigrant paupers. Thus, the accounts of the Sheffield capital burgesses contain the following typical entries:

'1569 gevyn to John Hornor for the caryeage of a pore man to the next constable . . . 1584 gyven to a poore man that had a Testimoniall from the Counsell at Yorke 4d . . . 1585 delivered to William Skargell to gyve to a poore wench of Crosebyes going to servic . . . 1595 payd Hugh Robertes the 14th Februarie 1595 to pay the Watchmen with when the Gipsees were in the towne.

Some parishes managed to convert their chantry lands into endowments for the poor and for other public purposes. At Ecclesfield fourteen feoffees were appointed in 1569 to administer 65 acres of former chantry land for the benefit of the church, the poor and the local highways; in 1638 feoffees' money usefully supplemented the poor rates when a parish poorhouse was built. In Sheffield the lands of the medieval burgery were divided in 1554 between two new bodies, the capital burgesses and the town trustees, and rents from burgess property were used to build the town's first workhouse in 1632. Rotherham's feoffees also helped the poor and eventually provided a school for local children. Such public provision was supplemented by private charity. W. K. Jordan has calculated that between 1480 and 1660 Yorkshire benefactors contributed £243,650.14s.0d. to charity, that no less than 8,632 people made

171

bequests to churches, schools and the poor, and that a third of these bequests went to some form of poor relief. A great flood of benefactions towards the relief of poverty began in the last decades of the sixteenth century and continued unabated to the Restoration (Jordan 1961: 217–35). Many of these bequests were small but some were major endowments. Few of the numerous almshouses or hospitals that were founded in Yorkshire during the century between the Dissolution and the Civil War survive in their original state, but a 1593 almshouse at Beamsley is still arranged in the ingenious manner of an Elizabethan 'device', with rooms forming segments of a circle and a central chapel rising to a lantern framed by tall chimney stacks; it was 'finished more profusely' in 1651 by Lady Anne Clifford.

In 1616 Gilbert, seventh Earl of Shrewsbury, ordered a survey of Sheffield and subsequently left £200 a year to provide for a hospital for twenty poor persons. The survey revealed that in the central, urban township 725, or about a third of the 2,207 inhabitants, were 'not able to live without the charity of their neighbours'. A further 160 householders did not contribute towards the poor rates, for they were 'not able to abide the storme of one fortnight's sickness, but would be thereby driven to beggary'. Only 100 householders paid for the relief of the poor and even they were 'but poor artificers; among them is not one which can keepe a teame on his own land, and not above tenn who have grounds of their own that will keepe a cow'. The greater part of the workmen and their children were 'constrained to worke sore, to provide them necessaries'. Some allowance has to be made for special pleading and perhaps for the particular circumstances of the winter of 1615–16 when this report was drawn up, but no doubt most of Yorkshire's other towns could have told a similar tale.

The almshouses and schools that were founded by lords of the manor or other wealthy individuals were not only the product of religious beliefs which stressed the importance of charitable works, but personal memorials to generous benefactors, who often adorned their buildings with suitable inscriptions and a coat of arms. It is not certain that any of the county's schools has a continuous history from the Middle Ages. At least 46 Yorkshire grammar schools were founded before the Reformation and few of them disappeared upon the dissolution of chantries, but no school in the county retains any medieval architecture. A further 68 schools are known to have been established between 1545 and 1603, including some in remote rural places. Many were taught by clergymen and may have been the successors to earlier schools held inside churches; schools of this period are commonly sited close to the parish church, and the single-storey, simple, Elizabethan or Jacobean school at Felkirk actually stands in the churchyard.

A typical development is illustrated by Worsbrough Grammar School, which was founded on a piece of waste ground immediately north of the churchyard in 1560 after the suppression of a chantry school; the present building probably dates from 1632 when John Rayney, a local man who had made his fortune in London, made a bequest to attract a well-qualified master to teach 'learning, cyphering [and] the grounds of religion'. Rayney was a puritan who also provided a lecturer to preach regularly in St Mary's Church. In all parts of England at this time men who had prospered in the capital or in some great provincial city remembered their birthplace when they came to make a will. One of the most attractive small schools in the county is at Burnsall, the lovely and lonely Wharfedale village where Sir William Craven was born. Craven became Lord Mayor of London and in his will in 1602 provided for a school to be built next to the church, with a house for the master and dormitories for boarders. Like another Jacobean school at Laughton, it is built in the local style of the domestic houses of the period. The former Otley Grammar School (1611) is also rooted in the vernacular tradition, but on a grander scale as befits a school that served a market town (Hey 1981: 131–9). Wakefield Grammar School was founded in 1591, largely through the generosity of George Savile and his son, puritan gentlemen who had prospered in the wool trade, and Halifax Grammar School (1600) was the inspiration of Dr John Favour, the Puritan Vicar of Halifax.

Religion and Politics

Twenty Roman Catholics were martyred at York between 1582 and 1589, a figure that is in sharp contrast with the lack of a single martyr in the whole diocese during the Marian persecution of Protestants a generation earlier. The most famous martyr was Margaret Clitherow, the wife of a prosperous butcher and stepdaughter of the mayor, who was pressed to death in 1586 for refusing to plead to a charge of harbouring priests. Many of the other martyrs were natives of the York district, but the Catholic stronghold was in the north-western dales, where it received the support of the rural gentry. Between 1580 and 1603 approximately three hundred Yorkshire households were consistently Catholic, and two hundred of these were of gentry status (Aveling 1980). On the whole the authorities successfully enforced conformity within the county, but in Nidderdale nearly all the leading families were Catholic and in the area between Pateley Bridge, Ripon and Spofforth recusants held important posts and were skilled in the art of evasion. The Ingilbys, Yorkes, Trappes, Plomptons, Middletons, Tankards and others were linked in a complex network of family connections, and in Richmondshire half the armigerous families were Catholics. Thirty-five North Riding men are known to have been trained in continental seminaries between 1582 and 1603, despite the treason laws, and the number of North Riding Catholics actually increased during this period (Jennings 1967: 381; Aveling 1966). By the 1620s persecution had largely ceased and the main burden for recusants had become

173

a financial one. The constant support of the squirearchy had seen Catholicism through its most dangerous years, and in north-western parts numbers increased again during the reigns of the early Stuarts. Elsewhere in Yorkshire, however, they formed an insignificant minority.

Meanwhile, the Church of England became dominated by Calvinists who regarded the Elizabethan settlement as too much of a compromise. Though they were small in numbers, they held influential positions. Their Puritanism was expressed in a desire for godly preaching. About 1604 one of them reported that only 3 of the 60 parishes of the deanery of Doncaster had ministers who were wholly devoted to the cause, 1 was sympathetic in some matters, and 13 were 'seeming weary of the ceremonies'; of the 80 clergy who served these 60 parishes, 42 did not preach, 26 were 'insufficient', and 12 were 'painful', i.e. painstaking, or Puritan (Marchant 1960: 27). Some despaired of making progress in England and ventured across the seas to the Dutch Netherlands or to New England; one such adventurer was William Bradford of Austerfield who sailed on the *Mayflower*, helped to found Plymouth, and was governor of the colony most of the time from 1621 until his death in 1657. Others found their part of Yorkshire congenial to their religious beliefs. Professor A. G. Dickens has written that,

> Local traditions and climates of opinion have a subtle and persistent strength . . . The communities which displayed the most marked Lollard-Protestant tendencies before 1558 proceeded in every case to develop puritan tendencies in Elizabethan and Jacobean times. The fact cannot be purely coincidental
> (Dickens 1959: 247).

Hull, Beverley, York and the West Riding industrial towns of Halifax, Leeds, Bradford, Wakefield and Sheffield became puritan strongholds, and so did the moorland chapelries. Some of the most eminent and extreme puritans served the twelve chapelries of Halifax parish and the chapelries of Morley and Woodkirk between Leeds and Dewsbury, which were dominated by the Puritan Saviles of Howley Hall. The role of the Puritan gentry in rural chapelries was as decisive as that of the Catholic squirearchy of the dales. Puritan squires built chapels on their own property and saw to it that services were organized on 'godly' lines by evangelizing clergy. These chapels were plain, stone oblongs with stone slate roofs, a bellcote, mullioned windows and simple interiors focused on the pulpit. Bramhope chapel, built in 1649 by Robert Dyneley, is the best surviving example but an impressive number were built in the large Pennine parishes before the Civil War. They were the forerunners of the dissenting chapels which were built in the years of toleration after 1689.

In 1632 Archbishop Richard Neile began a counter-attack on the puritans inside his diocese, as the northern counterpart to Archbishop Laud's efforts in the province of Canterbury. In such parishes as Halifax, Leeds and Sheffield Puritan ministers had been installed for forty years or more, with the enthusiastic support of their congregations. Now, Thomas Toller, vicar of Sheffield from 1598 to 1635, was forced to resign, and the powerful parishioners of Hull, Beverley, Doncaster and York were made to alter their churches by providing furnishings and altar rails and by emphasizing outward display. The number of Puritan clergy in Yorkshire had risen from 38 in 1603 to 96 in 1633, but by 1640 it had dropped to 65 (Cliffe 1969: 264). In Leeds, the medieval parish church of St Peter in Kirkgate could no longer house the greatly increased population, so in 1632 John Harrison, a wealthy alderman, built St John's in Gothic Survival style with a memorable display of woodwork and interior decoration; it is the finest church of the Laudian movement in the whole of England.

Clerical standards and the conformity of the lay population were maintained by the ecclesiastical courts at York and the archdeacons' visitations. After the brutal treatment of recusants in the 1580s the Church authorities successfully enforced their wishes without resort to harsh penalties. The practice of the diocese of York was to make drunkards, fornicators, swearers and others who offended the Church's moral code perform public penance in church. Offenders were obliged to stand on a form in front of the pulpit during divine service, draped in a white sheet and holding a white wand, and to repeat a confession and a request for forgiveness. Thus, in 1598 the archdeaconry of York tried a number of cases involving fornication or absence from church; at Doncaster a married couple were accused of living apart, three men had abused the churchwardens with vile speeches in church, two women were tried for fighting and scolding on the Sabbath day, Agnes Colier had abused the wife and children of Richard Thwaite, and three women were reputed common healers of persons with the French pox. At High Hoyland Ralph Clayton of Clayton West was presented for 'negligent cominge to the church and an excessive drinker', at Woolley Frances Hinchcliffe was reported to be a soothsayer, and at Silkstone Elizabeth Scruton of Bretton was said to be 'a blasphemer of gods holly word a Common Schoulder a Curser a Swearer a banner and a brawler'. Yorkshire did not suffer from the mania directed against supposed witches that erupted in some parts of the country. Between 1567 and 1640 117 cases of witchcraft were tried in the York courts; 62 involved charges concerning fortune-telling and the recovery of lost or stolen goods, and 37 involved spells cast on people or cattle, but only four or five cases specified cursing or black witchcraft. Those charged were treated lightly, and many cases were dismissed (Tyler 1969).

According to Dr J. T. Cliffe, Yorkshire had 557 gentry families at the beginning of Elizabeth's reign and 679 at the start of the Civil War. Many country squires could trace their descent from medieval knights and at least 270 Yorkshire gentlemen in Charles I's reign had ancestors who had been resident in the county since 1500. No less than 340 families appear in both the

1558 and 1642 lists, and about two in every five had increased their prosperity during that period. Many fortunes had risen spectacularly after former monastic estates and mineral rights had been acquired at the Dissolution. Upon James I's accession 60 Yorkshiremen were knighted, and later 35 were created baronets and ten raised to the peerage. But an equally large section of the gentry ran into financial difficulties either through bad management, costly litigation or living beyond their means. Many Yorkshire gentlemen still offered traditional hospitality of the sort provided by Sir Hugh Cholmley of Whitby in the reign of Charles I:

> I had between thirty and forty in my ordinary family, a chaplain who said prayers every morning at six, and again before dinner and supper, a porter who merely attended the gates, which were ever shut up before dinner, when the bell rung to prayers, and not opened till one o'clock, except for strangers who came to dinner, which was ever fit to receive three or four besides my family, without any trouble; whatever their fare was, they were sure to have a hearty welcome. Twice a week, a certain number of old people, widows and indigent persons, were served at my gates with bread and good pottage made of beef, which I mention that those which succeed may follow the example.

Cholmley's style of living was becoming less fashionable, but it was still favoured by many Yorkshire gentlemen (Cliffe 1969: *passim*).

When a petition for a new university at York was submitted to Parliament in 1641 the signatories confessed that 'we have been looked upon as rude and barbarous people', yet at that time 172 heads of gentry families had received a university education – mainly at Cambridge – and over 100 had travelled on the continent. Many gentlemen had an interest in music, plays, books and other cultural pursuits, and at least 40 wrote family histories, diaries or books of precepts for their sons. The Saviles of Bradley and Methley and the Fairfaxes of Denton were cultured families and George Gower, the leading portrait painter of the 1570s and 80s was a Yorkshire gentleman. It was probably at this level of society that a sense of being Yorkshiremen (and not just northerners) was first developed; county pride is evident in the way that Sir William Fairfax decorated his great chamber at Gilling Castle with the arms of the Yorkshire gentry. Yorkshire was administered largely through its Ridings, but that did not prevent the emergence of a sense of county community amongst the gentry, as in other parts of sixteenth- and seventeenth-century England, a sentiment that gave rise to the first county histories (though not for the vast county of Yorkshire) and to Christopher Saxton's series of county maps in the 1570s. The peculiarities of speech and character that distinguished Yorkshire people were evident to outsiders. In 1549 William Thomas observed, 'Betwene the Florentine and Venetian is great diversitee in speeche, as with us betwene a Londoner and a Yorkeshyreman', and the considered

176

opinion of Edwin Sandys, Archbishop of York (1577–88) was that 'A more stiff-necked, wilful, or obstinate people did I ever know or hear of.' In a *Brief Discourse between Yorkshiremen & Scottish-men* (1650) one of the participants declares, 'I am a Yorkshireman born and bred, I care not who knowes it; I hope true Yorkshire never denies his county.'

Only 25 Yorkshire gentlemen were Puritans in 1570, but by Charles I's reign their numbers had increased significantly to 138, or 20.3 per cent of the 679 gentry families. In Dickering and Buckrose wapentakes, along the northern fringe of the East Riding, they formed 46.6 per cent, but in the North Riding, where the Catholic tradition was strong, they numbered only 11.3 per cent. Many ancient families had become Puritan; indeed 90 Puritan families had resided in Yorkshire since at least the beginning of Elizabeth's reign. Nine baronets, 25 knights and a substantial number of professional and commercial men had also joined the cause; Puritan strongholds were found in the towns as well as in the countryside (Cliffe 1969: 262–77). Although the Civil War was not fought over religion, the Puritan gentry favoured Parliament by 64:24, with many other families neutral or divided. Dr Cliffe has analysed gentry loyalties as follows:

Table 3.1   Gentry families in the Civil War

	North Riding	East Riding	West Riding	York	Total
Royalists	68	44	125	5	242
Parliamentarians	35	37	54	2	128
Divided or changed	15	19	31	4	69
Neutral	77	42	110	11	240
Total	195	142	320	22	679

The majority of families were neutral in the summer and early autumn of 1642, and a striking number remained neutral throughout the war. Others drifted with the tide, but many sincerely believed that important issues of principle were involved. Political loyalties cut across personal relationships, and in some cases the head of the family fought on one side and his heir on the other. The Royalist party had a strong base in York, the seat of the archbishop and of the Council of the North, and Parliament was too far away in the South to have local influence, but Sir Thomas Wentworth, the Earl of Strafford, alienated some powerful Yorkshire families by his policy of 'thorough' and his general demeanour. Several Yorkshire landowners, including Lord Fairfax, Sir Hugh Cholmley, Sir Arthur Ingram and Henry Bellasis sat on the House of Commons committee that drew up the indictment that led to Wentworth's execution in 1641. On the whole, the Parliamentary gentry were better-off than their Royalist counterparts, but in absolute terms the Royalists included more rising families than did the Parliamentarians. Economic circumstances do not

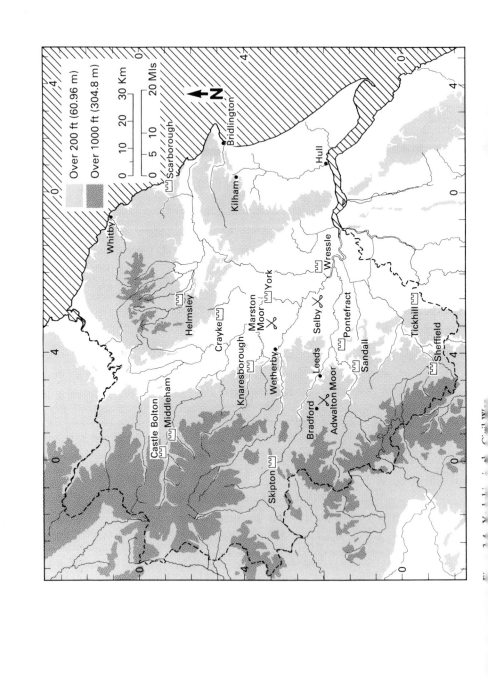

Over 200 ft (60.96 m)

Over 1000 ft (304.8 m)

N

0   5   10   20   30 Km

0   10   20 Mls

Whitby

Scarborough

Bridlington

Kilham

Hull

Helmsley

Crayke

Marston Moor

York

Wressle

Middleham

Castle Bolton

Knaresborough

Wetherby

Leeds

Selby

Pontefract

Skipton

Bradford

Adwalton Moor

Sandall

Tickhill

Sheffield

explain the choice of side. Rising and declining families fought on either side, and the Royalists as well as the Parliamentarians attracted commercial and professional support. Dr Cliffe's careful analysis makes it clear that there are no easy explanations. He does, however, note that one of the most striking features about both the Royalist and Parliamentary gentry is that only a minority of families were seated in the same locality in 1558 and 1642 (Cliffe 1969: 327–60).

After raising his standard at Nottingham on 22 August 1642, Charles I was soon in York. That summer Scarborough was also the scene of Royalist activity, as troops and supplies came in through the harbour. Charles attempted to establish a garrison at Hull, Yorkshire's major port, but he was denied entry; the war had begun. At first the Parliamentarians, led by Ferdinando, Lord Fairfax and his son, Sir Thomas, had some success in taking the West Riding clothing towns, but by July 1642 William Cavendish, Earl of Newcastle, had built up a substantial Royalist force at York and was able to defeat the Fairfaxes at Adwalton Moor and then drive them out of Leeds and Bradford. Soon the whole of Yorkshire was under Royalist control, except for the port of Hull, and several medieval castles were garrisoned. Newcastle's units, however, were needed to meet the challenge of the Scots, who had formed an alliance with Parliament and who threatened daily to invade. When Newcastle campaigned against this threat, the Yorkshire Royalists were unable to protect his rear. Sir William Constable led a contingent of Parliamentary forces out of Hull to a victory on the Wolds at 'Colham' (Kilham or Cowlam) and on to the capture of Bridlington and Whitby. Royalist counter-attacks under the leadership of John Bellasis were twice thwarted at Bradford, and in April 1644 Bellasis's army was decisively beaten by Sir Thomas Fairfax's troops at Selby. Newcastle was forced to hurry back to defend his base at York Castle (Newman 1980: 123–34). The advancing Scots joined the Parliamentary forces at Wetherby and went on to besiege the county capital. Newcastle was obliged to send for help to Prince Rupert, who advanced through the Welsh Marches and Lancashire, collecting recruits on his way, to Skipton and Knaresborough.

The stage was set for one of the most decisive battles ever fought on Yorkshire soil. On 2 July 1644 at Marston Moor Oliver Cromwell's cavalry routed Prince Rupert's horsemen then destroyed Newcastle's infantry in the centre: 'God made them as stubble to our swords', he said. During the next few months the remaining Royalist garrisons in the north fell one by one, and at the end of the war many of the old castles were dismantled so that they could never be fortified again. When Charles I was tried in 1649 fifteen Yorkshiremen were amongst his judges, and six were present at his execution. The Civil War caused substantial damage in Yorkshire and greatly disrupted trade; minor battles and skirmishes, unruly soldiers and general disorder caused by a breakdown in administration made life unpleasant and sometimes unbearable in many parts of the county.

The diary of Adam Eyre of Hazlehead Hall on the edge of the southern Pennines shows, however, that even for a Parliamentary captain life in the late 1640s could go on much as before (*Surtees Society*, LXV 1875). On 21 April 1647 he wrote,

> then I cam home, and in the way I fecht my hook I left yesternight; and, after dinner, I went down into the Second Royd on fishing, and lost my hook; and so came home again, where I spent the time idlely til night, for which I pray God forgive mee; and at night I took some alicompane for my cold, and so went to bed.

Life was full of such little trials for a Puritan minor gentleman: on 8 June 1647 he recorded,

> This morne my wife began, after her old manner, to brawle and revile mee for wishing her only to weare such apparell as was decent and comly, and accused mee for treading on her sore foote, with curses and othes; which, to my knowledge I touched not; nevertheless she continued in that extacy til noone.

He stiffened his resolve by attending sermons and by rising early to read the *Book of Martyrs*.

Chapter 4

The Later-Stuart and Hanoverian Era

Towns

During the reigns of the later Stuarts England's population was still overwhelmingly rural. Three out of every four people lived in the countryside and many others dwelt in small market towns which were essentially rural in nature. In 1700 the population of England and Wales was little more than five million, for the growth era of 1540–1630 had been followed by 70 years of stagnation. London, the largest city in Europe, had 575,000 inhabitants and remained a great magnet for rural immigrants in search of excitement and fortune. The leading provincial cities were tiny in comparison; Norwich had about 30,000 people, Bristol 20,000, and Exeter, York and Newcastle had even less. York had only 12,000 inhabitants in the 1660s, and a generation later the urban part of Leeds contained just over half that number. Some industrial towns and villages continued to grow even in the period of general stagnation, but it was not until the end of the seventeenth century that the national population began to rise again. This renewed growth was checked in the 1720s by the last series of great national mortalities brought about by fevers in the wake of disastrous harvests. In his *History of Hull* Thomas Gent remembered that during 1727 'in our Distress we were supplied with ship loads (of corn) from Italy, Flanders, Poland, and other distant parts, to the unspeakable Comfort of many house Keepers', and in 1729 a Vale of York vicar noted in his burial register: 'The greatest mortality that ever can be remembered, or made out to be in the parish of Arksey'. Arthur Jessop of Holmfirth completed his diary for 1730 with the words:

> conclusion of another year and many hath been taken away . . . reduced
> to great straits . . . forced to live upon coarse mean fare such as is not
> usual for man to eat but life was preserved to turn our scarcity into
> plenty and a plentiful crop the last year and . . . another plentiful crop
> this year.

During various years from 1723 to 1729 many parishes recorded more burials than baptisms, but not all communities were affected. Lancashire burial registers note fever, ague fever and pleurisy as causes of death, but elsewhere a variety of diseases were responsible. Few infants or children died in these troubled times, however, and from the 1740s onwards the growth of the national population was dramatic.

By 1801 the population of England and Wales had reached 9.2 million. This unprecedented rise was accompanied by an enormous shift in the distribution of the national population; the agricultural counties of southern and eastern England lost their dominance, one person in every three now lived in a town, and industrial Lancashire, Warwickshire, Staffordshire and the West Riding had assumed greater national importance. Manchester, Liverpool and Birmingham were now the most populous towns in the land, and of the old provincial centres only Bristol remained in the top six. Two out of every three Yorkshiremen now lived in the West Riding, that is 564,593 compared with 158,955 in the North Riding, 111,192 in the East Riding and 24,393 in York and its dependent wapentake, the Ainsty. A great shift of emphasis had occurred since the late Middle Ages. Leeds was now the largest town in Yorkshire and Sheffield came next. York was no longer the indisputed capital of the North.

Before this great transformation took place York fulfilled its traditional role as a major political, ecclesiastical, judicial, commercial and social centre. In 1686 it had 483 guest beds and stabling facilities for 800 horses, far more than the 294 beds and 454 stalls at Leeds. The Ouse remained a major thoroughfare and the city's markets and fairs were as busy as ever. Though Celia Fiennes found the streets narrow and the houses low, a poor contrast to a modern town like Nottingham, Daniel Defoe was enthusiastic:

> York is indeed a pleasant and beautiful city . . . there is abundance of good company here, and abundance of good families live here . . . No other city in England is better furnished with provisions of every kind, nor any so cheap.

County gentry like the Bourchiers of Beningbrough Hall had town houses in Micklegate or other fashionable streets, the Earl of Burlington designed assembly rooms and John Carr designed a grandstand for the Knavesmire racecourse, and York's skilled craftsmen continued to make jewellery, books, stained glass, etc. for the county clientèle. The great majority of the city's workforce were employed in service industries, catering for consumer demand.

The rural nobility and gentry continued to dominate the political life of the county. Only York and Hull generally managed to elect freely their own nominees to Parliament. In addition to the two county MPs (four from 1822 onwards) Yorkshire had fourteen boroughs with the right to return two members. Six others had lost their rights since the Middle Ages, and Leeds and

Halifax no longer had the privilege of electing one member each, which they had enjoyed briefly under Cromwell. Industrial towns such as Sheffield, Bradford and Wakefield had no members, yet 'pocket boroughs' like Knaresborough (controlled by the Duke of Devonshire) or Aldborough and Boroughbridge (dominated by the Duke of Newcastle) returned two members each. Elsewhere, the rich bought their victories, and county elections occasionally turned into an expensive battle for supremacy between the leading Whig and Tory aristocratic families. The famous 1807 election, when Lord Milton, the eldest son of Earl Fitzwilliam, defeated Henry Lascelles, the future Earl of Harewood, cost the two noble houses upwards of £200,000. Usually, however, the rival parties saved expense by agreeing to split the seats.

The 1686 War Office returns of the number of guest beds and stabling in towns and villages throughout the country demonstrate the continuing importance of old settlements such as Malton, Beverley and Ripon, and the growth of the major market towns in the industrial parts of the West Riding.

Table 4.1   The 1686 War Office returns

	Guest beds	Stabling
York	483	800
Leeds	294	454
Wakefield	242	543
Doncaster	206	453
Malton	205	543
Hull	199	349
Beverley	182	460
Halifax	130	306
Sheffield	119	270
Ripon	118	422
Thirsk	110	234
Richmond	99	228
Pontefract	92	235
Northallerton	82	83
Scarborough	74	114
Skipton	72	93
Howden	67	58
Barnsley	64	109
Rotherham	63	72
Selby	58	89
Bawtry	57	69
Bedale	52	44
Tadcaster	50	72
Boroughbridge	50	60

(*Source*: Public Record Office, WO/3/48)

Contemporary travellers spoke well of Yorkshire towns. Celia Fiennes thought Beverley preferable to any place she had visited except Nottingham, and Defoe

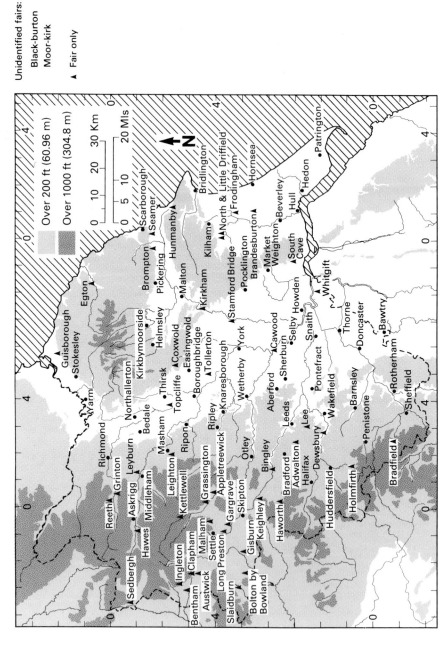

Over 200 ft (60.96 m)
Over 1000 ft (304.8 m)

Figure 4.1 Yorkshire's markets and fairs, 1770

thought that the 'very neat, pleasant, well-built town' of Ripon had 'the finest and most beautiful [market] square that is to be seen of its kind in England'. Ripon was famous for its horse fair, two great cloth fairs, wool fair and leather market, and when Viscount Torrington came on a visit in 1792 he found that 'the market place was crowded by cattle and holiday folk'. When he strolled through Skipton, however, he was disgusted by 'this nasty, filthily-inhabited town; for I never saw more slatterns, or dirtier houses'. Many of the old towns were rebuilt in stone or brick during the eighteenth century. Richmond remains an attractive Georgian and medieval settlement, but Doncaster is no longer the 'wealthy and beautiful town' that Joseph Hunter knew in 1828, nor 'one of the most clean, airy, and elegant towns in the British dominions', which is how Edward Baines described it in 1822; he went on to say that, 'There are few towns in the kingdom in which so great a portion of the inhabitants possess independent fortunes, and the neighbourhood is remarkable for opulent families.' Doncaster and Richmond remained great regional market centres. In 1749 Richmond had 'one of the best corn markets in the north of England', and the town's cheap provisions included sea-fish imported from Hartlepool and Redcar, flax, iron, tar, timber, salt and groceries which had come via Yarm or Stockton, and coal from County Durham. Even the growing industrial towns were still primarily market centres. In seventeenth-century Wakefield the market-place by the church was congested with the booths of the bakers and leather workers and surrounded by inns; names such as Shambles, The Cross, Bull Ring, Hog Market and Market Place indicated the heart of the town. The congestion was eased by the Improvement Commission appointed in 1771 to deal with the 'very ruinous condition of the streets' and by the enclosure of 2,633 acres under an Act of 1793. Before the end of the century Wakefield had an attractive Georgian square of brick terraces arranged around the new St John's Church.

Some of the smaller market towns also attracted favourable comments from visitors. Celia Fiennes thought Tadcaster 'a very good little town for travellers, mostly Inns and little tradesmens houses', and Defoe noted that Northallerton was 'remarkable for the vast quantity of black cattle sold there, there being a fair once every fortnight for some months', when oxen were bought to be fattened in the Lincolnshire fens or the Isle of Ely for sale in London. The townsmen 'boasted that they had not one Dissenter here, and yet at the same time not one Tory, which is what, I believe, cannot be said of any other town in Great Britain'. In 1751 Wetherby struck Dr Pococke as 'a poor town very pleasantly situated', and a generation later Viscount Torrington regarded it as small, gloomy and ill-built. Wetherby had suffered from the cattle plague and agricultural depression in the mid-eighteenth century and over half of its 70 or 80 properties had been destroyed by fire in 1723. The town had been established as a chapelry of Spofforth where the Great North Road crossed the river Wharfe and much of it had eventually come into the hands of the Duke of Devonshire. In 1776 the population stood at only 912, but Wetherby was nevertheless distinguished from its rural neighbours by the fifteen innkeepers in the High Street, Market Place and adjoining Chapel Yard, its eight professional families, its provision dealers and craftsmen, and its brewery, tannery and mills for grinding corn and crushing rape seed (Unwin 1982). Another typical minor market town with a simple craft structure supporting the basic economy of agriculture was Otley, where a market for corn and provisions was held each Tuesday and fairs for horned cattle and household goods were organized twice a year on 1 August and 15 November. Differences in the social and economic structure of town and countryside are highlighted by the hearth-tax returns; 37.2 per cent of the 118 households in the town had only one hearth, compared with 62.6 per cent of the 911 rural households in the outlying parts of the parish, and the townsmen had a much higher proportion of households with three to five hearths (Smith 1980).

Towards the end of the seventeenth century Yorkshire had over 60 market towns, and by 1770 the county held fairs in 97 different places. Ancient market rights had lapsed at Hornsea, Hunmanby, Frodingham, Kilham and elsewhere, but Thorne (1659), Huddersfield (1671) and Penistone (1699) had acquired new charters for weekly markets and annual fairs and several short fairs had been established in the countryside. Moreover, many villages now had shops to cater for their needs. At the close of the seventeenth century Abraham de la Pryme wrote that although Hatfield 'be not dignify'd either with a market or fair, yet it stands so conveniently that it is not far off of any', having Doncaster, Thorne and Bawtry nearby, but indeed it was itself 'so well furnished with one or two of almost every trade, as butchers, mercers, chandlers, joyners, cutlers, chirurgians, etc, that other places stands in more need of them than the latter of the former'.

A new type of town, the spa, took root during the Stuart era and blossomed in the eighteenth century. Spas offered cures and leisure, based on the supposed healing properties of sulphur and chalybeate springs. The fashion spread from the Low Countries and Germany to Bath, Epsom, Wells, Tunbridge Wells and to the northern resorts of Buxton, Harrogate and Scarborough. The chalybeate Tewit Well at Harrogate had been recommended by Yorkshire doctors since Elizabeth's reign; then in the seventeenth century three mineral springs were discovered on the commons at High Harrogate. 'Its all marshy and wett', wrote Celia Fiennes, and at first visitors stayed in nearby Knaresborough. During the later years of the seventeenth century it became the practice not only to drink from the springs but to bathe in tubs of heated sulphur water, so then it was necessary to provide accommodation. At Scarborough, where medicinal springs had been discovered on the sands in 1626, buildings were not erected nearby until about 1700. Sea-bathing was an added attraction, and Scarborough was probably the first place in England where it became popular. The poorer end of the town, in and around Newborough, now became fashionable, attracting inns, coffee shops and places of entertainment. It was said in 1705 that 'most of the gentry of the

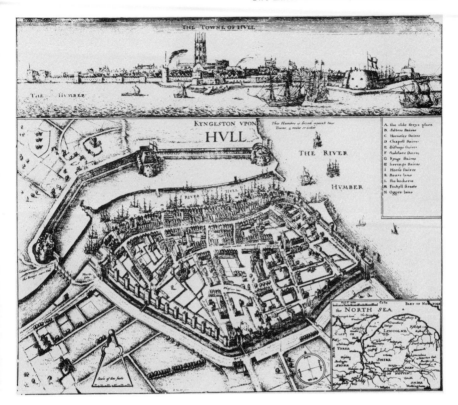

Plate 4.1 Wenceslaus Hollar's *View of Hull, c.* 1640. The town of Kingston-upon-Hull was still contained within its fourteenth-century walls when this view was taken on the eve of the Civil War. Plenty of space was still available for development within the old confines, though by the end of the seventeenth century Hull was badly congested. New streets were not laid out beyond the walls until the later eighteenth century when the first docks were constructed.

Hollar's view shows ships anchored in the river Hull near its confluence with the Humber and several stairs leading down to the quayside. The planned lay-out of the medieval town is evident and the massive brick walls and towers are intact. Hull stood firm for the Parliamentary cause and refused to let Charles I enter in the summer of 1642. For a time it was the only place in Yorkshire not under Royalist control.

North of England and Scotland resort hither in the season'. The harbour was also 'one of the most commodious of this kingdom' according to Defoe, 'yet scarce able to hold the ships belonging to the place'; a petition in 1702 claimed that about 160 sail or collier ships lay in the harbour during winter time. Fishing remained an important activity, and Scarborough also traded with the Netherlands and Norway, but the lack of a navigable river prevented its development into an important distribution centre (McIntyre 1978).

On the eve of the Civil War Hollar's view of Hull, Yorkshire's major port, shows much open ground within the medieval walls, but by the end of the century the town was badly congested. Defoe found it 'exceeding close built . . .

187

Plate 4.2 Whitby Harbour. The town of Whitby grew around the market place and harbour where the river Esk flows into the sea. The ruins of the medieval Benedictine abbey stand gauntly on the skyline overlooking the town.

The photograph was taken by Frank Meadow Sutcliffe (1853–1941), who was born at Headingley, Leeds, and who moved to Whitby in 1875 to open a photographic studio. Sutcliffe's photographs are renowned for their artistry and for the way they create a sense of place and community. The maritime character of Whitby is captured by this view of 'Dock End', taken in 1880. Bill Eglon Shaw's researches have established that the 'Alert' on the right was built in Whitby in 1802 as a sloop and later converted to a schooner.

'tis extraordinary populous, even to an inconvenience'. In 1700 the population of Hull and its northern suburb of Sculcoates was about 7,500; by 1831 it had risen six fold. During the reign of Queen Anne the leading merchants still lived in their counting houses in High Street, but by the beginning of Victoria's reign none of the thirteen aldermen-merchants lived in the town. A series of improvement acts after 1755 were necessary to deal with the building, traffic, sanitation, lighting and repair problems that accompanied this rapid growth, and the remaining medieval walls were destroyed by the three docks that were built between 1774 and 1829 (Gillett and MacMahon 1980: 198). The first dock, which covered nearly ten acres and sheltered more than a hundred ships, was the largest that had yet been constructed in England.

188

Hull's volume of shipping rose from a steady 11,000 tons per annum in the first quarter of the century to 135,000 tons in 1792. By then Hull was the fourth largest port in England, but it remained insignificant in comparison with London and much smaller than Liverpool and Bristol. Two or three dozen merchant houses, led by those of Crowle, Thornton, Maister, Sykes, Mowld, Somerscale and Broadley, dominated the export and coastal trades (Jackson 1972: 65–157). Whaling was a spectacular but relatively minor business. Oil obtained from Dutch whalers had been prized for lighting since Tudor times, but British seamen rarely ventured to Greenland or the Davis Straits until the 1730s. Hull became the major British whaling port, and great blubber houses were also built alongside the inner harbour at Whitby. Between 1766 and 1816 a total of 2,761 whales, *c.* 25,000 seals, 55 bearns, 43 narwhals and 64 sea-horses were brought to Whitby. William Chapman's contemporary 'Account of some of the Principal People of Whitby' records that

> In the year 1676 they had 76 ships, all of them small, except one or two fly-boats. In the year 1700 they had 113, two or three of which were of 20 keels (400 tons or upwards), but altogether did not equal the burthen of 30 of their present large ships. About the middle of the 18th century they increased very rapidly, both in size and number. The building of Dry Docks made an increase of trade and influx of inhabitants, and the war which began in 1744 increased them much by having many ships in the Transport Service. Since this they have increased much more in shipping, having sent 20 sail to Greenland this season – 1786.
>
> (Jeffrey 1971: 140–1)

Whitby was a busier port than Scarborough, and Filey and Bridlington were mere fishing settlements in comparison.

Farming

During the seventeenth and eighteenth centuries England became a network of integrated economies in which farmers concentrated upon what they could do best. In the North Riding, for instance, nobles and gentlemen-farmers acquired a national reputation for the horses which they reared for the coach and the saddle, while their tenant farmers specialized in dairying and sold good-quality butter to London or to continental factors and their inferior produce to the inhabitants of the northern industrial towns. In the heyday of the trade during

Charles II's reign nearly 42,000 firkins of butter per annum were carted up to 30 miles to Yarm, Stockton or Whitby for export. Farming activities were geared to the demands of the market and produce was transported long distances. Pennine farmers, for example, devoted their energies to dairying, rearing and industrial employments and were able to import their malt and bread corn via the navigable rivers, the market towns and the carrying services offered by local badgers.

The spirit of improvement infected all parts of the country. Thus in 1664 farmers in the liberty of Ripon claimed that,

> Many of late have pared dryed and burned their pasture and worser sorts of grounds – which doth yield three or four good Cropps, the first sowne in Aprill or beginning of May with Barley upon one Tillage; the second of Masline sown at Michaelmas following with one Tillage; the third Barley againe sowne in Aprill with two Tillages or ploweings; the fourth, Peas, beanes, or oates. And after these Cropps the spreading thereon a small Quantity of lime or dung, or marle and dung mixed, maketh good pasture grounds followe
>
> (Lennard 1932).

The practice of spreading lime was widely adopted when it was brought as back carriage to be burned in kilns at the head of navigable rivers and canals. One of the most successful farming innovations was the Rotherham plough, which was possibly based on Dutch models brought over by settlers in the Hatfield Levels. Patented in 1730 by Joseph Foljambe of Eastwood, yeoman, and Disney Staniforth of Firbeck, esquire, it became popular over a wide area and the basis for many metal ploughs in the nineteenth century (Marshall 1978).

Men of initiative, like Henry Best of Elmswell, tried to improve the quality of their livestock and were prepared to try the new crops that had been introduced in other parts of England. Where soils were suitable, turnips and clover were grown in many parts of the county during the late seventeenth and early eighteenth centuries; by the 1720s clover had replaced peas, and turnips had partly replaced rye, in the rotations of the townfields of Hatfield. Potatoes were not generally grown as a field crop until well into the eighteenth century, though small plots were cultivated in Masham and Nidderdale by 1712–13 and at Cowick in the southern Vale of York by the 1730s. They had been introduced into Lancashire and Cumbria by the mid-seventeenth century and had soon become a common sight in the western parts of the Lancashire Plain, especially in the reclaimed mosslands, but it was a century or so later before they were extensively adopted on the rich loams and warpings of Holderness and Howdenshire (Thirsk, ed. 1985: 70 Strickland 1812: 150). It was stated in 1800 that in the North Riding potatoes had become an object of field husbandry (as distinct from a garden crop) not more than 40 years previously, but now they were universal (Tuke 1800: 149). An older crop that gained in popularity was rape, which was grown in Holderness, the Vale of Pickering and other lowland areas as fodder for sheep and as a valuable supply of vegetable oil, much of which was exported to Holland. Amongst the newer crops were the hops which were cultivated around Doncaster and the liquorice that was grown in the gardens of Pontefract. As early as 1638 *Barnabees Journal* claimed that 'For the choicest Licorice' Pontefract was the place to go: 'Here Liquorice grows upon their mellowed banks, Decking the Spring with her delicious plants'. Liquorice was also grown in London, Godalming and Worksop in the middle years of the seventeenth century. It required plenty of dung, and as it took three summers for the roots to grow to a satisfactory size, vegetables such as onions and lettuces were cultivated on the same plots in the meantime. When Celia Fiennes visited Pontefract in the 1690s she saw gardens full of liquorice, but in 1770 Arthur Young observed that they often covered only 50 and never more than 100 acres.

Young wrote some disparaging words about those farmers who did not share the enterprising spirit of improving landowners such as the Marquis of Rockingham, and his criticisms were echoed by William Marshall: 'Poverty and ignorance are the ordinary inhabitants of small farms'. This conservatism was the other side of the coin to the progress that was undoubtedly made elsewhere. When, in 1729, the steward of the manor of Bilbrough in the northern Vale of York failed to get his tenants to grow less corn and to concentrate upon dairying, he wrote in disgust that they were 'like Old Cart Horses, one can't thrust 'em out of their old beaten track'. Most farms in the northern vale were under 30 acres; indeed much of the county was still farmed on this basis. In 1788 more than half the land in the Vale of Pickering was laid out in farms rented at less than £20 per annum, and perhaps three-quarters were let at under £50. Marshall observed that leases were unknown on most of the larger estates and that farms were let at will on a yearly tenancy; nevertheless, in practice they had been held as hereditary possessions through successive generations. Tuke made the same point about the North Riding generally and thought that few parts of England could produce a tenantry 'who, and whose ancestry have lived an equal number of years uninterruptedly on their farms'. Strickland claimed that East Riding tenants were just as secure without leases: 'Estates, in general, throughout the district, are let on very fair, and many even on moderate terms, and many of them have been occupied by the progenitors of the present tenants during two, three or four generations'. Tenure was just as secure in the West Riding, where Brown remarked upon 'the astonishing number of freeholders' and others with sound copyhold; the West Riding was one of the strongholds of small freeholders with less than 20 acres of land.

Nearly all the Pennine farmers within the Graveship of Holme were copyhold tenants of the huge manor of Wakefield. Common rights and dual occupations were vital to their well-being. In a chancery case of 1674 Oliver Roberts of Ox Lee, a yeoman copyholder of £30 per annum, accused Humphrey Bray of Hepworth, a copyholder of £10 per annum, of breaking a bond by continuing to pasture his sheep on the commons. Bray protested that he had signed the bond after an alehouse conversation on how the commons were overstocked, 'being hot with drinking and scarce understanding what he said or did'; his pasture rights were worth a further £10 a year and it would be impossible for him to farm without grazing his sheep on the commons and folding them on his lands for their manure. Probate inventories show that whatever their description – yeoman, husbandman, clothier, etc. – all the inhabitants of the graveship were farmer-clothiers in the traditional manner, though population pressure was causing the sub-division of many farms and the building of new ones on the edges of the commons. The 14,280 acres of commons and wastes belonging to the graveship in 1709 had been reduced to 9,200 acres at the time of the enclosure award in 1834. Similar trends can be recognized in the northern dales, where the common arable fields had mostly disappeared through piecemeal enclosure by the end of the seventeenth century. Wensleydale inventories taken between 1670 and 1700 show that only one in seven farmers in the lower parts and as few as one in twenty in the upper dale grew any crops. Small meadows and pastures lined the dale bottoms and large, stinted pastures covered the fell sides; common rights and subsidiary industrial employments were essential to the smallholders' economy. Though many weaver-farmers continued the old life-style, farms had generally dwindled in size and numerous cottagers were now principally dependent upon a craft; linen weaving rather than the manufacture of woollen cloth was now the mainstay (Fieldhouse 1980). In Swaledale also holdings became fragmented and their occupants turned increasingly to lead mining for extra income. As the scale of mining operations grew, some communities became more industrial than agricultural in character, so that by the late eighteenth century the men of Swaledale could be more properly described as miners who were part-time farmers (Raistrick and Jennings 1965: 310–13).

Long before 1700 many other Yorkshire townships had agreed to divide their open fields and sometimes also their commons into separate closes which could be grazed or tilled as the owner thought best. In the northern Vale of York strips farmed to common rotations rarely survived as late as the era of parliamentary enclosure. Field systems throughout the county were adapted to allow the cultivation of new crops or the conversion of some strips into grass leys to provide extra grazing. Piecemeal enclosure for such purposes meant that the fields of one township might be organized in a very different manner from those of their neighbours, for some were severely truncated and others were developed to their greatest extent and their most complex form. In the lower Dearne valley, for instance, Wath's regular common fields were affected only at the margins by piecemeal enclosure until their division by Act of Parliament in 1814, but at neighbouring Adwick two-thirds of the land had been enclosed by 1737 and though the remaining common-fields were still divided into strips they were held in compact blocks; in effect the landowner had enclosed the land by redistributing it amongst his tenants. Nearby Bolton had 1,715 acres of common arable fields, ings, pastures and wastes until 1761, with an authentic common-field system subject to common pasture rights where tenants' lands were scattered in every field, but in the early-nineteenth century Mexborough had only 700 acres of common fields, 160 acres of common ings and 90 acres of common pastures, for 300 acres were 'old enclosures' taken piecemeal from the three fields over the previous two centuries. Neighbouring settlements with similar soils and field systems could have a very different history of enclosure if the patterns of landownership and tenure were not the same; human factors were as important as the physical ones (Harvey 1974). In Holderness, for example, the long lands of the ancient two-field system remained intact in some townships, but in many parishes partial enclosure and the conversion of strips into temporary or permanent grass leys were commonplace. Holderness was a corn-and-cattle district with wheat and beans the principal crops and an average head of fifteen cattle per farm that was the highest in Yorkshire. Much land remained unenclosed here until the later eighteenth century.

Parliamentary enclosure was the last stage of a long process of conversion, the method that was resorted to when the full agreement of farmers could not be reached. If the owners of about three-quarters of the value of the land agreed upon the desirability of enclosure, their wishes could be enforced by private Act of Parliament. Between 1750 and 1850 over six million acres of land in England and Wales were enclosed by about 4,000 private Acts. Scattered strips were re-arranged into compact holdings, and those who had rights (notably of grazing and turf-digging) upon the commons and wastes were compensated with new closes. As these rights were related to the size of the farms, the largest allotments went to the biggest freeholders. The small cottager who previously had the right to graze a few animals often found that his compensation was inadequate and, moreover, expensive to fence. Though parliamentary enclosure was carried out with a scrupulous regard for the law, in practice the poorer sections of society fared badly. That this would be so was obvious to some of the Ackworth freeholders who refused to sign a petition to enclose their common land in 1772:

> Mr Joseph White said it will injure the Poor . . . Peter Wilson believes it for his Interest but that it will hurt the Poor . . . Mrs Turton said she would never consent to have the Common inclosed for it would hurt the Poor . . . Mary Rishworth's reasons were that it will injure the Poor be expence to her and that she would have things go on as they had done,

and Thomas Wood

kept a few Cows on the Common in Summer, took land of Mr Turton
at 40s. per Acre for Hay in Winter, and if it was not for the Commons
he could not pay Rent for his Land nor have Milk for his family.

However, the only occasion when opposition to enclosure turned to violence in
Yorkshire was when riots in Sheffield in 1791 temporarily halted the surveyors
at Crookesmoor, and even that disturbance must be seen in a wider context of
trouble at the time.

In 1729 Thurnscoe became the first West Riding township to obtain a
parliamentary Act to enclose. The South field had been divided by agreement in
1675, but further enclosures in 1717 must have run into legal difficulties for
they could not be 'rendered effectual to answer the purposes thereby intended
without the aid and authority of Parliament'. Later enclosures of the common
wastes in 1738 and 1825 were nevertheless completed by local agreements.
The expensive method of enclosing by private Act of Parliament was used only
as a last resort. Four West Riding Acts were passed before 1755, then 95 Acts
were obtained between 1756 and 1785 and a further 192 Acts between 1786
and 1820 before the pace slackened (Rogers 1952). In 1731 the Holderness
township of Cowick became the first place in the East Riding to be enclosed by
Parliament; by 1850 162 acts had reached the statute book. The Wolds were
particularly affected, for about 206,000 acres had been divided by 1810 and a
further 45,000 acres were enclosed by 1850. New, compact farms with
functional brick houses and outbuildings were planted in the countryside, dew
ponds were dug out for livestock, plantations provided shelter, and hawthorn
hedges transformed the Wolds landscape into large, rectangular fields. This
physical transformation was accompanied by a striking change in farming
practice, as old pasture was converted to tillage and even the rabbit warrens
were ploughed up. By 1812 two-thirds of the Wolds were farmed as arable
with a four-course rotation of turnips, barley, clover or grass, and wheat, or
with local variations adapted to different soils. New crops meant that store
cattle could now be fed through winter, but flocks of sheep remained an
essential part of this farming economy, for they were folded at night for their
manure (Allison 1976: 150, 158).

Moorland areas were also changed radically by parliamentary enclosure.
Miles upon miles of drystone walls gradually gave a new regularity to
thousands of acres of former commons and wastes, and long, straight roads
were built to standard widths of 30 feet or more. Farmsteads and field barns
were erected amongst the new fields, rough land was brought under the plough
for the first time, and the trim, green appearance of the new meadows and
pastures provided a vivid contrast with the unreclaimed moorlands beyond.
Thousands of acres of waste that could never be tamed remained as vast sheep

Plate 4.3 Penistone Cattle Market. In 1698 the leading inhabitants of Penistone parish attempted to revive a medieval charter which had allowed a weekly Tuesday market and an annual St Barnabas fair (10–12 June) at Penisale, a deserted site on the parish boundary. This proposal was opposed by the men of Barnsley and Huddersfield who wished to protect their own markets. However, a petition was drawn up by the Penistone schoolmaster and 2,140 signatures were collected from miles around. Barnsley withdrew its opposition when the proposed market day was changed from Tuesday to Thursday to avoid competing with Barnsley's Wednesday market. A royal charter was granted in 1699.

Dairy cattle were sold in the central streets until 1910 when the Thursday market was moved to its present site. The photograph was taken in Market Street not long before the venue was changed.

---

runs or now became private grouse-moors, with public access rights obliterated. But it was not just the large freeholders who favoured enclosure; small freeholders shared their concern at the rising number of squatters who nibbled away the moorland edges. Parliamentary enclosure brought to an end this centuries-old tradition.

Enclosure also brought other changes. Some parishes took the opportunity long before the Tithe Commutation Act of 1836 to make a deal with tithe-owners, and in the industrial parts of the West Riding former common land was used for building developments. Sheffield burst from its medieval bounds and houses and workshops were quickly built along 'The

Moor' when Ecclesall bierlow was enclosed in 1788 and in the Wicker when Brightside bierlow was enclosed seven years later. Five miles further north, a village diarist noted that 'In the year 1766 there was 20 single tenements abought Ecclesfield Common. Now in the year 1820 there is 45 single tenements'; the common had been whittled down from 95 acres in 1637 to 83 acres by the time it was enclosed in 1789. In low-lying agricultural areas enclosure was often the prelude to massive drainage schemes. The 4,000 acres of Potteric Carr, for instance, were enclosed in 1765–71 and drained in 1810–11, and the 5,000 or so acres of Wallingfen were enclosed in 1781 and drained by cuts leading into the Market Weighton canal. Prior to such schemes much waterlogged land resembled the 49 acre Great Ox Carr at Brandesburton, in Holderness, which was described in 1743 as 'coarse boggy land in which no cattle can go, it is in a Dry year always mown and the Sedge and Flaggs serve for young or dry cattle in the winter but this is under water 9 months at least and sometimes all year'. One of the most impressive drains was constructed in 1798 to take water fifteen miles along the western side of the Hull valley from Hempholme to Hull; the eastern bank was drained in 1832. Much of the Vale of Pickering was also drained after enclosure, but the heavy soils of many a lowland Yorkshire parish were not improved significantly until tile drainage was carried out on a large scale in the second half of the nineteenth century.

Houses

Yorkshire has no timber-framed houses that are later than 1680; by that time stone and brick were the favoured building materials in all but the most humble outbuildings. In some areas, notably the Wolds and the Magnesian Limestone belt, the rebuilding of villages was so thorough that few traces of former timber-framing survive, but in other parts of the county older frames are still concealed behind stone or brick shells. In his description of Hatfield at the end of the seventeenth century, Abraham de la Pryme, a grandson of a Flemish immigrant into the Levels, remarked that,

> The manner of building that it formerly had were all of wood, clay and plaster, but now that way of building is quite left of, for every one now from the richest to the poorest, will not build except with bricks: so that now from about 80 years ago (at which time bricks were first seen, used and made in this parish), they have been wholy used, and now there scarce is one house in the town that does not, if not wholy, yet for the most part, consist of that lasting and genteel sort of building; many of

which are also built according to the late model with cut brick and
covered over with Holland tyle, which gives a brisk and pleasant air to
the town, and tho' many of the houses be little and despicable without,
yet they are neat, well furnished, and most of them ceiled with the
whitest plaster within.

Gypsum plaster was 'digged up in great Quantity and plenty' in the nearby Isle
of Axholme, and the different nature of the local clays and the varying methods
used in the firing process produced bricks of diverse colours and textures. Brick
now became the usual building material in lowland Yorkshire, but in western
parts the first brick buildings were so distinctive that they were commonly
given the name of Red House. Nevertheless, by the middle years of the
eighteenth century brick was widely used in the West Riding industrial towns.
The Sheffield baptism and burial registers of 1698–1703 name only one
brickmaker amongst the 1,149 men whose occupations were recorded, but by
1764 the curate could report that 'The buildings are in general of brick.'

Brick houses were normally roofed with pantiles, the 'Holland tyle' of
Pryme's report. In 1694 Ralph Thoresby described Stapleton in the southern
Vale of York as 'a pretty village, where the Dutch tiles are much used'. They
were imported through Yarm from the Low Countries during the 1670s and
were soon manufactured locally, but it was well into the eighteenth or even the
nineteenth century before they were generally accepted. At Swainsby, for
instance, in 1807 almost all the houses were thatched, but by the 1840s they
had all been roofed with pantiles (Harrison and Hutton 1984: 148).
Converting roofs was a straightforward job, for the pitch did not have to be
altered, but pantiles were easily lifted by the wind and often allowed rain to
percolate the interior rubble of the walls, so a bottom course of stone slates was
commonly provided. Though Norwegian softwoods were imported via the
Humber and Tees in the eighteenth century and trusses were increasingly
copied from pattern books, simple traditional roof designs were used well into
the nineteenth century, especially in cottages and outbuildings. Another
change, widely adopted in brick buildings, was the replacement of mullions by
sash windows. Sliding-sashes were an innovation of the 1680s that combined
practical value with aesthetic appeal. Vertical sashes were soon a feature of
such gentry houses as Middlethorpe Hall on the southern outskirts of York,
but they did not appear at vernacular level until after 1700; for example, John
Hobson, a gentleman-tanner of Dodworth Green, near Barnsley, noted in his
diary for 20 September 1726 that, 'Guest put glass into the sash windows in the
buttery, being the first that ever was in this town.' Many a farmer preferred the
sideways-sliding type known as Yorkshire sashes that appeared about the same
time; they are still a feature of Grange Farm, Moss, which was built in 1705. In
stone houses, however, mullions continued in fashion until much later and can
be found in nineteenth-century buildings such as weavers' cottages.

Yorkshire has a wide range of vernacular houses dating from the seventeenth and eighteenth centuries. The former homes of yeomen-clothiers survive in their hundreds in the upper Calder valley. Built of solid millstone grit to a two-cell, three-cell or cross-wings plan with a workshop at the lower end, they confirm the evidence of the hearth tax returns of Charles II's reign that this was the richest part of rural Yorkshire. Harrison and Hutton have identified three main types of houses in north Yorkshire and Cleveland that are spread widely regardless of building materials. The hearth-passage plan seems to have been developed from both the medieval gentry hall, where a screens passage separated the main rooms from the service end, and from the more lowly longhouse, where a cross passage divided domestic accommodation from the cow byre. Such houses had three rooms on the ground floor, were one-room deep and were normally two-storeyed. The passage ran behind the chimney stack and divided the building into two unequal parts. Sometimes the low end contained two small service rooms of unequal size, but more often the whole space was taken for a kitchen. If an extra chimney was not provided at the low end, the cooking was done in the 'firehouse' or 'house', the main living room. Craven houses were often provided with handsome, stone-arched fireplaces, but elsewhere the fashion was to have a funnel-shaped timber and plaster firehood resting on a wooden beam. Beyond the 'house' lay the parlour, a retiring room which was commonly the best bedroom, and sometimes part of the top end was used as a small dairy. The chambers served as extra bedrooms, lumber rooms and occasionally as work rooms. The lobby-entrance plan was rather similar except that the chimney stack stood immediately behind the door, blocking the passage and providing heat to the rooms on either side. It was the dominant type in the Vale of York, Craven and the southern dales, but was rare in north-eastern parts of the county and apparently unknown north of the Yorkshire border. A third type, with the chimney stack at one end and a central door leading directly into the house, was also popular and widespread. Extra service rooms were sometimes added in the form of a wing or outshutt to the rear, or sometimes the back of the parlour end was partitioned off for this purpose. This simple plan continued in use in the nineteenth century, especially at the level of labourers' cottages (Harrison and Hutton 1984: 41–120).

Harrison and Hutton's survey points to wide variations in the quality and chronology of buildings between different areas. Surviving Yorkshire datestones indicate peaks of building between 1630 and 1719 and renewed activity between 1740 and 1770, though rebuilding in the East Riding was generally even later. The poorest and most backward areas were the North York Moors and adjacent parts of the coastal belt and the Vale of Pickering. In 1664 only one house in Goathland was taxed on more than one hearth and that belonged to a gentleman with two; Fir Tree House or Beck Hole, dated 1728, is the earliest house of two full storeys on these moors. The pattern in the northern Vale of York is of a few large farmhouses scattered amongst the much greater number of middling and small buildings that are clustered in nucleated villages and market towns. Farmers in the southern Vale of York, especially those in the riverside parishes, generally had a higher level of prosperity which was reflected in the large, upper storeys and kitchens of their farmhouses. As in medieval times, however, the quality of housing varied a great deal from village to village. Another wealthy area was Craven, which has some of the most picturesque old farmhouses in the country, built with a conscious element of display in a superb setting; in 1673 35 per cent of Craven houses had more than two hearths. Further north, the Dales smallholders lived in compact, unpretentious houses that were remarkably uniform in plan, structure and decoration, but on the whole they were well-furnished, even on the upper floor (Harrison and Hutton 1984: 201–43).

Parliamentary enclosure produced another characteristic Dales feature, the two-storeyed field barn standing in isolation among the rectangular-shaped fields. They are built into the slope so that hay can be pitched straight into the loft and the lower part can be used to house young cattle in winter. South of Craven, in the hilly country bordering the industrial West Riding, a distinctive type of building known to historians as the laithe-house combined farmhouse, barn and byre under a single roof. Much favoured by smallholders who pursued the traditional dual occupations, the type is unique amongst English buildings in remaining unchanged over nearly 250 years. The earliest known example is Bank House, Luddenden, dated 1650, but others were still erected in this style in the later Victorian period; it was the standard building on the reclaimed moors in the era of parliamentary enclosure (Mercer 1975: 45). The house part consisted of two-up, two-down accommodation with a central chimney stack and a separate entrance. Very few laithe-houses have internal communication and their most prominent external feature is the high, arched entry which allowed a loaded hay cart or sledge to enter the barn. All these buildings were constructed of local stone and given a stone-slate roof.

The vernacular tradition of building survived well into the nineteenth century, for the influence of pattern books was minimal and building materials remained local until the railways reduced the transport costs of Welsh blue-slates and machine-made bricks. Labourers' cottages were of course the last domestic buildings to be influenced by outside styles. In 1800 Tuke wrote that in the North Riding, 'The cottages of the labourers are generally small and low, consisting only of one room, and very rarely, of two, both of which are level with the ground, and sometimes a step within it.' Strickland had a higher opinion of East Riding cottages, which he considered were more comfortable than in many other parts of England, being mostly of the two-up, two-down kind. He went on to say that, 'The houses and farmeries of the tenantry are in general good, except upon the Wolds, where (chiefly in consequence of the nature of the materials of which they are constructed) they are miserably bad.' The old buildings on the Wolds were 'in general, composed of chalkstone, with mud instead of lime-mortar, and covered with thatch', but most East Riding buildings were by then made of bricks and pantiles and many were designed as

Georgian farmhouses with a central hall-way and sometimes as double-depth houses in styles that had become popular throughout England.

Yorkshire still has a great number of seventeenth- and eighteenth-century gentry halls and some of the finest noblemen's seats in the country. The later Stuart Age saw the beginnings of great changes in architectural styles and fashions of living. In 1682 Sir John Reresby celebrated Christmas in the lavish manner of his ancestors, 'with great mirth and ceremony'. On nine separate occasions between Christmas Eve and Epiphany he invited a total of 144 tenants, 61 gentlemen and their wives and twelve clergy, and noted contentedly that

> For musick I had two violins and a base from Doncaster that wore my livery, that plaid well for the country; two bagpipes for the common people; a trompeter and drummer. The expense of liquor, both of wine and others, was considerable, as well as of other provisions, and my guests appeared well satisfied.

But a lord of the manor's household no longer contained as many servants as it had in the past and this style of entertaining was generally regarded as old-fashioned. The designers of newer houses had abandoned the medieval concept of a great hall separated from the service rooms by a screens passage; the servants now had their meals in their own quarters near the kitchen and went about their chores via their own staircase, discreetly placed at the rear of the building. This new type of accommodation had been introduced into southern England by Royalist exiles returning from France and the Low Countries after the restoration of Charles II. The fashion spread to the North when provincial nobles and gentlemen, who resided for much of the year in the capital, approved the new designs and copied them at home. 'Restoration houses' were compact in plan, comfortable and warm to live in, and satisfying in their proportions. Gables were eliminated in favour of a double-pile house with a hipped roof and central lead flat, and though the buildings were normally only of two full storeys, they often also had a small attic floor and a basement. They were no longer vernacular in style, but readily lent themselves to classical shapes and details. Whereas the houses of the minor gentry usually had a plain, symmetrical elevation, the grander buildings had a flight of steps and a pediment adorned with the owner's coat-of-arms. The hall was now a grand entrance room with a great parlour beyond and smaller rooms to the side; above the parlour was the saloon, the successor to the great chamber as the most splendid room in the house.

Yorkshire's best 'Restoration houses' date from the last quarter of the seventeenth century and are found particularly in the Vale of York, notably Bell Hall at Naburn, Middlethorpe Hall, Newby Hall, Nun Monkton Hall and Slade Hooton Hall. One of the earliest is the fifteen-bay brick hall at Ribston on the banks of the river Nidd, erected about 1674 for Sir Henry Goodrick, who subsequently helped the Earl of Danby to secure York for William of Orange and was rewarded with the post of Lieutenant-General of the Ordnance and a seat on the Privy Council. On a similar scale is Beningbrough Hall, completed in 1716 for John Bourchier to the designs of William Thornton. Both the Goodrick and Bourchier families had resided on their estates since the sixteenth century, but fine houses were built for newcomers like Sir John Hewley, a lawyer and MP for York and owner of Bell Hall, and Sir Edward Blackett, MP for Ripon and the son of a Newcastle coal-owner, who erected Newby Hall.

The parliamentary victory in the civil war did not bring about great changes in landownership, for although heavy penalties were imposed on the losing side, many Royalist families were able to repurchase their forfeited estates. Nor did the Restoration seriously affect the fortunes of former Parliamentarians. For half a century or so after the outbreak of civil war very few great houses were built in Yorkshire, but during the long period of stability ushered in by the 1688 revolution stately homes that were sometimes as grand as palaces were erected all over England. The later decades of the seventeenth century saw the emergence of great estates in Yorkshire, as in many other parts of the country; a consolidation of property brought about by purchases, exchanges, enclosures, and above all by inheritance and marriage. Professional services offered by the growing number of stewards, agents and attorneys enabled landowners to secure their estates, and though the spread and consequence of the use of strict settlements has been exaggerated by historians, legal schemes were an effective aid in ensuring the transfer of property intact. Great landowners took pride in their family's past achievements and in their own standing in society, and they took their duty to future generations seriously. A failure of male heirs leading to indirect successions did not weaken this sense of obligation. Nevertheless, a detailed study of the ninety-three Yorkshire baronet families created between 1611 and 1800 has emphasized the way in which personal behaviour influenced dynastic fortunes (Roebuck 1980: 251–61). The importance of national office and court sinecures as extra sources of wealth was decisive to families aiming for the top. During the seventeenth and eighteenth centuries Yorkshiremen held some of the most powerful positions in the country and were able to amass great estates on which they built splendid houses and created landscaped parks. Some of the finest architects in the country were active in Yorkshire, designing houses in the English Baroque style, a development on a much larger scale of the rectangular, double-pile houses that had come into fashion after the Restoration. But Yorkshire also had some gifted native craftsmen such as William Thornton and the Ettys of York and talented gentlemen-architects like Lord Bingley and William Wakefield, who between them produced some of the county's finest buildings.

Those Yorkshiremen who played a prominent part in the 1688 revolution that placed William III on the throne quickly received their reward, none more so than Sir Thomas Osborne, who as Earl of Danby had been the greatest public figure after the monarch during the 1670s. Danby was appointed Lord President of the Council and created Duke of Leeds. The enormous wealth that he had obtained from public office enabled him to engage William Talman, who was then busy at Chatsworth, to design a new brick house at Kiveton Park (demolished in 1811), and to employ Laguerre and Thornhill for the interior decorations. Talman was approached by Charles Howard, the third Earl of Carlisle, to design a new house at Henderskelfe, to be called Castle Howard, but he quarrelled with his patron and lost the commission to Sir John Vanbrugh and Nicholas Hawksmoor. This astonishing building, the likes of which had never been seen before, was Vanbrugh's first serious attempt at architecture, and was remarkably successful in setting the style for the provincial palaces of the nation's leading figures. The earl was on two occasions the First Lord of the Treasury, the office soon to be equated with that of prime minister. His visitors were left in no doubt that they were at the home of a great man, long before they reached the state rooms or audience chambers. The Carrmire Gate, mock military structures on the crest of the hill, and a 100 ft obelisk mark the entrance to the 1,000 acre park, which is tastefully adorned with a lake, waterfalls, terrace, statues and some wonderful landscape buildings modelled on Italian structures seen on the Grand Tour. The Temple of the Four Winds, for example, was based on the Villa Rotonda at Vicenza.

Robert Benson had been to Italy to study architecture, and with the large fortune he had inherited from his father he was able to purchase an uncultivated estate at Bramham in 1699 to build a house and lay out formal gardens in the French style with high, clipped yews, long, straight vistas and intersecting rides, with water-works, temples and other eye-catchers. The gardens remain wonderfully intact, an outstanding example of the style of this period. Benson was MP for York, a favourite of Queen Anne, and from 1711 Chancellor of the Exchequer; in 1713 he was created Lord Bingley. At the height of his power and influence he supervised the building of Yorkshire's next great Baroque mansion, at Stainborough. Here, in the early 1670s, Sir Gervase Cutler had erected one of the county's earliest classical buildings (now the north range), but he was a spendthrift and in 1708 his son was forced to sell the estate to Thomas Wentworth, Lord Raby, the British ambassador in Berlin. Wentworth was a Tory who acquired a fortune as he rose in the army and diplomatic service under Queen Anne. The great nephew of his famous namesake, he was determined to outshine his Whig cousins who had inherited the ancestral estate at Wentworth. In Berlin he persuaded Johannes von Bodt, a leading continental architect, to design a new Baroque range with a long gallery running all along the top floor. Upon the death of Queen Anne he was forced to retire to his estates where he concentrated upon completing his house and gardens and upon a romantic scheme to build a mock castle on the site of the fort from which Stainborough's name was derived. By 1731 the estate was known as Wentworth Castle.

Plate 4.4 Cannon Hall, Cawthorne. Cannon Hall was the home of the Spencer family, the leading West Riding ironmasters, who came from the Welsh Borders in the mid-seventeenth century. The architect of their new home is unknown, but the house was shown without its wings in a sketch by Samuel Buck, *c.* 1720. John Carr, the famous Yorkshire architect, designed two wings in 1765 to serve as a dining room and library, but these were just one storey high. Carr also redesigned the interior, especially the entrance hall and the dining room, in 1778. The wings were given an additional storey in 1804–5, so the house was complete by the time J. P. Neale made this drawing in 1821.

In 1760 John Spencer employed Richard Woods of Chertsey (Surrey) to lay out a park and gardens. Cannon Hall and Cusworth Hall are the only examples of the work of this famous landscape gardener north of the Trent. Three lakes were constructed in 1762–64 and great numbers of trees and flowering shrubs were planted. The house and grounds are now maintained by Barnsley Metropolitan District Council as a museum and country park.

The challenge was taken up by Thomas Watson-Wentworth, the future Marquis of Rockingham, who inherited Wentworth Woodhouse from his father in 1723. He immediately set about building a brick Baroque range to face the village, but when this was finished in the late 1720s he found that the design was considered old-fashioned and imperfect. The strict Palladianism of the Earl of Burlington's circle was now the new orthodoxy. In 1715 Colen Campbell had championed this style in the first volume of *Vitruvius Brittanicus*, and in 1721 had designed Yorkshire's first Palladian villa, Baldersby Park, for Sir William Robinson, MP for York. Watson-Wentworth determined to build a vast east range, modelled on Campbell's Wanstead House in Essex, with the longest front of any country house in England, as a deliberate statement of his wealth, power and privilege. Meanwhile, the surroundings of the house were altered dramatically by Humphrey Repton and

203

others. By the middle of the eighteenth century the park had been so enlarged that it was over nine miles in circumference, and by 1800 the Wentworth estate had been doubled in size to 17,200 acres. The grounds were provided with a terrace, ha-ha and ponds, an enormous stable block was erected behind the house, and lodges and the grandiose follies known as Needle's Eye, Hoober Stand, Keppel's Column and the Mausoleum were sited on prominent points. Wentworth Woodhouse was a Whig palace dominating a large part of south Yorkshire. The second Marquis became leader of the Whig party and for two short periods Prime Minister, and the Earls Fitzwilliam who succeeded to the estate continued the paternalist Whig tradition.

The Earl of Burlington, the dominant aristocratic figure in the Palladian movement, spent most of his time in the capital but his ancestral estate was at Londesborough in the East Riding. The Earl designed the York Assembly Rooms in the 1730s, and his Bridlington protégé, William Kent, became an architect and designer of national repute. Prominent amateur architects in Burlington's Yorkshire circle included Sir Thomas Robinson, who designed his own hall at Rokeby on the banks of the Tees, and Colonel James Moyser of Beverley, who provided designs for Bretton Hall and Nostell Priory. Nostell was built for Sir Rowland Winn, who had married the wealthy daughter of a former Lord Mayor of London upon his return from a lengthy Grand Tour on the continent and particularly in Italy. The design was modelled on Palladio's drawings for the Villa Mocenigo, with features derived from buildings illustrated in Palladio's *Four Books of Architecture*, and the internal decoration was the work of the young James Paine, Antonio Zucchi and Joseph Rose, and subsequently Robert Adam; the furniture was created by Thomas Chippendale of Otley. Paine went on to acquire a national reputation and to design several other Yorkshire houses, including Heath House, Wakefield, the Mansion House, Doncaster, the garden front of Cusworth Hall, Wadworth Hall, Cowick Hall and the Earl of Scarbrough's villa at Sandbeck Park.

The style of a nobleman's house and the size of his estate reflected his political power and standing in local society. Eighteenth-century English aristocrats took their responsibilities seriously. Many of them tried to live like the senators and philosophers of the ancient world and regarded classical art, architecture and literature as ideals to be sought after. At Newby Hall, William Weddell, a renowned collector of art treasures, commissioned Robert Adam to design a gallery to display his classical sculptures. At Studley Royal John Aislabie created a superb approach to the ruined Fountains Abbey with such features as the moon pool, complete with a statue of Neptune, and a Temple of Piety. And high above the remains of Rievaulx Abbey Thomas Duncombe constructed a terrace with a Tuscan temple at one end and an Ionic temple at the other. The great houses and parks of the eighteenth-century Yorkshire aristocracy must be seen not just in a national but a European context.

The price of land was driven up by noblemen from remoter parts of the realm who wished to purchase an estate nearer the capital and by those who had made their fortunes in commerce and who wished to consolidate their position in the accepted way. On the Magnesian Limestone belt, for example, the manor of Edlington was bought in 1708 by Viscount Molesworth, an Irish peer who proceeded to build a suitable house, and a few years later the Scottish Earl of Kinnoul made Brodsworth his principal English seat. At Sledmere, tucked away in the Wolds, the Sykes family dramatically transformed the landscape. This dynasty of Leeds and Hull merchants had been founded in the mid-sixteenth century by a younger son of a Cumberland yeoman. The family acquired Sledmere in 1718, but it was not until Richard Sykes inherited the property in 1748 that great projects were put in hand. During the next half century Richard and Sir Christopher Sykes built a house close by the parish church and removed the village to a new site on the Malton–Driffield road beyond the park. The mere that had given the place its name was drained, roads were blocked, the park extended, and the house and church left in seclusion. Likewise, at Harewood Edwin Lascelles altered the landscape out of all recognition after he had inherited the estate from his father in 1759. Henry Lascelles was a director of the East India Company, whose wealth, acquired through the ribbon trade and collecting customs in Barbados, enabled him to purchase the Harewood-Gawthorpe estate. In the Middle Ages Harewood had been a flourishing market village protected by a castle but by the sixteenth century it had decayed. Edwin Lascelles removed all except the church, which now stands hidden in the trees, and demolished Gawthorpe Hall to make way for his new house and landscaped park. His architect, John Carr, designed a new village at the gates of the park, tastefully assembled to provide a widening vista of the entrance. Robert Adam and Thomas Chippendale were commissioned to decorate and furnish the interior.

Churches and Chapels

The restoration of Charles II led to the re-establishment of the former practices of the Church of England and to the ejection of those ministers who refused to conform to the Act of Uniformity of 1662. The Anglican Church entered a long period of stability and eventually of slumber. During the late seventeenth and eighteenth centuries church buildings were refashioned at such places as Boynton, Fewston, Thorganby, Wentworth, Wortley and Yarm, and new chapels-of-ease served the growing towns of Leeds and Sheffield, but few of these buildings had much architectural distinction. In the countryside the personal tastes of a squire produced structures as different in style as the neo-Norman church at Allerton Mauleverer and John Carr's Gothick design at Ravenfield. The modest classical church of St James at Tong was built in the

1720s on the Anglo-Saxon foundations of its predecessor by the Tempest family, who lived in the smart, new brick hall nearby; the church is still furnished with box pews (including the squire's pew with its small fireplace), three-decker pulpit, west gallery and all the other accoutrements of a 'prayer-book' church untouched by the reforming zeal of the Victorian High Church movement. Other Yorkshire churches still arranged in this way include the small buildings at Beauchief, Lead, Midhope and also St Andrew's, Slaidburn and Holy Trinity, York. The seating arrangements of such churches formalized the social structure of the parish, for the pews could not be alienated from the various farms and cottages to which they belonged.

The nation's most famous example of a church which preserves its Georgian interior intact is perched on the cliff by the ruined abbey, high above the port of Whitby. Here, between the late seventeenth and early nineteenth centuries the old Norman church of St Mary was gradually transformed into a building that could seat 2,000 people. Transepts were added in Gothick style and fitted with white-painted galleries reached by external staircases, and every space in the nave was crammed with dark-brown box pews, three-decker pulpit, baroque brass chandelier, and a stove whose flue disappears through the roof. But that is not all. The Cholmleys had their own peculiar seating arrangement in an elaborate pew adorned with garlands and cherubs' heads and supported by four 'barley-sugar' columns, built across the chancel arch where the medieval rood screen had once been, so that during service time the squire and his family faced the congregation, and breathed down the neck of the preacher. Keeping out the cold in winter time was a constant consideration. The floors of Yorkshire churches in the eighteenth century were commonly covered with rushes. When Dr Richard Pococke came down from Wensleydale in 1750 he arrived at Hornby, and

> observed some garlands in the church, and asking the meaning of them I was informed of the northern custom of rush-bearing, which is about St Jamestide. They fix a garland of flowers to a pole, and tye a bundle of reeds wrapt up in a cloth to the pole, a sufficient quantity according to the size of the church, put up the garlands of the skreen between the church and the chancel, and strow the rushes in the seats to keep their feet warm in winter; this ceremony is concluded with some feasting.

Lay support from rural gentlemen and urban tradesmen helped to preserve Nonconformity during the years of repression. Many ejected ministers served tiny congregations in a discreet manner, particularly in remote rural areas where patrons provided meeting-places and offered some protection from the law. In contrast, dissent was easily suppressed in estate villages where resident lords such as the Fountaynes and Montagus of High Melton or the Copleys of Sprotbrough ensured that their communities remained dependent upon the estate for tenancies and employment. The

Compton ecclesiastical census of 1676 shows that only 4 per cent of the nation's communicants were dissenters, but that some places had many more than the average. In Doncaster, where only eight of an estimated 3,000 communicants were Nonconformists, the mayor and corporation claimed five years later that, 'We can truly say without boasting that we have neither in our town nor corporation one dissenter from the present government in church and state', but a few miles away the industrial town of Sheffield had about 300 dissenters amongst its 3,000 or so communicants. Wakefield had 300 dissenters amongst 2,400 communicants, but Barnsley had only seven out of 638, despite the fact that it had a flourishing market and a wire-drawing industry and was merely a chapel-of-ease of Silkstone parish. Economic and topographical considerations favoured the spread of dissent but did not automatically produce it, and it is the lack of any urban pattern that is striking at this time. In the countryside, however, the moorland chapelries and those large lowland parishes that had links with Hull remained well-disposed towards the dissenting cause. The same geographical pattern is apparent in John Evans's 'List of Dissenting Congregations' in 1715; Nonconformity flourished in its urban and rural strongholds but attracted little support beyond. The 1,163 people who attended services in the Upper Chapel at Sheffield formed the largest dissenting congregation in Yorkshire and included some of the most important people in the town. Though dissenters were a minority group in the country at large, their influence in certain places remained strong (Hey 1973).

Bullhouse Independent Chapel has a continuous history of dissent from its foundation in 1692 to the present day. After the Restoration the Puritan vicar of Penistone, Henry Swift, continued to enjoy the support of his wealthiest parishioners – the Bosvilles of Gunthwaite, the Riches of Bullhouse and the Wordsworths of Water Hall – and despite his refusal to wear the surplice and use the approved prayer-book, he was never ejected. Upon his death in 1689 the Crown appointed a Conformist vicar, whereupon the Riches ceased to attend the parish church. Elkanah Rich registered Bullhouse Hall as a Nonconformist meeting-house under the new toleration laws and proceeded to build a chapel in his own grounds, with a minister's simple cottage attached. John Evans noted a congregation of 200 there in 1715. Men such as Elkanah Rich could dominate their meeting-houses just as effectively as an Anglican squire could dominate the church of his estate village.

The most widespread of the old dissenting sects were the Quakers, but their strongholds were the traditional ones. Their initial appeal was to the poor, but they soon attracted richer converts, notably many of the gentry ironmasters of the West Riding. Briggflatts meeting-house, high in a remote corner of the Pennines, was built as early as 1675 and preserves the original arrangements of its interior, and High Flatts meeting-house, on the edge of the ancient parish of Penistone, is still the focal point of a hamlet where all the farmhouses were once occupied by Friends. Endowed by the Jacksons,

207

yeomen-clothiers of Totties Hall, High Flatts served as a centre for a wide area, and in 1764 'many came out of different parishes' to swell the congregation to about a hundred. These and other meetings remained strong when others withered away as toleration, respectability and wealth lessened their spiritual zeal; by the mid-eighteenth century Quaker membership was on the decline. The Presbyterians and Independents also lost much of their force, and some congregations drifted into Unitarianism, whose rational approach attracted ministers and merchants but had little appeal to the poor. Neither the Established Church nor the old dissenting sects had the 'enthusiasm' to attract the growing masses in the towns and industrial villages. 'No other preaching will do for Yorkshire', wrote John Nelson to John Wesley, 'but the old sort that comes like a thunderclap upon the conscience. Fine preaching does more harm than good here.' The Methodists set out to remedy this situation.

On their first visits to Yorkshire the Wesleys and Whitefield sought rural farms and hamlets for their headquarters in the old dissenting areas, both in the lowland parishes within a few miles of Epworth and in the semi-industrial areas further west. They met with violent opposition when they ventured into the towns; 'Hell from beneath was moved to oppose us', wrote Charles Wesley in 1742, after his first attempt to preach in Sheffield. A local man reported in 1760 that, 'We have also preached at Barnsley, where they were very angry, cast rotten eggs at us, and gave us heavy curses.' The early Methodists co-operated with the Moravian groups led by the Revd Benjamin Ingham of Halifax, who in 1744 established a colony at Fulneck, near Pudsey. In time, Fulneck became a self-sufficient community with houses, schools and workshops arranged around a chapel. The West Riding had seventeen 'Ingham's Societies' in 1745, with a total membership of 856. The visits of famous preachers were highlights that encouraged local people to continue their efforts, but progress was slow and in many places preaching was abandoned. The vicar of Ecclesfield was convinced that the Methodists would 'not be of any long continuance', and the hostility of the Established Church was expressed by the vicar of High Hoyland in 1764 (referring, presumably, to the new industrial settlement of Clayton West at the edge of his parish): 'Some Interlopers from Places infected with Methodism are endeavouring to propagate their Notions, but gain few Proselytes. There is no licenced or other Meeting House, except a few private Houses may be called so; where the Above Crazy Visionaries sometimes assemble.' It was chiefly in the traditional dissenting district that recruits were obtained. Even so, by 1773 the Sheffield circuit (which included north Derbyshire and most of south Yorkshire except the eastern parishes) contained only 910 members. Methodism had not yet achieved the success that was to come its way in the nineteenth century (Hey 1973).

The Poor

During the later seventeenth and eighteenth centuries rural squires and other wealthy people continued the well-established tradition of building and endowing almshouses and schools. Surviving examples of former almshouses include the Fauconberg Hospital at Coxwold (1662), the Fountains Hospital at Linton (1721) and Mary Wandesford's Hospital for 'ten poor maiden gentlewomen' in the York suburb of Bootham (1743). Ledsham has two foundations close to its Anglo-Saxon church; in 1670 Sir John Lewis of Ledston Hall erected a range of eleven almshouses, and in 1721 his grand-daughter, Lady Betty Hastings, built an orphanage. But even these are modest structures compared with the grandiose Turner schemes at Kirkleatham, where Sir William Turner, a former Lord Mayor of London, and his great-nephew, Cholmley Turner, built a house, school and impressive hospital and provided the church with new fittings and their family monuments.

Except in times of dearth and depression, the effects of poverty were felt less acutely in eighteenth-century Yorkshire than in most other English counties. In normal times able-bodied men and women could find work, even if much of it was part-time or seasonal. The wages offered by industry meant that farmers had to pay their labourers more than the abysmally low levels of southern and eastern England; even the labourers in the agricultural North and East Ridings benefited in this way. The old, the sick, the infirm and dependent youngsters who together constituted the 'genuine poor', were on the whole treated sympathetically by their neighbours, but idlers and the poor of other parishes met with a hard-headed response. A typical attitude was expressed by 'A Yorkshire Farmer' who corresponded with the Board of Agriculture's West Riding reporters in the 1790s:

> Ride a horse with a slack bridle and he will stumble less: he will depend upon his own efforts. So it is with the lower order of mankind: the more bountiful we are, the more heedless and extravagant they are. I speak of the haughty and insolent; the aged and helpless will, I trust, ever meet with tenderness and compassionate assistance from their fellow-creatures.

Throughout England the later years of the seventeenth century saw a substantial decline in long-distance subsistence migration. Beggar bands no longer roamed the countryside in a desperate search for a living. As population growth slowed down and agricultural output increased, towns brought their social problems under control, and in rural communities old traditions of neighbourly help and paternalism flourished once more (Clark 1979). At the same time, new settlement laws and attempts to license itinerant traders hindered migration; even before the passing of the 1662 Act of Settlement some local authorities took a firm stance on wandering paupers for whom they were not responsible. In 1654, for instance, the clerk of Doncaster corporation noted: 'Given to Susan Stockham, being at her time, and ready to labore, to get shutt of her, 1s.', and 4d. more to carry her to the next parish. At meetings of the quarter sessions JPs found themselves increasingly occupied with settlement cases as contending parishes engaged lawyers to prove that paupers were legally settled elsewhere. In 1681 the overseers of Ecclesfield parish spent 2s. 8d. in proving that Hellin Carr was not their responsibility, plus 2s. 0d. for an order and 1s. 0d. for a horse to carry her away; nevertheless they provided her with a pair of shoes costing 3s. 0d. and gave her 6d. as she left.

The JPs heard tales of great hardship when trade was bad. In 1670 Barnsley people had wandered into neighbouring parishes to beg, for 531 inhabitants needed relief and only 'a few able persons' were able to provide it. Likewise, in 1657 the townspeople of Rotherham had 'falne in great decay much weakened in there estates and growne Numerous in their poore'; the feoffees of the town's principal charity were ordered to set the poor on work and not to give relief to those who refused employment. In 1664, when some of the Rotherham poor were said to 'neglect their worke and refuse to labour', the JPs threatened to put them in the house of correction. When the population began to rise again in the eighteenth century many places built workhouses to accommodate and employ the poor. For example, in 1719 Doncaster corporation erected a workhouse in Far St Sepulchre Gate 'to sett the pore of this town to worke, whoe are become very numerous', and thirty years later they ordered that paupers must wear a badge, that relief could be obtained only in the workhouse and that the doors must be kept locked except to allow the inmates to go out to work.

Attitudes towards the poor hardened during the second half of the eighteenth century as local rates began to rise and more squatters encroached upon the commons. In the North Riding expenditure on the poor rose from an average £5,581 per annum in 1748–50 to £12,702 in 1775–76 and £18,866 in 1783–85; nevertheless, only 9 of England's 42 counties spent less on their poor and 30 North Riding villages had no poor at all. By 1776 at least 35 workhouses, capable of housing 964 people, had been built by donation or subscription in the North Riding, and rising rates, together with the enabling powers of Gilbert's 1782 Act, led to the creation of 506 more workhouse places by 1802, but apart from Whitby (300 places), Scarborough (150–200) and Malton (120–50), North Riding workhouses were small (Hastings 1982). Even in the populous West Riding the poor were not an urgent problem in normal times. Sir Frederick Eden visited the large, semi-industrial parish of Ecclesfield in 1797 and reported that,

> Of the Poor, 64 are maintained in a Workhouse. 96 have regular weekly pensions and 38 have occasional relief. About half the Out-Poor have families. The Poor are farmed. The contractor received £760 in 1794, and £860 in 1795 [two exceptionally bad years]. The Workhouse

stands in a good situation, and the lodging rooms are tolerably comfortable, but not sufficiently sub-divided. There are 5 or 6 beds in each room, and 2 or 3 sleep in a bed, which are filled with chaff, and have each 2 sheets, 1 blanket, and 1 rug. Pillows are stuffed with chaff. Very little work is done, as the Poor are mostly old people and children. Bill of fare: Breakfast – every day, milk pottage and bread. Dinner – Sunday, Wednesday, butcher's meat, potatoes, broth and bread; Monday, Thursday, bread and 2oz. butter; other days, puddings with sauce and beer. Supper – Sunday, Wednesday, broth and bread; other days, milk pottage and bread. Oatbread is generally used, sometimes wheaten bread.

In the East Riding Eden noted that at Great Driffield, 'There are only 3 inmates in the Poor-house, many receive relief at home, which appears to be more convenient for them and not disadvantageous to the parish', and at Market Weighton, 'Very few paupers have ever been in the house, as they could be maintained at a cheaper rate on weekly pensions.' In the West Riding the 34 paupers in the Southowram workhouse were chiefly old people and children who appeared to be comfortable and well-fed. The general impression is that throughout Yorkshire the problem of poverty was under control for most of the time, though great hardship was endured in years of harvest failure and trade depression. Though the diet of the labourer was often monotonous, it was better than in many other parts of the country. Eden observed that at Settle, 'The food used by the labouring Poor is oatmeal, tea, milk, butter, potatoes and butcher's meat', at Stokesley 'bread, milk and tea, potatoes, and meat sparingly', and at Great Driffield 'barley bread, potatoes and perhaps 2 lbs of butcher's meat once a week, when they can afford it'. At Halifax he noted that, 'Butcher's meat is very generally used by labourers', and at Leeds,

> Wheaten bread is generally used. Some is made partly of rye and a few persons use oatmeal. Animal food forms a considerable part of the diet of labouring people. Tea is now the ordinary breakfast, especially among women of every description, and the food of both men and women is more expensive than that consumed by persons in the same station of life in the more northern parts.

After 1770 Britain was a net importer of cereals. The inhabitants of the West Riding towns and industrial villages were amongst the first to suffer in times of dearth for they were dependent upon the corn markets. The food riot, which compelled retailers to charge 'a fair price' and stopped movements of corn to places offering higher profits, was a common popular response to those who tried to gain financially from shortage. The worst crises occurred in 1795–96 and 1800–1, when poor national harvests and wartime blocking of continental supplies coincided with industrial depression. The summer of

1795, in particular, saw riots in several parts of the West Riding. Many more people died than usual, but a combination of public and private relief and self-help societies enabled the country to cope far better than during the old subsistence crises of previous centuries.

During the years 1815–22 and 1828–32 post-war depression brought widespread unemployment and reduced wages, and many agricultural labourers were forced to leave the countryside in the hope of work in the industrial towns or in search of a new life in Canada or the United States. At this time, the North Riding was a greater exporter of population than any other English or Welsh county, particularly from the North York Moors and the decaying lead settlements in the western dales (Hastings 1982). Nevertheless, the widespread use of self-help friendly societies and a general sympathy amongst ratepayers for the genuine poor checked the worst effects of poverty. The Speenhamland system, whereby wages were subsidized in relation to the price of bread, was not used in the north of England, where industrial wages forced up those earned by farm labourers. Captain Swing rioters received little support in Yorkshire, and the county was generally free of the serious social tension that afflicted the countryside in much of southern and eastern England. The burden of poverty was harsh enough for thousands of Yorkshire families in times of depression, but it did not weigh as heavily as in many other parts of the land.

Transport Improvements

During the seventeenth and eighteenth centuries the river Ouse remained a vital waterway, with numerous minor shipping points such as Cawood, Wistow, Stillingfleet, Naburn and Bishopthorpe, as well as important quays serving a large hinterland at York and Selby. In 1698 the mariners and watermen on the Ouse possessed

> several vessels of good burthen which are constantly employed in
> · carrying great quantities of woollen manufactures, lead, butter, corn,
> rape-seed, tallow and several other commodities, the products of this
> and the adjacent country, to Hull, London, Newcastle and several parts
> beyond the seas, from whence they bring all sorts of merchandise and
> sea-coals for supplying the city of York and the adjacent counties.

The typical Ouse vessel was the all-purpose 'Yorkshire' or 'Humber' keel, which was as well-suited to its river as was the trow to the Severn or the barge to the Thames (Duckham 1967: 57, 78). Water transport was much cheaper than land transport for heavy, bulky goods of relatively low value, so much of the industrial produce of the West Riding was brought by cart and packhorse along the Hambleton causey to the Ouse at Selby, until the Aire and Calder navigation provided a waterway from Leeds and Wakefield to the Ouse at Airmyn.

The industrial goods of south Yorkshire and the northern parts of Derbyshire were exported from Bawtry down the river Idle to the Trent, while good-quality continental iron, Norwegian deals and the groceries which were offered for sale in Sheffield shops came the other way. Daniel Defoe was much impressed by the bustle at Bawtry wharf:

> By this navigation, this town of Bawtry becomes the centre of all the exportation of this part of the country, especially for heavy goods, which they bring down hither from all the adjacent countries, such as lead, from the lead mines and smelting-houses in Derbyshire, wrought iron and edge-tools, of all sorts, from the forges at Sheffield, and from the country call'd Hallamshire . . . Also millstones and grindstones, in very great quantities, are brought down and shipped off here, and so carry'd by sea to Hull, and to London, and even to Holland also. This makes Bawtry Wharf be famous all over the south part of the West Riding of Yorkshire, for it is the place whither all their heavy goods are carried, to be embarked and shipped off.

Bawtry had the additional advantage of being 'upon the great post highway, or road from London to Scotland; and this makes it be full of very good inns and houses of entertainment'.

The mid-eighteenth century roads near Leeds consisted typically of

> a narrow hollow way little wider than a ditch, barely allowing of the passage of a vehicle drawn in a single line; this deep narrow road being flanked by an elevated causeway covered with flags or boulder stones . . . The raw wool and bale goods of the district were nearly all carried along the flagged ways on the backs of single horses.
>
> (Whitaker 1816: 81)

Long-distance carriers such as the men who took cloth to London or to the great Stourbridge fair had large teams of packhorses. Joseph Naylor of Rothwell had as many as 101 horses in 1718, but more typical was Abraham Pilling, the leading Doncaster carrier, who had 16 packhorses upon his death in 1695. Packhorses carrying a load of about 240 lbs were still the most economical form of land transport from Yorkshire to the capital; roads had to be passable in winter as well as summer and demand for carriage and back-carriage had to be substantial and regular for waggons to be used profitably. The West Riding in particular retains many landscape features that are redolent of the packhorse era; causeys, bridges and guide stoops that now seem old and quaint but which indicate the attempts that were made to improve the local highways and byways in response to the growing demands of an increased volume of traffic. Between 1660 and 1740 stone packhorse bridges replaced the old wooden ones, and in 1733 the West Riding JPs ordered the erection of guide stoops 'for the better convenience of travellers', particularly upon 'large moors and commons where intelligence is difficult to be had'; only Derbyshire has an equivalent, comprehensive set of route indicators from the pre-turnpike era. After 1738 West Riding guide stoops not only gave directions but the number of miles to the place whose name was inscribed; these were the old Yorkshire or customary miles of about 2,200 yards, which remained in use until the turnpike roads made the statutory mile of 1,760 yards more familiar (Hey 1980).

Wheeled vehicles were commonly used over shorter distances and a great deal of carrying was done on a part-time basis by farmers during slack spells, especially in the summer months when the roads were bad. A 1752 survey of the West Riding's bridges lists a great number that were sufficiently wide to take carts, wains and waggons. Leeds bridge had recently been widened to 17 feet and was the broadest in the riding; some county bridges were only 11 ft or 12 ft wide. By the early eighteenth century stage-waggon services were operating weekly from southern parts of the county to London. Stage-coaches had been offering quick connections with the capital via the Great North Road since the Commonwealth period; in 1658 Bawtry could be reached in three days at the cost of £1. 10s. 0d. and travellers could arrive in Wakefield in four days for £2. The road maps published in 1675 by John Ogilby indicated the routes of the two major highways into Yorkshire from the South; the Great North Road entered the county via Bawtry and Doncaster, and a more westerly line went via Mansfield, Rotherham, Barnsley, Huddersfield and Halifax all the way to Richmond. A post-road from London to Sheffield, established in 1663, went via Northampton, Market Harborough, Leicester and Derby, and it seems likely that a provincial network of carriers' services linking all the regions of England had been created before roads were improved by the turnpike trusts. John Warburton's map of Yorkshire (1718–20) marks the highways that led to the various market towns and shows that the turnpike roads of the eighteenth century made only minor deviations from routes that had been used from time immemorial. Thomas Jeffreys's much more detailed map of 1767–72 also shows a pattern of lanes and tracks that is still familiar today. Along such lanes pedlars, badgers and hawkers travelled to even the remotest hamlets and farmsteads in the land. These packmen grew significantly in number during the decades after the Restoration, thus helping to integrate Yorkshire even more closely into the national economy.

Improved waterways were as essential to economic progress as were better communications by land; the two systems were not rivals but were complementary to each other. By 1730 about 1,160 miles of English rivers were navigable for light craft and major efforts had been made in Yorkshire to improve the Ouse, Aire and Calder, Derwent, Hull and Don. An act to improve the river Derwent was obtained in 1702, about £5,000 was spent on the Ouse in the late 1720s and early 1730s and the Naburn lock, dam and weir were constructed in 1757, but far more important were the determined efforts to make rivers navigable into the heart of the industrial West Riding. A major step was taken in 1699 with the implementation of a scheme to extend the Aire navigation beyond its tidal limit at Knottingley to Leeds and along the Calder to Wakefield. Many improvements were subsequently made by means of cuts, locks and deeper beds. Previously, much of the produce of the textile district had been taken overland to Selby, but now the bulk went down river to join the Ouse at Airmyn. For two generations Selby languished, but by the later eighteenth century the Aire and Calder navigation could no longer cope adequately with the growing volume of traffic; in 1778–81 a canal was constructed from the navigation at West Haddlesey to Selby, which once again became the West Riding's chief port. After men and installations had been moved from Airmyn, a third of Selby's population was employed in building and repairing ships and in transferring goods from canal barges to the 200 ton vessels which sailed down the Ouse. By the 1820s over 800 vessels per annum were cleared at the local customs' house. Soon, however, Selby was to be eclipsed by Goole and to lose much of its trade to the railways (Porteous 1977: 31–2, 132–3).

The river Don was tidal as far as Wilsick House in the parish of Barnby Dun and navigable as far as Doncaster for nine months in the year. In 1721 the Hallamshire Cutlers company sought powers to make the Don navigable as far as Sheffield, but were frustrated by the combined opposition of Bawtry merchants, landowners below Doncaster who feared flooding on the scale of the disaster a century before when Vermuyden had drained the Hatfield Levels, and the Duke of Norfolk who was apprehensive about the supply of water to his forges and grinding wheels at Sheffield. A suitable compromise with the Duke, which stopped the navigation scheme at Tinsley, three miles from town, enabled two Acts to be passed in 1726–27 whereby Doncaster corporation improved the river downstream to Wilsick House and the Cutlers company assumed responsibility for the much more difficult stretch west of Doncaster. By 1735 Richard Dalton (who had moved from Bawtry to Sheffield) was able to import Scandinavian deals which 'never landed since they were put aboard at Stockholme until they came to Aldwork'. By 1739–40 a wharf had been constructed at Rotherham and in 1751 the scheme was completed all the way to Tinsley. The final stretch to Sheffield was not made until 1819. Bawtry lost its Yorkshire trade, and in 1777, when the Chesterfield canal provided a direct link with the Trent at Stockwith, Derbyshire lead and millstones went that way instead. But what Bawtry lost at its wharf it regained in its coaching inns and market place. Bawtry was handsomely rebuilt between 1780 and 1840 and did not become a 'sleepy old market town' until the age of railways.

For a quarter of a century the energies of the Cutlers company were

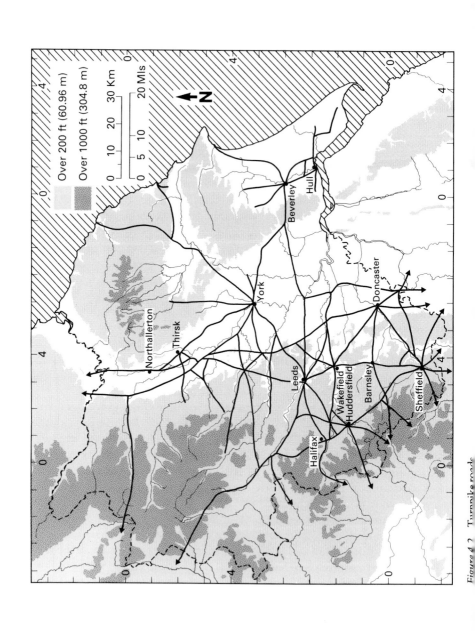

Over 200 ft (60.96 m)

Over 1000 ft (304.8 m)

20 Mls

30 Km

N

Northallerton

Thirsk

York

Beverley

Hull

Leeds

Wakefield

Huddersfield

Halifax

Barnsley

Doncaster

Sheffield

Figure 4.2 Turnpike roads

directed towards improving their waterway; they showed far less interest in land carriage, for they were in a sellers' market in the provincial towns. The West Riding lagged behind Lancashire in the provision of turnpike roads. Manchester merchants improved their Pennine highways as far as the county boundary in the hope that Yorkshiremen would repair their side, but the 1732 turnpike road to Saltersbrook was not extended to the Don navigation at Rotherham and Doncaster until 1741, and the 1735 Stanedge road was not completed to Huddersfield and Wakefield until 1759. The early turnpike trusts aimed not to replace existing highways but to maintain and improve them. Roads which proved unsuitable for wheeled traffic were eventually abandoned in favour of easier routes, but at first only a few minor detours were made to avoid the steepest hills. New routes along the valley bottoms, such as the Wadsley–Langsett road of 1805 via Deepcar and Stocksbridge came much later. At first, efforts were concentrated upon the Pennine crossings and the roads heading for the ports. The earliest Yorkshire turnpike road was the 1735 improvement to the Rochdale–Halifax route via Blackstone Edge. In 1741 six schemes dealt with links between Manchester or Rochdale in the west and Halifax, Bradford, Leeds, Wakefield, Selby and Doncaster in the east. All the petitions to Parliament emphasized the great amount of traffic that used these highways; the petition to improve the Saltersbrook route, for example, claimed that 'great Quantities of manufactured Goods, Cheese, Salt, and Potatoes, are carried from Manchester, Barnsley, and Parts adjacent to Doncaster, on Horses, and return loaded with Hemp, Flax and German Yarn'; and the Act for the Selby, Leeds, Bradford and Halifax turnpike observed that the road was 'much used and frequented for Carriage and Conveyance of Wooll, Woollen Manufactures, Dying Ware, etc.'. Other important early schemes included the 1744–45 turnpiking of the roads leading to Hull.

Turnpike trusts were concerned with the major thoroughfares, for 'the Benefit of Trade'. Minutes of individual trusts show that merchants were usually the most active trustees. Between 1751 and 1772 five Pennine routes were turnpiked and people began to speak of 'turnpike mania'. The heroic figure of John Metcalf – 'Blind Jack of Knaresborough' – who was responsible for many West Riding and Lancashire turnpike roads, represents the optimism of the age, but the lack of adequate technology and of experienced road builders meant that the early trusts had to be content with old methods of repair applied more thoroughly and regularly than before. A great deal of money was spent laying stones and gravel (and in some cases furnace cinders), on levelling and draining, and on maintaining an adequate surface at least 20 feet wide, but the primitive nature of many a moorland turnpike road is evident in the surviving stretches that were abandoned before major improvements had taken place, such as the Houndkirk moor portion of the 1758 Sheffield–Buxton road. Travellers' descriptions, even when an element of exaggeration is allowed for, leave no doubt about the condition of major highways even after they had been turnpiked. When Arthur Young travelled from Rotherham to

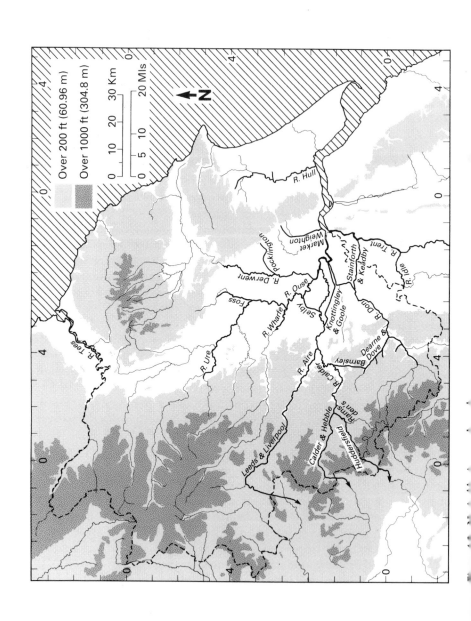

Over 200 ft (60.96 m)

Over 1000 ft (304.8 m)

Km
0   10   20   30

0   5   10   20 Mls

N

R. Tees

R. Ure

Foss

R. Wharfe

Selby

R. Ouse

R. Derwent

Pocklington

Market Weighton

R. Hull

R. Aire

Leeds & Liverpool

R. Calder

Calder & Hebble

Huddersfield

Rams dens

Barnsley

Dearne & Dove

R. Don

Knottingley & Goole

Stainforth & Keadby

R. Trent

R. Idle

Sheffield in 1769 he found that the road was 'execrably bad, very stony, and excessively full of holes'. As late as 1829 James Mill, the surveyor on the southern stretch of the Sheffield–Leeds turnpike road, commented that 'but a very small portion of this Road is compatible with the present rapid mode of travelling', and nine years later another observer reckoned that the whole route from Derby through Sheffield to Leeds was one of the worst roads in England.

Secondary routes which served the turnpike roads and connected minor settlements remained under the parish repair system. Those which crossed commons and wastes were improved during the late-eighteenth and early-nineteenth centuries by enclosure commissioners. Lanes were straightened and set out at a standard width and quarries were earmarked for the use of the overseers of the highways. On the Pennines in particular the modern road system owes much more to parliamentary enclosure than to turnpike mania. From an economic point of view, however, transport improvement has to be measured not by changes in physical condition, but by falls in the cost of carriage. During the eighteenth century English land-carriage rates were remarkably stable. The cost of tolls and of duties on carriage, together with the increased price of horse feed offset any gains; in fact, passenger rates doubled during the second half of the eighteenth century, but faster services meant that this rise was matched by savings on meals and accommodation (Pawson 1977: 297). In 1758 a House of Commons Committee was told by a Halifax merchant that the price of carriage along the 16 miles of the Halifax–Wakefield road was higher than it had been before the turnpike trust took over. This, he thought, was caused by 'the Increase of the Inhabitants, and their more extensive Trade', meaning perhaps that demand for carriers' services was greater than the available facilities and that heavy tolls were necessary to maintain the road. The most noticeable improvements made by the turnpike trusts were the great savings in time on long journeys and the widening of bridges so that wheeled vehicles could pass at all times of the year. The Halifax merchant went on to say that broad-wheeled waggons drawn by eight horses were able to carry 30 packs, each weighing 240 lbs, from Halifax to London. This load was $3\frac{3}{4}$ times heavier than the equivalent number of horses could carry on their backs. Turnpike roads widened the range of choice, whether of destination, of season, or of speed, expense and quality of travel. Their success can be judged by the fact that old roads which were not turnpiked, like the Pontefract–Hemsworth–Rotherham road, quickly declined in status.

Meanwhile, the river navigation system had been extended by cuts and canals into the heart of the Yorkshire coalfield and even across the Pennines. In 1779–80, for example, the Marquis of Rockingham had employed William Jessop to make the Greasbrough cut to the Don, with four broad locks and a reservoir, to facilitate the transport of coal from the Wentworth estate. Wooden railways of the type used in Northumberland and Durham since the seventeenth century were first used to connect these mines to the river in 1735, when John Hirst laid a track from his colliery at Ginnhouse. By 1763 three large collieries near Greasbrough, belonging to Messrs Hirst, Bowden and Fenton, had 'Newcastle roads' descending to the Don navigation. Until the canal era the Barnsley and Silkstone seams had been unable to compete in a national market through lack of access to coastal routes. In 1793 determined efforts were made to develop the potential of these seams by constructing canals towards both the Don and the Aire and Calder. An 11 mile canal linked Barnsley and Wakefield via an aqueduct over the Dearne and a long and deep cutting at Cold Hiendley, and at the same time work was begun on the 13½ mile Dearne and Dove canal from the Don at Swinton locks to Barnby basin, 4 miles beyond Barnsley. Two branches of the Dearne and Dove canal, each just over 2 miles long, went to Elsecar and Worsbrough. Coal was brought down wooden railways to the canal basins, and the lime that was brought as back carriage from the Magnesian Limestone quarries at Warmsworth, Levitt Hagg and Cadeby was burnt in kilns and sold to local farmers. The canal was vital to the development of the collieries and ironworks at Elsecar, and an entirely new community grew around the canal terminus at Worsbrough Bridge. White's *Directory* of 1838 reported that here were 'extensive iron, coal, lime, chemical, and flint glass works, with wharfs, boat-yards, a paper mill, and a large assemblage of houses, presenting a scene of bustle not often excelled in market-towns'. Soon, stone quarries, a glue manufactory and gunpowder works offered further employment, and the Wesleyans, the Wesleyan Reform movement and the Primitive Methodists each built a chapel. A new settlement had grown up around the canal basin that was completely different in outlook from the farming community gathered around the church and the hall at the top of the hill.

In 1758 John Smeaton began to extend the Aire and Calder navigation up the Calder and Hebble to Halifax, and twenty years later Sir John Ramsden constructed a small, private canal from this new waterway to Huddersfield. The next, ambitious step was to connect the industrial towns of the West Riding with those of Lancashire across the formidable barrier of the Pennines. Three ingenious and costly schemes eventually came to fruition. The first to cross the summit, but the last to be completed was the Leeds and Liverpool canal. Work began in the mid 1770s at the Aire and Calder terminus in Leeds, but was not finished until 1816; a series of ten locks enabled the canal to climb to Skipton and Gargrave and so on to Colne and Burnley, and a short branch from Shipley formed a link with Bradford. A second crossing, opened in 1804, was provided by the Rochdale canal, which entered Halifax. The third crossing was the most difficult of all, for it involved the construction of the Stanedge tunnel – at 5,456 yards the longest on any English waterway. This was the Huddersfield canal, which was opened in 1811 from Ashton under Lyne (where the Peak Forest canal led to other waterways in and around Manchester) to link with Sir John Ramsden's canal and the Calder and Hebble navigation at Cooper Bridge. These three trans-Pennine canals rank among the greatest engineering feats of their age.

The East Riding's three canals linked the market towns of Driffield, Pocklington and Market Weighton to navigable rivers, but their effect was less dramatic then in the west. A new settlement called Newport grew up where the Hull road crossed the Market Weighton canal, and by 1823 the seven manufacturers there were producing an estimated 2,000,000 bricks and 1,700,000 tiles per annum; the population had reached 777 by 1851. Another lowland canal, the Stainforth and Keadby (1793–1802), provided access from the Don to the Trent via Thorne for craft up to 200 tons. But the most important canal project in the Vale of York was undoubtedly the Knottingley and Goole canal, which opened in 1826, the Aire and Calder navigation company's final scheme to improve the route to the Ouse. The place-name Goole, first recorded in 1362, means a drain. A small, straggling settlement had grown up at the mouth of the Dutch river, but in 1821 the township contained only 450 persons. After 1826, however, when the navigation company put their enormous resources into developing a town and docks, Goole became the latest of a group of canal ports – notably Runcorn, Stourport and Ellesmere Port – that 'mushroomed' within a very few years into a thriving settlement. Today, at some 60 miles from the sea, it is England's most inland port, but when it was founded Yorkshire still had numerous loading points on rivers and canals much further upstream. The Canal Age had created a large number of small inland ports and had led to the rapid industrial growth of many existing settlements.

Collieries, Glassworks and Potteries

Until the late eighteenth century colliers normally had a dual occupation and were not regarded as separate from the rest of the community. Early coal mines were situated in or near towns and villages and the special rows that were built from the 1790s onwards were often close to existing settlements; only occasionally were new rows such as Belle Isle at Middleton erected in isolation near the pit shafts. Eventually, successful collieries fostered new communities, with rows developing into villages. The first parishes with a high proportion of colliers included those on the Rockingham-Fitzwilliam estates at Greasbrough and Elsecar. During the five years beginning 1 January 1773 the Greasbrough parish registers recorded the occupations of 111 men, 28 of whom were colliers; during the five years between 1789 and 1793 the 123 men included 40 colliers. Elsecar grew rapidly from the 1790s, for several families were employed at the local ironworks as well as in the mines. The colliers' houses that were erected in Elsecar in the 1790s to the designs of John Carr compare most favourably with contemporary farm labourers' cottages. The first planned colliery village seems to have been Waterloo, built on the banks of the

Aire for the Fentons on the boundary between Rothwell and Thorpe Stapleton; by 1821 it consisted of two rows and a school.

West Riding colliers received better wages than most craftsmen and labourers. In 1770 Arthur Young reported that miners near Rotherham earned 7–9 shillings a week and that those in the Wakefield district received 10–12 shillings; on Tyneside, however, colliers could earn up to 15 shillings a week. The scale of operations was still small in most mines, but the large Middleton colliery at Leeds employed 50 men underground and 27 on the surface in 1773 and a total of 230 men twenty years later; by 1820 the labour force at Middleton had risen to 380. No women or girls were employed in the larger West Riding collieries until the nineteenth century, and even then (apart from at Silkstone) only in small numbers. The recorded death of a woman in a Handsworth pit in 1799 is the earliest reference to female labour in Yorkshire mines (Goodchild 1978: 68–70).

Despite the extension of navigable rivers, West Riding coal was not shipped down the coast to London until well into the nineteenth century. However, the improved waterways provided access to markets in the North and East Ridings and Lincolnshire. When John Foster, a Woolley yeoman, died in 1721 he had £260 worth of coals 'sold to York, Lincolnshire & severall other places' and coals valued at £110 upon the 'stennard ' or wharf at Wakefield. Foster also had local sales worth £70, coals at Bimshaw pits worth £30, and a £110 valuation placed upon his mine and coals at Darton. He had installed two horse-drawn gins at Bimshaw, and his 24 picks, 22 baskets and seventeen sledges suggests a considerable enterprise for that time. Further east, in 1718 Richard Bingley of Goldthorpe had a winding gin and a horse gin with chains, worth in all £60, with coals valued at another £60; his direct descendants started the Elsecar and Low Wood collieries.

The first Thomas Newcomen atmospheric engine that was used to pump water out of a West Riding colliery was built about 1714 on Brown Moor, Austhorpe, five miles east of Leeds, but it was not a success and lasted only four years. A second engine was installed in the 1730s at Rothwell Haigh, the first large concern of the Fentons, 'coal kings' of the West Riding, who soon had other major collieries at Wakefield Outwood and Greasbrough. The Fentons had been yeomen or gentlemen-farmers at Woodhouse Hill on the south side of Hunslet since at least the sixteenth century, and one of their number, William Fenton, had been mayor of Leeds in 1658–59. They were also the owners of one of Yorkshire's largest glassworks at Rothwell Haigh and their varied interests included copper smelting in Cornwall and South Wales. Other colliery owners also invested in Newcomen pumping engines. In 1735 John Hirst installed one to drain Ginnhouse colliery near Greasbrough, and before 1750 the West Riding had eight; by the end of the century another 45 atmospheric engines and two Boulton and Watt engines were at work in the Yorkshire coalfield (Goodchild 1978). The only Newcomen-type engine still standing on its original site anywhere in the country is the one erected in

1794–95 to drain the Elsecar New Colliery.

West Riding collieries were at the forefront of improved winding and haulage technology during the late-eighteenth and early-nineteenth centuries. After the Duke of Norfolk had taken his Sheffield collieries under direct management in 1781 John Curr, his engineer from County Durham, installed underground waggonways and designed large corves which could be hauled fully loaded up the shafts; he also replaced the 1¾ mile wooden tramway from the collieries to the town with a new one built of cast-iron plates. The new era of steam transport started in 1802 when Richard Trevithick experimented with a locomotive at Coalbrookdale. Trevithick ran into technical problems, however, and these were not overcome until 1812, when John Blenkinsop and Matthew Murray built the *Prince Regent* and *Salamanca* to move coal from the Middleton colliery along the old waggonway across Hunslet Moor to the staithes on the Aire and Calder navigation. Each locomotive could pull twenty loaded waggons at a time and they attracted great interest throughout the world. One of the men who came to see them was George Stephenson, the engineer at Killingworth colliery in Northumberland, who was soon to make major advances in locomotive design.

During the seventeenth century the English glass industry was transferred to the coalfields. Between 1567 and 1615 Huguenot immigrants from Lorraine had introduced improved furnace designs using wood fuels into the Sussex Weald and subsequently into the Bristol Channel area, Staffordshire, Cheshire, Lancashire and some of the remotest parts of the North York Moors, such as Rosedale and Hutton Common. The Rosedale furnace, which was excavated in 1969 and then reconstructed in Ryedale folk museum, is thought to have been worked during the last quarter of the sixteenth century on similar lines to Lorrainer sites in the Weald (Crossley and Aberg 1972). One of the first furnaces on the coalfield was built on Sir Thomas Wentworth's estate at Glasshouse Green, Wentworth, in 1632, but it lasted for only a few years and had no connection with later enterprises, which were owned or managed by immigrants. In 1696 John Houghton claimed that Yorkshire had three glasshouses, which can probably be identified with Glass Houghton, Silkstone and Gawber. The Pilmays, who had established the Silkstone works by 1658, were immigrants who had previously worked in Hampshire, Gloucestershire, Staffordshire and Lancashire and who were connected by marriage to various other families from Lorraine such as Du Houx. Their technology was remarkably sophisticated. When Abigail Pilmay died in 1698 the Silkstone glasshouse was making not only green bottles, but crystal and flint glass. Very high quality sand from Brierley in Staffordshire and red lead were used for the crystal glass, rape ashes provided a source of alkali for green bottles, blue power and manganese were the main colourizing agents, and salt petre was used to avoid amber coloration in window glass and to convert any iron into a less-colouring state. Another prominent immigrant family were the Fenneys; Henry Fenney leased Glass Houghton, Joshua was at

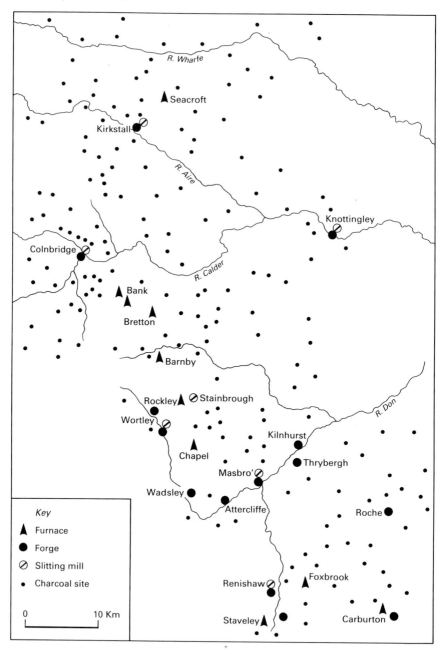

Figure 4.4 The charcoal iron industry in the early eighteenth century (after A. Raistrik, *Industrial Archaeology*, Methuen 1972, p. 123)

Rothwell Haigh, other members of the family worked at Thatto Heath in Lancashire, and in 1718 William married Mary Fox and became the manager of Bolsterstone glasshouse. In 1727 the Bolsterstone works used not only salt petre but starch, a chemical reducing agent that allowed the production of amber glass to be controlled precisely. Thirteen years later, William Fenney erected the Catcliffe glasshouse, whose cone is the oldest surviving structure of its kind in western Europe.

Many of these old glasshouses ceased production in the later eighteenth or early nineteenth centuries, and some were converted for a time into potteries; Silkstone was converted about 1750, Rothwell Haigh in 1768, Bolsterstone in 1778 and Gawber in 1821. Before the middle of the eighteenth century Yorkshire potteries were small local concerns, but the improved waterways offered opportunities for larger businesses where suitable clays and coals were available. The Leeds Old Pottery, established about 1755, was the first to operate on a large commercial scale, establishing a wide reputation for cream-coloured earthenware. The Green family, who had helped to found this enterprise, were also associated with other famous West Riding potteries, notably those at Swinton, the Don works and Castleford. The surviving cone at Swinton is another important and interesting piece of industrial archaeology. The pottery was established in 1745 but it achieved its greatest fame after 1826, when the Bramelds (in recognition of financial assistance from Earl Fitzwilliam) renamed their business the Rockingham Works and concentrated upon porcelain (Cox 1973). It achieved the greatest fame of all the Yorkshire potteries.

The Metal Trades

From the reign of Charles II to that of George II the West Riding and north Derbyshire charcoal iron industry was controlled by a group of gentlemen-ironmasters led by the Spencers of Cannon Hall, the Fells of Attercliffe and the Sitwells of Renishaw. By a complicated series of partnerships they owned or leased ironstone mines, coppice woods, blast furnaces, forges, wire mills and slitting mills, extending from Kirkstall and Seacroft in the north along the Tankersley seam of ironstone to Staveley and Renishaw in Derbyshire. Together they produced about 3,000 tons of pig iron per annum (Raistrick and Allen 1939). Their activities have left many a mark on the landscape, ranging from standing structures at Rockley furnace and Wortley forge to the foundations of wire mills and slitting mills at Wortley, and from the characteristic rows of bell pits near the former Bank furnaces east of Emley to numerous springwoods on the Coal Measures and adjacent parts of the

Plate 4.5 Nethercut Wheel, Rivelin valley. The rivers and streams in and around Sheffield were dammed at frequent intervals to provide water power for grinding cutlery and edge tools. By the 1930s this was the only grinding wheel still at work in the Rivelin valley. Known as Marshall's Wheel in 1726, for much of its history it was concerned with the grinding of scythes. This old photograph shows how water was channelled from the dam via a pentrough to an overshot water wheel which was geared to several grindstones inside the hull (as the building was called). Most grinding wheels were set in a similar rural situation.

Shepherd's Wheel on the Porter Brook has been restored by Sheffield City Museums, but most sites are known only from dams and foundations and many have been obliterated.

Magnesian Limestone. Even when it was close to Sheffield, most of this industry was carried on in a rural setting.

Local iron was of sufficient quality for the hundred or so nailers who in 1672 worked in villages, hamlets and isolated farmsteads near the Wortley, Masborough and Renishaw slitting mills, both to the north and to the south of the cutlery district. Nailmaking was essentially a rural craft that required little capital or technical knowledge and which was normally combined with farming until the population explosion destroyed this old way of life. In 1739 William Murgatroyd of Wortley forge observed that between March and August clasp nails were made for the London market, during harvest time nailmaking stopped, in the autumn flat points were made for Virginia until Martinmas, then sharp points were made for the Leeward Isles and Jamaica. Local chapmen supplied the nailers from the slitting mills and saw to sales in distant fairs and markets, but from the 1730s onwards the Spencers became directly involved in exporting nails down the rivers and along the coast to Deptford, where London merchants collected them for redistribution in southern England and America. The local nailing industry was second only to that of the Black Country, and demand in the 1730s was such that youngsters were leaving after serving only two years of their apprenticeship and setting up as masters themselves. The 1733 Ecclesfield agreement, which was eventually signed by 210 nailmakers (126 with a mark) tried to enforce the old regulations and complained that those who had abandoned their apprenticeships 'do frequently marry very young and inconsiderately and by that means have often a great charge of children to maintain before they scarce know how to maintain themselves'. Economic opportunities allowed earlier marriages and more children. The humble nailing craft not only helped to sustain population growth by offering employment, it provided much of the capital and leadership needed to launch an industrial revolution. Samuel and Aaron Walker, who became the leading ironmasters in the North of England, started their careers as typical nailer-farmers, and the new iron and steel works which they established at Masborough in 1746–48 was financed by John Booth, the leading nailchapman in south Yorkshire (Hey 1972).

Tankersley ironstone was good enough for the local nailers, wiredrawers and panmakers, but was of insufficient quality to provide the cutting edge needed by the cutlers and tool-makers, who had long relied upon continental imports. By the later seventeenth century Swedish iron from the Dannemora district was being brought via Oregrund and Hull and the navigable rivers. At first, Sheffield cutlers relied upon Newcastle cementation furnaces to convert Swedish iron into steel, but by the 1690s similar furnaces were operating in south Yorkshire. Nevertheless, Thomas Oughtibridge's 1737 view of Sheffield shows only one pair of cementation furnaces in the town; Sheffield's fame as the world's greatest centre of quality steel production still lay in the distant future. The new age was signalled in 1742 when Benjamin Huntsman, a Doncaster clockmaker, settled in Handsworth and began to recast cementation steel in fireclay crucibles, using coke fires and a natural draught. His melted steel was much more uniform and pure and ideal for his watch springs and for the fine cutting edges required in the cutlery trades. Huntsman 'laid the foundations on which all ingot-making steel-melting processes are based' (Barraclough 1976).

The hearth-tax returns of 1672 suggest that about 5,000–5,500 people lived in the large parish of Sheffield. The population of the central, urban township had risen a little since 1616 to between 2,300 and 2,700 people. From about 1630 to 1700, in line with national trends, the number of burials recorded in the parish registers exceeded the baptisms, and during the last decade of the seventeenth century the total deficit was 636. Short-distance migration sustained the population level in the town; a study of the places of origin of all apprentices in the cutlery trades between 1624 and 1799 has shown that throughout this period only 15–20 per cent came from more than five miles away and that two-thirds of these distant immigrants travelled less than 21 miles (Buckatzsch 1950). After 1700 Sheffield's population trends changed dramatically, and during the first two decades of the eighteenth century baptisms exceeded burials by 979. By 1711 the Cutlers company was worried about increasing numbers entering their trades. During the 1720s heavy mortalities reduced the surplus of baptisms to 38, but in the following decade baptisms outnumbered burials by 842. By 1736 the town's population stood at 10,121 and that of the entire parish at 14,531. Daniel Defoe was suitably impressed:

> The town of Sheffield is very populous and large, the streets narrow, and the houses dark and black, occasioned by the continued smoke of the forges, which are always at work. The manufacture of hard ware, which has been so antient in this town is not only continued but much increased.

Sheffield did not have a merchant class, for its trade was dominated by the rural ironmasters and urban attorneys and factors who dealt with London merchants, but in contrast with James I's reign it now had many more people who were reasonably well-off and able to contribute to the poor rates. Of the townspeople in 1672 58.2 per cent had only one or two hearths, but another 34.8 per cent had three to five hearths and seven per cent had more. The town had 224 smithies, that is one to every 2.2 houses and the eastern half of the parish had already acquired an industrial character; Attercliffe township had almost the same concentration as Sheffield with 51 smithies to 123 houses, and the neighbouring township of Brightside had 30 smithies to 100 houses, but the western parts of the parish had only 37 smithies to 286 houses.

Sheffield township contained 38 per cent of the 600 or so smithies recorded in south Yorkshire and north Derbyshire. Common penknives, forks, nails, scythes and sickles were made in the rural parishes and high-quality cutlery was manufactured in the town. The Sheffield baptism and burial registers for the five years beginning 1 October 1698 recorded 1,149 occupations, half of which were concerned with cutlery or other metal trades; the 763 urban craftsmen included 264 cutlers and 51 scissorsmiths and comprised 57.3 per cent of the recorded male population. Most of the newer crafts pursued by bladesmiths, snuff-and-tobacco-boxmakers, shearsmiths, buttonmakers and file cutters were found in the town rather than in the rural parts of Sheffield. At the beginning of the seventeenth century filemaking was not a separate craft, for cutlers made their own files; a few filesmiths were recorded locally during the Commonwealth period and 21 were accepted into membership of the Cutlers company in 1682; at the end of the century Joseph Brammall was a small employer with over 600 dozen files recorded in his probate inventory ready to sell to London merchants, and soon the craft spread to surrounding villages. Even more dramatic was the rise of the Old Sheffield Plate industry following Thomas Boulsover's discovery in 1743 of a method of fusing silver with copper and Joseph Hancock's realization of its commercial possibilities. This expansion of local trades provided the wealth for new houses and much rebuilding. A 1725 tourist observed,

There has been a great part of the town, which was made up chiefly of wooden houses, rebuilt within these last few years and now makes no mean figure in brick particularly towards the north side of it, where there are abundance of new erections upon new foundations by which the town has lately been considerably enlarged.

Another account in 1764 noted that most of the buildings were of brick, 'but from the great quantity of smoke occasioned by the manufactory, the newest buildings are apt soon to be discoloured'. By 1760 Horace Walpole could describe Sheffield as the foulest town in England, though set in the most charming situation (Hey forthcoming). Between 1736 and 1801 the population of the parish of Sheffield rose from 14,531 to 45,758 and that of the central urban township increased from 10,121 to 31,314. The town burst beyond its medieval limits when the Duke of Norfolk allowed building on Park Hill and Alsop Fields and when the surrounding greens and commons were enclosed by Parliament, and in 1784–86 the livestock markets and slaughter houses were removed from the central streets.

Gales and Martin's 1787 directory lists twenty steel converters and refiners, seventeen manufacturers of silver and plated goods, five founders and fifteen merchant houses which had all been established during the previous half-century, but the 'little-mester' remained the characteristic Sheffield figure. Industrial expansion was based on water power. Although a stream-grinding factory had been built in 1786, the number of grinders' 'hulls' on the local rivers increased considerably. A writer in 1750 claimed, moreover, that in recent years fifteen tilting mills had been erected on Sheffield rivers to reduce forged iron to sizes suitable for the secondary metalworkers. By that time Sheffield had a greater concentration of water-powered sites than anywhere else in England. The cutlery industry was still dominant, and expansion was achieved by the multiplication of small establishments of the traditional kind. 'Upon the whole', wrote Arthur Young in 1769, 'the manufacturers of Sheffield make immense earnings' of between 9 shillings and 20 shillings a week. These skilled, well-paid and independent craftsmen lived in a town without a mayor and corporation, without a resident lord and without even a resident magistrate. They became ardent supporters of a new political radicalism, which burst into life in the early 1790s, inspired by the French Revolution. Over 5,000 people joined a demonstration in November 1792 to celebrate the success of the French armies at Valmy, and the local Constitutional Society was the strongest in provincial England. The reformers were supported by many local professional men and by Joseph Gales's radical newspaper, *The Sheffield Register*, so that by May 1792 they had obtained nearly 10,000 signatures to a petition demanding that all men should have the right to vote. The authorities were able to control this agitation by repressive measures in 1794–95, but by then a new political movement had been born.

The Textile Industries

During the seventeenth and eighteenth centuries the English woollen industry was carried on in the same regions as it had been in the late Middle Ages; all counties had at least a scattering of weavers, but East Anglia, the West Country and the West Riding were pre-eminent. The progress of the West Riding industry was steady but unspectacular for most of the seventeenth century, when its main export outlet was through Holland and Germany, for keen continental competition and the Dutch wars hindered expansion. After the opening of the Aire and Calder navigation in 1700, however, Leeds merchants were able to penetrate home and overseas markets previously dominated by London, Norwich and Exeter merchants, particularly the south European trade and from the late 1750s the American trade. Long before the great changes that transformed the woollen cloth industry from the 1770s onwards the West Riding had outstripped its competitors. Its production of broad cloths in 1770 was nearly 3½ times what it had been in 1727 and the number of its narrow cloths in 1785 was more than double the output for 1740. Yorkshire's share of the total English production grew from less than 20 per cent in 1700 to about 60 per cent a century later (Heaton 1965: 277–81). Meanwhile, the growth of the West Riding worsted industry had been nothing less than sensational. Worsteds had been manufactured here during the Middle Ages but had been abandoned during the sixteenth century in favour of kerseys and dozens. After the Restoration worsted manufacture was reintroduced and once the Aire and Calder navigation had substantially reduced the cost of importing long wools from Lincolnshire and Leicestershire the industry expanded enormously. By 1770 output in the West Riding had reached the same level as that of Norwich, the traditional leading centre of worsted manufacture.

It was a source of strength for the West Riding to have this unique combination of woollen and worsted industries in close proximity. By 1700 Halifax was not only the leading centre of kersey manufacture but also of worsted shalloons. Worsteds were made in the upper valleys of the Calder and Aire as far north as Haworth and Keighley, and as far east as Bradford (the later centre) and even Wakefield and Leeds. Kerseys and other narrow woollen cloths were manufactured in Pennine districts stretching south of Halifax to Huddersfield (the later centre of fancy woollens) and Penistone. And broad cloths were made in the district bounded by Leeds, Wakefield, Huddersfield, Halifax and Bradford, with Leeds as the finishing and marketing centre; white or undyed cloths were produced in the Calder valley and coloured cloths were made in the parish of Leeds and in the villages to the west and south. Daniel Defoe passed through some of these populous villages on his journey from Halifax to Leeds and thought they presented, 'A noble scene of industry and application'.

As early as 1627 the inhabitants of Leeds, Wakefield and Halifax had declared that 'there is not the quantitie of cloth made in these three towns and their precincts as is made in the severall and dispersed towns and villages about us'. Villages such as Woodhouse, Beeston, Armley, Hunslet, Haworth, Holbeck, Churwell and Morley grew steadily as the cloth industry expanded (Heaton 1965: 288). In his account of the parish of Mirfield in 1755 the Revd J. Ismay noted that the parish contained over 400 houses and 2,000 people, of whom 400 were employed in carding, spinning and preparing wool for the looms and 200 in making broad cloth for Leeds market. The hamlets within the parish included

> The dwellings at or about Hopton Hall [which] are increased in less than forty years from three to eleven, and the inhabitants from seventeen to eighty . . . There are forty pairs of looms for weaving of white broad cloth in the hamlet. [Not far away,] about two years ago only three families lived on the north side of Lee Green, but now the number amounts to twenty-three and more new buildings are about to be erected.

Lee Green had three pubs, a workhouse and a new Moravian chapel (Crump and Ghorbal 1935: 57). Few cottages were without a piece of land, for the West Riding was one of the strongholds of a dual economy that emphasized both farming and a craft. When John Nobles, a Kirkburton kersey clothier, made his will in 1715 he instructed his supervisors to 'chuse such a master for my son where he may learn both the clothier trade and husbandry'. An analysis of 3,300 probate inventories for the West Riding cloth area has shown that 77.6 per cent of clothiers had agricultural goods worth £1 or more and that in the rural parts of Halifax parish the proportion was as high as 86 per cent (Dickenson 1974). Only in the towns and in the villages near Leeds was weaving divorced from farming. Daniel Defoe's famous description of his journey over the Pennines to Halifax depicts this way of life vividly:

> The nearer we came to Hallifax, we found the houses thicker, and the villages greater in every bottom; and not only so, but the sides of the hills, which were very steep every way, were spread with houses, and that very thick; for the land being divided into small enclosures, that is to say, from two acres to six or seven acres each, seldom more; every three or four pieces of land had a house belonging to it.
> Then it was I began to perceive the reason and nature of the thing, and found that this division of the land into small pieces, and scattering of the dwellings was occasioned by, and done for the convenience of the

business which the people were generally employ'd in, and that . . . though we saw no people stirring without doors, yet they were all full within; for, in short, this whole country, however mountainous . . . is yet infinitely full of people; those people all full of business; not a beggar, not an idle person to be seen, except here and there an alms-house . . . This business is the clothing trade . . . We found the country, in short, one continued village, tho' mountainous every way, as before; hardly a house standing out of a speaking distance from another . . . we could see that almost at every house there was a tenter, and almost on every tenter a piece of cloth, or kersie, or shalloon . . . Every manufacturer generally keeps a cow or two, or more, for his family, and this employs the two, or three or four pieces of enclosed land about his house, for they scarce sow corn enough for their cocks and hens . . . Among the manufacturers houses are likewise scattered an infinite number of cottages or small dwellings, in which dwell the workmen which are employed; the women and children of whom, are always busy carding, spinning, &c so that no hands being unemploy'd, all can gain their bread, even from the youngest to the antient; hardly any thing above four years old, but its hands are sufficient to it self.

Contemporaries believed that the West Riding's success was due to the peculiar structure of its industry, which provided opportunities for men of enterprise and initative. Certainly, the county had no advantage in terms of wool supplies or export markets, and the differences in labour costs were minimal. The West Riding was a much more complex and forward-looking industrial area than its competitors, whose cloth manufacture took place in an otherwise agricultural setting, and the variety of woollens and worsteds produced meant that manufacturers could switch relatively easily from product to product as occasion demanded. Moreover, the West Riding concentrated upon the cheap end of the market with cloths of excellent value which were bought eagerly by the rising population both at home and abroad.

But the most notable feature of the Yorkshire industry was the domestic system of organization. Whereas East Anglian and West Country manufacture was dominated by wealthy merchants and clothiers who employed numerous outworkers for wages, the characteristic West Riding enterprise was the independent family unit which produced one piece of cloth each week for the local market. Only a small amount of capital was needed for such a venture, which was often profitably combined with the running of a smallholding. This type of organization, with its investment in breadth, enabled the industry to expand enormously; the new inventions did not transform the industry, but were taken up by the small clothiers. Nevertheless, a number of large-scale employers did emerge and in Leeds the merchants dominated the trade. The worsted industry had been organized on a capitalistic basis from the start and the masters had many workers at their command. Samuel King of Making

Place, Soyland, was such an employer. Letters written early in 1738 show that he sold almost 1,000 pieces of worsted cloth in less than three weeks, which implies a workforce of at least 200 weavers and many more spinners (Atkinson 1956: 1–18). As the population rose, cottagers were increasingly obliged to work for an employer on a piece-rate basis at a specialist occupation such as weaving, spinning or combing.

During the seventeenth century the manufacture of woollen cloth was still widespread in Yorkshire. York played an important role as a marketing centre, Doncaster woolstaplers brought in good quality wools and cloth fairs were held in Ripon, Pontefract and Barnsley. But even before the opening of the Aire and Calder navigation Leeds and Wakefield markets were pre-eminent. In 1628 it was claimed that 'Wakefield now is the greatest markett and principal place of resorte of all sorts of Clothiers, Drapers, and other traffickers for Cloath in all these parts', and in the early eighteenth century Defoe observed that 'Wakefield is a clean, large, well-built town, very populous and very rich ... and yet it is no corporation town'; the Friday cloth market was held 'after the manner of that of Leeds, tho' not so great'. The Tuesday and Saturday cloth markets at Leeds were 'a progidy ... not to be equalled in the world'; clothiers set off in the early hours of the morning to be in Briggate for 6 a.m. in summer and 7 a.m. in winter, and all transactions were completed by 8.30 a.m. During the eighteenth century a succession of cloth halls were built to protect these activities from inclement weather. Halifax had such a one by 1708, and in 1779 a large new Piece Hall of 315 rooms around a central courtyard, the only major one to survive. The Wakefield cloth hall of 1710 caused the Leeds merchants to erect their own in 1711; in 1755 Leeds acquired a large White Cloth Hall and in 1774 another large hall, and in 1776 Wakefield merchants built their Tammy Hall. At the southern edge of the textile region the small cloth market established at Penistone in 1743 was transferred to a cloth hall twenty years later and at Huddersfield, where kerseys had been exposed for sale on the churchyard wall every Tuesday since the granting of a market in 1671, a cloth hall was built in 1766 at the expense of Sir John Ramsden. In 1775 Gomersal men tried to draw away some of the Leeds trade by erecting a cloth hall and in 1773 Bradford acquired its Piece Hall. Bradford was still a small place with only about 4,200 people in 1780, and though the worsted industry thrived around it, the town was not yet firmly established as the centre of trade (Heaton 1965: 359–82).

In the later seventeenth century 9–10,000 people lived in Leeds borough, two-thirds of them in the urban part that was no more than half a square mile in size. The borough's jurisdiction extended over the 21,000 acres of the parish and included the populous industrial villages of Holbeck, Hunslet, Armley and Bramley to the south and west of the town. The woollen manufacture stopped one mile to the north of the urban centre in pleasant, well-wooded, undulating country around Headingley, Chapeltown and Potter Newton. In all parts of the town the houses of the rich and the poor were intermingled with

233

workshops, though Briggate had the most substantial dwellings, and the eastern district from Mabgate to Marsh Lane had poor domestic accommodation among the dyehouses and fulling mills. The hearth-tax returns of 1664–72 show that Leeds had relatively few paupers; about two in five of the inhabitants had one hearth, a similar proportion had two or three hearths, and one in five had more (Fraser, ed. 1980: 8–19). In 1698 Celia Fiennes wrote,

> Leeds is a large town, severall large streets clean and well pitch'd and good houses all built of stone, some have good gardens and steps up to their houses and walls before them; this is esteemed the wealthyest town of its bigness in the Country . . . they have provision so plentifull that they may live with very little expense and get much variety.

She also noted that the town was 'full of Dissenters'; the Presbyterians built a chapel in Mill Hill in 1674 and by the 1690s the Congregationalists and Quakers also had their meeting places.

In 1686 Leeds had 294 guest beds and 454 stables. Packhorse routes headed west into the Pennines but the eastern routes to the inland ports on the Ouse were used by carts and waggons; the road to Selby was particularly busy and the West Riding JPs spent over £500 on it during the last sixty years of the seventeenth century. The opening of the Aire and Calder navigation to Leeds bridge in 1700 was of major importance to the commercial and industrial development of the town. Leeds expanded more rapidly than any other Yorkshire settlement. The population rose by natural increase and by immigrant apprentices and journeymen labourers and after 1740 the rate of growth accelerated. By 1771 the town's population stood at 16,380 and four years later at 17,121; yet all these new people were accommodated within the old confines, and almost everywhere the workplace was the small craft shop. Economic expansion was not restricted to the cloth trade; in fact, the proportion of both the workforce and the firms involved in textiles declined after 1740. The number of firms engaged in other trades rose three fold between 1720 and 1797, long-established industries involving coal, bricks and wood or building, dressmaking, tailoring, shoemaking and printing expanded and new industries such as the manufacture of pottery, linen, chemicals, soap-boiling and sugar-refining took root and flourished.

Progress in all these fields was gradual rather than revolutionary, with few significant changes in the size of economic organization before the 1790s. Apart from the Leeds pottery, the Middleton colliery and the Aire and Calder navigation, only the biggest merchant houses in the cloth trade were unusually large in terms of capital investment. The 73 cloth firms that were based in Leeds in 1781 varied considerably in size; two-thirds of the cloth trade was organized by the 24 largest firms, but even they had at most 30 dressers and a few packers, pressers and clerks. Leeds merchants were mostly descended from substantial yeomen or smaller landed families, such as the Wades and Sykeses, rather than from clothiers. They were closely connected through marriage and dominated the town's political and social as well as economic affairs, but few of these family concerns continued for more than half a century. Fourteen of the fifteen illustrations of solid, respectable houses that adorn the margins of Cossin's 1725 plan of Leeds belonged to merchants. They were an affluent body with numerous links with neighbouring gentry on a personal, business and social basis. The town's corporate status gave it a dignity that was rarely matched by other West Riding towns. Leeds was as fashionable a social centre as many a county town, with attractions ranging from horse-racing on Chapeltown moor and cockfighting to a theatre which brought performers from London, dancing, card assemblies and musical concerts (Wilson 1971; Fraser, ed. 1980: 24–43).

During the 1790s Leeds acquired two enormous water-powered factories that became celebrated throughout the land as wonders of the age. In 1792 John Marshall, who three years earlier had installed Cartwright power looms at Scotland mill in the parish of Adel, built the largest flax-spinning mill in England at Holbeck and established Leeds as an important centre of the linen trade alongside Knaresborough and Barnsley; by 1804 the mill operated 4,000 spindles. Even more impressive was the Bean Ing woollen mill which Benjamin Gott of the Leeds cloth merchant house of Wormald and Fontaine erected on the banks of the Aire. Bean Ing was the first mill in the West Riding to have a Boulton and Watt steam engine. By 1797 Gott's 12,000 workers were making 4,000 broad cloths per annum, mainly cheap clothing and blankets for the army in the French wars. In 1800 Gott constructed a second mill and a mansion at Armley and soon became a noted philanthropist. He had few imitators at first, however, and the nineteenth century was well advanced before the West Riding had many large woollen mills. Even by the beginning of Victoria's reign mills employing more than 400 workers were unusual.

The factory system that gradually transformed the West Riding textile industry was introduced into the cotton and worsted branches from Lancashire. Keighley, which attracted Dr Pococke's attention in 1750 as a place where 'woosted, calimancoes, shaloons and stockins' and 'the small wares of Manchester' were manufactured, acquired several cotton mills in the 1790s, notably Ponden mill (1791) and Turkey mill at Goose Eye (1797). In Leeds, Richard Paley, soap boiler, ironfounder, potash manufacturer and property developer, built two steam-powered cotton mills at the Bank in 1790, though ultimately he went bankrupt and the Leeds cotton industry failed. Todmorden was more successful. In 1786 Joshua Fielden, a worsted manufacturer, put all his capital into a cotton business; by 1827 the Fieldens' Waterside mill had ten power looms and numerous spinners and weavers had moved across the border from Lancashire to gain employment as outworkers (Thornes 1981: 26–7). By 1835 the Craven district had 44 cotton mills, most of them water-powered, with Skipton, Barnoldswick and Settle as the main centres. Further south, Saddleworth also shared Lancashire's interest in fustians, linens and cottons as well as having a domestic woollen industry.

The West Riding's first worsted-spinning mill with Arkwright machinery was established at Addingham in 1787 to produce yarn for Bradford weavers. Five years later a similar mill was constructed at Mytholmroyd by Thomas Edmondson, one of the partners of Britain's earliest worsted-spinning mill at Dolphinholme, near Lancaster, and by 1800 the West Riding had 22 worsted mills. During the second half of the eighteenth century market forces had persuaded the inhabitants of the Pennine settlements west of Bradford, including those in the great parish of Halifax, gradually to abandon the manufacture of kerseys in favour of worsteds. As the local population rose to unprecedented levels more and more families were unable to find a smallholding to supplement their craft wages and were forced to work full-time for an employer on piece-rates, albeit in their own homes until it became apparent that worsted yarn could be spun by water power equally well as cotton. Except in the combing process, where the technical problems were formidable, the transition to factory production was far more rapid in the worsted than in the woollen trade. The longer stapled wools of the worsted manufacturer were more suited to machines than were those of the woollen clothier, who was unable to introduce powered spinning for another two or three decades. By the 1820s worsted-spinning mills had an employment structure similar to that of the cotton industry, based on female and juvenile labour, but water power was only just becoming applied to worsted weaving. The relatively high wages of the combers and weavers attracted thousands of the rising population into the worsted trade, many of them from agricultural districts as far apart as Cumbria and Devon or the North Riding and Leicestershire. An estimated 20,000 weavers and combers were employed in the Bradford area in 1825 on the eve of a bitter 23 week strike, which ended in total defeat for the strikers. The wool-combers who had once been privileged artisans were now humble outworkers (Thompson 1963: 282).

Most of the early woollen mills were erected not by wealthy merchants but by small manufacturers who had previously been involved in the trade. Until the 1820s domestic production of woollen cloth remained far more important than factory output and small mills and workshops were always more typical than the large concerns. At first, the domestic industry welcomed the new machinery from Lancashire; Kay's flying shuttle was in general use in the West Riding by 1770, and when Hargreaves's spinning jenny was introduced into Holmfirth about 1776 it was 'hailed as a prodigy'. In upland villages and hamlets small manufacturers installed a few hand-looms and jennies in their 'warehouses' and employed others to spin and weave at home. Machines based on Arkwright's carder appeared in the mid-Calder valley, the old centre of the cardmaking trade, in the 1770s, but in the early years they were operated by hand or by a horse-drawn gin. Soon, however, the preparatory processes of carding and scribbling were adapted to water-power, and later to steam. Newcomen-type steam engines manufactured by local foundries were used to pump water back into the dams so that the water wheels had a regular supply. Boulton and Watt engines were expensive and so were adopted slowly, but they allowed mills to be sited away from the rivers. Gradually the skylines of the West Riding mill towns and villages were pierced by a growing number of tall chimneys. A typical development can be observed in miniature in a secluded moorland clough half a mile east of Meltham, where in the 1780s a scribbling mill and then a fulling mill were erected near the old manorial corn mill, and where a new settlement known as Meltham Mills soon flourished (Crump and Ghorbal 1935: 59–74). Three miles away, the changes in the Holmfirth district were on a much larger scale. Until the late eighteenth century nearly all the inhabitants lived high above the river valleys; Holmfirth was a district name that originally denoted the hunting chase of the medieval lords of the huge manor of Wakefield. The valley bottom that is now occupied by the town of Holmfirth had few buildings apart from the manorial corn and fulling mills until 1784, when John Fallas, a woollen clothier acquired those properties and added a scribbling mill. In 1822 Edward Baines's directory observed

> The houses are scattered in the deep valley, and on the acclivities of the
> hills, without any regard to arrangement, or the formation of streets . . .
> The traveller, at his first view of this extraordinary village, is struck
> with astonishment at the singularity of its situation and appearance . . .
> This is a place of great trade, and the principal part of the inhabitants
> are employed in the manufacture of woollen cloth.

Jeffreys's map of 1767–72 marked eighteen mills on the local rivers and streams, and new valley settlements also grew up at Holmbridge, Hinchliffe Mill and at New Mill, the site of the new manorial corn mill of the early fourteenth century. Holy Trinity Church, built between 1777 and 1787 at the bottom of the valley, served these new communities but Holmfirth did not become an independent parish until 1858. The rows of two- or three-storeyed terraced houses that characterized these new settlements were very different in scale and plan from the previous detached cottages. They were soon to become the normal type of accommodation for industrial workers in the West Riding mill towns.

Factory machine spinning was introduced into the woollen industry in the 1820s, but the weavers stayed in the hills and their craft long remained a domestic occupation. Villages and hamlets as well as towns took part in the tremendous expansion of the textile trades. Houses were clustered in folds or arranged along the streets with an upper range of mullioned windows extending all along the front so as to catch the maximum amount of light on the looms. The traditional economy of the weaver-farmer, whose workplace was his home, flourished well into the Victorian period, but with the great rise in population weavers were increasingly a wage-earning class, whose cottages

237

were rented from the manufacturers. Many weaving villages were linked with newer settlements in the valleys, where the yarn was prepared and spun; Skelmanthorpe, for example, was a typical upland community with warehouses and weavers' cottages, whereas the scribbling and spinning mills were down in the river valley at Scissett and Denby Dale. By the middle years of the nineteenth century the worsted industry was dominated by factories, but the woollen trade still employed numerous domestic workers.

The exploitation of female and child labour, the long hours and hard working conditions that became such familiar features of the factory system had long been characteristic of domestic industry, but workers in the textile mills now had the additional burdens of strict discipline and the tyranny of the clock. Moreover, many skilled craftsmen were replaced by the new machines. The early activities of the Luddites won widespread public sympathy, including that of many 'respectable inhabitants' appalled at the new system which threatened to destroy the old social order. Machine-breaking began in 1811 in Nottinghamshire, Leicestershire and south Derbyshire, where framework knitting was rapidly becoming a depressed craft. In the spring of 1812 the knitters' example was followed by West Riding croppers and shearmen, those skilled well-paid craftsmen who 'finished' the cloth and who now found their livelihoods threatened by the gig mill and shearing frame.

Figure 4.5   The townships of Staincross wapentake

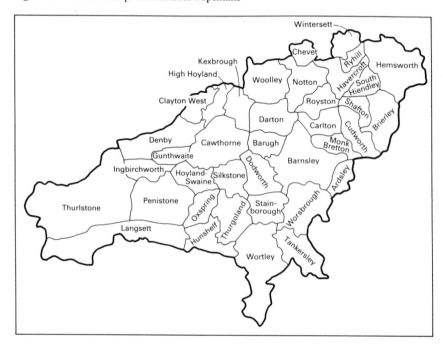

Between 1806 and 1817 the number of gig mills in Yorkshire rose from 5 to 72 and the number of shears worked by machinery increased from 100 to 1,462. As a result, 1,170 of the 3,378 shearmen were thrown out of work and 1,445 received only part-time employment (Lipson 1921: 191). Unskilled men and children were able to work the machines. The attacks began in Leeds, then in Huddersfield and the Spen Valley, where the greatest number of machines had been installed. Then in April 1812, six or seven weeks after the first acts of destruction, the Luddites turned to more desperate measures.

On 9 April an estimated 300 men set fire to Joseph Foster's mill at Horbury and destroyed all the machines. Two days later, 150 Luddites, led by George Mellor, a young cropper from Longroyd Bridge, attacked William Cartwright's Rawfolds mill in the Spen Valley, but were met by a hail of musket fire. Expected reinforcements from Halifax failed to arrive and the Luddites were forced to retreat, leaving two members dead and five wounded. William Horsfall of Ottiwells near Huddersfield was equally determined to defend his mill and was as loud as Cartwright in his condemnation of Luddism. On 28 April, on his return from Huddersfield market, he was shot dead by George Mellor from behind a wall on Crosland Moor. The assassination was a turning point, for public sympathy changed and 'Yorkshire Luddism petered out amidst arrests, betrayals, threats and disillusion' (Thompson 1963: 572). In January 1813 Mellor and sixteen other Luddites were executed at York and seven others were transported to Australia.

Patterns and Contrasts

By the beginning of the nineteenth century many parts of the West Riding had been deeply affected by industrial change and Leeds and Sheffield were well on their way in becoming two of the leading cities in the land. Nevertheless, it remained true that an older, more traditional way of life was everywhere to be found alongside the new. Farming parishes in eastern parts of the riding proceeded in their own unhurried way and estate villages remained immune to social change. In many parts of the West Riding industrial expansion was achieved not so much by new factories as by the ancient hand-crafts. Even in Sheffield industrialization so far had largely meant the multiplication of existing small establishments using immemorial forms of organization.

The 1806 militia returns for the 40 townships of Staincross wapentake record the names and occupations of men aged between 18 and 45 who could be called upon to resist a French invasion. They provide information on employment in an area which stretched from the county boundary high upon the Pennines across the coalfield to Hemsworth and Brierley, and from the

239

banks of the river Dearne in the north as far as the Little Don in the south. The wapentake contained a flourishing urban centre at Barnsley, a small market town at Penistone and a considerable variety of rural communities. The north-eastern parts were still almost entirely agricultural, for the days of great mining activity were yet to come; no colliers were recorded in either Brierley or Hemsworth, and the halls and parks of the landed gentry dominated several small settlements. Even when deep mines were sunk during the reign of Victoria, places such as Chevet, West Bretton and Woolley were hardly affected, for no industry was allowed to pollute their surroundings. Like many another deserted medieval village Chevet was under the control of a single family; the fifteen men liable for militia service comprised a baronet, two farmers, a butler and eleven servants. West Bretton was larger, with carpenters, joiners, blacksmiths and masons as well as the men who formed the entourage of the hall. No two estate villages were completely alike, and the inhabitants of Woolley were less dependent upon their squire; they included not only a gentleman and his 4 grooms, 3 keepers, 2 butlers, 2 ushers, valet, footman, coachman, 23 farm labourers and 9 farm servants, but also 6 farmers, 6 carpenters, 5 miners, 3 masons, 3 blacksmiths, 3 shoemakers, 2 tailors, a basketmaker and an innkeeper.

The squires of such villages refused to allow migrant labourers to settle in their townships in case they became a burden upon the poor rates. In 1834 Woolley was said by the Poor Law Commissioners to have only three residents who had come into the parish and consequently it had no unemployment problem. Nearby Notton was another 'close' village with no paupers, no industry and no religious dissent. By way of contrast, a large 'open' township with less social control often had a large number of immigrants working at a variety of industrial employments. In 1806, for instance, Cawthorne township had 201 men liable for militia service who between them had 33 different jobs. This diversity of occupations was more pronounced amongst some early-nineteenth-century open townships than ever before, and while estate villages developed slowly and imperceptibly, most open communities grew at an astonishing rate. A generation after the compilation of the Staincross militia list, the Poor Law Commissioners noted that in addition to the more substantial buildings 238 cottages were occupied in Cawthorne township; the number of colliers living in these cottages had recently increased from 32 to 85. The patterns of land ownership which determined whether a village was open or close, or somewhere between the two extremes, had often been settled long before the nineteenth century. However, the number and variety of open villages had recently been increased by new industrial settlements on the borders of ancient townships and parishes.

By 1806 some crafts had become concentrated in certain districts. Linen weaving, for example, had once been thinly spread over the south Yorkshire countryside, but in 1744 William and John Wilson, two Quaker brothers, established a warehouse and bleach works in Barnsley and provided houses and looms for weavers. There are no records of how many women and children assisted the men at their looms in damp cellars, but the rapid growth of the trade can be assessed by the militia returns. In 1806 Barnsley had 174 weavers, 42 manufacturers, 32 bleachers and ten warehousemen. Baines wrote in his 1822 directory:

> Wire drawing was formerly the principal trade of this town, but it has now given place to the manufacture of flax, bleaching of linen yarns, weaving of linen cloth, ducks, diapers, damasks, etc, which is carried on to a very considerable extent. About 36 tons of these articles are sent out of Barnsley every week, the average value of which is about £500 per ton. There are upwards of 3,000 looms employed in this town and the neighbouring villages.

By 1806 linen weaving and bleaching were well established in Ardsley, Barugh, Dodworth, Monk Bretton and parts of Worsbrough; 48 of the 79 men in Ardsley were weavers and 21 were labourers or farm servants. Not only was this type of local community totally different from that at Chevet or West Bretton, its craft specialization made it unlike open townships such as Cawthorne which had a wide range of occupations. Early-nineteenth-century Ardsley was very much a product of recent industrialization.

The manufacture of woollen cloth had likewise become confined to a special district. Penistone parish lay on the southern borders of the textile zone, and its weavers were numerous only in the townships of Denby and Thurlstone. The villages and hamlets further north specialized to the same degree as did the linen-weaving communities around Barnsley. Of the 129 men recorded in Thurlstone township, 41 weavers, 21 clothiers and 7 others were employed in the woollen industry. In Denby and Denby Dale 70 per cent of the 111 men were textile workers, and Cumberworth, the most specialized township of all, had 89 weavers, 6 clothiers, 3 cutters and 11 tradesmen compared with only 31 men who were not employed in cloth manufacture. Cumberworth township ranked fourth in Staincross wapentake in terms of population but was fifteenth in range of occupation.

Another type of industrial village specialized in metalware. The heart of the nailmaking area was beyond the wapentake boundary, but Mapplewell and Staincross, two of the hamlets of Darton parish, were recognized centres. In 1806 the 165 men liable for militia service in the parish of Darton included 66 nailers, that is half the number recorded in the wapentake. Twenty others were working in Hoylandswaine, an open township with 14 weavers, 8 clothiers, 11 farmers, 10 labourers, 5 servants and 11 other craftsmen. The nailers were already facing severe competition from machine-made nails, and the decline of their trade was soon to be rapid. However, they were still more numerous than the 115 colliers in Staincross wapentake. Cawthorne had 32 colliers, but Barnsley had only 23 and Silkstone a mere 11. The wapentake contained a large part of what is now the old coalfield, where by the end of the nineteenth century pit villages had emerged as distinctive communities, but in 1806 there were only 7 miners in Dodworth, 6 in Cudworth and none at all in Hemsworth.

At the beginning of the nineteenth century Staincross wapentake also had a variety of small crafts and family businesses such as basket weaving, glass making, pottery manufacture and tanning, and those who could be called upon to join the militia included 125 joiners and carpenters, 117 shoemakers and 102 masons. Farming remained the major occupation, for the returns list 277 farmers, 551 labourers and 289 farm servants, who together formed 36 per cent of the recorded work force. In addition the wapentake contained many butchers, millers and an incalculable number of craftsmen who combined their trade with the running of a farm or smallholding. Even on the coalfield agriculture was still of paramount importance.

But the signs of a new industrial age were plentiful to see. The old charcoal iron industry had given way to a technology based on coal and to operations on a much larger scale. In the middle of the eighteenth century the Walker brothers had taken over the site of the Masborough slitting mill so as to be near the navigable river, after the success of their experiments with an 'Air Furnace in the old nailor's smithey, on the backside of Saml. Walker's cottage at Grenoside', and later John Cockshutt had adapted Wortley forge to the new techniques of coke-fuelling, puddling and rolling. Meanwhile, Richard Swallow, the heir to the Fells of Attercliffe, had converted Chapel furnace and Attercliffe forge to the production of steel and iron by the use of coke fuel. He was described in the 1787 directory as steel converter and refiner, and by 1806 his son and namesake was making 3,737 tons of metal per annum. The scale of production had risen considerably, for the average output of the old Chapel furnace had been a mere 450 tons. Chapeltown had long been known simply as Chapel on account of its medieval origins as a chapel-of-ease in the northern part of the parish of Ecclesfield, but now it grew out of all recognition.

In 1793 George Newton and Thomas Chambers moved from Sheffield to begin a lease of Earl Fitzwilliam's iron and coal mines at Thorncliffe, just up the valley from Swallow, and to build a foundry. By 1806 their output was 2,500 tons a year and they employed some 300 miners, furnacemen, foundrymen and labourers (Hey 1977). Further north, the iron industry was concentrated not only near ironstone deposits but where coal was of suitable quality for coking. In the Bradford district, for example, Emmet's ironworks was established at Birkenshaw in 1782, six years later the Bowling ironworks began manufacturing pig iron and such cast-iron domestic goods as fire-grates, fire-irons and frying pans, and in 1789 the Low Moor Iron Company, the best-known of all, started production. The Low Moor works was founded by John Hardy, a Bradford solicitor, John Jarratt, a draper, Richard Hind, a woolstapler, and the Revd Joseph Dawson, a nonconformist minister; as none of the partners had any previous ironmaking experience, the technical side of the business was left to the engineer, Edward Smalley (Thomas 1981: 31). The French Revolutionary Wars stimulated the iron trade through lucrative government contracts for armaments, and during the course of the nineteenth century the West Riding became an important centre for the engineering industry.

The workforce for these new industries was overwhelmingly local in origin. Yorkshire had not yet experienced large-scale immigration. The pattern throughout rural England was still the ancient one of considerable movement between neighbouring parishes, especially amongst the labourers, but relatively little migration beyond the nearest market towns. Local communities remained markedly different in their customs, speech and employment. 'The County of York', observed George Walker of Killingbeck Hall, 'offers perhaps a greater variety and peculiarity of manners and dress than any other in the kingdom.' His *Costume of Yorkshire*, published in 1814, depicted various occupations, pastimes and amusements in 40 colour plates. The 'humble individuals' who attracted his attention were shown in 'their simple and sometimes squalid garb' in an attempt at a true portrayal of ordinary Yorkshire people. 'These men', he said of the West Riding cloth-makers, 'have a decided provincial character.' Though gentry families had begun to speak a standardized English by the end of Elizabeth's reign, regional differences in speech at other social levels remained marked. Dryden wrote of one who was 'Like a fair Shepherdess in her Country Russet, talking in a Yorkshire tone'. According to John Aubrey, Ben Jonson took his 'hint for clownery' when writing *The Tale of a Tub* from the Yorkshire words and proverbs spoken by John Lacy, a player of the King's House who had come to London from Doncaster in 1631.

Scholars first became seriously interested in the peculiarities of local speech later in the seventeenth century. The first dialect dictionary was John Ray's *Collection of English Words* (1674), which was augmented from Yorkshire in 1691 by a list of East Riding words from Francis Brokesby, rector of Rowley, and in 1703 by a catalogue of words spoken in the Leeds area from the antiquary, Ralph Thoresby. An unknown author published his *Yorkshire Dialogue between an Awd Wife, a Lass and a Butcher* at York in 1693, and four years later George Meriton's *The Praise of Yorkshire Ale* included a section entitled 'A Yorkshire Dialogue in its pure Natural Dialect as it is now commonly spoken in the North parts of Yorkshire', followed by 'Some Observations concerning the Dialect and various Pronunciations of words in the East Riding'. Most of the early dialect writing in Yorkshire came from the North and East Ridings, perhaps because the speech of those areas differed from the standard language more than did the West Riding vernacular (Ellis 1981). Histories of Yorkshire towns also appeared in the early eighteenth century, with Ralph Thoresby's *Ducatus Leodiensis: or, the Topography of Leeds and the Parts adjacent* (1715), Thomas Gent's *The Ancient and Modern History of the Famous City of York* (1730), the same author's *History of Kingston-upon-Hull* (1735), Francis Drake's *Eboracum: or the History and*

243

Antiquities of the City of York (1736) and later the Revd John Watson's *History of Halifax* (1775) which appended a list of local words. The most notable attempts to cover wider areas were Thomas Dunham Whitaker's *History and Antiquities of the Deanery of Craven* (1805) and his *Loidis and Elmete* (1816), followed by the Revd Joseph Hunter's *History of Hallamshire* (1819), *History of South Yorkshire* (2 vols, 1828–31) and *The Hallamshire Glossary* (1829), which recorded words spoken by 'the rustic and the mechanic', many of which were archaic words which had disappeared elsewhere. Yorkshire never got a complete county history, however, for it was far too large for a single author to attempt the task.

Chapter 5

Victorian and Edwardian Times

Population

In many respects Victorian and Edwardian England was vastly different from the country that had been ruled by the Stuarts and the Hanoverians. Though life in the countryside went on in much the same way as before, the astonishing increase in the urban population was a totally new phenomenon which transformed the townsman's environment and his way of life. Falling death rates, brought about by fewer epidemics and lower infant mortalities, coupled with an increasing number of early marriages and therefore more births led to a spectacular population rise that was unparalleled in the previous history of the world. In 1801 the population of England and Wales stood at about 8.9 million (or 9.2 million if allowance is made for under-recording); by 1851 it had reached 17.9 million; and by 1911 it had soared to 36.1 million. At the beginning of the nineteenth century England was still largely a rural country; only one in three Englishmen lived in a town, and only one in five inhabited a town of more than 20,000 people. The nineteenth-century population explosion shifted the balance dramatically, however, so that by 1851, for the first time in history, more English people lived in an urban environment than in the countryside. By 1881 only one in three Englishmen was a countryman, and by 1911 the proportion had fallen to one in five. Yorkshire's population quadrupled during the nineteenth century and that of the West Riding increased nearly five times. At the beginning of the nineteenth century the West Riding's population was already double that of the combined totals of the other two ridings; by the end of the century it was $3\frac{1}{2}$ times as high. In provincial England only Lancashire and the West Midlands surpassed this rate of growth and showed a greater trend towards urbanization.

When county councils were created in 1888 Wakefield, Beverley and Northallerton became the administrative centres of the three Ridings, with county halls, and offices and prisons. The West Riding's pre-eminence in Yorkshire was such that by the end of the century it had twenty county and municipal boroughs compared with only four each in the other two ridings. The Parliamentary Boundary Commission of 1832 concluded rightly that

Table 5.1   The population of Yorkshire, 1801–1901 (from census returns)

Year	Yorkshire	West Riding	East Riding	North Riding	York + Ainsty
1801	859,133	564,593	111,192	158,955	24,393
1811	977,820	650,168	132,415	167,779	27,458
1821	1,173,106	800,444	153,854	188,201	30,607
1831	1,371,966	957,458	168,891	192,255	35,362
1841	1,592,059	1,154,068	194,936	204,734	38,321
1851	1,797,995	1,315,885	220,983	215,225	45,902
1861	2,033,610	1,497,787	240,227	245,267	50,329
1871	2,436,330	1,821,340	268,476	293,274	53,240
1881	2,886,536	2,165,056	315,478	346,264	59,738
1891	3,208,502	2,429,632	348,426	367,911	62,533
1901	3,584,675	2,733,688	392,392	391,011	67,584

York was no longer 'a northern metropolis', for together with such other ancient urban centres as Beverley, Richmond and Ripon it had long since been overtaken by the burgeoning industrial towns. In 1801 Leeds was far bigger than York and it ranked seventh amongst English towns in terms of population. Whereas the city of York had 17,238 inhabitants, the central urban township of Leeds had 30,669 people and the whole borough contained 53,162. By the mid-nineteenth century the only English cities with larger populations than Leeds were London, Liverpool, Manchester and Birmingham. Sheffield stood seventh in the national ranking in 1851, for it too had expanded enormously. Comparisons between towns are not easy to make, for many urban settlements included large rural hinterlands within their borough boundaries. Sheffield borough, for instance, comprised the 22,370 acres of the ancient parish, which contained several villages and many hamlets and isolated farmsteads; most of these were gradually absorbed in the urban sprawl, particularly when huge steel-works were built in the eastern part of the borough during the second half of the nineteenth century. In 1801 the population of the entire parish was only 1.46 times higher than that of the central township, but by 1901 it was 4.2 times as high. Comparisons between towns are also complicated by shifting boundaries. During the early years of the twentieth century Sheffield took in Tinsley, Hillsborough, Owlerton, parts of Wadsley and Wincobank and the whole of Norton Woodseats (which formerly lay in Derbyshire), thus enabling it by 1911 to become the largest city in Yorkshire and prompting the Master Cutler to remark, 'I'm glad we've beaten Leeds'.

The same difficulties over boundaries are encountered when tracing the growth of nineteenth-century Bradford and Hull, Yorkshire's next largest towns. In 1801 Bradford township was still physically distinct from the rest of the parish, but by the later Victorian period the borough was the meaningful unit. After the Napoleonic wars Bradford grew at an astonishing rate as it became a world centre for the manufacture of worsted cloth. Its population growth exceeded 50 per cent during every decade between 1811 and 1851, and during the ten years between 1821 and 1831 it grew by a sensational 65.5 per cent. Until the mid-Victorian period Hull's growth was largely confined to the ancient limits of the city, but by then little room was left for further housing and the rising population had to seek accommodation within the adjoining 'county'. Whereas in 1851 only 5,943 people lived in the county compared with 50,670 in the town, by 1901 the county's 76,949 population almost matched the 82,245 inhabitants in the old urban centre.

Table 5.2   The population of Yorkshire's largest towns, 1801–1901

Year	Leeds Borough	Town	Sheffield Parish	Town	Bradford Parish	Town	Hull County	Town
1801	53,162	30,669	45,755	31,314	29,794	6,393	25,294	22,161
1851	172,023	101,343	135,310	83,447	149,543	52,493	56,613	50,670
1881	308,628	160,109	284,508	91,806	251,553	68,372	101,517	78,222
1901	428,572	177,920	380,793	90,398	290,297	73,454	159,194	82,245

By 1851 Yorkshire had thirteen towns with over 10,000 inhabitants. All but three – Hull, York and Scarborough – lay in the West Riding. The difficulty of deciding which boundary to use makes the task of defining a large town a rather arbitrary one, but if the definition is limited to the central urban township and no allowance is made for the outlying parts, then the ranking is as follows: Leeds 101,343, Sheffield 83,447, Bradford 52,493, Hull 50,670, York 36,622, Huddersfield 30,880, Scarborough 25,830, Halifax 25,161, Wakefield 16,989, Barnsley 14,913, Dewsbury 14,049, Bingley 13,437 and Doncaster 12,052. The story of population growth and of the economic developments that sustained it is not confined to the towns, however; the industrial villages of the West Riding played a very important role.

Table 5.3   The population of three West Riding parishes, 1801–1901

Year	Halifax (82,543 acres)	Birstall (13,988 acres)	Keighley (10,132 acres)
1801	63,434	14,657	5,745
1851	140,257	36,222	18,259
1881	193,707	62,781	30,395
1901	221,061	67,424	42,106

The sprawling parish of Birstall at the heart of the textile district provides a suitable illustration. It had no urban centre, but included within its boundaries the settlements of Cleckheaton, Drighlington, Gomersal, Heckmondwike, Liversedge, Tong and Wike, whose combined population increased 4.6 times during the course of the nineteenth century. Further west,

247

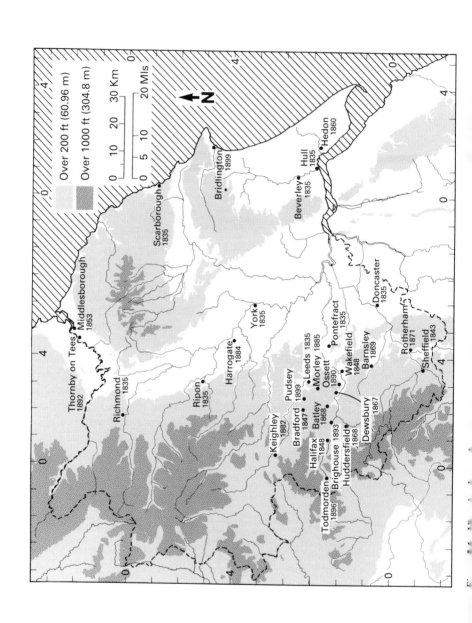

Over 200 ft (60.96 m)

Over 1000 ft (304.8 m)

N

0   5   10   20   30 Km

0   10   20 MIs

Scarborough
1835

Bridlington
1899

Beverley   Hull
1835   1835

Hedon
1860

Middlesborough
1853

Doncaster
1835

Thornby on Tees
1892

York
1835

Pontefract
1835

Rotherham
1871

Richmond
1835

Harrogate
1884

Leeds 1835
Morley 1885
Wakefield
1848

Barnsley
1869

Sheffield
1843

Ripon
1835

Pudsey
1899

Ossett
1890

Keighley
1882

Bradford
1847

Batley
1868

Dewsbury
1867

Halifax
1848

Brighouse 1893

Huddersfield
1868

Todmorden
1896

on the Pennine fringes, Halifax was not only a town but the centre of the largest parish in England. In 1851 the population of the parish was 5.6 times that of the town, and rural growth accounted for most of the 348 per cent increase in the parish's population during the course of the nineteenth century. A similar story can be told for such parishes as Keighley.

The other side of the coin was rural depopulation. The railways provided opportunities for young men and women to move easily to the towns, and the Great Agricultural Depression turned choice into necessity. From the 1860s and 1870s onwards scores of purely agricultural villages experienced a net loss of population and many an old market town stagnated or declined. The contrast between the rural North and East Ridings and the industrial towns and villages of the West Riding became even more pronounced. At the same time, Yorkshire experienced a phenomenon that it had not known since the time of the Viking settlers: the arrival of thousands of immigrants from across its borders. They came from Lincolnshire, East Anglia and other agricultural areas and from settlements whose industries had disappeared, and they came to the towns in search of work. In 1851 less than half the inhabitants of Bradford had been born in the borough. Two special groups of immigrants helped to swell urban populations; Yorkshire had 50,664 Irish people in 1861 (compared with 245,933 in Lancashire and Cheshire), and Jews arrived in Leeds in large numbers in the 1880s. Immigration from beyond the county boundaries played a large part in the spectacular growth of Middlesborough, which had only 239 inhabitants in 1801 but a population of 90,936 a century later. Middlesborough was unique in Yorkshire and had few parallels elsewhere. The county's other Victorian towns were ancient urban centres or at least former market towns. By the end of Victoria's reign Middlesborough was far larger than Beverley or Ripon, Pontefract or Richmond, or even the city of York. These old places had grown at rates that would have astonished an earlier age, but they were eclipsed by the even more surprising performance of the industrial towns.

The arrival of large numbers of poor immigrants put enormous strains on urban resources, particularly in times of trade depression. The 1834 Poor Law Amendment Act inaugurated a new system of relief based on unions of parishes and the workhouse, but when assistant commissioners were sent north to organize unions in 1837–38 they were greeted with riots in Bradford, Dewsbury and Todmorden. An Anti-Poor Law movement was organized in the West Riding and Lancashire by Oastler, Fielden and Stephens, who felt that in the north the old system had worked in both a humane and economic way. They said that workhouses were irrelevant in industrial areas, for few able-bodied paupers were to be found when trade was good and the unemployed masses were too numerous to be accommodated in workhouses when trade was bad. Their point was eventually conceded; the workhouse test was never enforced in the West Riding and Lancashire and outdoor relief was granted in the old manner (Rose 1972). The poor relief system reduced the possibility of death from starvation. Despite the population explosion, the death rate in England during the first half of the nineteenth century was on the whole a great deal lower than that of countries far less urbanized and industrialized (Clark 1962: 95). Nevertheless, many families lived in dire poverty during the Victorian and Edwardian Age, until the Old Age Pension Act (1908) and the Unemployment Insurance Act (1911) provided some relief. Seebohm Rowntree's 1899 survey of York showed that 20,302 people, that is 27.84 per cent of the city's population, were living in either primary or secondary poverty.

Most towns probably had a similar number of poor; Charles Booth estimated that in contemporary London 30.7 per cent were living in poverty. Rowntree counted 7,230 people in the worst class of primary poverty whose total family income was less than 18 shillings a week; most were in that desperate plight because of the removal of the wage-earner by death or desertion or by their inability to earn better wages because of illness or old age. But few people spent all their days in primary poverty; if trade was good and the children had grown up they could look forward to easier times. The 13,072 people who lived in secondary poverty had barely sufficient earnings to live from hand to mouth, but could sink into primary poverty at any moment; mutual help and the pawnshop kept them going. York's slums were not confined to any particular quarter, for the miserable, overcrowded dwellings of the poor were scattered throughout the working-class district of the city (Rowntree 1901).

The enormous population growth and industrial developments of the nineteenth century made Victorian towns and cities into great arenas for political struggles. The election of John Marshall, the Leeds flax-spinner, as MP for Yorkshire in 1826 announced the arrival of a new urban élite in county politics and the beginning of a protracted conflict between the Liberal and Dissenting merchants and manufacturers and the old Tory and Church of England establishment. A partial and pragmatic attack upon grievances turned in the 1840s into a major assault upon the Established Church (Fraser 1977). Towns were the major venues for the great political campaigns of the day, notably that of the Anti-Corn Law League. Ebenezer Elliott's *Corn Law Rhymes* (1831) made him Yorkshire's popular champion of this cause and in 1854 Sheffield workmen paid for a bronze statue of him to be erected in the market place. Huge Chartist meetings were held in the towns when the voice of the working classes was first heard on a national scale during the 1830s and 40s. Chartism gathered support in all parts of the country, but its greatest strength lay in the manufacturing districts, where it was a protest movement that provided a vigorous outlet for diverse hopes and demands. Industrialization had produced a working-class culture that was radically different from that of the labouring poor of previous centuries. Towards the close of Victoria's reign the labour movement, based on trade unions, co-operative societies and the Independent Labour Party, had become a force to be reckoned with.

The Railways

The optimism of the Victorian age was nowhere more evident than in the ambitious ways that railways were planned, financed and constructed. A complex system of lines, authorized by hundreds of private Acts of Parliament, grew haphazardly without central direction, in the same manner as the network of canals and turnpike roads of the previous era. Within a couple of generations of George Stephenson's Stockton-to-Darlington and Liverpool-to-Manchester lines railways had reduced journey times and costs so triumphantly that the turnpike trusts faltered into bankruptcy and the canals became mere backwaters. Places that did not have a main line station found it hard to compete and began to decline, but those fortunate enough to be well-placed reaped economic benefits: York recaptured some of its former glory, Doncaster became a major engineering centre as well as a thriving market town, and on the coast Bridlington, Filey, Scarborough and Whitby catered for the new holiday traffic. Businessmen quickly saw that railways were vital to the continued growth of their industrial towns, in terms both of freight and passengers.

Appropriately enough, the first place in Yorkshire to adopt Stephenson's technology was Leeds, the county's major industrial and commercial centre and the home of the pioneering Middleton colliery railway. Leeds businessmen and Hull merchants (who feared the rise of Goole) commissioned George Stephenson and Joseph Locke of Barnsley to construct a line that would link the industrial heart of the West Riding with the county's major port. In 1834 the line was opened from Leeds to Selby, and six years later it was extended to Hull. Meanwhile, in 1836 Leeds had also backed an early scheme to cross the Pennines to Manchester under the supervision of George Stephenson and James Walker. About 1,000 navvies completed the Littleborough tunnel by 1840. In Yorkshire the route followed the Calder valley all the way from Todmorden to Normanton so as to connect with Stephenson's York and North Midland railway of 1836–38, which was part of a wider scheme to link the capital with the North. By 1841 it was possible to travel all the way from London via Derby, Rotherham, York and Darlington, and seven years later a more direct route via Doncaster and Selby to York made for an even quicker and more economical journey.

Such early successes led to the 'railway mania' of the mid-1840s, an era personified by George Hudson, twice Lord Mayor of York and the most ebullient of the first railway magnates. Hudson's reign as 'railway king' ended in shame in 1849 when his financial chicanery was exposed, and he eventually left the country in disgrace, but his contribution to the development of the national railway system was nonetheless of permanent value. Above all, he realized that as the small private companies which had built the early lines had

251

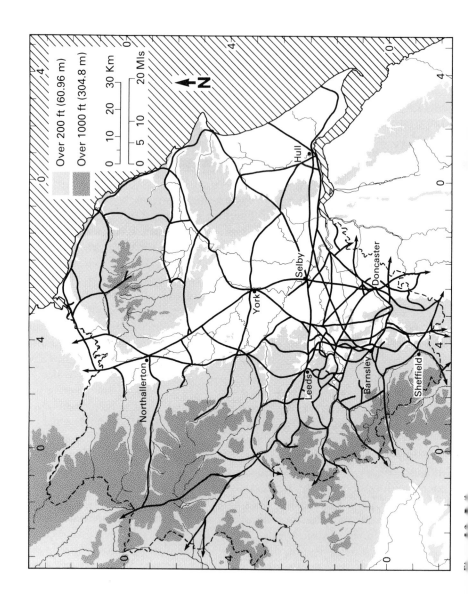

Over 200 ft (60.96 m)

Over 1000 ft (304.8 m)

0   10   20   30 Km

0   5   10   20 Mls

N

Hull

Selby

Doncaster

York

Northallerton

Leeds

Barnsley

Sheffield

insufficient resources, amalgamation was the key to progress. He pioneered the way with his Midland railway company of 1844 and at the height of his powers five years later he had financial control of almost all the railway system of Northumberland, Durham and the North and East Ridings, his Midland company had a monopoly in Nottinghamshire, Leicestershire and Derbyshire, and his was the dominant interest in East Anglia (Simmons 1961: 12–24). Under Hudson, York's fortunes were restored as it became a great railway administrative centre with accompanying waggon and coachbuilding works.

Other important amalgamations created the Manchester, Sheffield and Lincolnshire railway company in 1846–47 and the North Eastern railway company in 1854. The North Eastern owned about 1,700 miles of line and worked another 300. By the mid-1850s nearly all the major English railway lines had been completed or were under construction, though it was not until 1899 that the Manchester, Sheffield and Lincolnshire railway (by then known as the Great Central railway) opened its trunk line to London with a new terminus at Marylebone. In Yorkshire, branch lines were built in all three ridings during the 1860s and 70s, and it was not until 1885 that a coastal route was opened from Redcar to Whitby and Scarborough and a new rail link forged between the coalfield at Barnsley and the port of Hull. Great feats of engineering and the hard labour of enormous gangs of navvies overcame the rugged terrain of upland Yorkshire. The thirty-two tall arches of the Lockwood viaduct (1846–48) west of Huddersfield, the gently curving Ribblehead viaduct on the scenic Settle to Carlisle line (1875) and many massive embankments, cuttings and tunnels overshadowed the achievements of the canal age. Some railway companies sought dignity in the architecture of their stations; J. P. Pritchett's classical façade at Huddersfield (1847–48) was the best building in town; and at York in 1877 Thomas Prosser replaced an earlier station with a 800 ft long shed, supported on iron columns and built on a curve.

The most ambitious railway engineering project undertaken in Yorkshire was the Woodhead tunnel, which provided a link through the Pennines between Sheffield and Manchester. Begun in 1839, it took six years to complete and at 3 miles 13 yards was by far the longest tunnel in Britain at that time. At the height of the operation over 1,500 navvies worked night and day, including Sundays, tunnelling from twelve different rock faces at once. The tunnel crossed the moors at about 1,000 feet above sea-level, and the longest ventilation shaft was sunk to a depth of 579 feet. All but 1,000 yards of the tunnel had to be lined with masonry to prevent falls from the roof. The work was dangerous and unpleasant. It involved standing ankle-deep, and some-times knee-deep, in mud, and if the parched men drank the water which ran down the walls they soon suffered from chronic diarrhoea. In a celebrated reply to a question at a parliamentary enquiry in 1846, Wellington Purdon, the assistant engineer to Joseph Locke, agreed that perhaps the safety fuse was a better way of conducting explosions than the one he employed, 'but it is attended with such a loss of time, and the difference is so very small, I would not recommend the loss of time for the sake of all the extra lives it would save'. At least 32 men were killed while building the tunnel, and (incomplete) records detail 23 cases of compound fractures, 74 simple fractures and 140 serious cases involving burns, contusions, lacerations and dislocations. As Edwin Chadwick remarked, the 3 per cent killed and 14 per cent wounded nearly equalled the proportionate casualties of a military campaign or a severe battle.

The navvies lived with their wives, mistresses and children in stone huts at the Yorkshire end of Dunford Bridge and in worse conditions at Woodhead. They were attracted by high wages, and when they were paid every 9–13 weeks, they invariably went on a drunken rampage. Stories of their wild, dissolute, heathen life alarmed the respectable inhabitants of the towns and villages a few miles away. Public concern about Woodhead led to the establishment of a parliamentary enquiry into the employment of railway labourers in 1846. A second bore was constructed alongside the original tunnel in 1847–52, and this time working conditions were better and fewer men died; an outbreak of cholera killed 28 navvies at Woodhead, however, in 1849 (Coleman 1965).

The impact of the railway age is nowhere more evident than at Doncaster, where the Great Northern Railway from London arrived in 1848. Four years later a major railway engineering works known as the Plant was established on the west side of the town for the construction and repair of locomotives, coaches and waggons; here were built the famous locomotives of Sturrock, Stirling and Gresley that became known throughout the world. By the end of 1853 the Plant employed 949 workers; by the early 1890s, when it extended over two miles, its workforce had risen to about 3,500. The workers came mostly from the countryside to live in monotonous streets of little brick and slate houses, separated by corner shops, pubs and places of worship, in Hexthorpe and Balby, next to the works. They formed a very different type of community from those of the small, agricultural villages which had previously surrounded Doncaster. The railway led to further industrial and commercial development and gave a boost to Doncaster's ancient role as a regional market centre; major alterations were made to the market place from the 1840s onwards, culminating in the large, new corn exchange of 1873. Edward Baines had described Doncaster in 1822 as 'one of the most clean, airy and elegant towns in the British dominions', but now it was transformed from a prosperous Georgian and Regency borough into a bustling Victorian and Edwardian town. After a disastrous fire in 1853 the noble parish church of St George was rebuilt to a grand design of George Gilbert Scott's, several other churches and chapels were erected in the town centre and suburbs, new public buildings included the baths (1862), infirmary (1865), free library (1889) and schools, and between the 1890s and 1914 the transformation was completed by the erection of large shops in the town centre and by further suburban expansion after the opening of an electric tram system in 1902 (Holland 1980: 46–51).

The railways put Hull in a strong competitive position on the east coast and helped it to remain Britain's third port behind London and Liverpool. Hull's overseas trade was still predominantly with north-east Europe and its major imports were Baltic iron, timber, grain, flax, linseed and rape-seed. Seed-crushing was a well-established dockside industry by the 1860s and it was soon followed by flour-milling and ancillary trades associated with fishing, such as the curing of herrings. Hull adapted quickly to the age of steam, it reduced its railway rates and dock dues, and after much argument extended its docks and built ornate dock offices in an Italianate style. The Victoria Dock of 1850 and the Albert Dock of 1869 were overshadowed by the St Andrew's Dock of 1883 (the largest fish dock in the world) and the Alexandria Dock of 1885, which enclosed 46 acres of water at a depth of 33 feet. Finally, in 1907 the Riverside Quay between Albert Dock and the Humber provided docking facilities for large ships at any state of the tide. Hull thrived and its population rose rapidly. In 1870 the local shipping industry was run by a number of small firms, but by the end of the First World War it was dominated by the Wilson Line. Trading links had been extended beyond Europe to the river Plate, Bombay and Alexandria, nevertheless in 1913 nearly two-thirds of the total tonnage entering Hull's docks still came from Russia, Scandinavia, Denmark, Germany, Holland, Belgium and France (*VCH East Riding, I* 1969: 245–9).

The Textile District

The West Riding textile industry entered its most prosperous era during the middle decades of the nineteenth century. By then it had easily outstripped its ancient rivals in East Anglia and the Cotswolds. Great shifts of population had transformed the ancient patterns of settlement as the mills attracted new and populous communities in the deep river valleys. All the way down the Calder valley mill towns crammed every available space around the factories. The contrast between the old and the new is perfectly illustrated at Heptonstall and Hebden Bridge, a few miles into the Pennines west of Halifax. On the lofty summit of a bleak hill stands Heptonstall, a weaving village full of dark vernacular houses and cottages clustered haphazardly together, a sturdy Pennine community that remains a wonderfully preserved period piece from the days of the old domestic economy. The village continued to thrive in Victoria's reign but its inhabitants must have been astonished at the youthful vigour and spectacular growth of the settlement down below at Hebden Bridge. Before the nineteenth century a few houses had gathered near the old bridge over the river Hebden just above its confluence with the Calder but now they were engulfed by rows of houses perched on the steep bank sides in places which earlier settlers had instinctively avoided. The opening of the Rochdale canal and then the Lancashire and Yorkshire railway encouraged the expansion of new communities in the Calder valley, especially when Hebden Bridge, Mytholmroyd and Sowerby Bridge were provided with railway stations. White's 1853 directory noted that Sowerby Bridge had 'extensive cotton worsted, and corn mills, commodious wharfs, and several chemical works, iron foundries, etc'. By then Sowerby Bridge was more populous than the old village of Sowerby, Mytholmroyd had outgrown Midgley, and further down the valley the former hamlet of Brighouse had become larger than neighbouring Rastrick. A similar story could be told about developments in the Colne and Holme valleys and about the towns that sprawled along the banks of the Aire.

The hill villages and hamlets did not decline in absolute terms, for weaving long remained at the domestic stage of manufacture and mining, quarrying and the usual range of village crafts provided other employment. The old dual economy of the smallholder-craftsman lingered on late into the Victorian era. Baines reported that even in 1859 as many woollen workers were employed outside the factories as within. In the fancy trade in particular hand-looms long remained in use. Nevertheless, by the time of the Great Exhibition of 1851 it was clear that within another generation or so the changeover to the factory system would be complete. The number of West Riding woollen mills rose from 129 in 1833 to 606 in 1838 and to 880 by 1850, and steam engines rather than water wheels were now the major source of power. Meanwhile, in the worsted industry hand-weaving declined rapidly, while between 1838 and 1850 employment in factories more than doubled. New combinations of alpaca and mohair with cotton warps enabled the worsted trade to compete with cotton in the market for cheap, light fabrics. By 1838 the West Riding produced about 85 per cent of the nation's worsted goods, and twelve years later its share had risen to 90 per cent (Darby, ed. 1973: 494, 462).

By the 1830s widespread unease at the regimented working conditions in the textile mills, which had broken the ancient link between home and place of work, burst into an indignant revulsion for the new system. This disgust was expressed by Richard Oastler of Fixby Hall in a famous letter to the *Leeds Mercury* on 16 October 1830 in which he condemned 'those magazines of British infantile slavery – the worsted mills of the town and neighbourhood of Bradford'. Child labour in these mills, wrote Oastler, was worse than negro slavery in America. Recalling his early days in Pudsey, where he was born in 1821, Joseph Lawson remembered that large numbers of women and girls were burlers of cloth who picked out specks with small irons after the scouring process and that the slubbers who drew out the cardings and wound them ready for the spinners earned twice as much as the weavers. Children, however, were paid a pittance of only 3*s*. or 3*s*. 6*d*. for standing at their work sometimes 90 hours a week.

Some of the slubbers behaved very badly to these young boys and girls, beating them most cruelly. In winter times fathers might be seen carrying their children on their backs by five o'clock in the morning through deep snow to their work at the mills. Many with crooked legs might be seen – the result of standing fifteen, and sometimes sixteen hours a day piecing.

Oastler was typical of many small West Riding squires whose sympathies lay with the mill-workers rather than the owners. They were Tory paternalists concerned with restoring the old social order rather than Radicals who dreamed of a new one. John Fielden of Todmorden, John Wood of Bradford and Michael Sadler, the Tory MP joined Oastler in the Ten Hours Movement to limit the daily hours of work in textile mills. They met furious opposition from the mill owners, particularly from the Ackroyds of Halifax, who at a meeting on 5 March 1831 drew up 'fourteen points' against Oastler. Many of the local Church of England clergy spoke out on behalf of the masters, but in 1832 the philanthropists got their way with the establishment of a royal commission, whose sympathetic questioners elicited damning evidence of the abuse of child labour. Samuel Cooke's replies were typical of many:

At what age did you begin work in the factories? I began betwixt seven and eight years old.
At whose mill did you begin? Benjamin Woodhead's.
Was this at Holmfirth? Yes.
How far did you live from the mill? Better than a quarter of a mile.
State at what time in the morning you went to the mill. In summer, before six o'clock; in winter, between seven and eight.
At what time did you give over at night? At dark.
Did you ever work as late as ten o'clock? Yes, sometimes.
Had you any time given you for breakfast? No.
What time was allowed for getting your dinner? Half an hour sometimes.
Then you had fifteen hours daily labour when you were seven-and-a-half years old? Yes.
What wages had you? I had 3s 6d per week when I could piecen a side. [He worked for nothing for six months until he had learnt his job].
Have you ever been beaten severely with a billy-roller? Yes, when I worked at William Woodhead's, I had my head broke with it.
Did your mother ever make any complaints as to your treatment? Yes.
What was said to your mother when she complained? The slubbers all said, if they did not like it they might take us away.

Could your parents do without your little wages? They could not do without our working.

What effect has it had on your health, being thus confined and thus beaten? My eyes were getting very bad with it.

Have you ever been at a day or a night school? No, I went on a Sunday.

Can you write? No.

Can you read? No.

As a result of the commission an Act was passed in 1834 which prohibited the employment of children under the age of 9 in textile mills; those aged 9–13 were limited to a 48 hour week; those aged 13–18 were allowed to work 60 hours a week but could not be employed on the night shift. The Act also established the important principle that government inspectors should ensure that the law was applied strictly. Thirteen years later Oastler's campaign achieved its objective with the passing of the Ten Hours Act.

In Leeds the textile industries, particularly the manufacture, dyeing, finishing and marketing of woollen cloth, remained pre-eminent throughout the first half of the nineteenth century. John Marshall's flax mill, opened in 1840, was one of the architectural wonders of the age, and by 1855 Leeds had 37 flax mills which employed 9,500 people, mostly women, children and Irish immigrants. Nevertheless, in 1851 the borough still had twice as many workers in the woollen and worsted industries than in flax. Leeds also had a significant trade in carpets, cotton yarn and silk, and the textile trades provided an important market for the machines and steam engines that were produced in local engineering works. Founding and engineering became major Leeds industries during the first half of the nineteenth century, and between 1851 and 1914 they became the leading sector of manufacture. John Marshall considered that local manufacturing prosperity rested upon secure property, good machinery and the plentiful supply of cheap coal. To this might be added entrepreneurial skill, the availability of a large and flexible labour force, and constant concern with transport improvements. By 1850 Leeds was a town of many trades. Tanning provides a good example of local adaptability. At the beginning of the nineteenth century Leeds had overtaken Wakefield as the leading centre of leather production in west Yorkshire, and by 1817 the borough had six fellmongers, ten curriers, 66 bootmakers and nine tanners, and the largest leather market outside London. Businesses were on a small scale until the Kirkstall Road tannery was opened in 1828; by 1850 Leeds had a dozen extensive tanneries and skinworks. The use of new tanning agents such as gambier and shumac instead of the traditional oak bark was quickly accepted and by 1870 Leeds had become the leading centre for sheepskins and the second national centre for the tanning of hides (Fraser, ed. 1980: 142–76).

Between 1851 and 1914 the manufacture of cloth declined in importance and the production of flax almost ceased in the face of Belfast and foreign competition. As the textile industries declined the engineering, leather and chemical industries expanded and new trades arose in clothing, footwear and printing, so that by the eve of the First World War Leeds had a much more diverse economy. The engineering industry grew rapidly in the 1840s and 50s. John Fowler, the most famous name, began to manufacture traction engines and steam ploughs in 1850, but Leeds's early specialization in steam engines and textile machinery became only part of a great metalworking tradition based on local iron and coal. The production of wrought iron in local foundries fell towards the end of the Victorian era as local ores became exhausted, but engineering firms used Cleveland and Sheffield steels and continued to prosper. The labour force needed in the new clothing trade was provided by Jewish immigrants and the thousands of women and girls who had previously worked in the flax industry. Sewing machines were introduced into the city's workshops about 1855, and the band-saw which could cut many thicknesses of cloth simultaneously, about a decade later. Many small workshops in Leeds were overcrowded and unhygienic and rates of pay for long hours were abysmally small; Leeds had a great many 'sweatshops' by the end of the century. By 1914 Leeds had about 100 wholesale clothiers with perhaps 80 factories and over 300 small workshops crammed in whatever space was available. The most famous business to rise from this background was that of Montague Burton and Company, founded in Sheffield with a capital of £100, and soon transferred to Leeds (Fraser, ed. 1980: 142–76). Leeds also became the leading provincial printing centre, specializing in quality colour printing, mostly for the local market, and the city was indisputedly 'the commercial metropolis of Yorkshire'. At the end of the century the central shopping area was developed by widening Briggate and Boar Lane and by creating shopping arcades and a new market. The multiple shop and departmental store owe some of their beginnings to Leeds, for in 1881 Thomas Lipton, the pioneer of the multiple grocery trade in Scotland, opened his first English shop there and in 1884 Michael Marks opened his first Penny Bazaar in the covered market.

In 1884 J. D. Kohl thought that 'Leeds like all the great manufacturing cities in England is a dirty, smoky, disagreeable town . . . perhaps the ugliest and least attractive town in all England'. The population of the central township rose from 30,669 in 1801 to 101,343 in 1851, and that of the out-townships grew apace. Nevertheless, in 1849 A. B. Reach found Leeds less crowded than other industrial cities, partly, he reasoned, because the Pennines formed a barrier against sudden influxes of Irish immigrants. Leeds did not become as squalid as Manchester and Liverpool. However, during the 1840s and 50s many Irish immigrants did reach Leeds; nearly 15,000 of them were there by 1861 and they formed by far the largest Irish community in Yorkshire. Leeds was also a magnet for Jewish immigrants after the Russian pogroms of the 1880s. Only ten Jewish families resided in the borough in 1841, by the late 1880s Leeds contained some 6,000 Jews, especially in the Leylands district where some streets were 85 per cent Jewish. National restrictions were placed on immigration in 1905, but by the eve of the First World War Leeds had a community of about 20,000 Jews (Fraser, ed. 1980: 46–71).

The rapidly rising population was densely packed into yards and folds that lacked running water and sanitation facilities. At the beginning of Victoria's reign 341 people were crowded into 57 rooms in the notorious Boot and Shoe yard. An official report in 1842 noted that in a typical Irish weaver's cottage in Leeds

> the kitchen is not only appropriated to culinary purposes, but is the house, the sleeping-room, the hen-house, and the piggery; whilst upstairs are three or four looms, all but touching each other; and perhaps, in a corner, a bed on the floor for one of the owners of these looms.

Beyond the old town centre, alongside the main highways were built row after unvaried row of brick back-to-back houses. Piecemeal, unplanned development began in 1787 when Richard Paley acquired land to build speculative housing or to sell in lots to developers. Paley built 275 houses before he went bankrupt in 1803 and 290 houses had been erected by other builders on his plots. The long, narrow fields that adjoined the town were ideal for the back-to-back method of construction. By 1850 Leeds had 360 streets of back-to-backs. Professor Beresford has calculated that half the houses that were standing in Leeds on the eve of the First World War had been built before 1841 and that two-thirds of these were back-to-backs (Fraser, ed. 1980: 72–112). In the southern townships of Holbeck and Hunslet three times as many houses were built during the first half of the nineteenth century than in the northern townships of Headingley, Potternewton and Chapel Allerton. Crowded folds and back-to-back terraces vied for space with great flax mills, foundries, gasworks, railway sidings and brickyards. In the central township the pace of growth began to slacken in the 1870s when some residential streets were given over to retail shops, warehouses, banking, insurance and commerce, and transport improvements encouraged the middle classes to move north away from the smoke and the noise. Horse-drawn omnibuses ran daily to Headingley and Roundhay from 1858 onwards, and the first horse-drawn tram service to Headingley commenced operations in 1871.

Great wealth could be earned in Leeds but it was also a city of filth and squalor. Overcrowding was made worse by primitive sanitation facilities and an inadequate water supply.

> The Aire below is doubly dyed and dammed;
> The Air above, with lurid smoke is crammed

punned William Osburn in 1857, yet 2,000 homes took piped water from the Aire and the rest relied upon wells, boreholes and itinerant water-carriers. Tuberculosis, typhus, typhoid and dysentery were the major killers of the age, but it was the great cholera epidemics that aroused the nation's conscience and drew attention to the horrors of the urban slums. In Leeds at least 700 people died of cholera in 1832 and over 2,000 died in the outbreak of 1848–49. Throughout the land the turning point did not come until the 1870s when deaths from tuberculosis and typhoid fell dramatically and cholera and typhus almost disappeared. Meanwhile, the Leeds Borough Council, which had been reformed under the Municipal Corporation Act of 1835, expressed its civic pride in slum clearances, road widening schemes, the making of public squares and the construction of public buildings. Their most ambitious project was the grandiose town hall of 1853–58, designed by the young Hull architect, Cuthbert Brodrick. When Queen Victoria came to open it she was welcomed by a record crowd of 32,110 Sunday school children on Woodhouse Moor, which remained Leeds's principal recreational area until the purchase of Roundhay park in 1872 provided the city with the finest park in England.

As the wealth and population of the town grew, so did the inhabitants' interest in cultural affairs. The eighteenth century had seen the establishment of the *Leeds Mercury* (1718) and the *Leeds Intelligencer* (1754, which became the *Yorkshire Post* in 1866), the first music concerts, assemblies, the opening of a library (1767) and a theatre (1771), and the creation of a scientific group around Joseph Priestley, John Smeaton and William Hey. By the Victorian period Leeds took part in a national and even an international culture as wealthy families, notably the Gotts, toured the Continent and collected art objects for local galleries and museums. The first Leeds music festival was held in 1858, the reference and central libraries were opened in 1871–72, the art gallery in 1888 and the Yorkshire College in 1874 (the forerunner of the university 30 years later). Leeds had not been alone amongst northern industrial towns in experiencing a sharp decline in standards of literacy during the late eighteenth and early nineteenth centuries, but the first Sunday school in the borough had started in 1784 and by 1817 few churches or chapels were without one. The Evangelical movement emphasized the importance of religious education and by 1858 Leeds had over 130 schools which provided places for about 35,000 pupils, (Fraser, ed. 1980: 200–49). A Mechanics Institute for working men had been founded in 1824, but despite all this voluntary activity educational provision for the masses was woefully inadequate before the building of board schools after 1870.

At the time of the Great Exhibition of 1851 British industry produced over 40 per cent of the world's total output of manufactured goods. Textiles, coal, iron and steel dominated the industrial scene, but Britain now had a far wider range of industries than ever before. The Victorian era was an age of innovation based on steam power and the railways. Britain's colossal share of the world market was not dominated by foreign competition until the last quarter of the nineteenth century. The country had become the greatest in the world, exporting her manufactured goods to all parts of the globe, but for millions of her people who lived and worked in appalling surroundings the benefits of this leading position were far less obvious than their immediate plight. The world had never seen anything like a Victorian city, nor had it encountered grave social problems on such a massive scale. The great cholera outbreaks of 1832 and 1848 made public health a major issue of the day, and parliamentary investigators, novelists and reporters drew the nation's horrified attention to overcrowded houses, insanitary surroundings and repressive conditions at work.

At the beginning of Victoria's reign the industrial towns lacked the organization, the power and the will to remedy the unprecedented problems which they faced. Voluntary rather than municipal effort was the order of the day, but although much was achieved – notably in church and chapel building and their associated schools – the continuous and huge rise of population overwhelmed the resources of the voluntary bodies. Only in the last quarter of the century did the municipal corporations respond adequately with sewage farms, water works, slum clearances, hospitals and schools. No two towns acted in the same way. Though Leeds, Bradford, Halifax, Huddersfield and Wakefield had much in common as West Riding textile towns, their buildings and topography, their economic and social structures and their responses to their problems were all different from each other. They each prided themselves on their independence and their particular character, and so did the smaller communities of the woollen and worsted conurbation (Briggs 1963: 32). Despite their proximity and similarities, their rivalry was intense.

While Leeds had a wide range of industries, Victorian Bradford was pre-eminently a textile town, the 'worstedpolis' that had overtaken Halifax as the leading centre of worsted manufacture in the north. The industry was carried on in steam-powered factories; Bradford had only one steam mill in 1801, but forty years later it had 67 in production. Some of the most prominent manufacturers came from Germany, men with names like Behrens, Flersheim, Furst, Gumpal, Hertz, Mayer, Schlesinger and Sichel, who like their counterparts in the Manchester cotton industry gave a cultural as well as a business lead to the town. In 1864 Charles Seman from Dantzig became Bradford's first foreign-born mayor. The central township's rapid growth from 6,393 inhabitants in 1801 to 52,493 in 1851 was largely the result of youthful immigrants seeking work in the town. At the time of the 1841 census 50 per cent of the population were under the age of twenty; a decade later only 25 per cent had been born in the borough. This staggering growth rate brought immense problems in housing, sanitation, water supply and atmosphere pollution. One of the Health of Towns Commissioners described Bradford as 'the dirtiest, filthiest and worst regulated town in the kingdom'. Its infant mortality rates were the fifth highest amongst the towns investigated, and at twenty years the average age at death was the lowest in Yorkshire. Drainage was provided by open sewers which saturated the surrounding soil and ran down to the Bradford canal, a major health hazard known locally as the 'River Stink'. The prosperous middle classes lived in pleasant villas in Manningham

Lane, but the town-centre slums were amongst the worst in the country, particularly in the Wapping and White Abbey districts where woolcombers lived and worked in crowded cellars. A local chartist described such a dwelling in Manchester Road in 1845:

I advanced along the floor saturated with rain-water which flowed in torrents from the door and recognized a female form laid on what it would be a shame to call a bed. She had been ill for some time and had a husband and five children living with her in this wretched hole. Her husband, a woolcomber, had worked in that cellar until his health was completely undermined.

(Briggs 1963: 145–51)

During the 1830s and 40s Bradford gained a radical reputation as its youthful and oppressed society rioted against the Poor Law (1837), took part in the plug-drawing riots (1842) and enthusiastically supported the Chartists (1839 and 1848). The borough was also noted for its religious nonconformity and in 1837 was the first town to have a Temperance Hall. Later in the century, in 1893, Bradford was the birthplace of the Independent Labour Party. Early attempts to tackle the massive public health problems were hampered by the chaotic local government structure before Bradford achieved its borough status in 1847. The lord of the manor held his courts leet and baron and controlled the markets, fairs, slaughter houses and weights and measures; the ratepayers met as a vestry at Easter to elect church-wardens, constables, surveyors of the highways and overseers of the poor, until the establishment of a board of guardians in 1837 and a board of surveyors in 1843; the justices of the peace supervised the vestry officials and served as local magistrates; and from 1803 the 58 Improvement Commissioners, appointed by a local Act of Parliament, were in charge of cleansing, lighting and watching the town centre streets and the removal of nuisances and obstructions. Even those involved in administration were unsure of the exact scope of their rights and responsibilities, and no body had adequate powers to cope with disease and social disorder (Elliott 1979).

After 1847 the corporation tackled the problems of water supply, draining and building regulations and Bradford became one of the first provincial towns to have a police force. Civic pride asserted itself in the building of St George's Hall in 1851–53, with a concert hall, restaurant, gallery and accommodation for 3,100 people. Bradford developed a strong choral tradition, had regular visits from the Hallé orchestra, and in time acquired two theatres and two music halls. Lockwood and Mawson, the local architects who designed St George's Hall, built the other major public buildings, including the Exchange (1864), Victoria Hotel (1867), Town Hall (1873), Independent College (1874), Markets (1877) and Bradford Club (1877). They were also commissioned by Titus Salt to design his model village at Saltaire after he had moved his alpaca and mohair mills out into the countryside near Shipley. Salt was mayor of Bradford in 1848, MP in 1859 and was made a baronet in 1869. His new mill was opened with great celebrations in 1853 and by the following year 150 houses were ready for his workforce; eventually 820 houses were completed in rectangular blocks of sixteen properties arranged in a grid pattern. Each house had a parlour, kitchen, two or three bedrooms and a back yard, though no garden. The public buildings included Congregational and Methodist churches, school and institute and a bridge leading to an attractive park. Salt wanted his estate to combine 'every improvement that modern art and science had brought to light', including the banning of public houses. This Congregationalist businessman imposed his ideals on his new community as effectively as an Anglican squire dominated his estate village. Saltaire attracted enormous interest in the High Victorian period, though it was overshadowed later by the garden villages of other enlightened, paternalist employers.

Huddersfield was another textile town that grew at an astonishing rate during the first half of the nineteenth century; the central township had 7,268 inhabitants in 1801 and 30,880 people fifty years later. In 1868 the town was elevated to the status of a borough. Huddersfield was the centre of the fancy trade, whereby figured silk and wool or worsted yarns were woven into patterns to make flowered waistcoats and other fancy goods. The trade had developed during the later eighteenth century under the stimulus of the Lancashire cotton industry, and in 1822 Baines's directory listed 102 'Manufacturers of Fancy Goods who attended Huddersfield Market, with their places of abode and Inns or Warehouses' gathered in cluttered yards near the cloth hall. Outworkers took part in the trade in villages to the east and south of Huddersfield, at Kirkheaton, Dalton, Almondbury, Lepton, Honley, Shepley, Cumberworth, Skelmanthorpe, Denby Dale and Thurlstone. A manufacturer paid £5 of the cost of a loom, and £2 was paid by the weaver out of his wages. The trade was at the mercy of changing fashion but it expanded considerably in the mid-Victorian era.

Huddersfield attracted conflicting opinions from visitors. One outsider in 1849 thought it 'by no means a well-built town' with three-quarters of the working-class districts consisting of back-to-back houses, but five years earlier Friedrich Engels wrote that 'Huddersfield is the handsomest by far of all the factory towns of Yorkshire and Lancashire, by reason of its charming situation and modern architecture'. The paternal influence of the Ramsden family and the powers granted by improvement Acts in 1820 and 1848 ensured an orderly lay-out with proper drainage facilities when the town expanded beyond its old limits around the church, market square and cloth hall. The streets were given ample widths on a grid pattern and decent two-storeyed houses and public buildings. When John Wesley 'rode over the mountains to Huddersfield' in 1757 he noted, 'A wilder people I never saw in England. The men, women and children filled the streets and seemed just ready to devour us.' Evangelical religion channelled this energy to more constructive uses, however, and

1836 saw the foundation of a choral society that was to become world famous.

By the end of Victoria's reign the West Riding woollen and worsted district had been urbanized to such an extent that it contained six county boroughs and seven municipal boroughs. In provincial England only the west Midlands and south Lancashire had experienced similar momentous changes. Several West Riding villages had grown at a spectacular rate during the nineteenth century and had achieved the coveted status of municipal borough. One of these was Pudsey, a chapel-of-ease of the parish of Calverley with only 4,422 inhabitants in 1801, but 18,469 people a hundred years later. Joseph Lawson recalled that in his childhood in the 1820s the houses were mostly scattered, for people built their homes to suit their personal whims regardless of taste, order or sanitary conditions. Narrow local prejudices existed between neighbouring villages and even between clans in different parts of the same village. Strangers were regarded with suspicion and pelted with stones. But,

> however bad Pudsey might be at that time [he wrote] Yeadon was much worse, and had a large number of reckless and low characters in proportion to its population . . . It was a common remark . . . that Yeadon was the last place God made, and that He made it out of the refuse

or shoddy. On the other hand, the Moravian colony nearby at Fulneck 'had a kind of charm for us, and we remember thinking and saying that it always looked like Sunday there, all being so quiet and clean, and most of the people well dressed'. The rural communities of the West Riding were as varied in their individual characters as were the great industrial towns.

Sheffield and Middlesborough

In 1801 the population of Sheffield's central township stood at 31,314; fifty years later it had reached 83,447 and most of the old open spaces had been filled up. The urban population had spilled over into the neighbouring townships of Ecclesall and Brightside, so that by 1851 about 120,000 of the borough's 135,310 population lived in the built-up area. By that time the larger of the central dwelling houses were being converted into workshops or factories so their owners moved to the newer middle-class residential areas along the Glossop Road and in Broomhall. The national population doubled during the first half of the nineteenth century, but that of Sheffield trebled. Though the death-rate was higher than the national average, immigration, chiefly from the surrounding villages, sustained the rising numbers; in 1851

36.3 per cent (and 49 per cent of those aged more than 20) were born outside the boundaries of the borough. The next few decades saw an enormous expansion of the population of the two eastern townships of Sheffield when huge new steelworks were established on the banks of the Don.

Table 5.4 The population of Sheffield's two eastern townships, 1801–1901

	1801	1851	1881	1901
Brightside Bierlow	4,030	12,042	56,719	73,088
Attercliffe cum Darnall	2,281	4,873	26,965	51,807

At the same time, such strongholds of the light trades as Crookes and Walkley expanded at a more modest rate, and Heeley's population rose threefold in the twenty years after 1871. Despite this growth, however, an 1889 report claimed that,

> The population of Sheffield is, for so large a town, unique in its character, in fact it more closely resembles that of a village than of a town, for over wide areas each person appears to be acquainted with every other, and to be interested with that other's concerns.

In 1843 J. C. Symons described Sheffield as 'one of the dirtiest and most smoky towns I ever saw', and in 1861 *The Builder* reported

> A thick pulverous haze is spread over the city which the sun even in the long day is unable to penetrate, save by a lurid glare, and which has the effect of imparting to the green hills and golden cornfields in the high distance the ghastly appearance of being whitened with snow.

By 1864, when a local by-law forbade further buildings of this type, Sheffield had 38,000 back-to-backs cheek by jowl with the cutlery works and factories. Built of bricks and roofed with slate, they were only one-room deep and consisted of a cellar, living room, bedroom and an attic. About half of them opened into confined yards which contained communal privies and a standpipe or water pump. But when trade was good Sheffield workmen were reasonably well-off by the standards of the time. Relief claims made after the disastrous 1864 flood, when the Dale Dyke reservoir burst its banks, drowning 258 people and causing £500,000 worth of damage, suggest that most families possessed such basic items of furniture as bedstead, table and chairs, sideboard or chest-of-drawers and that a man in work normally had two sets of clothes, one for weekdays and one for Sunday. Sheffield did not have the dismal cellar accommodation of some Victorian cities, but its courts and alleys had all the usual health hazards of a major industrial town. Over four hundred people died in the cholera outbreak of 1832 and during the second half of the nineteenth century local death rates from contagious and infectious diseases were amongst the highest in the country (Pollard 1959: 1–25).

Sheffield had the inestimable advantage of being within reach of spectacular countryside, so that Sunday walks to the moors and reservoirs were a frequent pleasure, even if access was limited by moor owners and their gamekeepers to a limited number of rights of way. The town of Sheffield was well provided with public open spaces, such as the gifts of Norfolk Park and Firth Park and the corporation's purchase of Weston Park, Meersbrook Park, Endcliffe Woods and Hillsborough Park and several recreational grounds in closely built-up areas. Public health measures included the opening of a general cemetery in 1836, the subsequent closure of churchyards and the building of a sewage works at Blackburn meadows in 1866. Between 1864 and 1871 a private company piped water to the west end, Walkley and Crookes and soon another company installed gas lighting in many working-class homes. Meanwhile, self-help societies had built small estates at Crookes and Heeley and a residential garden suburb at Walkley, the 'Working Man's West End'. But Sheffield still had a disgraceful number of slums and more privy middens than any other large industrial city.

In 1894 the corporation embarked on its first slum clearance scheme, rehousing seven hundred people in the Crofts in blocks of flats. The gloomy nature of the new accommodation provoked such dismay, however, that the corporation's next step was to build an estate on industrial land at the north-eastern edge of the borough, at High Wincobank. The first 41 houses were let in 1906 and 617 had been completed by 1919. They attracted national attention and praise from the leaders of the Garden City movement. The installation of an electric tram system from 1899 onwards also meant that working-class suburbs could be built well away from places of work. New estates were built around the tram termini at Woodseats and Hillsborough and along the main routes out of town. Nevertheless, the hard core of the slum problem remained untackled by the eve of the First World War. In 1914 nearly 17,000 families still lived in back-to-backs and another 8,000 families in houses which needed repairs and alterations to make them suitable for habitation. And though determined efforts to replace middens with water closets had been made since 1892, by 1914 11,000 privy middens still served 16,600 of the city's 107,000 houses (Pollard 1959: 184–90).

Sheffield's traditional light crafts expanded rapidly in the early Victorian age. Cutlers, edge-tool makers, file-cutters and craftsmen in silver and silver-plated goods manufactured a great variety of articles in countless different patterns and qualities, each requiring specialist skills. Machines therefore came late to the industry. Greaves's Sheaf Works of 1823 was the first cutlery factory, but by 1850 only half a dozen or so cutlery firms employed more than a hundred workers and even they put out much of their work to independent 'little-mesters'. Employment conditions in the light trades were varied and

Plate 5.1　Sheffield's first electric tram. On 5 September 1899 Sheffield's electric tramcar No. 1 began a new era of public transport. At Tinsley on the city's eastern boundary the Lord Mayor, the Electrical Engineer and Councillors and their families posed for a photograph to record the historic occasion. For the first four years all double-deck tramcars had open tops, then in 1903 the first tram was covered and from 1907 onwards glass protected the drivers; 1911 saw the first tramcar that was totally enclosed. Electric trams produced a faster and more efficient service than the old horse-drawn trams and fares were reduced to ½d a stage. Cheap transport encouraged the development of working-class suburbs well away from the steel and cutlery works.

complex and though the craftsmen were traditional in their outlook and methods, they responded readily to innovations in patterns and products. Little-mesters were men of great skill but small capital who received high wages when trade was booming and whose products were sold throughout the world. Foreign competition and the erection of tariff barriers began to tell in the mid 1870s, and after the McKinley tariff of 1890 exports to the USA almost ceased, but this blow was softened by the opening of markets in Central and Southern America and throughout the British Empire. Mechanization was a more dangerous enemy to the traditional structure of the industry. A sixteen-week strike against the installation of file-cutting machines in 1866 ended in defeat, and by the 1890s it was obvious that the higher wages that could be earned in works using machines had made the old hand-craft a sweated trade primarily for women and children in rural communities such as Ecclesfield. In the cutlery industry the typical unit was still the small family concern; by the 1890s Joseph Rodgers employed nearly 2,000 workers and Walter & Hall, Mappin & Webb, George Wolstenholme and James Dixon & Sons employed nearly 1,000 each, but even they were partly dependent upon out-work (Pollard 1959: 132).

The unions resisted attempts to install machinery and some took extreme measures to force workers into membership. The 'Sheffield Outrages' of the late 1850s and 1860s became a national scandal which led to the 1867 Royal Commission of Inquiry into Trade Unions. With the granting of legal immunity it gradually became clear that twelve of the local unions had been involved in assault and in 'rattening' practices whereby a non-union worker's tools and wheel bands were stolen and gunpowder was placed in chimney stacks and grinding troughs. William Broadhead, landlord of the Royal George in Carver Street, secretary of the saw grinders and treasurer of the Associated Trades of Sheffield, was forced to admit that he had incited and paid for murderous assaults. The enquiry led to the passing of the 1871 Trade Union Act which enabled unions to meet openly rather than in secret. Despite all this upheaval the real earnings of workers in the skilled crafts undoubtedly rose during the second half of the nineteenth century. In 1889 John Wilson believed that the workmen as a whole

> were never better fed, better clothed or better housed than they are at present . . . Now in the homes of many you will find the floor covered with oil cloth, a good table and sofa, and even a piano – although perhaps purchased on the hire system.

Meanwhile, the heavy trades had expanded phenomenally. In 1850 they had employed only about a quarter of the numbers who worked in the light trades. At that time Sheffield had about 1,250 crucible holes and 150 cementation furnaces and its forges and rolling mills were only just being converted to steam rather than water power. But during the third quarter of the nineteenth century giant steel and engineering works, the like of which Britain had never seen before, were laid out alongside the railway and the river at the eastern end of the borough. This new generation of steelmen generally came from a background in the light trades; Charles Cammell started as a filemaker and a steel and file merchant, John Brown began as a cutlery maker and factor, and when Thomas Firth's Norfolk Works opened in 1851 it included not only crucible and cementation furnaces, tilt hammers and rolling mills, but departments that specialized in making files, saws and edge-tools. At first these new works concentrated upon serving local cutlers and tool makers but soon railway demand for steel springs and axletrees created a large-scale market from beyond the region. The development of east end works, such as the massive River Don works of Naylor, Vickers and Co., was very rapid during the 1850s and 60s. It was achieved by the multiplication of existing types of furnaces, so that crucible steel production reached an all-time peak during the 1870s, until all was changed by the discovery of large-scale methods of making steel.

Henry Bessemer invented his converter in 1856 and built his own works in Sheffield two years later. A converter could produce 800 times the output of a single crucible in a 30 minutes period; the era of cheap steel had arrived. Steel that was converted in this manner was not of high quality but it proved better than iron for making railway lines. In 1860 John Brown installed four Bessemer converters in his works; five years later 75 per cent of his output was sold to the railway companies. But when English demand declined Sheffield was badly placed geographically to take advantage of overseas markets; Brown's Atlas Works closed its rail mill in 1874 and nine years later Wilson Cammell moved their Dronfield works to Workington. Of more lasting importance were the Siemens open-hearth furnace and the James Nasmyth steam hammer, which was first tried at Firth's in 1849. Instead of concentrating upon railway stock, Sheffield steel firms now concentrated upon castings for the engineering and shipbuilding industries; by the end of the century single items weighing up to 100 tons were being made. By then the other major buyer of Sheffield steel was the armament industry, for both British and foreign governments were bulk purchasers of guns, shells and armour plate. Hadfield's East Hecla works concentrated almost entirely upon war materials. Sheffield offset the disadvantages of its geographical position by manufacturing high-quality steel for special purposes. Robert Mushet and Robert Hadfield pioneered the scientific understanding that was necessary to produce such steels, and in 1912–13 Harry Brearley discovered a formula for making stainless steel, which at first was used for rifle barrels but after the war soon transformed the cutlery industry.

The steelworks employed large labour forces on an unprecedented scale. John Brown had 200 men in 1856 and 5,000 by 1872, Cammell's workforce had risen to 4,000 in 1872, and by 1890 2,000 men were employed at Firth's and another 2,000 at Vickers. Other large-scale employers included Hadfield's, Jessop's, Turton's, Steel, Peech & Tozer and Brown, Bayley & Dixon. Two shifts each of twelve hours' duration became the rule, with 1½ hours allowed for two meal intervals. The typical worker in the heavy industries was very different from his counterpart in the traditional light trades. He was often an immigrant attracted by high wages, who moved on in times of depression. Steelworkers acquired a reputation as rough-and-ready men who were heavy drinkers. Despite being gathered together in a single works, they were rarely interested in trade union activity; the national unions gained a foothold only in the 1890s (Pollard 1959: 233–42). They lived close to the works in rows of brick, terraced houses, blackened by the smoke that belched forth from the industrial and domestic chimneys. John Murray's *Handbook for Travellers in Yorkshire* (1874) claimed that Sheffield was 'beyond all question the blackest, dirtiest and least agreeable' town in the county: 'It is indeed impossible to walk through the streets without suffering from the dense clouds of smoke constantly pouring from great open furnaces in and around the town.'

The steelmasters built grand houses away from the smoke in the spacious countryside to the west of the town. John Brown's Endcliffe Hall and Mark Firth's Oakbrook Hall were both built in an Italianate style about 1860 and Ranmoor was developed as a fashionable quarter. But the town centre lacked dignified buildings and well-laid-out streets. In the early Victorian period Sheffield was unusual amongst England's industrial towns in having few wealthy manufacturers to provide a lead in civic projects, but even when the gap between master and men widened with the advent of the heavy trades little was spent on improving the central streets and public buildings; a suitable town hall was not available until Queen Victoria opened the present building on the occasion of her diamond jubilee in 1897. Sheffield did not attract a group of energetic outsiders to lead the way, unlike Birmingham, which had a similar economic system but could claim to be 'the best governed city in the world'. Nor were the working classes much interested in municipal reform. In many ways Sheffield was not a city but a collection of communities often physically separated from each other by steep hills and deep river valleys. Several contemporary commentators remarked upon the uniqueness of Sheffield, which had 'scarcely yet emerged from the status of an overgrown village'.

Though Sheffield had acquired a reputation for radicalism during the French Revolutionary wars and though large crowds supported the Chartist agitation, political activity remained a minority interest and never developed into class conflict. Sheffield society was unusually homogeneous and wages were normally high, so on the whole the borough remained peaceful. By the beginning of Victoria's reign Sheffield had acquired a network of 'respectable' voluntary societies dedicated to the moral improvement of the inhabitants. Primary education was largely provided by religious bodies. In 1850 Sheffield had fourteen National schools, a Lancastrian school, boys' and girls' charity schools, a newly-founded ragged school and denominational infant schools as well as private 'academies' and the so-called Free Grammar school and Free

Plate 5.2   File-cutting at Ecclesfield in the late nineteenth century. In his *History of the Parish of Ecclesfield* (1862) the Revd Jonathan Eastwood wrote,

> The chief trade of the village is the cutting of files, the teeth of which are formed by a series of cuts made by a small chisel and hammer of peculiar construction, and the sound of constant tapping thus made never fails to excite the curiosity of strangers to the mystery, especially in cold weather, when the otherwise open windows of the hulls, or small shops in which each family carries on the trade at home, are closed by screens of oiled paper which let in sufficient light for a process which depends more upon a sense of touch than of sight.

Seventy heads of households worked at the trade in 1851 and a great many women were employed. Women were able to make up to 250 cuts per minute on small files.

File-cutters were liable to become hunch-backed and bow-legged and to have deformed thumbs and wrists. When one side of a file was completed it was turned over and set on a lead block so that the work would not be harmed when the other side was cut. This caused the additional hazard of lead in the atmosphere.

Just one fileshop remains in the village. Work ceased there in 1921.

Writing school. About three-quarters of Sheffield's children went to Sunday school but only about half attended day-school; 50 per cent of Sheffield workmen could neither read nor write (Pollard 1959: 33–4). Sheffield responded quickly to the 1870 Education Act by building board schools, but managed to cope with the rising numbers of school children only by gross overcrowding. Meanwhile, Sheffield was at the forefront of the adult education movement. The People's College, opened in 1842 by the Revd R. S. Bayley, minister of Howard Street Congregational chapel, became famous as the first place in Britain to make higher education available to all classes. The success of

272

the Cambridge University Extension Movement inspired Mark Firth to found Firth College in 1879, which together with the Medical Institution and Technical School provided a firm base for the University that was established in 1905. However, the pub continued to be the most common place where the Sheffield workman spent his leisure hours. St Monday, St Tuesday and birthday ales were still celebrated in the traditional manner. Relatively high wages, the independence of the 'little mester' and his irregular working hours and the demands of hard physical work were commonly believed to be the cause of excessive drinking habits. But at weekends Sheffielders enjoyed organized sports and outdoor activities and many were keen gardeners. The arrival of cheap transport allowed families to escape from the smoke and the grime into the attractive countryside surrounding the town.

Middlesborough was Victorian England's most astonishing town. Most of the great, nineteenth-century industrial boroughs had been urban centres long before their phenomenal growth; only a handful of new towns such as Crewe and Barrow in Furness sprang from nowhere. In 1801 Middlesborough consisted of four houses with 25 inhabitants, in 1831 the tiny population stood at 154, but ten years later it had risen to 5,463 and by 1901 it had soared to 91,302. The massive development of the site began in 1829 when a group of quaker industrialists led by Joseph Pease of Darlington extended the Stockton to Darlington railway into the bleak salt marshes on the southern bank of the Tees where they constructed large wharves to export coal. Two years later, Pease laid out a new town on a symmetrical plan behind the wharves, around a market square, church and town hall, and a pottery and a foundry and rolling mill provided extra jobs for the thousands of immigrants who poured into Middlesborough. Chapels, schools and a mechanics' institute were also founded, but despite the quaker paternalism of the developers Middlesborough's immigrant population soon acquired a reputation for rowdiness and drunkenness. By 1840 $1\frac{1}{2}$ million tons of coal were exported every year from the new port, but the development of a national rail network meant that the sea-borne coal trade soon declined sharply. This setback was more than compensated for by the spectacular growth of the local iron industry, however.

The man most responsible for Middlesborough's change of course and continued growth was Henry Bolckow, who came from Mecklenburg to Newcastle in 1827 at the age of 21 and who fourteen years later established an ironworks on the banks of the Tees. His partner, John Vaughan, had previously worked at the Dowlais ironworks and at Carlisle and Newcastle. For several years their business was a small concern dependent upon imported ore, but during the 1850s they began to exploit the ironstone deposits in the nearby Cleveland hills at Eston, which had previously been considered of poor quality. Supplies of coke came a short distance from County Durham. When Middlesborough was incorporated in 1853 Bolckow became the town's first mayor; five years later he was elected unopposed as the town's first MP. A staunch Liberal and Wesleyan, he was a noted philanthropist, the leading subscriber to every good cause and a benefactor who provided schools and a public park. Where Bolckow and Vaughan led the way, other ironmasters such as the Bells and Wilson, Pease and company, soon followed. By 1873 the north-eastern ironfield was producing over two million tons of pig-iron per annum, i.e. about a third of the total British output. The Teesside furnaces were larger and more efficient than the older plant elsewhere in the country, and the high wages enjoyed during the boom years of the later 1860s gave workers as well as masters a shared sense of prosperity. Local Cleveland ores still provided 84 per cent of Teesside requirements in 1883, but from then onwards the area became increasingly dependent upon overseas ores, so that by 1913 local supplies accounted for only 60 per cent of consumption. A change of emphasis from iron to steel came in the mid 1870s under the leadership of Arthur Dorman and Albert de Lande Long. Teesside became a major centre for the production of Bessemer steel, then that of the open-hearth process and of sheet steel for ship plates. By 1913 the North-East produced over two million tons of steel per annum, or nearly half the national output (Briggs 1963: 247–82).

Middlesborough attracted immigrants from far afield. In 1871 nearly half its population were born outside Yorkshire, including a large Irish contingent of 3,622 people, 1,531 from Wales, 1,368 from Scotland, 1,169 from the west Midlands and about 600 who were born overseas. The various buildings that were erected to cater for immigrant religious beliefs included a Jewish synagogue and a Roman Catholic cathedral serving a new bishopric. Middlesborough's population rose quickly during the second half of the nineteenth century, from 7,431 in 1851 to 19,416 (1861), 39,563 (1871), 55,934 (1881), 75,532 (1891) and 91,302 (1901). A guide to the town written in 1899 admitted that,

> At first sight Middlesborough is not calculated to create a particularly favourable impression upon the visitor. Its utilitarian aspect is somewhat too pronounced. With its numerous ironworks lying between the town and the river, the town itself being built upon a low level stretch of country on the south side of the river, and its streets composed for the most part of plain brick houses, it presents essentially a business town, and little that is picturesque to attract and please the eye.

The growing town burst beyond the original grid pattern, and in the 1880s a new centre was laid out on the other side of the railway line around the grand town hall of 1883 and other public buildings of that period. Working-class houses were built as near to the place of work as possible until an electric tram system was installed in 1898; they were as overcrowded as those of any other industrial town. But in 1911 Middlesborough could boast of one major feat of engineering when the Transporter Bridge was built by the Cleveland Bridge and Engineering company; 850 ft long and 215 ft high, it was the largest bridge built on the gantry principle anywhere in the world.

Coal

During the reign of Queen Victoria the Yorkshire and north Midland coalfield, stretching from Leeds to Nottingham, became the largest in Britain. An estimated 8 million tons of coal were mined there in 1851; by 1913 the coalfield's annual output had risen to 73 million tons. The labour force in the nation's mines rose from c. 50,000 at the beginning of the nineteenth century to over one million on the eve of the First World War. In Yorkshire old agricultural communities on the exposed coalfield such as Featherstone and Hemsworth were transformed into pit villages, the ancient market towns of Wakefield and Barnsley acquired a new dimension, new settlements such as Fitzwilliam and Denaby Main were founded at the edges of old parishes, and from the 1870s onwards colliery muck stacks began to rise and became a dominant feature of the landscape. In western parts of Yorkshire the colliers were mostly natives, but during the third quarter of the nineteenth century deeper mines were sunk further east and thousands of immigrant miners came in search of work. The changes were without parallel in the county's history. Then, in the late-Victorian and Edwardian era the concealed coalfield under and beyond the Magnesian Limestone belt was exploited and many of the old farming parishes of the Doncaster district were altered beyond recognition. Only the squires of trim estate villages managed to preserve their rural setting whilst benefiting from royalties earned from the mining of coal below their land. Thus Hickleton is still the pleasant village that Sir Francis Wood rebuilt in the early 1840s in the vernacular style of the sixteenth and seventeenth centuries, but the colliers who worked at Hickleton Main lived at the foot of the limestone escarpment at Goldthorpe and Thurnscoe, two farming hamlets that became pit villages as large as towns but lacking their amenities.

Few great estate owners other than the Fitzwilliams or the Lister-Kayes were directly involved in exploiting their mineral resources as well as benefiting from royalties and mineral rents. Most coalmasters were a new breed who came from a minor landowner, professional or business background. The most successful were the Charlesworths of Chapelthorpe Hall, the successors to the Fentons. Joseph Charlesworth began mining at Crigglestone in 1799 and his son, John, expanded the family's interests enormously in west and south Yorkshire. The Charlesworths prospered by using advanced technology and commercial methods and by cultivating good industrial relations. In Victoria's reign they were able to join the ranks of the West Riding gentry and send two members to Parliament (Goodchild 1978: 94–121).

William, the fourth Earl Fitzwilliam (1748–1833) was one of the greatest landowners in England. In 1756 he succeeded to a large estate at Milton, near Peterborough, and to more than 80,000 acres in Ireland; then in 1782 he inherited the Wentworth Woodhouse and Malton estates of his uncle, the

275

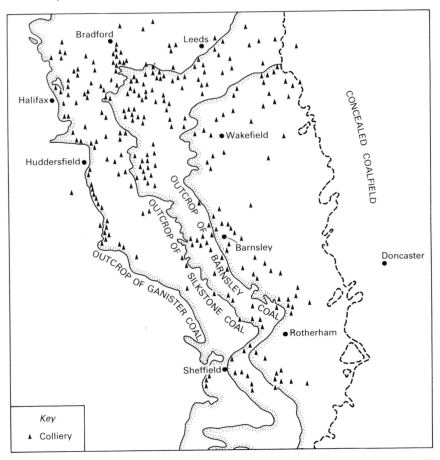

Figure 5.3 Yorkshire collieries in 1855 (after G. D. B. Gray, fig 2.2, in J. Benton and R. G. Neville (eds), *Studies in the Yorkshire Coal Industry*, Manchester U. P., 1976, p. 36.)

second Marquis of Rockingham, together with a London town house in Grosvenor Square. He and his son, Charles, the fifth earl (1786–1857) shared a paternalistic concern for those dependent upon them for home and employment and a conviction that the ruling classes should recognize their responsibilities and work to promote God's kingdom on Earth. These beliefs cost Charles his posts of Lord Lieutenant of the West Riding and of Ireland when he spoke out against the massacre of Peterloo. In comparison with most coal owners at that time the Fitzwilliams were outstanding employers. They were fortunate to be well-served by Joshua Biram and his son, Benjamin, two remarkable mining engineers and viewers, and they exploited their coal reserves at Elsecar, Park Gate and Stubbin so successfully that eventually their mineral income greatly exceeded their revenue from agriculture (Mee 1975: 24–34).

From the 1790s onwards Elsecar was developed as an industrial estate village of the Fitzwilliams. In 1795 the Elsecar New Colliery was sunk to the Barnsley seam and provided with a Newcomen-type pumping engine, and that year the number of colliers on the Wentworth estate increased from 45 to 79. At the same time, John and William Darwin leased ironstone and coal mining rights and built the first Elsecar furnace; a second furnace followed in 1800 and the firm prospered till about 1812 making pig iron, domestic ranges, spoutings and rails for colliery tramways. The heyday of the Elsecar ironworks came after 1850 when George and William Dawes from Birmingham ran the business until its closure in 1884; they were also the founders of the Scunthorpe iron and steel industry. Meanwhile, less than a mile away, at the end of the eighteenth century the Walkers of Masborough had established the Milton ironworks. The reputation of the works was enhanced in 1824 when William and Robert Graham came from London to manufacture pig, rod, hoop and sheet iron, castings, steam engines and boilers, suspension and other bridges, iron boats and general millwork. Lime kilns, coke kilns and a tar distillery followed the opening of a branch of the Dearne and Dove canal in 1799, and a major boost to production came in 1850 when the South Yorkshire Railway provided access to the London market via Doncaster.

Local coal sales rose from 70,000 tons in 1800 to 300,000 tons in 1856, and by 1856 869 miners were employed at Elsecar, Park Gate and Strafford Main (Mee 1975: 23–4). The workforce were accommodated in good-quality housing provided by the earls. Elsecar grew from a scattered hamlet to a considerable village during the course of two generations. Between 1796 and 1801 Station Row and Old Row were built to the designs of John Carr, the famous Yorkshire architect who had worked on the great house and stables at Wentworth Woodhouse. The long, curving terrace of Reform Row was added in 1837 and the Miners' Lodging House in Fitzwilliam Street was built in 1854 for 'young colliers' at the newly-opened Simon Wood colliery nearby. Milton Hall was opened as a model hostel in 1870 and contemporary houses survive in Cobcar Lane. The new community was provided with a Wesleyan Methodist chapel (1842), Holy Trinity church (1843) and a Church of England school (1852), which replaced the 1836 National School. All these buildings, together with the flour mill (1842) and the earl's private railway station (1870), survive intact in a designated conservation area.

In the days of shallow pits mining had normally been a safe occupation, but the large-scale development of the Yorkshire coalfield in the Railway Age brought all sorts of hazards and hardships. The dust at the coal face wore away a hewer's lungs and the work was exhausting. Seventeen-year-old Andrew

Roger, who worked at the Chapeltown colliery, said in 1841, 'Sometimes I can hardly get my breath, and it is often hot . . . I can hardly get washed of a night till nine o'clock, I am so tired.' A Barnsley man was killed in a 'firedamp' explosion in 1672 and three men 'were slain by the damp in Mr Boden's coal pits, near Genne Lane', Worsbrough in 1755, but few major accidents occurred in Yorkshire pits before deeper mines were sunk to the fiery Barnsley seam. In 1803 30 men were killed in an explosion at Barnby, and during the next two generations the death toll rose appallingly. In 1847 an explosion at the Oaks colliery killed 73 men; two years later 75 died at Darley; in 1857 189 miners were killed at Lundhill; seven years later 59 died at Edmunds Main; and then, in 1866, in the worst calamity of all, 361 men were killed in a second disaster at the Oaks colliery. Recommendations made after the 1847 explosion had not been put into effect; too much reliance had been placed upon safety lamps for detecting gas rather than upon improving the ventilation system. The blast on 12 December 1866 was heard three miles away and only six of the 340 miners who were working at the time survived. Tragically, the following day a second explosion killed 27 rescue workers. National opinion was horrified and £48,747 was collected by the Lord Mayor of London's fund. The Oaks disaster was the worst the country experienced until 439 Senghenydd miners were killed in an explosion in Glamorgan in 1913. But although it was the largest calamity that occurred in Yorkshire, it was not the last; 143 miners were killed at Swaithe Main in 1875, only a short distance from the Oaks colliery, and in 1912 an explosion at Cadeby killed 90 men.

The collective conscience had been stirred a generation earlier by an accident of a different kind. An ugly Gothic monument, as stark and black as the event it commemorates, records the burial of 26 children in Silkstone churchyard. These fifteen boys and eleven girls were drowned at the Husker pit, 1½ miles away from the church. One of the boys was only 7 years old, five children were aged 8, and the average age of all the children was 10. The monument is inscribed with biblical texts and a record of the event. The cumbersome Victorian prose must have done little to comfort the bereaved parents and the underlying theology is revolting to the modern reader. It says:

This Monument was erected to perpetuate the remembrance of an awful visitation of the Almighty which took place in this Parish on the 4th day of July, 1838. On that eventful day the lord sent forth his Thunder, Lightning, Hail and Rain, carrying devastation before them, and by a sudden irruption of water into the Coalpits of R. C. Clarke Esqr twenty six human beings whose names are recorded here were suddenly Summon'd to appear before their Maker. Reader Remember! Every neglected call of God will appear against Thee at the Day of Judgement. Let this Solemn Warning then sink deep into thy heart, and so prepare thee that the Lord when he cometh may find thee Watching.

A similar note was struck by the Bishop of Ripon on the occasion of the Oaks disaster. He wrote to the *Barnsley Chronicle* on 22 December 1866, 'Let it be a warning to others to attend more seriously than they ever have done before to their eternal interest.'

No-one could be blamed for this accident. It was normal at that time for children to be at work, and boys were employed throughout the coalfield. However, most Yorkshire collieries did not employ girls amd Clarke's pits were unusual (though not alone) in having so many. A total of 91 boys and 53 girls were employed in Clarke's coalpits in 1841. The youngest children sat by themselves in the dark and opened the ventilation trap doors whenever a corve came along. Henry Goddard of Chapeltown was 'ten years old last Christmas. I attend a trap door. I sit in the dark generally, but sometimes they give me a light . . . The corves pass sometimes every five minutes.' In some parts of the coalfield the youngest trappers were only 5 or 6 years old. The older children were employed as hurriers. Their job was to push the loaded corves along rails from the coal face to the bottom of the shaft. Three-quarters of the children in Clarke's pits were hurriers, aged between 8 and 17, with an average age of 11 for the boys and 9 for the girls. In one of the Silkstone pits investigated by J. C. Symons, the parliamentary commissioner in 1841, the hurriers worked in pairs pushing a load of 8 cwt on the 150 yard descent and an empty corve weighing 2 cwt back up the ascent.

The normal day's work involved twenty journeys with an aggregate distance of 3½ miles. On the western edge of the coalfield, on the thin seams between Huddersfield, Hepworth and Stocksbridge, the hurriers had the hardest task of all. At Foster Place colliery near Hepworth the agent reported, 'There are no rails. We hurry on sledges and with belt and chain. With empty ones they thrust behind, and the full ones they hurry going before.' Symons reported,

> One of the most disgusting sights I have ever seen was that of young females, dressed like boys in trousers, crawling on all fours, with belts round their waists, and chains passing between their legs, at day pits at Hunshelf Bank and in many small pits near Holmfirth and New Mill.

As a result of his and other reports, an Act was passed in 1842 prohibiting the employment of females in mines and forbidding the use of boys under the age of ten. Three years later a commissioner noted that,

> The temporary privation occasioned to some of the females formerly employed in the pits has nearly passed away. Almost all have found other occupations. Several expressed to me their content at the alteration: 'they were glad to be out of the pit', 'it wanted doing most sadly', and 'it will be a deal better for all now it is done'.

Symons's report also revealed the neglect of the children's education. As most children were at work, the Silkstone day-school was 'wholly insignificant'. On the other hand, a high proportion of the children attended the Sunday schools of the Church of England and of the Wesleyan and Primitive Methodists. 'The object of these schools is to give secular instruction; religious instruction is secondary to it, and the system is wholly mechanical.' However,

> the statistics of education, though they exhibit the meagreness of its extent, convey no adequate idea of its deficiency in quality. In nineteen out of every twenty instances the mind of the child is as much uninformed even after a couple of years' tuition as before it went to school.

Hannah Clarkson (age 16) was illiterate, Mary Shaw (19) and Matilda Carr (12) could not write, and John Batty, an eight years old trapper, did not go to Sunday school: 'My father and mother won't let me; so I do nought but lake on Sundays.' When an agreement was made between Clarke and 81 of his adult workers in 1838, 61 signed the document with a mark. It was the same throughout the coalfield. Daniel Drenchfield worked in a pit at High Green. He did not know when his birthday was, what three times ten made, which was the biggest city in England, nor who Jesus Christ was. He had been to Sunday school at Wortley and knew 'I shall go to hell if I am not a good boy.' He knew his catechism off by heart but had no idea what it meant. He must have been typical of many.

It was about this time that the miners made a united effort to increase their wages. In 1842 the Miners' Association was formed at Halifax and on 20 February 1844 nearly 4,000 men attended a demonstration at Hood Hill near Chapeltown. This impressive display of solidarity caused the employers to gather at Wakefield to discuss the 'unsettled disposition of the colliers'. The masters resolved to lock out any employee who joined the union and declared their intention not to raise wages. Their announcement provoked a series of strikes all over the coalfield and on 12 May 1844 most of the West Riding colliers ceased to work. R. C. Clarke was one of the 'hardliners' who were determined to crush the strike at all costs, even by ejecting the strikers from their homes. A large and hostile crowd watched the ejections and made a collection on behalf of the homeless families. The miners were defeated and it was not until 1858 that their union was revived, but the events of 1844 were a foretaste of many bitter conflicts to come.

During the middle years of the nineteenth century more pits were sunk in the older parts of the coalfield – to the 'ganister' seam at Stocksbridge in 1840 and to the Barnsley bed at Tinsley Park (1842), North Gawber (1850) and Orgreave (1851), for example – for companies preferred to invest their capital where coal had been proven rather than take risks further east. The Yorkshire pits that worked the 9 ft Barnsley seam were often given the distinctive name of Main (though Silkstone Main lay further west), a usage almost without parallel in Britain's other coalfields. When a new pit was opened in 1868 at the eastern extremity of the exposed coalfield the name Denaby Main was also given to the settlement that was founded alongside it. It lay 4 miles north-east of Kilnhurst and 5 miles east of Wombwell, the nearest of the older colliery communities, and was markedly different in character from its neighbours. In 1861 the small village of Denaby, settled nearly a thousand years earlier by a group of Danes, contained only one coalminer amongst its inhabitants. By 1871 the new pit village of Denaby Main sited on the eastern parish boundary housed 166 colliers, only 10 of whom were born in Yorkshire; more came from Derbyshire (56), Nottinghamshire (17), Staffordshire (16), Ireland (14), and Durham (12) than from their adopted county. Other employees lived nearby in Old Denaby, Conisbrough and Mexborough; 74 of Mexborough's 258 miners were born in Yorkshire, but they were outnumbered by those born in other counties, notably Cheshire (34), Staffordshire (33), Lancashire (27) and Derbyshire (14). The pit employed 473 men and was the largest in Yorkshire. It was sunk by a partnership of west Yorkshire coalowners, led by Richard Pope and John Buckingham Pope of Leeds, George Pearson of Pontefract, Joseph Crossley, the Halifax carpet manufacturer, Edwin Baines, the Leeds MP and newspaper proprietor, and George Huntriss of Doncaster. Denaby Main was a 'company town' consisting almost entirely of colliery-owned terraced houses—two up, two down brick cottages with no bath and only an outside WC—and colliery-provided public buildings. This raw 'frontier' community was vastly different from earlier Yorkshire pit villages which had developed from an older nucleus. The owners were hard-headed men who had taken considerable commercial risks, and the miners were immigrants welded by their shared working experience into a closely knit and militant community. Conflict broke out as early as 1869 when notice was served on those who had joined the miners' union; the 350 miners who went on strike at the beginning of March were evicted from their homes, but on 16 September the owners admitted defeat. Further major strikes occurred in 1877, 1885 and 1902–3 (MacFarlane 1976).

The Miners Federation of Great Britain, founded in 1889, faced its first major test in 1893, when 300,000 workers in the central coalfields were locked out after refusing to take a 25 per cent reduction in wages to help offset a 35 per cent fall in prices. The dispute was largely peaceful, but in some West Riding pit villages such as Hoyland and Orgreave the militia were called out to quell disturbances. The Riot Act was read at Featherstone on 7 September and two men were killed and sixteen wounded when the militia opened fire. On 17 November the miners returned to work victorious. In 1912 a dispute over guaranteed minimum wages led to the first national miners' strike, involving over one million men. A national ballot showed that the strike was supported by 4:1 miners and that in Yorkshire the proportion was as high as 6:1. By the eve of the First World War the Yorkshire coalfield had a firm reputation for militancy.

Denaby Main remained the most easterly pit on the coalfield until the same company opened Cadeby colliery in 1893. In 1905–8 Brodsworth Main was sunk to the Barnsley seam in the concealed coalfield in a joint operation between Hickleton Main Colliery Company and the Staveley Coal and Iron Company. The principles of housing and urban design that had been developed since the 1890s at Port Sunlight, Bourneville and other model villages were advocated by Arthur Markham, Liberal MP and one of the owners of Hickleton Main, who commissioned Percy Houfton of Chesterfield to build an estate known as Woodlands that was totally different from the monotonous rows of terraced houses that characterized most of the old pit villages. All houses had at least three bedrooms, a bathroom and hot water and the density of building was kept as low as six houses per acre. A full-time social worker helped to run the various clubs and societies and two Methodist chapels opened immediate-

Plate 5.3 Orgreave Pit during the 1893 lock-out. In 1893 the coalowners proposed to reduce wages by 25 per cent on the grounds that prices had gone down 35 per cent over the previous three years. This proposal was resisted by the Miners' Federation of Great Britain, which had been formed in 1889, and so the owners locked the miners out during the last week of July. About 300,000 miners were without wages until they resumed work on the old conditions on 17 November. The dispute was mostly peaceful but violence flared at some West Riding pits where 'blacklegs' were employed, and police or the militia were sent in. The photograph shows soldiers outside Orgreave colliery, which worked the Barnsley seam, at the time of the September troubles.

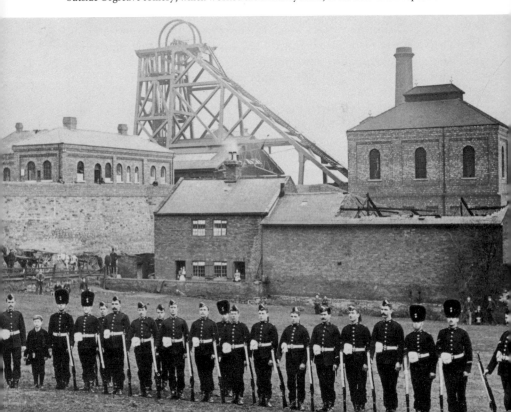

ly, followed in 1913 by All Saints Church. Woodlands was sited close to the mine but beyond the Brodsworth boundary in the parish of Adwick le Street. It was the forerunner of many other model colliery villages and of inter-war council estates.

Pit villages such as New Edlington were more common than the model estates, however. While the Yorkshire Main colliery was being sunk from 1909 to 1911 by the Staveley Coal and Iron Company, the sinkers lived in huts and gained a notorious reputation for gambling, drinking and fighting. An investment company meanwhile started to build the village. For a time the new settlement was known as Staveley Street but it was eventually named after the older village of Edlington gathered round its Norman church at the top of the hill. The roads were like a quagmire as bricks were brought by traction engines from Conisbrough and Balby. The houses were erected in units of four or six, with large flower and vegetable gardens to the rear. On the ground floor was a living room with a Yorkshire range and small side-boiler, a scullery with a sink and copper to heat water for washing clothes and for bathing in a portable zinc bath, a small pantry, a sitting room and two outshuts serving as WC and coal-place. Upstairs were two bedrooms and a boxroom. The manager's house was a large brick villa set in its own grounds, and the other officials lived in semi-detached houses. For a year or so a few mobile carts and travelling shopkeepers came on regular visits, but the nearest shops, schools, post office and pubs were at Warmsworth and Balby. The miners came chiefly from Derbyshire and Nottinghamshire, where their own pits had been worked out. A temporary 'tin tabernacle' doubled as chapel and social hall until better facilities could be provided. By 1914 New Edlington had a church, school, co-operative store, pub and concert-cum-dance hall (Holland, ed. 1971: 47–50).

The construction of the South Yorkshire Joint Railway in 1909 was a vital aid to the development of the concealed coalfield. In *Brother to the Ox* Fred Kitchen describes the transformation:

> Then a loco came, fussing and snorting like some prehistoric monster, scattering the sheep and cattle from their grazing. It brought behind it engine-sheds and fitting-shops, so that the miller's field, which had once been a sanctuary for birds, rang all day with the clatter and bang of hammers and the snorting of steam-engines. It came one day with a whole town of tin – at least it was called Tin Town, though most of it was made of wood – and it brought in a strange race of people, who taught us new ways and habits. They married and inter-mixed with the natives, so that in a few years you couldn't tell a Norwood [Maltby] yeoman from an alien.
>
> It wasn't the settled inhabitants of Tin Town, so much as the nomadic race of navvies, that shook the village to the very foundations. A paternal government had not then docketed and labelled each workman

Plate 5.4   Installation of a pumping engine at Nunnery Colliery in the late 1860s. In 1868 the Nunnery Colliery Company Ltd began to mine the Parkgate and Silkstone seams on land belonging to the Duke of Norfolk east of Sheffield. A large pumping engine, known affectionately in later years as Old Sal, was built by Walker and Eaton Ltd at the Spital Hill Engineering Works and dragged by 45 horses to the engine house. The photograph shows how wheels and wooden runners were used to raise the beam into position. The engine was often worked 24 hours a day, lifting 1,000 gallons of water per stroke, at the rate of $2\frac{1}{2}$–3 strokes a minute. It continued in use until 1933 and the 65 ft high engine house remained standing until the early 1960s.

with a labour card. They just came and went, hundreds of them; where to, or where from, nobody knew or cared, and the quiet country lanes became infested with as scurvy a lot of weary willies as ever got bitten with a louse . . . Much beer and blood began to flow in the street on Saturday nights and Sundays. Drunken brawls, revellings and revilings, drink-sodden navvies sprawling in the gutter, tramps sleeping in barns, tramps threatening housewives for a crust, and tramps massaging their stinking feet at the village drinking trough . . . Never since the time of the Danes had our village suffered such an invasion . . .

When he returned to Maltby after six years absence:

It seemed as though a town of bricks had been carried bodily through the air and dropped on Little Norwood, leaving bits of stone cottages showing here and there. The two inns had been done up, while a miners' institute and a fish-and-chip shop showed how greatly Little Norwood was developing . . . A model village, with church, chapels, and a fine new council school had sprung up where oats and wheat and barley had followed each other in about a dozen different fields . . . But with the opening out of the coal-field a difference came over the rural population; they tried to imagine themselves a grade finer in the grain than were their forefathers, and even in the stables the old songs died out, along with the old games.

Rural Yorkshire

Those Victorian and Edwardian market towns that serviced the agricultural parts of the county proceeded unhurriedly in their time-honoured way. In his *Little Guides* to the three Ridings, published between 1904 and 1911, Joseph Morris described Bedale as 'a very small, very sleepy old market-town', Great Driffield as 'an old-fashioned red-brick market town' and Howden as 'a dull and depressing little town'. Thirsk, he thought, was 'a rather dingy old town, almost left stranded by the railway, which passes nearly a mile to the west' and Selby was 'as dull a little town as any in the [West] Riding'. Tadcaster struck him as 'a small, old-fashioned town, dominated, whether seen from far or near, by the chimneys of its enormous breweries'. Pocklington was typical of many of these old centres in that it had held a weekly market since the early Middle Ages and by the seventeenth century it had seven annual fairs and a regular Saturday market, but then it failed to take advantage of the improved means of transport; it was by-passed by the 1764 York-to-Beverley turnpike road, in 1815 the canal stopped short of the town, and the railway that came in 1847 was of only limited importance. Though Pocklington's population rose from 1,502 in 1801 to 2,546 in 1851, this rate of growth was slow compared with that of the West Riding industrial towns. Pocklington remained a retail and service centre for a small rural hinterland with numerous shopkeepers and craftsmen and a social elite dominated by a few solicitors, doctors and wealthy tradesmen (Neave 1983). This enclosed and in many ways unprogressive world was very different from that of the Victorian borough but it was an environment that was familiar to tens of thousands of Yorkshiremen and one that remained profoundly characteristic of the age.

Most Victorian market towns had some small-scale industry, perhaps a brewery or an ironworks, a tannery or a corn-milling business, but the local economy was firmly based on the varied activities of numerous skilled craftsmen, who created and sold their goods on their own premises and sometimes hawked them around the countryside. These craftsmen typically turned their hand to a variety of work, for demand was rarely sufficient to enable them to specialize. In the 1850s Tadcaster's 2,500 inhabitants included nearly 300 small masters, journeymen and apprentices; a third of them were tailors, shoemakers and dress-makers, another third were employed in the building trades, and in a society dependent upon horse transport the 6 wheelwrights, 10 saddlers and 10 men who worked in the three blacksmiths' smithies fulfilled an essential role (Brewster 1970). Market towns also provided professional and trade services and on market day they created a sense of excitement and pleasure as well as of business. Fred Kitchen remembered 'the smell of tarpaulin, leather, cow-cake, apples, calves, pigs and poultry' and 'the biggest babel of dialects since the time of Noah' when he went to the hiring fair at Doncaster in a carrier's cart. Country carriers had adapted well to the age of the railways; many of them had other occupations for the rest of the week, but on market day they brought passengers, goods, shopping lists and messages to town and returned in the evening with purchases and many a fine tale to tell. By the 1880s or 1890s the great annual livestock fairs were a thing of the past. The railways had hastened their decline and their absorption into the weekly market system, but they were retained in a few places for the annual hiring of servants and for merrymaking. However, even the growing numbers of village shops did not replace the thought of market day in some nearby local town as an event to look forward to.

Many a small market town was able to take advantage of improved communications and to prosper in a modest way. In 1874 John Murray described Thorne as 'an active market-town, carrying on considerable trade in corn, coal, and timber . . . the Quay called the Waterside, [is] resorted to by sailing-vessels, and when the tide permits, by steamers from Hull'. Ships were built at Thorne and the port flourished during the second half of the nineteenth century when the peat-cutting trade grew in response to the enormous demand for bedding material for horses. Dutchmen came to provide technical skills and capital and by 1889 about a hundred immigrants lived in a Dutch colony at

Thorne Moorends. In 1896 five companies amalgamated to form the British Peat Moss Litter Company which worked the peat moors between Hatfield and Goole. Demand for peat declined sharply after the First World War when motor transport began to replace the horse.

In Victorian times rural society was polarized more than ever before between the rich and the poor. At the bottom of the social hierarchy the ranks of the farm labourer had been swollen by the population explosion, and at the top gentry families had become more exclusive as younger sons no longer took their place among the middling farmers but served in the army, the church or the professions. In the country as a whole landed estates and their tenants farmed about 85 or 90 per cent of the available land, leaving only a small proportion for owner-occupiers, and the landlord–tenant relationship had a customary, almost feudal air about it (Mingay, ed. 1981: 14). In the East Riding in 1873 11 men with over 10,000 acres each owned about 28 per cent of the land, another 24 great landlords with 3,000 to 10,000 acres each owned a further 18 per cent, and 58 men with 1,000 to 3,000 acres each owned 13 per cent. The Crown was by far the largest corporate owner with 12,230 acres, but this estate was nowhere near as large as those of Sykes (34,010 acres), Londesborough (33,006 acres), Cholmley/Strickland (20,503 acres) and several others who employed London or provincial firms as professional land agents (English 1984). In the West Riding agricultural incomes were considerably increased by coal-mining royalties, which helped to pay for building projects and other improvements.

Nineteenth-century country house owners at first built in a Grecian style or they aped the Tudor and Jacobean age with gables and mullioned-and-transomed windows. Anthony Salvin's Moreby Hall in the East Riding ôr the hall built at Broomhead on the edge of the Pennine moors for James Rimington, a Sheffield barrister, were conscious revivals of a style that had gone out of fashion nearly two hundred years earlier. In south-west Yorkshire Thrybergh Park and Sir Jeffry Wyatville's Banner Cross Hall are rare examples of the castellated or Gothic mode of building. In the West Riding the Grecian style gave way to the Italian at Grimston Park, the home of Lord Howden and his wife, a Russian princess, and then to the unrestrained Italian display of Sir Charles Barry's alterations at Harewood House, the halls built for Sheffield steel manufacturers at Endcliffe and Oakwood, and Brodsworth Hall, built in 1861–63 for the Thelluson family to a design of the Cavaliere Casentini of Lucca (Pevsner 1959: 57–60). The Gothic style was occasionally used in later Victorian houses but was more commonly employed in churches and public buildings. A neo-Norman style was fashionable for churches in Victoria's first decade but Gothic soon became accepted as the only conceivable style.

In the towns numerous new churches were needed to serve the spiritual needs of the rapidly expanding population. In the countryside many churches were ruthlessly restored or completely rebuilt. Victorian zeal saved many a crumbling edifice but the enthusiasm for stripping walls of their plaster and for removing the galleries, box-pews and other fittings so familiar to their Georgian ancestors eventually provoked an outcry against what was being done in the name of restoration and improvement. Though the archaeological study of ancient churches reached new scholarly levels, much that was old and worthy was undoubtedly lost. The East Riding churches were most badly used, but new buildings there were amongst the very best. Escrick St Helen by F. C. Penrose (1856–57) and South Dalton St Mary (1858–61) by J. L. Pearson are the most memorable. Sir Tatton Sykes (1826–1913) built a dozen churches on his Sledmere estates and restored another eight. In the West Riding Earl Fitzwilliam commissioned Pearson to build Wentworth Holy Trinity on a scale befitting the great estate at Wentworth Woodhouse, to replace the modest medieval chapel-of-ease further down the hill. Such churches stood alone, often at the end of the drive to the great house, and they served as landmarks for miles around. Most of the great Victorian architects – Scott, Pearson, Street and Butterfield, etc. – were active in Yorkshire. Butterfield was particularly busy in the North Riding, and at Baldersby he not only designed St James's Church (1856–58) on a lavish scale for Viscount Downe at Baldersby Park, but also the vicarage, school and brick cottages for the tenants.

Scores of schools were erected in Victorian Yorkshire, both in the towns and the countryside, especially after the passing of the 1870 Education Act, though many date from the 1840s and 50s. Estate villages were generally well provided before 1870, or if not their squires were quick to build rather than have a board school which was out of their control. The parsonage was another important Victorian building in the countryside, and in estate villages such as Hooton Pagnell or Wortley the incumbent lived in comfortable style in a house that was second only to that of the lord of the manor. When Sir Joseph William Copley of Sprotbrough Hall rebuilt Sprotbrough and Cadeby villages in the late 1840s, the parsonage and estate steward's house stood a little apart from the cottages in the village street. The Revd John Fardell, the incumbent, thought the cottages were 'replete with the comfort and necessaries of that station of life . . . so that the poor now enjoy houses not to be excelled by the poor of any parish around'. About the same time, Sir Francis Wood rebuilt the homes of his Hickleton tenants in the vernacular style of the Elizabethan and Stuart Age, with Magnesian Limestone walls and pantile roofs, all tastefully assembled beyond the grounds of the hall. The 'close' village of a great landowner provided a strong visual as well as a social contrast with the more numerous 'open' villages which no single landlord could dominate.

By the beginning of Victoria's reign the long-term effects of parliamentary enclosure were being felt in those agricultural regions where the movement had been most active. In Holderness the old two-course rotations that had been suited to the arrangement of the open fields were replaced by four courses (including a bare fallow) and small farms were engrossed into larger arable ones. More wheat was grown on the Wolds and turnips were introduced into crop rotations so that sheep might be fattened; here farmers had to be men with capital who were responsive to new ideas, for farms of 800–1,000 acres were in greater demand than those of only 300 acres (Long 1969: 30). Most of the eighteen agricultural societies that had been founded in Yorkshire by 1835 were in the East Riding or the Vale of York, at Beverley, Boroughbridge, Bridlington, Doncaster, Driffield, Goole, Hedon, Holderness, Howden, Malton, Pocklington, Richmond, Scarborough, Selby, Thirsk, Wetherby, York Central and York East Riding (Mingay, ed. 1981: 247). The Yorkshire Agricultural Society was founded in 1837 and held its first show the following year in York, while the Royal Agricultural Society, also established in 1837, attracted 145,738 people to its show at Leeds in 1861 and further large crowds at Hull (1873) and York (1883). One of the improvements that was widely advocated was the under-drainage of land that was naturally heavy and wet. About 30 per cent of the Earl of Scarbrough's south Yorkshire estate, for example, was drained during the second half of the nineteenth century (Phillips 1972). Between 1848 and 1893 Yorkshire lost 774 acres to coastal erosion, some of which was deposited on Spurn Point, so that by 1851 this stretch of sand was 2,530 yards longer than it had been in 1676 (Sheppard 1912: 2). At the same time, however, 2,178 acres were reclaimed within the Humber estuary, and warping (the process by which fine, muddy deposits were left by the tides) was encouraged in the Humberhead Levels by the construction of dikes and embanked fields in which potatoes and other root crops were grown.

At the start of Victoria's reign few machines were used on English farms, but by the end of the century the same farms were the most mechanized in Europe. By then, Fowlers of Leeds and other agricultural engineers supplied steam engines and a range of machinery far beyond the capacity of the old country workshops which turned out ploughs and cultivating implements. Though traditional tools and methods survived, especially on small hill farms, elsewhere wire fencing became common in the 1860s and 70s, dairy farmers started to use oilcakes and other cattle feeds, chemical fertilizers were accepted, and farmers responded to the needs of the growing urban population by producing more meat, vegetables, dairy produce and hay for the townsmen's horses. Incomes, rents and wages all rose during the prosperous years of high farming, particularly during the 1860s, and the amount of arable land farmed in England and Wales rose from 12 to 15 million acres. By 1900, after a quarter of a century of agricultural depression, all this extra land under the plough had again been put down to grass. As Professor Thompson has written, 'The English countryside has probably never looked more prosperous than it did in the 1860s . . . The countryside has seldom looked more dejected than at the turn of the present century.' In 1851 over two million men and women were employed in farming, horticulture and forestry, the largest single source of employment, which provided jobs for well over one in five of the workforce. By the end of the century only one in eleven were employed in this way and the

289

labour force had declined to under 1½ millions (Mingay, ed. 1981: 4, 103, 200–13).

From the late 1870s to the mid-1890s imported corn from the prairies and steppes increased in such volume that home prices came tumbling down. Wheat prices fell by a half and those of barley and oats by about a third. The corn-growing districts such as Holderness and the Wolds were hit very badly, and the distress of the arable farmers was made worse by the atrocious weather of 1878–82. The Wolds farmers suffered further because wool prices fell sharply in face of Australian competition. Many were the tales of personal hardship and tragedy. But the story was not one of uninterrupted gloom. Although refrigerated meat and dairy imports caused English prices to fall by 15–20 per cent, the superior quality of English beef and mutton helped to maintain sales. During the 1880s beef and dairy cattle became the mainstays of many farmers. Those who concentrated on meat and milk, potatoes, hay, poultry, eggs and fresh vegetables managed to survive the worse years of the depression, and some were able to prosper. Though the gross output of English agriculture fell by 13 per cent between 1871 and 1891, by 1911 it was back at its 1871 level (Mingay, ed. 1981: 103–17).

For about a hundred years or so, during the second half of the eighteenth and the first part of the nineteenth centuries, the number of Englishmen employed as farm labourers had risen substantially. The great increase in the size of the national population had not only swelled the ranks of the industrial workers but had provided cheap labour on the farms, so that long before Victoria's reign rural society in non-industrial districts had been divided into three classes: landlords, tenant-farmers and labourers. In 1851 the agricultural labour force of England and Wales reached a peak of 1.88 millions; thereafter, it declined both in relative and absolute terms. The permanent agricultural workforce fell by 20 per cent during the three decades after 1851; whereas one in four adult males had been engaged in agriculture at the middle of the nineteenth century, by the eve of the First World War the proportion had fallen to one in ten. During the great agricultural depression the total number of farmers remained roughly the same, but they survived by reducing their labour force. A shift of emphasis from arable to pasture meant that fewer hands were needed, and demand for manual labour was reduced further by the adoption of seed drills, horse hoes, mowers and reaping machines in the 1850s and 60s, followed by self-binding reapers in the 1880s. Women left the fields first, and they more than men swelled the ranks of those searching for work in the towns and industrial villages. Without this migration rural areas would have suffered widespread unemployment. The poor quality of cottage accommodation increased the determination of some country families to move to the towns, though the standard of rural building improved in the 1880s, particularly in estate villages where squires were anxious not to see their workers leave. In some estate villages the population rose again during the last quarter of the nineteenth century, while that of neighbouring 'open' villages declined.

The Poor Law Commissioners of 1834 reported that labourers in York-shire were often employed on a piece-work rather than a permanent basis, and that little work was available for women and children. In Campsall and Norton vagrancy was regarded as a threat to the social order: 'The neighbour-hood swarms with vagrants. Gangs of gypsies infest the country and frighten the farmers and overseers by threatening to fix their settlement with them.' Elsewhere, farmers in the East Riding were dependent, as of old, on the seasonal migration of labourers from the moors and dales to help with gather-ing the harvest, and the landlords of 'close' villages needed the services of labourers from surrounding 'open' villages on a more regular basis. Local communities still tended to be charitable towards their own poor but to be wary of outsiders. A typical attitude was found at Tickhill workhouse, where 'the object is to make the old and infirm as comfortable as they can, and the able-bodied, if dissolute characters, as uncomfortable as they can'.

The nineteenth century saw the decline and sometimes the disappearance of old rural industries. In the North Riding the woollen knitware trade and the alum industry, two successful projects of the Elizabethan and early-Stuart era, had collapsed before Victoria came to the throne, and the scattered linen industry withered soon afterwards in face of Irish and continental competition. The lead fields, however, continued to thrive, despite prolonged periods of depression in 1816–18 and 1824–33, and miners farmed moorland intakes in the manner of their ancestors. Production reached new peaks in the middle years of the nineteenth century but some lead fields were soon exhausted. Grassington's population declined by 123 in the 1850s and then by a further 400 between 1861 and 1881. In Swaledale Muker lost a quarter of its inhabi-tants in the 1850s, some going to the industrial parts of the West Riding or Lancashire, others emigrating to the United States or Canada. But the main exodus occurred during the 1880–82 depression, when many mines were abandoned. During the year ending October 1882 Reeth School lost more than half the children on its register, and between 1871 and 1891 the population of Swaledale declined by nearly 50 per cent (Raistrick and Jennings 1965: 323–7). The characteristic Dales farms of today are often amalgamations of even smaller holdings that were vacated when the lead industry decayed.

Life in the remoter parts of nineteenth-century Yorkshire was recollected in two remarkable accounts by distinguished local scholars, the Revd J. C. Atkinson, vicar of the North York Moors parish of Danby, and J. R. Mortimer, the archaeologist and geologist who spent his boyhood in the Wolds village of Fimber. In *A Victorian Boyhood on the Wolds* (Hicks, ed. 1978), Mortimer recalled that in the 1830s:

The farmers of Fimber were a very plain and homely class [who] worked and took food with their servants, acting, in fact, as foremen. They mostly wore the same kind of clothing as their labourers, which consisted mainly of fustian jackets and long frock-smocks, either white

291

or brown, of a coarse material named duck. Their agricultural implements were few, and of a very primitive kind, and to my recollection there was not a cart with springs in the whole parish . . . At that time, in the country villages, much plainer food was eaten than now. Very little fresh butcher's meat was consumed, bacon and salted beef being almost the only animal food indulged in, supplemented, largely, by old milk cheese (nicknamed 'Old Wengby') which many farmers then made for the consumption of their own household . . . Small oatmeal dumplings (derisively named 'Dogwhelps') cooked in boiling milk were, along with bread, the most frequent breakfast and supper dishes. Bread at that time was of a very coarse and inferior kind.

The villagers drank water from the two stagnant meres until draw-wells were sunk. And as the Wolds had neither timber nor coal, fuel was often so scarce that dried cow-dung had to be burnt. Living conditions for the poorest families were very primitive. Henry Cawood, for instance, lived with his wife and four children

in one of the smallest single-roomed cottages I ever saw. This house had a mud floor full of holes, was open to the roof, and had three steps leading into it, resembling a cellar. The side walls were so very low that I, with other boys have crept up the thatched roof . . . There were four or five more similar cottages in the village at that time.

However, Mortimer observed a considerable improvement in housing standards during his boyhood, when the old cruck-frame buildings were replaced by farmhouses and cottages

with walls consisting of chalk and road scrapings mixed with small chalk gravel, called 'mortar-earth', which is found in abundance on the hill sides near many of the villages of the wolds. Most of the old labourers were then able to build these chalk walls, also thatch the roofs of the houses.

J. C. Atkinson also witnessed much improvement during his long incumbency, but remembered vividly his visit to an ancient house in Danby in 1870:

We entered on a totally dark and unflagged passage. On our left was an enclosure partitioned off from the passage by a boarded screen four or five feet high, and which no long time before had served the purpose originally intended, namely that of a calves' pen. Further still on the same side was another dark enclosure similarly constructed, which even yet served the purpose of a henhouse. On the other side of the passage opposite this was a door, which on being opened gave admission to the living room, the only one in the dwelling. The floor was of clay and in holes, and around on two sides were the cubicles or sleeping boxes . . . of the entire family. There was no loft above, much less any attempt at a 'chamber': only odds and ends of old garments, bundles of fodder, and things of that sort.

Danby was a parish of small farms: 'in all, there may be now six or eight farms of more than 100 acres; all the rest, in number if at all under seventy, and exclusive of small holdings or cow-keepings, scarcely average seventy-five acres each'. Even so, these farms were larger than in earlier times for their number had been reduced by 25 per cent since the mid-seventeenth century. The quality of the livestock had improved in recent years but the system of crop management had remained unaltered in every particular during Atkinson's long incumbency. He had seen much moral improvement – rowdyism had declined and drunkenness carried a stigma – and he felt quiet satisfaction at the achievements of church, chapels and schools, regretting only that education had led to 'the decay of the old pure Yorkshire speech'. Contemporaries who shared his concern to record dialects included Samuel Dyer, whose *Dialect of the West Riding of Yorkshire* appeared in 1891, and another Yorkshireman, Joseph Wright, whose monumental *English Dialect Dictionary* was published in six volumes between 1898 and 1905.

Atkinson was fascinated by the survival of an older culture and knew that 'still there is a singular amount of old and unchanged custom, habit, feeling, among us'. When he had arrived in the parish at the beginning of Victoria's reign most of the moorfolk believed in fairies, beneficial or otherwise, small people like the Hart Hall Hob in Glaisdale who dwelt in the prehistoric burial mounds scattered on the moors. Burial parties clung steadfastly to hallowed routes or church-ways, for fear that if they took a short-cut the ghost of the deceased would rise again to haunt them. Superstitious beliefs were widely accepted and were similar to those that Mortimer remembered on the Wolds. Both men wrote, for example, about bee-customs that secured the future prosperity of the hive upon an owner's death; Mortimer recalled that hives were decked with strips of black crape and given ale on a plate or a saucer before their dead owner was taken to his grave. Every rural area supposedly had its resident witch, whose evil powers could sometimes be countered by witch-wood (rowan or mountain ash) or other magical charms or by visiting a wise-man with a reputation for remedying misfortunes.

One old man told Atkinson how he had once travelled eleven miles over a rough, wild, lonely road to see John Wrightson of Stokesley, 'Au'd Wreeghtson, t'wahse man o' Stowsley', to seek a cure for his uncle's bullock:

After some little delay he was admitted. The Wise Man was seated in his consulting room, dressed in some sort of long robe or gown, girded round him with a noticeable girdle, and with a strange-looking head-covering on. There were some of the accustomed paraphernalia of the character assumed and its pretensions – a skull, a globe, some mysterious-looking preparations, dried herbs, etc, . . .

'Well, John, thou's come to ask me about Tommy Frank's black beast, that is carried on in yon strange way', began Wrightson to his visitor's amazement; the wise-man diagnosed a cancer that was past curing. Wrightson performed the role of a primitive vet and herbalist; he was a semi-magical figure who reassured those who feared they were bewitched and who frightened thieves into returning stolen property. As such he was a valuable member of rural society.

The communities on the edge of the Pennine moors were equally remote and lacking in refinement. In the 1850 edition of her sister's great novel *Wuthering Heights* Charlotte Bronte acknowledged that strangers

> will hardly know what to make of the rough, strong utterance, the harshly manifested passions, the unbridled aversions, and headlong partialities of unlettered moorland hinds and rugged moorland squires, who have grown up untaught and unchecked, except by mentors as harsh as themselves.

She explained that as her own remarkable family were

> resident in a remote district, where education had made little progress, and where, consequently, there was no inducement to seek social intercourse beyond our own domestic circle, we were wholly dependent on ourselves and each other, on books and study, for the enjoyments and occupations of life.

Their writings did not receive immediate acclaim, but today Haworth parsonage is one of the most popular literary shrines in the world.

Religion and Recreation

The only census of church attendance ever held on a national level in this country revealed that on 29 March 1851 well over half the population of England and Wales did not participate in any religious service at all. Worshippers formed about 35 per cent of the West Riding's population, and in the great Victorian cities of Birmingham, Liverpool, Manchester, Newcastle and Sheffield fewer than one person in ten attended either church or chapel; the urban working classes were largely absent. A second shock to the established church came with the revelation that of the 40.5 per cent of the national population who were present at a service almost half (48 per cent) preferred a chapel to the Anglican church. In the West Riding the proportion of Nonconformists was considerably higher. In Leeds a new vicar observed in 1837 that 'The *de facto* established religion is Methodism.' There the Anglicans had lost control over the Improvement Commission by 1829 and the town council after 1835. Dissenters also wrested control of the vestry, which set the church rate and managed the financial affairs of the parish, and by 1833 formed a majority of the churchwardens (Fraser, ed. 1980: 250–69).

Table 5.5 Attendance at religious services in the West Riding, 29 March 1851

	Morning	Afternoon	Evening	Total
Church of England	113,683	87,712	36,387	239,792
Methodists (all types)	97,116	92,707	106,291	296,114
Others	75,743	51,694	37,383	164,820
Total	286,552	234,113	180,061	700,726

Total population of West Riding: 1,325,495

(*Source*: *Northern History*, XVII (1981): 200)

The situation in 1851 was very different from what it had been in the late seventeenth century when dissenters formed only 4 per cent of the nation. The Unitarians and Quakers were unmoved by the Evangelical Revival, but the other old dissenting sects – the Independents (Congregationalists) and Baptists – joined in the new religious fervour. The new Independency was a product of industrial areas and it appealed chiefly to the better-off. But now Wesleyan Methodism was easily the strongest Nonconformist sect. The triumph of Methodism was not limited to the older strongholds of dissent; nearly all areas had their Nonconformists now. Whereas the old dissent had become largely the concern of the respectable classes, Methodism attracted people of all social backgrounds in almost every type of community. It was particularly successful in industrial towns and villages, especially in outlying settlements that lay well away from the parish church. For instance, Darton had its Anglican church and Wesleyan chapel, but further out in the parish the two nailmaking communities of Mapplewell and Staincross had three more Wesleyan chapels. The hill-top village of High Hoyland had only its established church, but in the valley below the new textile settlement of Clayton West had chapels for its Wesleyans, Independents, Particular Baptists, Methodist New Connection and Primitive Methodists and the Wesleyan Reform movement gathered 150 people in Aaron Peace's warehouse. Only those estate villages that remained under the firm grip of an Anglican squire still resisted dissent.

Up till then, Wesleyan Methodism's greatest building period had been in the 1830s. Like some of the older dissenting sects, it had already become respectable. In 1847 the Mill Hill Unitarians in Leeds became the first West Riding congregation to build a chapel in the Gothic style that had been so enthusiastically resurrected by the Anglicans; during the 1860s the style was frequently adopted by the wealthier denominations. Soon the West Riding had chapels that were far removed in spirit from the simple boxes of earlier times, pompous and showy buildings like Cleckheaton Central Methodist (1875–79) and Heckmondwike Upper Independent (1890). The industrial poor turned increasingly to the Methodist New Connection or to the Primitive Methodists, who also appealed to the humbler sections of rural communities. The 'Ranters' as the Primitives were known were the second strongest Nonconformist sect in 1851. In the towns they could attract large numbers, such as the 1,550 who attended evening service at the Sheffield Bethel, but in the countryside many of their meetings were small affairs, like the group of twelve who met in a cottage in the limestone-quarrying community of Levitt Hagg. Their main period of strength was still to come (Hey 1974).

1851 was in no way a terminal date, for many more churches and chapels were erected during the second half of the nineteenth century, but a new pattern had become clear. The Church of England had woken from its eighteenth-century slumbers, however, and had begun to tackle the problems caused by the population explosion. In Sheffield, for instance, ten new churches were erected under the terms of the Million Act between 1825 and 1850, and in 1846 the medieval parish was divided into twenty-five new units; in 1851 large congregations met in the borough's Anglican churches – 1,200 at St Peter's (the ancient church), 1,300 at St George's, 750 in the Wicker, and between 375 and 600 at four other churches – but even so the combined numbers of worshippers at the Established Church did not match those of the numerous dissenting sects. By 1851 the Church of England was stronger in Leeds than it was in Sheffield or Bradford. The Revd Walter Farquhar Hook, vicar from 1837 to 1859, led a spirited counter-attack, emphasizing a deep social as well as a spiritual concern; unlike most Anglican clergymen in the West Riding at that time he was a High Churchman. The new ritualism of the High Church movement was well accommodated in Scott's Doncaster church (1854–58) and Norman Shaw's church at Bingley (1866–68) and elsewhere it led to the drastic reorganization of church interiors; out went Georgian pulpits, box-pews, galleries and plastered walls in favour of a bare, uncluttered look, and many churches were restructured in a medieval Gothic style.

During Joseph Lawson's youth at Pudsey 'there were only two places to go to in spending spare time away from one's own house – the church or chapel, and the alehouse; the former were seldom open, while the latter was seldom closed'. The pub was often a cheerful place that provided gossip, games and songs, but cheap drink made drunkenness common and convivial evenings often ended in fighting. Men gambled on prize fights, games of pitch and toss,

296

cock fighting and dog battles, and at that time no police force existed to keep order. 'Dumb animals were formerly much more cruelly treated', Lawson remembered, and 'both horses and donkeys were worked in a most horrid and pitiful state, having such wounds and sores.' J. R. Mortimer recalled that on the Wolds dog-fighting and badger-baiting were common cruel sports; bull-baiting was also indulged in by the larger villages but was too expensive for his native Fimber. The evangelical revival offered a respectable alternative to this rough tradition. Chapel and Sunday school festivals and anniversaries and the Whitsuntide processions vied with the beerhouse and village feasts, and clergymen and magistrates were eventually able to stamp out the more disorderly of the old pastimes. This process was hastened by the depopulation of much of the countryside, for though many countrymen took their customs and practices with them to the towns they rarely passed them on to their descendants. By Edwardian times the traditional rural recreations had largely disappeared. Folklorists were just in time to record songs, dances, mummers' plays and ceremonies that had enriched rural life for generations.

Parish feasts and the Martinmas hiring fairs were the major rural festivals of the nineteenth century. At Darrington the annual feast was the occasion for all to make merry: 'everybody kept open house; friends and relations who had left the village came back to it, sometimes from far distances, and there was a great reunion of families' (Fletcher 1910: 143–4). The hiring or 'stattis' (statute) fair in Edwardian Doncaster attracted farmers and labourers from south Yorkshire, north Yorkshire, north Lincolnshire and parts of Nottinghamshire and Derbyshire:

> The streets were crowded with farm chaps seeking new masters, and all were dressed in breeches and leggings, while most of them wore favours in their caps, such as one gets by throwing at Aunt Sallies, and, on account of the pubs being open all day, many of them had obtained a staggering gait at an early hour.

Bargains were clinched by a 'fastening-penny', which varied in value according to the generosity of the farmer; a head-waggoner usually got five shillings, a seconder half-a-crown, and lads a shilling. To Fred Kitchen it always seemed a wretched business, especially for a lad of thirteen or fourteen to be taken like a sheep or calf to market and sold to the highest bidder. However, Martinmas did provide a welcome week's holiday for the farmworker.

The concept of a holiday was revolutionized by the coming of the railways, which provided opportunities for outings to the seaside at a reasonable cost. Bridlington attracted its first bathers about 1770, but its development alongside the quay away from the old priory church and market town was modest until a railway reached the town in 1846. Bridlington soon became popular with holiday-makers from Hull, the West Riding and the north-east midlands. The railways also prompted the growth of Filey as a

297

seaside resort, and a grid of new streets begun there in the 1850s was completed
by 1890. Further north, Scarborough catered for the rich as well as for the
working classes, with cliff-top villas and hotels beyond the ancient limits of the
town; Cuthbert Brodrick's Grand Hotel dominates the front, rising thirteen
storeys on the side facing the sea. The railways also enabled Yorkshire families
to visit Cleethorpes and places on the Lancashire coast or to get to Harrogate,
England's smartest inland spa, which was replanned and rebuilt as a superior
Victorian resort. Ilkley became another fashionable watering place and smaller
spa centres continued to attract a local clientèle. J. M. Wilson's *Imperial
Gazetteer* (1875) noted that Askern was 'not long ago, a paltry hamlet, but is
now a pretty place, with hotels and lodging-houses, much frequented by
invalids and others' seeking cures for rheumatism and scorbatic diseases.
Improved communications also helped to make towns into entertainment
centres, attracting visitors to racecourses, sports grounds, concert halls,
theatres and music halls. Doncaster, for instance, was said in 1874 to be 'best
known to the world for its Races, which take place annually in September, and
last four days. They are among the most celebrated in England, attracting a
vast assemblage of persons, and contributing not a little to the prosperity of the
town'.

New traditions forged in the towns and industrial villages improved the
quality of life, particularly in the field of music. Many a home had its piano and
most places in the West Riding had a brass band. Joseph Lawson thought that
'perhaps there is nothing in which Pudsey has made so much progress during
the last sixty years as it has in music'. The music performed by the Pudsey Old
Reed Band on clarinets, trumpets, bugles, trombones, French horns, brass
horns, serpents, bassoons, fifes and big drum was but 'child's play' compared
with the standards of later bands. Choral societies were founded at Halifax
(1818), Bradford (1821), and Huddersfield (1836), where Mrs Susan
Sunderland of Brighouse reigned supreme until her retirement in 1864.
Nonconformity had brought discipline and religious fervour to communal
singing at a time when German oratorios had almost replaced the traditional
anthems. The towns provided the large number of performers that were needed
and buildings big enough to accommodate them.

The towns were also focal points for the various historical, literary,
philosophical and scientific societies that enlivened nineteenth-century
provincial England. The Yorkshire Archaeological Society grew out of
meetings begun in Huddersfield in 1863, six years later it published the first of
its annual journals and in 1885 began to print its invaluable record series. The
North Yorkshire Record Society produced its first volume in 1884. The
Thoresby Society at Leeds published its first transactions in 1889 and the
Hunter Society at Sheffield followed in 1914. The first volume of the *Victoria
County History of Yorkshire* appeared in 1907, but the initial momentum has
been lost except in the East Riding. Meanwhile, a number of good local
histories had appeared, often written by parsons, for example the Revd

Plate 5.5 Yorkshire County Cricket Team, 1875. This is the earliest known photograph of a Yorkshire County Cricket Team, taken at the match with Surrey at Sheffield on 14–16 June 1875. The county club had been founded at Sheffield twelve years earlier. The match took place at Bramall Lane, which in 1854 had replaced earlier grounds at Darnall and Hyde Park as the major venue for cricket in Sheffield. Back row: G. Martin (umpire), J. Thewlis; middle row: G. Pinder, G. Ulyett, T. Armitage, J. Rowbotham (captain), A. Hill, A. Greenwood; seated: T. Emmett, J. Hicks, E. Lockwood, C. E. Ullathorne.

Jonathan Eastwood's *History of the Parish of Ecclesfield* (1862), or by prominent townsmen such as John Tomlinson, former mayor of Doncaster, whose *Doncaster from the Roman Occupation to the Present Time* was published in 1887. And the books which are now regarded as the classic pioneering studies of vernacular architecture, namely S. O. Addy, *The Evolution of the English House* (1898) and C. F. Innocent, *The Development of English Building Construction* (1916) were based on old houses within a few miles of Sheffield. Louis Ambler, *The Old Halls and Manor Houses of Yorkshire* (1913) extended this interest into the heart of the West Riding.

Organized sport, particularly cricket, was actively encouraged by those who saw it as a peaceful, enjoyable and manly alternative to cruel sports and violent activities. Eventually cricket acquired strict rules and an established code of conduct for players and spectators. The oldest clubs in the north, at York and Hallam (Sheffield), can trace a continuous history back to at least 1804. The first organized games were professional challenge matches, such as the one held in 1771 between Sheffield and Nottingham, or those featuring William Clarke's top-hatted All England XI. Clarke's team toured the country

299

Plate 5.6 Sheffield United Football Club, 1901. Sheffield United were the most successful football team in the country at the turn of the century. They were league champions in 1898, FA Cup winners the following year and cup finalists when this photograph was taken in 1901.
    They were founded in 1889, thirty-five years after the formation of the cricket club whose ground at Bramall Lane they shared.
    Ernest Needham, their left-half and captain, is standing on the far right. Billy Foulke, their heavyweight goalkeeper, is seated second from the left. Most of the players were internationals.

and played up to forty matches a season, often against twice as many opponents; they attracted a crowd of 16,000 when they came to Hyde Park, Sheffield, in 1846. This ground had been opened twenty years earlier as a better venue than the previous main Sheffield ground at Darnall, but after 1855 it was overshadowed by the new Bramall Lane site at the edge of the town. Yorkshire County Cricket Club was founded at Sheffield in 1863, but it did not fare particularly well until its reorganization in 1893 and the ending of Sheffield's monopoly. Under Lord Hawke (a Yorkshireman by ancestry though not by birth) the team became county champions in 1893, 1896 and 1898, then between 1900 and 1902 they lost only two of their eighty matches; they were champions again in 1905, 1908 and 1912 and were never far from the top. A new tradition had been born that enabled Yorkshiremen to identify themselves with their county. The players were all Yorkshire born, and the best of them, George Hirst and Wilfred Rhodes, were the greatest players in the game. The Roses match with Lancashire attracted 79,000 people in 1904.

    Meanwhile, the ancient, popular game of football had also been organized on a regular, competitive basis and had attracted enormous support amongst the working classes. Sheffield Football Club, founded in 1857, is the oldest football club in the world. A newspaper report of a London *v.* Sheffield match at Battersea Park in 1866, which London won by two goals and four touch-downs to nil, records that 'the game was a very hot one; although Sheffield were over-matched, many of the Londoners were badly knocked about'. The National Football Association, founded in 1863, and its FA Cup of 1871 were products of the public school interest in the game, whereas the Football League, established in 1888 (with two divisions from 1892), reflected the desire of working-class supporters for regular entertainment. Numerous local leagues were also created and teams sponsored by bodies as diverse as churches, chapels and pubs. Sheffield's two Football League teams grew out of organized cricket. In 1867 the Wednesday Cricket Club decided to keep its members together during the winter months by playing football, and in 1889 the United Cricket Club gave birth to a football team that was soon one of the most successful in the land. Between 1897 and 1901, under the captaincy of Ernest Needham and starring their giant goalkeeper Billy Foulke, they won the league championship once, were runners up twice, won the FA cup once and were also beaten finalists. Barnsley FC won the FA Cup in 1912, but Sheffield United's achievement was bettered by another Yorkshire club only when Huddersfield Town (founded 1907) dominated the football scene in the 1920s. Huddersfield was also the home of another type of organized football, for it was here at the George Hotel that representatives of twenty clubs met in 1895 to discuss the formation of the Northern Rugby Union, which from 1922 has been known as the Rugby League. On the eve of the First World War Harold Wagstaff's Huddersfield team were the finest in the industrial North.

Chapter 6

Since the First World War

War memorials in every town and village in the land speak of the appalling carnage of the First World War. Thus, at Easingwold, a small town with about 2,000 people in Edwardian times, a prominent cross erected at the edge of the old market square records the names of 57 local men who died 'For King and Country'. Yorkshire families were as involved as much as those of any other region of Britain; indeed, a disproportionate number of soldiers came from the northern industrial cities and from Scotland and Ireland. Yorkshiremen enlisted in many regiments, but particularly in the York and Lancaster, the West Yorkshire, the East Yorkshire, the Yorkshire, the Duke of Wellington and the King's Own Yorkshire Light Infantry. The reality of war was witnessed at first hand by some who stayed at home when the Zeppelin raids began and when Scarborough was shelled by two German ships. The bombings provided a foretaste of what was to happen in 1940 and 1941. Those who returned from the war were promised 'a land fit for heroes', but the pace of reform was unhurried and in most ways life went on much as before.

The last two generations have seen a gradual decline in Yorkshire's importance in the national economy as the old manufacturing industries contracted in face of international competition. After the collapse of the post-war boom in the 1920s, British industry lost much of its competitive edge in international markets, then the world-wide depression of 1929–31 brought unprecedented levels of unemployment. By 1932 Britain had nearly three million people, or 23 per cent of the labour force, out of work; the industrial districts of the North and the Midlands were hit hardest of all, with unemployment levels well above the national average.

Before the First World War British steel production had fallen behind that of the USA and Germany, but urgent wartime demand for ships, shells and armour plating and the brief boom that followed the war revitalized the industry. Investment in new plant at Redcar and elsewhere on Teesside enabled the North-East to claim nearly one-third of British pig iron production by 1920 and about one-fifth of British steel. During that year sixty-nine north-eastern furnaces, using both Cleveland and foreign ores, were in blast. Most of these furnaces were small, however, and their equipment elderly. In this they were typical of much of the British steel industry. Though the major part of national output was controlled by a relatively small number of companies, the industry was still characterized by numerous small firms. The inter-war years saw a series of amalgamations that created giant companies with widespread interests not just in steel, but in coal, shipbuilding and heavy engineering. Thus, in 1916 the Sheffield firm of Steel, Peech & Tozer began to erect their new Templeborough works with fourteen open-hearth furnaces, two billet mills, a nearby rod mill and bar and strip mills; two years later they amalgamated with Samuel Fox of Stocksbridge, the Workington Iron and Steel Co., the Frodingham Iron and Steel Co. and the Rother Vale collieries, so that they controlled coal mines and ore fields as well as all stages of iron and steel production (Vaizey 1974: 29–30, 41).

The post-war boom collapsed in 1921. During that year national crude steel production fell from 9 million tons to less than 4 million tons. Production levels improved somewhat in 1923–24, though prices failed to rise, and a modest recovery got underway in the late 1920s, but then came the world-wide depression. During the early 1930s steel output was halved and 45 per cent of the work-force were unemployed, for steel's main customers in the heavy engineering and shipbuilding industries were hit disastrously by a loss of trade. After 1931 Sheffield's unemployment rate rose to 34 per cent of the insured population. Amalgamation was the order of the day. In Sheffield John Brown merged with Mark Firth, while Vickers Armstrong joined forces with Cammell Lairds to form the English Steel Corporation. On Teesside Dorman Long amalgamated with Bolckow Vaughan in 1929, four years later with the South Durham Iron and Steel Co., and in 1936 with Bowesfield Steel at Stockton. But recovery was delayed until 1936 when a national rearmament programme began to meet the threat of Hitler's Germany.

The same economic forces brought hardship and bitterness to the coalfields. The number of men employed in the nation's coal mines dropped sharply after the post-war export boom, from 1,227,000 in 1920 to 827,000 in 1932 and to 704,000 by the time the pits were nationalized in 1947. The 1913 peak of production was never reached again. In 1913 96 million metric tons were mined in the nation's coalfields but by 1924 output had fallen to 81 million tons and by 1938 to 47 million tons. On the eve of the First World War Britain's share of the world export trade in coal had amounted to 55.2 per cent but a quarter of a century later it had fallen to 37.6 per cent. Falling exports led to a contraction of the industry and to the major strikes of 1921 and 1926. The miners' refusal to accept wage cuts led to a lock-out on 1 April 1921; at the beginning of July the men returned to work demoralized, having been forced to accept the new conditions. Five years later the owners proposed not only to cut wages but to increase the working hours from seven to eight each day. The miners' secretary, A. J. Cook, responded with the slogan: 'Not a penny off the pay, not a minute on the day'. Widespread sympathy for the miners' cause brought British industry to a standstill. From 4 May 1926 the country experienced the only General Strike in its history, but after nine days TUC support was withdrawn. The miners stayed out for a further seven months before they submitted. The bitterness of this struggle has remained fresh in the folk memories of the mining communities and has helped to create their unity, defiance, pride and insularity; Yorkshire's typical mining settlements are towns in terms of size but villages in most of their characteristics. Shared experiences have bound the mining families tightly together. Their social cohesiveness has become legendary.

The West Riding textile industries also suffered decline during the inter-war years, though unlike the experience of the Lancashire cotton industry this was not due to the effects of international competition. Rather, it simply reflected the general fall in the amount of world trade, particularly after 1929. West Riding woollen and worsted firms relied less on exports than did cotton and more on the home market, and their quality trade remained unchallenged. Nevertheless, unemployment levels rose steadily and were well above the national average. The knock-on effects of the decline of Yorkshire's staple industries were felt in Hull, where half of the city's 8,240 dockers were out of work in 1931. For the long-term unemployed these were grim years. The 1906–11 Liberal government had alleviated much of the poverty described in Rowntree's 1899 survey, but during the early 1930s many families still lived below the poverty line. In 1936 6.8 per cent of York's working classes were living in primary poverty according to the Rowntree definition, compared with 15.46 per cent in 1899, and 31.1 per cent of the working classes (or 17.7 per cent of the total population of York) were living in either primary or secondary poverty (Pollard 1983: 190–1). The story is not one of unrelieved gloom, however. Those in work during the inter-war years saw a steady rise in their standards of living in terms of housing, furniture, nutrition and health. Re-creational activities flourished as opportunities increased. Sports events attracted massive crowds as the Yorkshire Cricket Club continued to dominate the county championship and local football teams did well, and the cinema provided a new form of mass entertainment. By 1935 Hull, for instance, had thirty cinemas with a total of 40,000 seats, a repertory theatre and three variety theatres with the exotic names of Alexandra, Tivoli and Palace; together they attracted 200,000 patrons a week (Gillett and MacMahon 1980: 382).

The Labour Party made spectacular advances after the widening of the franchise in 1918. Before the First World War Yorkshire had only six Labour MPs and few seats on local councils. In the 1919 local elections Labour made big gains in Leeds, Sheffield and other industrial towns and for a year or so had a slender majority in Bradford, the home of the Independent Labour Party. The number of Yorkshire Labour MPs rose from 21 in 1922 to 40 in 1929 but fell to seven in the debacle of the 1931 election. Numbers rose again to 27 in 1935 and to 44 in 1945 when the Parliamentary Labour Party was able to form its first majority government. Meanwhile, Labour had taken control of some important local councils, notably Sheffield, where the party has remained in power since 1926 except for two brief periods in 1932–33 and 1968–69.

304

Leeds and Hull also fell to Labour for a time in the late 1920s, but at Huddersfield the Liberals retained an overall majority from 1868 to 1945. As in other matters, the west Yorkshire textile towns went their separate ways; their political history does not conform to a simple, general pattern.

During the inter-war years the legacy of crumbling nineteenth-century houses, blackened with smoke, lacking basic facilities and crammed into every available yard of space near the steel works or textile mills posed formidable problems. In 1937 George Orwell wrote, 'Sheffield, I suppose, could justly claim to be called the ugliest town in the Old World.' The sulphurous stench from the steel works was all-pervading.

> If at rare moments you stop smelling sulphur it is because you have begun smelling gas. Even the shallow river that runs through the town is usually bright yellow with some chemical or other. Once I halted in the street and counted the factory chimneys I could see; there were thirty-three of them but there would have been far more if the air had not been obscured by smoke
> (Orwell 1962: 95).

Labour-controlled authorities made a determined effort to clear the slums and to erect council houses. Edwardian housing schemes, such as the 603 new houses built in Garden Village, Hull, between 1907 and 1916 set the standards for post-First World War building. By 1935 Hull had 74,000 houses, 19,000 of which had been built since the war; 8,600 were the responsibility of the corporation, the landlord for about 10 per cent of the city's population (Gillett and MacMahon 1980: 382). In Sheffield huge new council estates with semi-detached properties and short rows of terraces set in spacious surroundings were built to the south-east of the town at Manor, Wybourne and Arbourthorne and to the north at Shiregreen and Parson Cross. At the same time, the middle classes spread into the countryside to the west to make Fulwood, Dore and Totley the new desirable residential areas.

The most ambitious housing scheme between the wars was undertaken by Leeds City Council on Quarry Hill, the site of one of the city's worst slums. When a Labour council was returned by a narrow majority in 1933, some 75,000 back-to-backs still stood within the city's bounds and little attempt had been made at slum clearance. The Revd Charles Jenkinson, the new chairman of the Housing Committee, saw to the appointment of R. A. H. Livett as Leeds's first City Architect and embarked on a massive rehousing programme with huge suburban estates. Quarry Hill became the largest council estate in England when between 1935 and 1941 slums were replaced by 938 high-rise flats, a shopping parade, communal laundry and other amenities, all constructed in a modernistic style. Sheffield tried this high-rise method in the 1950s and attracted international attention by its schemes, but this type of accommodation has since proved deeply unpopular and has now been abandoned. The Quarry Hill flats have been demolished and when Sheffield's working-class suburb of Darnall was rebuilt in the 1970s and 1980s it was constructed in traditional terraces (albeit of a modern design) in an attempt to retain the old community spirit. The persistence of local and family identities even among an urban sprawl was observed by Richard Hoggart in Leeds:

> To a visitor they are understandably depressing, these massed proletarian areas; street after regular street of shoddily uniform houses ... But to the insider, these are small worlds, each as homogeneous and well-defined as a village ... they know it as a group of tribal areas ... This is an extremely local life in which everything is remarkably near.
>
> (Hoggart 1957: 52–3)

A national housing survey of 1956 revealed that, together with east Lancashire and the Durham coalfield, the west Yorkshire conurbation had the largest proportion of obsolescent housing in England and Wales. One in every eight houses – twice the national average – was considered unfit for people to live in. By 1962 Bradford had managed to clear 20,000 of its worst 30,000 houses, but in the smaller towns the pace of renewal was slower. The drive to clear the slums seemed never ending.

The devastation caused by German bombs during the Second World War, especially in Hull, multiplied the problems faced by councils that were trying to clear their slums. The worst raids on Hull came on 13 and 18 March 1941. By the end of the war over 5,000 Hull houses had been destroyed, together with half the central shopping area, over 3 million square feet of factory space, 27 churches and 14 schools or hospitals. Hull's coastal position made it particularly vulnerable and Sheffield's steel works were a prime target. German bombers failed to find the steel works but they bombed Sheffield city centre in December 1940. The towns in the textile conurbation did not suffer to the same extent.

The 1950s saw the beginnings of a wholesale redevelopment of city centres. By the 1970s local identities had been lessened in a new environment of glass and concrete, with national or multi-national departmental stores, supermarkets, multi-storey car parks and ring roads. The old urban centres had long ceased to be residential areas, and reliable public transport and the growing number of family cars hastened the movement to the outer suburbs and beyond into the countryside. Many an old rural community was engulfed in the urban sprawl and environmental groups sprang up to defend the countryside by successfully advocating the creation of national parks and of green belts around the towns. But the most astonishing and welcome change of all was the transformation of the grimy Victorian towns and cities by the vigorous application of the 1956 Clean Air Act and the later use of government grants to clean public buildings. Sheffield was no longer 'the foulest town in England' but the cleanest industrial city in western Europe, set in some of the most attractive countryside in Britain.

Since the First World War every decennial census has noted an increase in the population of each of the three Ridings, though the phenomenal growth rates of the nineteenth century have not been maintained. Yorkshire's population growth in recent decades has in fact been lower than the national average.

Yorkshire's Victorian cities have shared the familiar national experience of migration from the old urban centres into the suburbs or the surrounding countryside. Changing boundaries make comparisons difficult, but between the wars population growth was most noticeable in the smaller towns and after the Second World War in the suburban estates built either by a council or by private developers. By 1971 sixteen Yorkshire boroughs had each over 40,000 inhabitants. (See Table 6.1, over.)

Polish, Ukranian and Hungarian refugees arrived in Yorkshire during the 1940s and 1950s to find work in the textile mills and the coal mines and a new

Plate 6.1 A Sunday School anniversary, Thurlstone, 1924. Churches and chapels retained large congregations in the inter-war period and anniversaries were popular occasions. The annual Whitsuntide procession of witnesses was a major event in the local calendar. The children of each Sunday school would parade with their parents from their church or chapel to join other groups at regular stops. Each Sunday school walked proudly behind its own banner and the entire procession was led by a brass band. At each stop, such as the one shown in the picture, hymns would be sung and prayers said. This was an occasion for wearing one's best clothes, indeed new clothes were often purchased for Whitsuntide and were expected to last a year. After the procession each Sunday school organized a tea and games. Such events have become much less popular in recent years.

Table 6.1   The population of Yorkshire, 1911–71

	West Riding	North Riding	East Riding	Yorkshire: total
1911	3,131,357	483,957	432,759	4,048,073
1921	3,270,266	529,437	460,880	4,260,583
1931	3,446,477	553,770	482,936	4,483,183
1941	(no census taken)			
1951	3,586,274	623,710	510,904	4,720,888
1961	3,680,547	664,563	526,510	4,871,620
1971	3,785,015	725,658	543,316	5,053,989

* Includes the County Borough of York
(The figures are taken from *Census 1971: England and Wales, County Report*, HMSO, London 1973.)

Table 6.2   Yorkshire's largest
boroughs, 1971

	Population
Sheffield	520,327
Leeds	496,009
Bradford	294,177
Hull*	285,970
Huddersfield	131,190
York	104,782
Halifax	91,272
Rotherham	84,801
Doncaster	82,668
Barnsley	73,395
Wakefield	59,590
Dewsbury	51,326
Scarborough	44,440
Morley	44,345
Batley	42,006
Spenborough†	40,690

* The adjoining urban district of
Haltemprice (created in 1935) had a
population of 52,273.
† Created a municipal borough in 1955.

influx of Irish immigrants arrived at the same time. Bradford had the largest proportion of Poles among its inhabitants than any other British town. Nevertheless, Central and Eastern European immigrants were relatively small in numbers and were easily absorbed into existing communities. Immigration of a totally different kind began in the late 1950s and continued on a large scale until the 1970s. Thousands of families from the New Commonwealth countries – from Pakistan, India, the West Indies and former British territories in Africa – arrived in search of work and an improved standard of living or to escape from persecution. They flocked to the large towns, particularly the West Riding mill towns, where they were prepared to take on menial jobs and work unsocial hours. In the early 1950s it was still rare to meet a coloured person in Yorkshire, but two decades later Asian or West Indian immigrants had taken over many of the old quarters of the Victorian cities. Their distinctive appearances, languages, religions and cultures, and their overwhelming numbers, made them a bewildering phenomenon to their neighbours. Racial tension has rarely flared into the ugly scenes witnessed in some other English cities, however, and local authorities have made determined efforts to cope with the unprecedented problems that have arisen.

Over four-fifths of the coloured immigrants in Yorkshire settled in the west Yorkshire conurbation. Though the West Riding had far fewer Commonwealth immigrants than London or the Midlands, some of its towns attracted large numbers. Bradford had the third highest total of immigrants in the country and Leeds and Huddersfield were both among the first ten. These three towns accounted for nearly 90 per cent of the immigrants who came to live in the textile district.

Table 6.3   Estimates of immigrants into the West Yorkshire conurbation by 1966

Town	Total population	Immigrants	West Indians	Pakistanis	Indians	Others
Bradford	298,000	21,000	2,000	15,000	4,000	
Leeds	508,000	12,000	6,000	2,400	3,000	600
Huddersfield	132,000	12,000	6,000	3,000	2,400	600
Halifax	89000	1,500		1,500		
Keighley	56,000	1,200		1,200		
Dewsbury	53,000	2,000		1,500	500	
Batley	40,000	2,000			2,000	
Other parts		1,300		900	100	300
Total	1,914,000	53,000	14,000	25,500	12,000	1,500

(*Source*: E. Butterworth *et al.*, *Immigrants in West Yorkshire: Social Conditions and the Lives of Pakistanis, Indians and West Indians,* Institute of Race Relations, 1967.)

The West Riding has the largest Pakistani community in the country, with the overwhelming majority based in Bradford, Halifax, Dewsbury and Keighley. The Indians made for Bradford and Leeds and to a lesser extent Batley and Dewsbury. The West Indians flocked to Leeds and Huddersfield and also to Bradford. Further south, by 1968 Sheffield had about 5,000 West Indians and a similar number of Asians. Some immigrants found jobs on public transport, but most made good the labour shortage in the staple industries. Night shifts in particular were dependent upon immigrant labour. In Bradford the new families settled in the inner wards, so that by 1966 Listerhills and Exchange had probably the highest proportions of immigrants of any local electoral area

309

in the country; 1,275 of the 1,417 lodging houses known to the council were owned or occupied by Indians and Pakistanis. These lodgings were mostly large houses formerly occupied by middle-class families and much sub-divided after their original owners had moved out of the inner city. The immigrants did not occupy the old back-to-back houses in the working-class quarters (Butterworth 1967).

The depopulation of the countryside continued well into the twentieth century until the mass-ownership of motor cars reversed the trend. Farming remained depressed between the wars and the mechanization of agriculture and the disappearance of rural industries meant fewer job opportunities for the countryman. Families moved out of the Dales in such large numbers when the lead mines closed that the population of Swaledale is now only a quarter of what it was 150 years ago. Shops were closed and services withdrawn so even more people decided to leave. The population has become elderly and many properties have been bought by outsiders as weekend cottages or holiday homes (Fieldhouse and Jennings 1978: 473). In less remote areas that are within commuting distances from the cities rural communities have often benefited from the enthusiasms of new residents who have restored houses and have taken an active part in village social life. Within the last few decades the provision of electricity, gas, piped water, water closets, telephones, radio and television has dramatically improved rural standards of living and has reduced the isolation of country life. Meanwhile, the power of an aristocratic family in their country house or the squire in his hall has been weakened considerably and has in many cases vanished altogether. Castle Howard, Burton Agnes, Burton Constable, Bramham Park and Newby Hall have to attract summer tourists to remain family homes, the National Trust has taken over Nostell Priory, Beningbrough Hall and some smaller houses such as Nunnington and East Riddlesden, and local authorities have accepted responsibility for Temple Newsam, Cusworth Hall and Cannon Hall, but Wentworth Woodhouse and Wentworth Castle have become colleges, Kildwick Hall and some other gentry houses have been converted into restaurants and inns, and Sprotbrough, Wheatley and numerous smaller halls have been demolished. An interest and pride in historic buildings has blossomed in recent years, however, and many old halls and manor houses that had declined to mere farmhouses or had been converted into cottages have been restored with all the added advantages of modern comforts.

During the inter-war years farming remained a laborious occupation that offered little financial reward. James Herriott's humorous stories capture the tenacious spirit of farmers in the northern hills where strenuous work on a smallholding was little different from what it had been for centuries. The horse era did not come to an end until the 1960s. Most parts of rural Yorkshire still follow the traditional concerns of the past three hundred years. The Dales farmer, for instance, still keeps dairy cattle on the lower slopes and sheep on the higher land, though since 1956 all Wensleydale cheese has been made in factories rather than on the farm. On the North York Moors the biggest change has occurred since the 1920s, when the afforestation programme began; by 1959 about 23,000 acres were covered with trees. Elsewhere, the management of deciduous woodland declined after the First World War when demand for traditional products fell. In the arable parts of the county the mechanization of cultivation and harvesting has continued apace as government and Common Market subsidies have made farming a profitable business. In the lowland vales the mixture of livestock and corn is much the same as before, except that more barley is now grown and more emphasis is placed on cash root crops such as potatoes, sugar beet and carrots; the bright yellow fields of early summer show how much oil rapeseed is grown in response to generous subsidies. In Holderness more than three-fifths of the land is under the plough at any one time, for corn yields well, but dairy cows remain important as Hull is so near. Corn and sheep are still the mainstay on the Wolds, where an arterial grid now supplies water to the farmsteads and fields. In 1943 the military authorities took more than a third of the Wolds as a training ground on which to prepare for the Normandy invasion, but all traces of this activity have now gone (Long 1969: 25–39).

Wartime needs between 1939 and 1945 re-emphasized the value of the traditional manufacturing base and in the post-war era the mining, metallurgical and textile industries remained dominant. A new era of full employment seemed assured. The full force of foreign competition was soon to be felt, however. During the 1960s and 1970s, many old-established firms went out of business and major enterprises were forced to reduce their scale of operations. In Sheffield, for instance, the cutlery industry was undercut by the cheap products of the Far East and the city was seen to be dangerously reliant upon the steel industry, which was faced with a world glut as other countries established their own furnaces and rolling mills. No other city in Britain was so dependent upon the fortunes of a single industry. A catastrophic decline in demand in the late 1970s and 80s cost thousands of jobs. Another traditional source of employment to disappear at this time was the Hull fishing industry, which received a death blow in 1978 when Iceland imposed a ban on fishing for cod within 200 miles of its shores. Hull remained Britain's third largest port and the long-dreamed of Humber Bridge has at last been completed, but the docks handled far less trade than London or Liverpool. Meanwhile, throughout the land new technology replaced many traditional crafts and greatly reduced the need for unskilled labour. The economic and demographic trends are away from the old northern industrial centres to London and the South-East.

The coal industry has also undergone major changes since the war. On 1 January 1947 the newly established National Coal Board took over a work-force of 704,000 men who mined 184 million tons of coal a year in 958 pits. The NCB operated in a seller's market until 1956–57 when the effects of cheap imported crude oil were first felt. Uneconomic pits were closed and machines

311

replaced men until by 1976 only 247,100 worked in the nation's mines. As the older pits became exhausted or were declared uneconomic, the centre of the Yorkshire coalfield moved east to Doncaster. All the pits on the Silkstone seam were eventually closed and so were many that worked the Barnsley bed. During the 1960s the miners slipped from third to twelfth position in the national wage-earning league. The era of cheap oil came to an end in the early 1970s; this strengthened the bargaining power of the National Union of Mineworkers and successful strikes restored the miners to their premier position as industrial wage-earners. The Yorkshire coalfield was one of the most militant in Britain and it was here that the disastrous 1984–85 strike began when Cortonwood colliery was threatened with closure. It was this militancy as much as the area's central position that had encouraged the NUM to move their headquarters from London to Sheffield. The contraction of the old coalfield continues, but the vast reserves of coal that have been found in the Vale of York will ensure Yorkshire's pre-eminent position in the national coal industry.

The desirability of attracting new industries and of reducing the dependence on a single form of employment is evident to all, but the legacy of industrial dereliction – of colliery muck stacks, vast acres of despoiled land, decaying buildings and rusting machinery, pollution and an all-pervading grime – has made the old manufacturing districts uninviting to investors. In recent years reclamation schemes and financial inducements to start new businesses in depressed areas have begun to make an impact, but official surveys of consumer trends consistently show that most Yorkshire families are well below the national average in terms of purchasing power. Regions such as Yorkshire which rely heavily on traditional industries have fallen behind in relative terms even though the county has shared in the unprecedented rise in national standards of living since the 1950s. This higher standard of living is immediately apparent in the coal-field. During the 1950s it was still common to see colliers in their pit dirt, with their snap tins and Dudley bottles, joining the queues for public transport near the pit head at the end of a shift, but all that has changed with the provision of baths and changing facilities at the pit and with wage levels that allow the purchase of a car.

The great changes that have occurred in all aspects of life since the Second World War and particularly since the late 1950s are a national rather than a regional story. In such matters as social attitudes, education, religion and leisure activities Yorkshire has conformed to national trends. The plight of the poor was improved radically after the war by the establishment of the Welfare State and by an international rise in the standard of living experienced by all western democracies from the mid-1950s onwards. The last generation has seen a consumer revolution brought about by the mass-production of cheap, high-quality goods and an unprecedented rise in the purchasing power of ordinary families. The advent of quick communications, cheap travel and mass culture has weakened regional identities and has reduced the influence of the provinces on the great social and political issues of the day. Yet despite the local

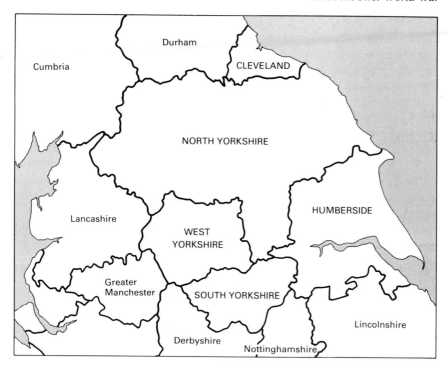

Figure 6.1 The new counties, 1974

government boundary changes of 1974 Yorkshire remains a recognizable entity, not only to its residents but to outsiders, whether or not they approve of distinctive Yorkshire characteristics and well-known personalities. The affairs of the Yorkshire County Cricket Club are widely reported as a constant source of national wonder. The novels and plays of Alan Bennett, John Braine, Stan Barstow, Barry Hines, David Storey and Keith Waterhouse brought national acclaim for a group of West Riding authors. Local roots have also been important for Henry Moore and David Hockney who have achieved international distinction in the arts, for Ted Hughes, the new Poet Laureate, and for many who have been successful in other fields, notably Henry Asquith and Harold Wilson, two West Riding men who became Prime Ministers. Yorkshire remains firmly in the public mind even if it no longer survives as a distinctive unit.

Throughout the old county it is possible to find evidence on the ground of the long and varied history of Yorkshire's urban and rural communities and its great families and institutions. York, Beverley and Richmond immediately spring to mind when thinking of England's historic towns; the abbeys and castles of north Yorkshire, the churches of Holderness, Castle Howard, Wentworth Woodhouse and other great country houses, the vernacular buildings on

313

the Pennine foothills are all well-known nationally as an essential part of historic Yorkshire. They are showpieces, but everywhere in the county towns and villages that do not have an immediate appeal to outsiders contain relics of the activities of past generations in such forms as street names, field patterns, historic buildings half-obscured by later alterations, ancient churches in the most unlikely surroundings, mysterious earthworks with legends attached to them, nineteenth-century chapels and other public buildings whose historical importance is now being recognized or diverse remains of vanished local industries. The majority of Yorkshire families have long been resident in the county and many have the distinctive local surnames that their ancestors adopted in the Middle Ages. Yorkshire speech is still unmistakeable and minor variations enable the listener to place a speaker within one of the county's sub-regions. But Yorkshire no longer exists as an administrative unit, nor do its ancient Ridings. After a thousand years of history the county of Yorkshire was abolished on All Fools Day 1974.

Bibliography

Abrams, P. and Wrigley, E. A. (eds) (1978) *Towns in Societies*. Cambridge

Allison, K. J. (1976) *The East Riding of Yorkshire Landscape*. London

Ambler, L. (1913) *Old Halls and Manor Houses of Yorkshire*. London

Andrews, C. (ed) (1934–38) *The Torrington Diaries*. London

Atkinson, F. (1956) *Some Aspects of the Eighteenth Century Woollen and Worsted Trade in Halifax*. Halifax Museums

Atkinson, J. C. (1893) *Forty Years in a Moorland Parish*. London

Aveling, J. C. H. (1966) *Northern Catholics: the Catholic Recusants of the North Riding of Yorkshire, 1558–1790*. London

Aveling, J. C. H. (1980) Catholic Households in Yorkshire, 1580–1603, *Northern History*, XVI, 85–101

Awty, B. J. (1981) French immigrants and the iron industry in Sheffield, *Yorkshire Arch. Journal*, 53, 51–6

Aylmer, G. E. and Cant, R. (1977) *A History of York Minster*. Oxford

Bailey, R. N. (1980) *Viking-Age Sculpture*. London

Baker, A. H. R. (1966) Evidence in the 'Nonarum Inquisitiones' of contracting arable lands in England during the early fourteenth century, *Econ. Hist. Rev.*, 2nd series, XIX, 518–32

Baker, A. H. R. and Butlin, R. A. (eds) (1973) *Studies of Field Systems in the British Isles*. Cambridge

Barraclough, K. C. (1976) *Benjamin Huntsman, 1704–1776*. Sheffield Central Libraries Local Studies leaflet

Barrow, G. W. S. (1969) Northern English Society in the twelfth and thirteenth centuries, *Northern History*, IV, 1–28

Bartlett, J. (1959) The expansion and decline of York in the later Middle Ages, *Econ. Hist. Rev.*, 2nd series, XII, 17–33

Beresford, M. W. (1955) The lost villages of Yorkshire, part II, *Yorkshire Arch. Journal*, 38, 215–40

Beresford, M. W. (1967) *New Towns of the Middle Ages*. London

Beresford, M. W. (1975) Leeds in 1628: A 'Ridinge Observation' from the City of London, *Northern History*, X, 126–40

Beresford, M. W. and Hurst, J. G. (eds) (1971) *Deserted Medieval Villages*. London

Beresford, M. W. and Finberg, H. P. R. (1973) *English Medieval Boroughs: A Hand-List*. Newton Abbot

315

Beresford, M. W. and St Joseph, J. K. (1979) *Medieval England: an Aerial Survey.* Cambridge, 2nd edn

Brathwait, R. (1932) *Barnabae Itinerarium: Barnabees Journal.* London

Brewster, D. M. M. (1970) Tadcaster in 1851: the population of a market town, *Annual Report and Bulletin of the West Riding (Northern Section) Committee of the National Register of Archives.* Wakefield

Briggs, A. (1963) *Victorian Cities.* London

Brooks, F. W. (1966) *Domesday Book and the East Riding,* East Yorkshire Local History series, **21**. York

Brown, R. *et al.* (1799) *A General View of the Agriculture of the West Riding.* London

Browning, A. (ed.) (1936) *The Memoirs of Sir John Reresby.* Glasgow

Buckatzsch, E. J. (1950) Places of origin of a group of immigrants into Sheffield, 1624–1799, *Econ. Hist. Rev.,* 2nd series, II, 303–6

Burton, J. E. (1979) *The Yorkshire Nunneries in the Twelfth and Thirteenth Centuries,* Borthwick Papers, **56**. York

Butler, L. and Given-Wilson, C. (1979) *Medieval Monasteries of Great Britain.* London

Butterworth, E. (1967) *Immigrants in West Yorkshire: Social Conditions and the Lives of Pakistanis, Indians and West Indians,* Institute of Race Relations. London

Cartwright, J. J. (ed.) (1888) *The Travels through England of Dr Richard Pococke,* I. London

Chibnall, M. (1969) *The Ecclesiastical History of Orderic Vitalis,* II. Oxford

Clark, G. K. (1962) *The Making of Victorian England.* London

Clark, P. (1979) Migration in England during the late seventeenth and early eighteenth centuries, *Past and Present,* **83**, 57–90

Cliffe, J. T. (1969) *The Yorkshire Gentry from the Reformation to the Civil War.* London

Coleman, T. (1965) *The Railway Navvies.* London

Cox, A. and A. (1973) *The Potteries of South Yorkshire.* Sheffield Museums

Crossley, D. W. and Ashurst, D. (1968) Excavations at Rockley Smithies, a water-powered bloomery of the sixteenth and seventeenth centuries, *Post Medieval Archaeology,* **2**, 10–54

Crossley, D. W. and Aberg, A. (1972) Sixteenth-century glassmaking in Yorkshire: excavations at furnaces at Hutton and Rosedale, North Riding, 1968–71, *Post-Medieval Archaeology,* **6**, 107–59

Crump, W. B. and Ghorbal, G. (1935) *History of the Huddersfield Woollen Industry.* Huddersfield Museum

Darby, H. C. (ed.) (1973) *A New Historical Geography of England.* Cambridge

Darby, H. C. and Maxwell, I. S. (1962) *The Domesday Geography of Northern England.* Cambridge

Davis, R. (1964) *The Trade and Shipping of Hull, 1500–1700,* East Riding Local History series, **17**. York

Defoe, D. (1962) *A Tour Through the Whole Island of Great Britain,* Everyman edn. London

Dickens, A. G. (1959) *Lollards and Protestants in the Diocese of York, 1509–58.* Oxford

Dickenson, M. J. (1974) *The West Riding Woollen and Worsted Industries, 1689–*

1770: an Analysis of Probate Inventories and Insurance Policies, Nottingham University PhD thesis

Dobson, R. B. (1973) Admissions to the Freedom of the City of York in the later Middle Ages, *Econ. Hist. Rev.*, 2nd series, XXVI, 1–21

Dobson, R. B. (1974) *The Jews of Medieval York and the Massacre of March 1190*, Borthwick Papers, 45. York

Dobson, R. B. and Taylor, J. (1976) *Rymes of Robyn Hood*. London

Drake, M. (1962) An elementary exercise in parish register demography, *Econ. Hist. Rev.*, XIV, 427–45

Duckham, B. F. (1967) *The Yorkshire Ouse: the History of a River Navigation.* Newton Abbot

Elliott, A. (1979) The incorporation of Bradford, *Northern History*, XV, 156–75

Ellis, S. (1981) Huddersfield and Yorkshire dialect, *Old West Riding*, I, 23–5

English, B. (1979) *The Lords of Holderness, 1086–1260.* Oxford

English, B. (1984) Patterns of estate management in east Yorkshire, *c.* 1840–*c.* 1880, *Agricultural Hist. Rev.*, 32, 29–48

Farrer, W. (ed.) (1914) *Early Yorkshire Charters*, I, Yorkshire Archaeological Society Record Series, extra series

Faull, M. L. and Moorhouse, S. A. (eds) (1981) *West Yorkshire: an Archaeological Survey to AD 1500.* Wakefield

Fieldhouse, R. T. (1980) Agriculture in Wensleydale from 1600 to the present day, *Northern History*, XVI, 169–95

Fieldhouse, R. and Jennings, B. (1978) *A History of Richmond and Swaledale.* Chichester

Firby, M. and Lang, J. (1981) The pre-Conquest sculpture of Stonegrave, *Yorkshire Arch. Journal*, 53, 17–30

Finberg, H. P. R. (ed.) (1972) *The Agrarian History of England and Wales, I: II, AD 42–1042.* Cambridge

Finn, R. W. (1972) *The Making and Limitations of the Yorkshire Domesday*, Borthwick Papers, 41. York

Fraser, D. (1977) Voluntaryism and West Riding politics in the mid-nineteenth century, *Northern History*, XIII, 199–231

Fraser, D. (ed.) (1980) *A History of Modern Leeds.* Manchester

Gibson, E. (ed.) (1695) *William Camden: Brittania.* London

Gillett, E. and MacMahon, K. A. (1980) *A History of Hull.* Oxford

Girouard, M. (1978) *Life in the English Country House.* New Haven and London

Girouard, M. (1983) *Robert Smythson and the Elizabethan Country House.* New Haven and London

Goodchild, J. (1978) *The Coal Kings of Yorkshire.* Wakefield

Griffin, A. R. (1977) *The British Coalmining Industry: Retrospect and Prospect.* Ashbourne

Hall, T. W. (1914) *Descriptive Catalogue of the Jackson Collection at Sheffield Public Library.* Sheffield

Halliwell, J. O. (1904) *A Dictionary of Archaic and Provincial Words.* London, 6th edn

Harrison, B. and Hutton, B. (1984) *Vernacular Houses in North Yorkshire and Cleveland.* Edinburgh

317

Harvey, J. C. (1974) Common field and enclosure in the lower Dearne valley, *Yorkshire Arch. Journal*, **46**, 110–27

Harvey, M. (1978) *The Morphological and Tenurial Structure of a Yorkshire Township: Preston in Holderness 1066–1750*. London

Harvey, M. (1983) Planned field systems in eastern Yorkshire: some thoughts on their origin, *Agricultural Hist. Rev.*, **31**, 91–103

Hastings, R. P. (1982) *Poverty and the Poor Law in the North Riding of Yorkshire, c. 1780–1837*, Borthwick Papers, **61**. York

Heath, P. (1968) North-Sea fishing in the fifteenth century: the Scarborough fleet, *Northern History*, III, 53–69

Heaton, H. (1965) *The Yorkshire Woollen and Worsted Industries from the Earliest Times up to the Industrial Revolution*. Oxford, 2nd edn

Hey, D. (1972) *The Rural Metalworkers of the Sheffield Region*. Leicester

Hey, D. (1973) The pattern of nonconformity in south Yorkshire, 1660–1851, *Northern History*, VIII, 86–118

Hey, D. (1975) The parks at Tankersley and Wortley, *Yorkshire Arch. Journal*, **47**, 109–19

Hey, D. (1977) The ironworks at Chapeltown, *Trans Hunter Arch. Soc.*, X, 252–9

Hey, D. (1979) *The Making of South Yorkshire*. Ashbourne

Hey, D. (1980) *Packmen, Carriers and Packhorse Roads*. Leicester

Hey, D. (1981) *Buildings of Britain, 1550–1750: Yorkshire*. Ashbourne

Hey, D. (forthcoming) Sheffield on the Eve of the Industrial Revolution. *Trans Hunter Arch. Soc.*, XIII

Hey, D. and Magilton, J. R. (1983) St Peter's Church, Warmsworth, *Yorkshire Arch. Journal*, **55**, 27–60

Hicks, J. D. (ed.) (1978) *A Victorian Boyhood on the Wolds; the Recollections of J. R. Mortimer*, East Yorkshire Local History series, **34**. York

Hoggart, R. (1957) *The Uses of Literacy*. London

Holland, D. (ed.) (1971) *The South Yorkshire Historian*, I. Doncaster.

Holland, D. (1980) *Changing Landscapes in South Yorkshire*. Doncaster

Horrox, R. (1983) *The De la Poles of Hull*, East Yorkshire Local History series. York

Hoskins, W. G. (1976) *The Age of Plunder*. London

Hunt, Pantin and Southern (eds) (1948) *Studies in Medieval History presented to Frederick Maurice Powicke*. Oxford

Hunter, J. (1819) *Hallamshire*. London

Hunter, J. (ed.) (1830) *The Diary of Ralph Thoresby*. London

Jackson, G. (1972) *Hull in the Eighteenth Century*. Oxford

Jeffrey, P. S. (1971) *Whitby Lore and Legend*. Whitby, 3rd edn

Jennings, B. (ed.) (1967) *A History of Nidderdale*. Huddersfield

Jennings, B. (ed.) (1970) *A History of Harrogate and Knaresborough*. Huddersfield

Jensen, G. F. (1978) Place-names and settlement in the North Riding of Yorkshire, *Northern History*, XIV, 19–46

Jewell, H. M. (1982) 'The bringing up of children in good learning and manners': a survey of secular educational provision in the North of England, *Northern History*, XVIII, 1–25

Jordan, W. K. (1961) *The Charities of Rural England, 1480–1660*. London

Kapelle, W. E. (1979) *The Norman Conquest of the North: the Region and its Transformation, 1000–1135*. London

Kaye, J. M. (1979) The Eland murders, 1350–1: a study of the legend of the Eland feud, *Yorkshire Arch. Journal*, 51, 61–80

Kershaw, I. (1973) *Bolton Priory: the Economy of a Northern Monastery, 1286–1325*. Oxford

Kitchen, F. (1983) *Brother to the Ox*. Harmondsworth

Lawson, J. (1978, reprint) *Progress in Pudsey*. Horsham

Lennard, R. V. (1932) English agriculture under Charles II, *Econ. Hist. Rev.*, IV, 23–45

Lennard, R. V. (1959) *Rural England, 1086–1135: a Study of Social and Agrarian Conditions*. Oxford

Le Patourel, H. E. J. (1973) *The Moated Sites of Yorkshire*, Society for Medieval Archaeology monograph series, 5. London

Le Patourel, J. (1971) The Norman Conquest of Yorkshire, *Northern History*, VI, 1–21

Lipson, E. (1921) *The History of the Woollen and Worsted Industries*. London

Long, W. H. (1969) *A Survey of the Agriculture of Yorkshire*. London

MacFarlane, J. (1976) Denaby Main Colliery, *Colliery Guardian*, March. London

McIntyre, S. (1978) The Scarborough Corporation quarrel, 1736–1760, *Northern History*, XIV, 208–26

Magilton, J. R. (1979) Tickhill: the topography of a medieval town, *Trans Hunter Arch. Soc.*, X, 344–9

Magilton, J. R. (1980) *The Church of St Helen on the Walls, Aldwark*. York

Manby, T. G. (1965) Medieval pottery kilns at Upper Heaton, west Yorkshire. *Archaeological Journal*, 121, 108–10

Marchant, R. A. (1960) *The Puritans and the Church Courts in the Diocese of York, 1560–1642*. London

Marshall, G. (1978) The Rotherham plough, *Tools and Tillage*, III, 3, 150–67

Mayes, P. and Butler, L. A. S. (1983) *Sandal Castle Excavations, 1963–1973*. Wakefield

Mee, G. (1975) *Aristocratic Enterprise: the Fitzwilliam Industrial Undertakings, 1795–1857*. Glasgow and London

Mercer, E. (1975) *English Vernacular Houses*. London

Miller, E. and Hatcher, J. (1978) *Medieval England: Rural Society and Economic Change, 1086–1348*. London

Mingay, G. E. (ed.) (1981) *The Victorian Countryside*. London

Morris, C. (ed.) (1949) *The Journeys of Celia Fiennes*. London

Morris, J. (1904) *The North Riding of Yorkshire*. London

Morris, J. (1906) *The East Riding of Yorkshire*. London

Morris, J. (1911) *The West Riding of Yorkshire*. London

Murray, J. (1874) *Handbook for Travellers in Yorkshire*. London

Neave, D. (1983) *Pocklington Town Trail*. Bridlington

Newman, P. R. (1980) The defeat of John Belasyse: Civil War in Yorkshire, January–April 1644, *Yorkshire Arch. Journal*, 52, 123–34

Orwell, G. (1962) *The Road to Wigan Pier*. Harmondsworth

Pacey, A. J. (1966) Ornamental porches of mid-seventeenth century Halifax, *Yorkshire Arch. Journal*, XLI, 455–64

Palliser, D. M. (1979) *Tudor York*. Oxford

Palliser, D. M. (1983) *The Age of Elizabeth, 1547–1603*. London

319

Pawson, E. (1977) *Transport and Economy: The Turnpike Roads of Eighteenth Century Britain.* London

Pevsner, Sir N. (1959) *The Buildings of England: the West Riding.* Harmondsworth

Pevsner, Sir N. (1966) *The Buildings of England: the North Riding.* Harmondsworth

Pevsner, Sir N. (1972) *The Buildings of England: York and the East Riding.* Harmondsworth

Phillips, A. D. M. (1972) The development of underdrainage on a Yorkshire estate during the nineteenth century, *Yorkshire Arch. Journal,* **44,** 195–206

Phythian-Adams, C. V. (1975) *Local History and Folklore: a New Framework.* London

Platt, C. (1969) *The Monastic Grange in Medieval England.* London

Platt, C. (1976) *The English Medieval Town.* London

Platt, C. (1978) *Medieval England: A Social History and Archaeology from the Conquest to 1600 AD.* London

Pollard, A. J. (1978) Richard Clervaux of Croft: a North Riding squire in the fifteenth century, *Yorkshire Arch. Journal,* **50,** 151–70

Pollard, S. (1959) *A History of Labour in Sheffield.* Liverpool

Pollard, S. (1983) *The Development of the British Economy, 1914–1980.* London, 3rd edn

Porteous, J. D. (1977) *Canal Ports, The Urban Achievement of the Canal Age.* London

Postles, D. (1979) Rural economy on the grits and sandstones of the south Yorkshire Pennines, 1086–1348, *Northern History,* XV, 1–23

Postan, M. M. (1972) *The Medieval Economy and Society: an Economic History of Britain in the Middle Ages.* London

Prestwich, M. (1976) *York Civic Ordinances, 1301,* Borthwick Papers, **49.** York

Raistrick, A. (1968) *The Pennine Dales.* London

Raistrick, A. and Allen, E. (1939) The South Yorkshire ironmasters, 1690–1750, *Econ. Hist. Rev.,* old series, IX, 168–85

Raistrick, A. and Jennings, B. (1965) *A History of Lead Mining in the Pennines.* London

Redmonds, G. (1973) *Yorkshire: West Riding,* English Surnames series. Chichester

Redmonds, G. (1982) *The Heirs of Woodsome.* Huddersfield

Robinson, D. (1969) *Beneficed Clergy in Cleveland and the East Riding, 1306–1340,* Borthwick Papers, 37. York

Roebuck, P. (1980) *Yorkshire Baronets, 1640–1760.* Oxford

Rogers, W. S. (1952) *The Distribution of Parliamentary Enclosures in the West Riding of Yorkshire 1729–1850.* Leeds University M Comm thesis

Rolls Series (1885) Vol. 75

Rose, M. E. (1972) *The Relief of Poverty, 1834–1914.* London

Rowley, T. (ed.) (1981) *The Origins of Open Field Agriculture.* London

Rowntree, B. S. (1901) *Poverty: A Study of Town Life.* London

Ryder, P. F. (1982) *Medieval Buildings of Yorkshire.* Ashbourne

Sawyer, P. H. (ed.) (1976) *Medieval Settlement.* London

Selden Society LVI (1937) *Rolls of the Justices in Eyre for Yorkshire*

Sheppard, J. (1966) Pre-enclosure field and settlement patterns in an English township, *Geografiska Annales,* XLVIII, 64–9

Sheppard, J. (1974) Metrological analysis of village plans in Yorkshire, *Agricultural Hist. Rev.,* XXII, 118–35

Sheppard, T. (1912) *Lost Towns of the Yorkshire Coast*. London

Simmons, J. (1961) *The Railways of Britain*. London

Smart, V. J. (1968) Moneyers of the late Anglo-Saxon coinage, 973–1016, *Commentations de nummis saeculorum IX–XI in Suecia repertis*, II. Stockholm

Smith, A. H. (1961) *The Place-Names of the West Riding of Yorkshire, I*. Cambridge

Smith, L. T. (ed.) (1964) *Leland's Itinerary*. London

Smith, R. B. (1970) *Land and Politics in the England of Henry VIII: the West Riding of Yorkshire, 1530–1546*. Oxford

Stenton, Sir F. M. (1947) *Anglo-Saxon England*. Oxford, 2nd edn

Stevenson, W. H. (1912) Yorkshire surveys and other eleventh-century documents in the York Gospels, *English Hist. Rev.*, XXVII, 1–25

Strickland, H. E. (1812) *A General View of the Agriculture of the East Riding of Yorkshire*. London

Surtees Society, XXXIII (1857) *Rural Economy in Yorkshire in 1641, being the Farming and Account Books of Henry Best*

Surtees Society, LIV (1869) *The Diary of Abraham de la Pryme, the Yorkshire Antiquary*

Surtees Society, LXV (1875) *Four Yorkshire Diaries*

Smith, D. E. (1980) Otley: a study of a market town during the late seventeenth and eighteenth centuries, *Yorkshire Arch. Journal*, 52, 153–6

Thirsk, J. (ed.) (1967) *The Agrarian History of England and Wales, IV: 1500–1640*. Cambridge

Thirsk, J. (1978) *Economic Policy and Projects*. Oxford

Thirsk, J. (1985) *The Agrarian History of England and Wales V: 1640–1750*. Cambridge

Thompson, A. H. (1914) The pestilences of the fourteenth century in the diocese of York, *Yorkshire Arch. Journal*, LXXI, 97–154

Thompson, E. P. (1963) *The Making of the English Working Class*. London

Thornes, R. C. N. (1981) *West Yorkshire: 'A noble scene of industry'*. Wakefield

Tuke, J. (1800) *A General View of the Agriculture of the North Riding of Yorkshire*. London

Tyler, P. (1969) The Church Courts at York and witchcraft prosecutions, 1567–1640, *Northern History*, IV, 84–110

Unwin, R. (1982) An eighteenth century census: Wetherby, 1776, *Yorkshire Arch. Journal*, 54, 125–40

Vaizey, J. (1974) *The History of British Steel*. London

Victoria County History, *City of York* (1961)

Victoria County History, *East Riding*, I (1969)

Victoria County History, *East Riding*, II (1974)

Victoria County History, *East Riding*, III (1976)

Waites, B. (1967) *Moorland and Vale-Land Farming in North-East Yorkshire*, Borthwick Papers, 32. York

Walker, G. (1814) *The Costume of Yorkshire*. London

Wardell, J. W. (1957) *A History of Yarm*. Sunderland

Whitaker, T. D. (1816) *Loides and Elmete*. London

Wightman, W. E. (1975) The significance of 'waste' in the Yorkshire Domesday, *Northern History*, X, 55–71

Wilson, R. G. (1971) *Gentlemen Merchants: the Merchant Community in Leeds, 1700–1830.* Manchester

Wrigley, E. A. and Schofield, R. S. (1981) *The Population History of England, 1541– 1971.* London

Yorkshire Archaeological Society Record Series, XLI (1908) *Yorkshire Star Chamber Proceedings*

XLIV (1911) *Three Yorkshire Assize Rolls*

LXXX (1931) *Miscellanea, Vol. III*

CVII (1943) *Fasti Parochiales, Vol. II*

CXVII (1952) *The Diary of Arthur Jessop*

CXXV (1959) *Tudor Treatises*

CXXVI (1960) *A Survey of the Manor of Settrington*

CXLI (1983) *Selected Rentals and Accounts of Medieval Hull, 1293–1528*

Yorkshire Archaeological Trust (1978) *2,000 Years of York: the Archaeological Story.* York

Young, A. (1771) *Tour through the North of England, I.* London

Index

169, 181, 190, 192, 197, 198,
199, 200, 221, 289, 312
Vanbrugh, Sir John, 114, 202
Vaughan, John, 273, 274
Vavasour family, 93, 161
Vermuyden, Cornelius, 145, 215
Viking-age sculpture, 12–13
Vikings, 1, 4, 11, 12, 13, 16, 22, 23,
24–6, 31, 57, 249
villeins, 19
Vitalis, Orderic, 26

Waddeswyk, William, 106
Wadsley, 153, 217, 224, 246
Wadsworth, 21
Wadworth, 2, 89, 108, 153, 203
Wainstalls, 73
Wakefield, town and manor, 18, 22, 33,
34, 38, 42, 43, 70, 71, 72, 73,
74, 75, 83, 84, 102, 103, 108,
109, 115, 116, 118, 120, 121,
122, 130, 151, 152, 155, 167,
171, 173, 174, 183, 184, 185,
192, 203, 207, 213, 214, 215,
216, 217, 218, 219, 220, 222,
230, 231, 233, 238, 245, 247,
248, 258, 262, 276, 280,
305
Wakefield, William, 201
Wales, 14, 16, 17
Wales, Gerald of, 117
Waleswood, 111
Walker, George, 138, 243
Walker, Samuel and Aaron, 227, 242,
277
Walkington, 140
Walkley, 266, 267
Walling Fen, 140, 194
Walpole, Horace, 229
Waltheof, Earl, 24
Wandesford, Mary, 209
Wansford, 101
wapentakes, 4, 16, 114
Warburton, John, 214
Warenne family, 34, 59
Warley, 160, 166, 167
Wars of the Roses, 102–3

Warter, 58, 60, 65
Wasplington, 101
Waterhouse, Keith, 313
waterhouses, 90
Waterloo, 221
water-power, 85, 120, 151, 154, 163,
255–6
Wath upon Dearne, 150, 193
Watson, Revd John, 244
Watton, 58, 64
Wawne, 20, 22, 80
Weaverthorpe, 54
Weddell, William, 204
Weedley, 85
Weighton, Little, 69
Well, 116
Welwick, 89
Wensley, 121
Wensleydale, 22, 70, 84, 99, 100, 138,
146, 148, 192, 206, 310
Wentbridge, 114, 158
Wentworth Castle, 202, 310
Wentworth family, 82, 164, 177, 202,
223
Wentworth village, 201, 204, 217, 223,
288
Wentworth Woodhouse, 160, 164, 203,
276, 277, 288, 310, 313
Wesley, John and Charles, 208, 264
Wessex, 1, 24
West Indian immigrants, 308–9
Westmorland, 3, 4
Weston Hall, 161
Wetherby, 114, 171, 178, 179, 184,
185–6, 289
Wetwang, 141
whaling, 189
Wharfe, river, 18, 46, 152, 185, 218,
224
Wharfedale, 65, 70, 84, 110, 161, 173
Wharncliffe, 81, 123
Wharram le Street, 14
Wharram Percy, 79, 92, 109, 141
Wheatley, 310
Wheldrake, 21, 77, 79, 90
Whernside, 7, 73
Whiston, 16, 72, 112, 158
Whitaker, T. D., 243

Tees & Yarm

Hull / Baltic / Leas & London 133
         Leas & Bawtry
         (with Verm)   135

         Doncaster
         Seaward port   136

Navigation : early 46
          late 215

Gt. N. Road alterations 114
Beds (overseer (68£) 183

'Market' award / industry 176-7

~ Amari town 174
    Housing 169-70